Economics of Global Business

Economics of Global Business

Rodrigo Zeidan

The MIT Press
Cambridge, Massachusetts
London, England

This book was set in Palatino by Toppan Best-set Premedia Limited. Printed and bound in the United States of America.

Library of Congress Cataloging-in-Publication Data

Names: Zeidan, Rodrigo, author.
Title: Economics of global business / Rodrigo Zeidan.
Description: Cambridge, MA : MIT Press, [2018] | Includes bibliographical
   references and index.
Identifiers: LCCN 2017058666 | ISBN 9780262535625 (pbk. : alk. paper)
Subjects: LCSH: Economic development. | International economic relations. |
   Economic policy. | Monetary policy.
Classification: LCC HD82 .Z45 2018 | DDC 338.88--dc23 LC record available at https://lccn.loc.
gov/2017058666

10 9 8 7 6 5 4 3 2 1

Contents

Preface

When I was a kid in the 1980s in Brazil, I had a job to do once every month. My task was to rush around our local supermarket and toss items on my mother's list into a cart, trying to keep one step ahead of employees armed with price guns who regularly marked up prices on the day my mom received her paycheck. The goal was to spend 60% of the check on nonperishable groceries that would last us through the month. It was a time of hyperinflation in Brazil, and as a youngster, I was experiencing firsthand many effects of inept economic policies. Now, as an adult, I regularly spend one summer month in Denmark, where problems are those of a developed country, and most of the year in China, literally breathing in the implications of global policymaking along with millions of others who choke on air polluted for the sake of industrial development.

Books are often propelled into life by underlying tensions between conflicting ideas, ideologies, or identities. This book has been borne out of several types of conflict—that between theory and practice, rigor and narrative, convention and unfamiliarity, emergence and development, and nationalization and globalization. But perhaps the most important disparity is the one between what is and what ought to be. Economists invited to work for governments soon notice that public authorities rarely address problems by using the most efficient paths—what we call first-best solutions. In real life, third-best, fourth-best, or even downright spurious policies are the norm, with first-best solutions as the rare exceptions. Many economic textbooks are concerned with what the policies ought to be, but few examine the actual policies as they are, complete with all their tradeoffs and unintended consequences. This goes beyond a clash between theories and practice. It touches on ideology. I trust science over ideology. This trust is not naive. I know that even the choice of a research question is often the result of political decisions. That notwithstanding, economic theory provides testable hypotheses that are refined over time. Theoretical breakthroughs do happen. And in the end, empirical works broaden our understanding of economic processes.

It is impossible for all these conflicts to be resolved. Some authors favor theory over practice, and others look for a rigorous approach. But even though there is no shortage of books on economy, I have never found one I was entirely comfortable with when teaching macroeconomics and the global economy to business students. Some focus mostly on the United States, others are too technical for my typical audience, and a few are out of touch with the real world. There is nothing wrong with most of the economics textbooks in the market. Other authors simply choose a different path than the one taken in the book you are holding in your hands or reading on your electronic device.

I decided to write a nontechnical manual of public policy that has examples from all over the world and presents all the difficult tradeoffs that policymakers face. The book can be used by students in emerging and developed countries alike, and, most important, should be engaging. Dry technical manuals sometimes are inevitable, but that is definitely not the case for economics textbooks. We are inundated with news regarding the choices made by public authorities: Will the Federal Reserve hike the target interest rate? Will the Japanese public deficit increase yet again? Should the Argentinian authorities sell foreign currency to prop up the peso? There is plenty of real-life material to keep the average reader interested.

If there is one ideology I developed throughout my career and by experiencing the contradictions in all the countries I have lived, then it is radical skepticism. I am uncomfortable with simplistic thinking. We live in a world in which most people seek easy answers to complex issues. Political discourse is full of extreme arguments that focus entirely on costs or benefits but rarely takes a nuanced approach that balances the two. When people favor policy A, then they highlight only its benefits to society. The narrative trumps facts. That is not the case here. Economic systems also need to be thought about in dynamic terms. This requires that the evolution of the economy should be taken into account when we develop arguments pro and contra certain policies.

There are no easy solutions. Economic policy is context-dependent. Textbooks today must address issues like income inequality and the impact of the great financial crisis, innovative policies like quantitative easing and negative interest rates, and climate change. True development, where people are not left behind and we do not destroy the environment, is extremely hard. And it takes time.

The Structure of the Book

The book follows a straightforward structure with one exception: the main details regarding the social outcomes of economic policy are at the end of the book, instead of the beginning. I chose to do it this way because I have found that going over the precise definitions of gross domestic product (GDP), inflation, income inequality, and unemployment in the first few weeks of a macroeconomics introductory course alienates some students. I have found it more useful to return to these definitions after we understand how these outcomes are determined in distinct macroeconomic markets and how policies affect social welfare. One does not need to know right away that GDP includes only final goods and services to understand that economic growth is a relevant social outcome.

Other than this, the structure of the book is quite conventional. The first part deals with closed national economies, and the second part integrates the national economy with the rest of the world. Monetary and fiscal policies are described in the first part of the book and are revisited, alongside currency management, in the second part. The last chapter integrates all the macromarkets in a comprehensive framework that allows readers to analyze the impact of an economic shock through all the markets and evaluate the possible consequences of a reaction by public authorities.

Given that the detailed definitions of social outcomes come only in chapter 14, readers can read chapters 1 and 14 before reading the rest of the book if that sequence works better for them rather than reading chapters consecutively.

In addition to this book, instructors have access to all the materials necessary to teach a course based on the book. Slides that highlight the main points of each chapter, additional case studies, and exam and review questions are provided so that the book can function as an introductory or intermediary macro and international economics course for undergraduate or graduate students. The book also can be used as a complement to more technical manuals, illustrating concepts and models with real-life examples.

Acknowledgments

I owe much to my teachers, coauthors, colleagues, and students. But I want to focus here on the people who gave me their valuable time to improve this book. Svetlana Fedoseeva, Michel Fleuriet, and Jacek Matuszak read the entire manuscript with an attention to detail that I often lack. No lazy or incomplete argument got past them. Jay Rubin, Cristina Terra, and Ernani Torres provided very useful comments. Steven Lehrer was a great ideas soundboard. Dan Guttman and Oran Young helped ensure that the climate change chapter delivered a coherent narrative that is in line with the research in the area. Tensie Whelan advised on making the climate change aspects of the book more relatable to a business school audience. Claudio Considera and Irineu de Carvalho Filho made sure that the chapter on national accounts reflected best practices. Finally, Paul Wachtel welcomed me warmly into the New York University faculty. Without his support, I never would have had the confidence to take on this project. He is a specialist in comparative economics, has taught the subject for over thirty years, and inspired me to make *Economics of Global Business* into a truly global course.

Introduction

Economics can be truly exasperating. The US president Harry Truman grew so frustrated with the inconclusive advice of his economic experts that he is reported to have said, "Give me a one-handed economist. All my economists say, 'On the one hand … on the other hand …'" He longed for clear and straightforward economic pointers without any ifs and buts. Although many people would find the existence of one-handed economists comforting, the truth is they do not exist. Policymaking in a global economy is always about tradeoffs. Whatever issue needs to be addressed, the use of economic tools leaves scars. The old joke that bad doctors are preferable to bad economists is more valid than ever. Bad medical care may harm a handful of patients, but bad economic advice wreaks havoc on a much larger scale.

The ultimate goal of this book is to provide a clear gauge for understanding how and why governments make decisions on economic policies, including the tradeoffs and constraints that policymakers face and the reasons that they can make mistakes. The book's main theme is that there is rarely a right answer to an economics dilemma. Should banks be bailed out? Should the European Commission have forced countries like Greece and Portugal to adopt austerity measures? Should the Federal Reserve (the Fed) increase the interest rate?

The purpose of the book is not to answer these and other questions definitively but to provide a rationale for both yes and no answers. You decide. Playing a fiscal or monetary authority is hard, and government officials, even if we assume competence and honesty, are constrained by uncertainty and contradictory political (among other) factors.

First, we need to look at the major tradeoffs of economic policies. No economic decision comes without consequences. Every time a government intervenes, somebody loses. This is true about taxes, trade policy, public spending, and the interest rate, to name a few of the tools at the disposal of public authorities. Inaction also has its costs.

Second, we need to develop a context for economic policies. Economic modeling combines mathematics and human behavior and tests them through statistical techniques. But economics has no universal model about how countries develop. Countries differ in many dimensions, including the quality of their institutions, levels of economic development, cultural and social norms, and relative number of poor people. In the end, the efficacy and efficiency of economic policies depend on a given economy at a particular moment. Sometimes even completely counterintuitive policies may be tenable. A good example is quantitative easing. Most young people learn that printing money leads to inflation. Yet quantitative easing is almost akin to a public announcement that the government is going to print copious amounts of money. Many developed economies tried this in the twenty-first century. From 2009 to 2014, the United States bought $5 trillion of financial assets during three rounds of quantitative easing. Yet inflation never arrived. In fact, policymakers wanted inflation to pick up a bit. If in the same time frame a middle-income or poor country had tried a similar strategy, however, inflation likely would have exploded.

Another example of context dependency is related to currency control. In China, the government manages the price of the renminbi (or yuan). India allows the rupee to be traded but not freely, and Australia abstains from intervening in the price of its dollar. Each choice is viable and comes with its own costs and benefits.

Tradeoffs and context dependency are the cornerstones of this book. Globalization, income inequality, and the great financial crisis are examples of context dependency. From 1994 to 2008, integration among countries was the major driver of economic growth. Integration can be either financial (where banks and other institutions can act globally) or commercial (where the trade of goods and services is increased). Globalization is the advancement of these two types of integration. Many countries are part of all global markets, but some are not. China's financial system, for instance, is not integrated with the rest of the world. Its capital controls do not freely allow foreign currency in and out of the country and mostly limit foreign funds from investing in local capital markets.

The period that runs from the launch of the World Trade Organization (WTO) in 1995 until the great financial crisis of 2008 is considered the golden age of recent globalization. In 2007, just before the crisis, there was hope around the world, and most countries were growing rapidly. China led the way, and many emerging countries followed. European countries paraded their virtues to attract more immigrants and offset the effects of an aging population. Spain marketed itself as the premier destination for citizens of the Latin American countries it had colonized. The major global fear was inflation, fueled by the increases in energy and food prices: prices were high because the world was getting immensely richer. Then the great financial crisis hit, and the world changed dramatically. Growth stalled. Oil prices crashed. Effects have been long-lasting. Ireland bailed out its central bank, Greece almost left the euro, and the United Kingdom voted for Brexit (its exit from the European Union). Inflation concerns mostly disappeared. Most immigrants are now unwelcome. Since then, we have learned more about how climate change is a major existential threat. Unorthodox policies like quantitative easing and negative interest rates (when the central banks charge negative interest and depositors should pay to keep their money in the banking system) became normal, at least in developed countries. Discontent with economic policies fueled civil unrest in many Arab countries. Chinese growth started to slow down. Latin American countries crashed. Income inequality became a major issue in Europe and the United States. Yet the world economy moves in cycles of recessions and expansions. Later we will see under which conditions countries leave recession behind. Here, we integrate the features of the world postfinancial crisis into the general framework that informs economic policies.

Broadly speaking, three macroeconomics instruments influence social welfare—monetary, fiscal, and currency policies. The first deals with the interest rate, the second with taxes and public spending, and the third with the management of a currency regime. The interest rate is important because it is the cost of borrowing or the benefit from saving. The choice of currency regime affects everyday life, the companies that want to sell or invest abroad, and the multinationals that want to invest locally. For instance, the United States has a flexible exchange rate regime, and China maintains control over the path of its currency. The exchange rate of the US dollar with other currencies fluctuates all the time, but Chinese policymakers define the interval of trading of the Chinese renminbi (yuan) daily. Think of public authorities as surgeons and monetary and of fiscal and currency policies as their scalpels. Policymakers yield their instruments to excise problems and mend their patient, the national economy, trying to bring it back to health and promote prosperity with controlled inflation. Unlike physicians, government officials do not necessarily have the best training. Misdiagnosis or unnecessary exploratory surgeries happen much more often than they should.

This book is called *Economics of Global Business* because the path of a country's economy cannot be analyzed in isolation, even though some opponents of globalization wish that it could. Decisions made in the United States influence governments all over the world. Hiccups of Chinese markets have global effects. Economic policy is the domain of dilemmas. Economists use the metaphor of the "free lunch" for economic policies that public authorities dream of—a policy that brings only prosperity without leaving society worse off in any way. Free lunches are rare. A better metaphor for policy advice is that of low-hanging fruit. They are plentiful. National and international authorities ignore them all the time, mostly because political costs outweigh the benefits.

Welcome to *Economics of Global Business*. Whatever your ideology, you will find justification for it in this book. But be aware of the costs of the policies you favor. Acknowledging and understanding the policy dilemmas are the only ways to build true prosperity for all.

1 The Economics of Global Business: The Basics

In this chapter,
- Social welfare and the evolution of national economies
- Prosperity vs. economic growth
- Economic policies and tradeoffs
- The role of governments
- The importance of context-dependency

Imagine that you are a policymaker in Europe and that you have to decide if you should support the European Central Bank and other institutions in their austerity demands to the Greek government.[1] You need to make a simple rational decision. Would it be better for the Greek government to stop profligacy, increase revenue through new taxes, and go through a recession so it could emerge a more solid economy, or should it try to shorten the recession by expanding public spending?

Now, assume that you are a member of the Board of Governors of the Federal Reserve, the central bank in the United States, and you have to decide if the US economy is ready for an increase in the interest rate. You may be worried about inflation or a rapid increase in the prices of financial assets. But you also should be concerned about jobs and economic growth.

Economic systems are alive with action. Markets are interconnected. Policymakers can decide on something today but miss the right time to act. Or their action can come with unintended consequences given unexpected reactions by economic agents.

1. Central banks are government institutions (or supranational institutions, in the case of the eurozone—the European countries that use the euro as their currency) that have the power to issue currency, regulate financial markets, and determine economic policies regarding the exchange rate or the price of the local currency in relation to foreign money.

1.1   Social Welfare

Economics is about improving the standards of living. Countries and people should do better over time. Yet what does doing better mean for the average person? In a dynamic world, desires are left unfulfilled, and government officials are driven to meddling and trying to shepherd nations through evolving times, more alchemists than decision makers.

The first building block of our edifice is the relationship between people's aspirations and measurable outcomes. For that purpose, economists define a social welfare function as a way that summarizes in as few concepts as possible all that makes us better human beings. This impossible endeavor is flawed yet necessary. All material dreams are condensed in a single variable called gross domestic product (GDP), with its arcane methodology and abstract relation to reality. Unemployment measures people who cannot find a job, but it fails to take into account disillusioned individuals who leave the labor force because they cannot see a path to an acceptable occupation. Inflation computes increasing prices for an average household that does not exist. For every individual, goods and services become more or less expensive depending on his or her predilections and distinct choices at each possible moment. Income inequality and poverty are multidimensional. Everybody wishes poverty could be vanquished, but no society has ever been able to do it.

No variable can capture all that makes society more prosperous, yet economists try to do so by distilling everything into the smallest possible number of components. For that purpose, we can start by trying to answer a simple question: how can we define a developed country by looking only at its surface, its economic data, and which criteria do we use to analyze a nation's development over time?

The simplest version of a social welfare function consists of only three terms—GDP per capita, inflation, and unemployment. Today we should add income inequality and the environment as well.

GDP per capita is a measure of purchasing power of a typical individual in a given country. For instance, if GDP is US$20 trillion and 320 million people live in the United States, then American society generates an average of US$62,500 per person. This does not mean that everybody gets this amount, but it is a good approximation of how much the society is producing and consuming. Income inequality is a measure of how this income is distributed among residents. Unequal income distribution means that most of national income flows to relatively few people. As money gets distributed more evenly, income inequality decreases. No modern society strives for perfect equality because this would take away the incentives for individuals to work and create wealth.

The rate of unemployment measures the relative number of people looking for work who cannot get a job. If it is 10%, it means that of 100 individuals willing to work at that time, ten cannot find a job. Inflation is the rate at which prices are increasing, on average. If it is 5% per year, prices of goods and services are increasing by 5%. Low unemployment and inflation are clearly good for society.

A developed country is a nation where people are rich (as measured by GDP per capita), inflation and unemployment are low, income inequality is such that the median (and not only the average) family is rich, and society tries to minimize the impact of economic activity on the environment. The focus on the median family is important because some countries are classified as high-income or upper-medium-income by the World Bank but are not developed societies.[2] Equatorial Guinea, for example, is blessed by natural resources and riches from oil exports, but money flows to few individuals. The average resident does not share in the country's fossil fuel production.

Throughout history, there have been many attempts to identify the determinants of prosperity that distinguish the rich and developed countries from the less fortunate ones. Deirdre N. McCloskey has explored the role played by the bourgeois,[3] and Daron Acemoglu and James Robinson have examined the strength of the rule of law and property rights alongside other institutions that mold each country's economic system.[4] Nations take different paths in their search for prosperity. Past choices constrain present policy options. History matters. Macroeconomics, the study of national economies, and international economics are context dependent, and public authorities work and make decisions with limited information.

Economic policy can have tremendous impact in areas that are not directly tied to these outcomes. Take, for instance, social inequality. Social dimensions such as gender, religion, and culture are extremely relevant to the well-being of society. In a contemporary political economy course in Copenhagen, my students and I confronted myths about Danish society and compared them with myths about Latin America and Asia. In Brazil, for instance, there is a pervasive idea that society has achieved racial justice. Brazilians are not supposed to be racist because they come in all skin colors a result of significant immigration flows. In addition to its tribal nations and Portuguese colonizers, Brazil was a major player in the

2. Details on the income classifications are available at "How Does the World Bank Classify Countries?," World Bank, https://datahelpdesk.worldbank.org/knowledgebase/articles/378834-how-does-the-world-bank-classify-countries.
3. Deirdre N. McCloskey's bourgeois series starts with the excellent *The Bourgeois Virtues: Ethics for an Age of Commerce* (Chicago: University of Chicago Press, 2006).
4. Daron Acemoglu and James Robinson, *Why Nations Fail: The Origins of Power, Prosperity, and Poverty* (New York: Crown, 2012).

slave trade and was the last country to abolish slavery. Even after slavery was formally abolished in 1889, the practice continued in remote regions for more than a generation. In 1913, in Sergipe, in the poor northeast, a slave owner who still treated his workers as property was told by the public authorities that he should free them. He did so but not before amputating the fingers of their right hands so they could never do manual labor again. Still, not every immigration was tragic. Japanese, Lebanese, Italian, German, and Polish immigrants arrived in the late nineteenth century and early twentieth century. Today's Brazilians are the result of this melting pot, and people are not supposed to care about skin color. Although many Brazilians maintain that race is not an issue in the country, racial prejudices are deeply entrenched in people's behavior and social outcomes.

In Denmark, the self-myths are different: many people believe that the country has successfully dealt with both racial and gender inequality. When I asked an African student who was spending a year in the country if he thought that Danish people were racist, however, his answer was, "Hell, yes!" The same was true when I informally polled a couple of gay students. Gender disparity also exists. A female student said that female job applicants should not mention in job interviews that they have a boyfriend because maternity benefits are high and create an incentive for companies to hire fewer young female workers.

Economic policy can act to remediate such issues. Macroeconomics alone will not bring about an enlightened society, but it certainly has a role to play. To understand income inequality, we need to understand the relationship between economic policies and social outcomes.

Prosperity is not happiness, and for some nations, simple measures of accumulation may be insufficient targets for policymakers. After all, a 5% increase in income is much more important for a poor person than for a rich one, and the same is true when comparing the economic performances of a poor African country and a Scandinavian country. Yet in most of the world, there is a continuous struggle for some measure of prosperity, which is inevitably tied, at least initially, to rising income. There is a difference between prosperity and development, and the world has paid a significant price for learning this. By any economic definition, the United Kingdom is a prosperous nation. It has one of the highest incomes per capita in the world as measured by GDP, relatively low unemployment compared to the other European Union countries, and little inflation. Despite all of this, on June 23, 2016, its citizens voted for a clean break from the larger European Union (Brexit), believing that the country's future development was tied to an autonomous path instead of integration with its neighbors across the English Channel.

In the first fifteen years of the twenty-first century, the world economy lifted more than a billion people out of poverty, but billions more are still waiting. The economics of global business is about prosperity, but it is also inherently tied to development. Economic growth is still the harbinger of material wealth, an almost universal aspiration that informs the actions of policymakers, who are enthralled by robust growth and restless when recessions hit. Economic growth is important because slow growth imposes substantial social costs. Stagnation is corrosive and contributes to rising nativism and protectionist policies. Such effects are more pronounced in emerging countries, where sluggishness may precipitate coups, but they also affect developed economies. There is little question that stagnation in Europe has caused political fragmentation in the European Union in general and the eurozone in particular.

Governments try to promote prosperity through economic policies, and they intervene in different markets to change the path of economic growth, unemployment, and inflation. There is no consensus on the success of such interventions. Some economists defend inaction, and others advocate for strong countercyclical policies. The goal here is not to enter the debate on economic modeling and on the best responses to economic issues but to explore the decision-making processes of public authorities, knowing that their inclinations are toward action and never inaction.

We are not interested in what the governments *should* be doing but in how they actually make decisions that are supposedly in the best interests of society. There are always other alternatives, with their own sets of costs and benefits, for every economic policy decision, which is how that figure of folklore, the two-handed economist, is born. The two-handed economist is the reticent noncommittal expert on world affairs. Everyone should begin as a two-handed economist and then use ideology to inform an appropriate course of action.

There are some caveats. The analysis of all possible sets of actions assumes that policymakers are dealing with market economies. There are certainly tradeoffs between market-based economies and other kinds of social arrangements, but these topics are outside the scope of this book. Monetary policy should not even exist in a true communist regime because prices would not work in clearing markets. Here, the economics of global business is the domain of capitalist economies.

The United States and Denmark are developed economies, and the BRICS (Brazil, Russia, India, China, and South Africa) are not. Not only are the US and Danish GDPs per capita much higher than GDPs in the BRICS, but these countries usually face lower inflation and unemployment than the BRICS. In the last thirty years, China has been a success story because its economy grew tenfold without major inflationary pressure. The Chinese experience is an interesting case because the country has been able to raise its citizens from poverty to middle-class status. Today China is a developing country with a middle-class income, but there is still a significant distance between its incomes and those in more developed ones like the United States and Denmark. Rising income is part of a social welfare function, and public authorities should be concerned with improving the economic well-being of their citizens.

Today incorporating sustainability as a major goal in the social welfare function is paramount to true development. Countries that pursue only growth-based strategies face significant income and environmental tradeoffs, and these should be made explicit in the execution of economic policy. For instance, expansionary fiscal policies should concentrate on sustainable projects instead of on across-the-board subsidies or tax benefits. Nevertheless, most economic models still consider the classical tradeoffs between unemployment and inflation or growth and inflation. Even though this book concentrates on traditional economic models, minimizing the negative environmental and social impacts of economic action should be a major concern for society.

The present work is directed at students who are looking for a foundational course that combines macroeconomics and international economics with a contemporary approach that considers the most important obstacles that we face today—such as the middle-class squeeze in some rich countries, extreme poverty and abject institutions in developing countries, gender and racial inequality, and migration waves. It focuses on the main events that have shaped the last decade (globalization and the great financial crisis) and the one that is the major threat to our continued existence (climate change). The book is called *Economics of Global Business* because of its focus on the decisions of policymakers, their impacts on social welfare, and their implications for business managers. It is especially suitable for business school students. Senior managers need a solid grounding in the functioning of national economies because the fortunes of a company depend on the encompassing environment, in general, and on economic policy, in particular. Changes in interest rates, foreign currency regimes, and public budgets influence the behavior of all kinds of companies, from small and medium-sized enterprises to large multinational corporations.

The study of global economics is about understanding economic policy and its effects on the different variables that affect every individual as well as the rest of the world. Businesses and governments capsize if the economy is not performing well, unemployment and inflation destroy economic well-being, and the search for economic growth has immense consequences for people and nature alike. Companies today face a "license to operate" that comes from a tacit agreement between their management and their stakeholders, such as consumers and the local community. As such, ignoring social and environmental issues greatly diminishes a company's lifespan. Every person benefits from understanding the tradeoffs associated with distinct economic policies.

The structure of macroeconomics and international economics is straightforward, and their outcomes are measurable. Nevertheless, there are gaps in our knowledge of economic processes, and we cannot predict perfectly (or sometimes even imperfectly) how policies will affect all dimensions of international markets. A national economy is composed of millions, if not billions, of economic agents that act interdependently. It is a complex adaptive system, like the ones studied in biology. It is impossible to predict accurately outputs from such systems because they show hypersensitivity to the initial conditions. The science behind economics, then, is about making conditional forecasts expressed in statements like "If the central bank raises its target interest rate, inflation should fall in line with its intended interval" or "The government can choose only two of the following—a fixed exchange rate, an autonomous monetary policy, and a free flow capital."[5] Such conditional forecasts inform policymakers, and by the end of the book, readers should be able to write their own forecasts and discuss the costs and benefits of real economic policies anywhere in the world.

Our social welfare function is far from perfect, but it indicates that if we find the right balance of social outcomes, countries are prospering. Yes, GDP is messy and ignores many important economic activities, such as caring for our parents and cooking food for our children. The focus here is not solely on GDP, however. After we take into account the rate of unemployment, inflation, inequality, and the environment, we can talk about development instead of mere economic growth. Governments should strive to improve these social outcomes when deciding on economic policy. Our job is to understand how they go about trying to do just that.

1.2   Mechanisms, Policies, and the Role of the Government

Redistribution is a dirty word in the United States because for many people it is intimately linked to socialism. It shouldn't be. The state has three main economic goals—to provide public goods and correct market failures, to maintain macroeconomic stability, and to determine how much and through which means income should be redistributed.

This first goal—providing public goods and correcting market failures—is related to microeconomics. The state affects certain markets by directly producing goods and services, by outsourcing them, and by regulating the companies that supply markets. Every country has regulatory and supervisory agencies for the financial system. The provision of public goods is clear: the state has two main monopolies—national defense and the judicial system. Other semipublic goods,

---

5. Countries can choose between allowing free movement of capital or imposing restrictions. When there is free capital flow, companies and people can move their money in and out of a country freely.

like education and health care, are provided by public, private, or mixed agencies. In most countries, health care is universal, but rich families have access to private hospitals and clinics.

Throughout modern history, the state has always played a role in economic development. It is responsible for allocating resourcing to certain industries while investing in infrastructure and the provision of public goods. In some countries, governments use state-owned companies to foster investment, and in others, public banks play a significant role. Even in the United States, supposedly the epitome of a market economy, the government intervenes in the healthcare market. The Patient Protection and Affordable Care Act (also known as Obamacare) was a healthcare reform enacted in 2010 to increase insurance affordability through direct or indirect public subsidies.

Redistribution is a fundamental role of governments that has nothing to do, in principle, with socialism or any strong ideological bent. Every society has recognized that economic gains are not equally distributed, regardless of the economic or political system. In some countries, elites fight to keep income concentrated in their hands. In others, the societal arrangement favors income redistribution, a situation that is found throughout the rich world. Income tax, pension systems, and universal access to education are all examples of the role played by the state in redistributing income. There is no rich country in which governments do not redistribute income. What is more, income redistribution is a precondition to development. There cannot be true prosperity without it spreading to all of society to some degree.

In most rich countries, there is a fundamental tradeoff regarding equity and equality. The US system favors efficiency, the Danish one equity, and the Brazilian lags behind in both dimensions. The United States has more top universities than any other country, but it does not have universal access to college degrees. In Denmark, every college student gets the same subsidy from the state (around 700 euros per month). There is no discrimination: every student has access to a college degree, and subsidies are evenly distributed. This creates moral hazard, with many young people going to universities even if they have no particular interest in a college degree. But it is an egalitarian system, or as egalitarian as we can get at this stage of humankind development. In most developing countries, the education system is elitist and inefficient. In such countries, the system could be made more efficient without becoming more unequal or made more egalitarian without losing efficiency. The political system decides on the design of the education system, and it determines income redistribution by deciding on the amount of equity embedded in the system.

Redistribution does not come solely from handouts or a progressive marginal income tax rate. Morality plays a role in how countries determine their redistributive systems. Efficiency concerns constrain it. Here, there is no a priori choice between equity and efficiency. The Danish university system is more egalitarian, and the US system has more elite universities. Both are valid choices. We do need to make tradeoffs explicit, however. Income inequality is at the forefront of the economic and political issues in many countries, poor and rich alike. In the United States, middle-class discontent helped propel Donald Trump's candidacy for president. In China, as growth slows and stops lifting all boats, concerns about inequality are increasingly more relevant. Every economic policy decision has distributive effects. We cannot disassociate macroeconomic policies from distributive concerns.

Given all this, we can describe the role of public authorities in the context of macroeconomic policy as using economic policies to affect different macroeconomic markets with the purpose of influencing economic growth, stability in price levels, employment, income inequality, and sustainable development. As we have seen, governments have at their disposal, in general terms, monetary, fiscal, and currency policies.

The difficulty with the economics of global business stems mostly from the fact that each policy option affects different markets and the policies interact with each other. For instance, contractionary monetary policy (when governments increase the interest rate, making borrowing more expensive) increases public debt, whereas defining a fixed exchange rate may limit a country's autonomy to influence the target interest rate. Additionally, each policy has its own mechanisms. Fiscal policy acts through taxes and government spending, and central banks conduct conventional monetary policy through open-market operations on government bonds. Quantitative easing (QE), a new instrument added after conventional policy had reached its limits, is an unconventional approach to the way central banks operate. Under QE, central banks buy government and corporate bonds from the market; in effect, they are printing money. Nowadays, some central banks in developed economies are printing money as a way to influence economic activity. Although most people learn in high school that printing money begets inflation, this is not happening. Conventional and unconventional economic policy tools and their impacts on society are discussed later in the book.

A comprehensive knowledge of the economics of global business entails proficiency in the workings of different markets, the distinct mechanisms of each policy option, the interrelations between markets and policies, and measurement issues regarding policy targets. The book follows a structure that starts with an operational definition of macroeconomic markets, goes on to explore the short- and long-run dynamics of the market for goods and services, introduces the relationship between the financial and real sides of the economy, analyzes the tradeoffs

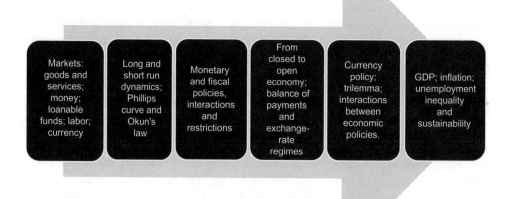

The structure of the book

between economic policies, and finally examines the implications of an open economy.

The linear structure of the book seems logical, but given the multiple interactions among the parts of the economic system, it is impossible to divide economics into pieces that follow a unique trajectory. For every relationship analyzed in the text, many are left unexplored. Unlike most textbooks, in this text, methodological discussions on the measurement of macroeconomic outcomes are at the end of the book. The aim is to bring forward the most interesting parts of economic policies and its implications. Details on the methodology for calculating the social outcomes of international economics—GDP, inflation, unemployment, inequality, and sustainability—appear at the end of the book. Such details are important for understanding national accounting but less so for analyzing the implications of governments choices.

1.3 Assumptions and Equilibria

Economic models work on assumptions and are supposed to be ideologically neutral. Ideally, they should describe the real world and allow for reliable conditional forecasts. One simple assumption is that people are rational and work in their best interest. It might seem trivial that a researcher needs this assumption to build a micro- or macroeconomic model, but the rationality assumption has profound implications for economic theorists. Take, for example, the rational expectations revolution. Robert Lucas, a Nobel laureate in 1995, was the first to incorporate the rational expectations assumption into macroeconomics, and he showed how to make it operational mathematically.[6] Rational expectations theory states that people's expectations are the same as the forecasts of the model developed to describe the decisions made by those people. Most current sophisticated models use this working hypothesis to constrain individuals' behavior. This is a strong assumption. In fact, Daniel Kahneman won his Nobel prize in 2002 by showing how innumerable biases affect our decision-making abilities. We are not rational. Nevertheless, the counterintuitive thing about assumptions is that even if economic models are based on questionable assumptions, they can be quite useful and describe reality quite well.

Assumptions are necessary and certainly limit the number of testable statements from models, but they do not need to be a perfect descriptor of reality to be incorporated into a model. Yet it is important to understand which results from a model are closely related to the underlying assumptions and which are not. For instance, if a researcher assumes that a society has zero tolerance for inflation, then the behavior of the central bank is different than if the society accepts, like in almost every country, some level of inflation that is adequately low. In the United States, the Federal Reserve has an implicit target for inflation of 2% per year. Results of macroeconomic models depend on their underlying assumptions, and there is a pressing need to make all relevant assumptions explicit.

Building models based on simplified assumptions is at the core of science. Most of the models in this book are simple to facilitate exposition, but they are a fair representation of how the world economy evolves and how public authorities decide on their economic policy. For instance, most government officials do not promise to control inflation and promote economic growth at the same time because there is usually a tradeoff between economic activity and price levels. They also choose between a fixed or flexible exchange rate regime based on perceived costs and benefits.

In introductory textbooks, the focus is on comparative statics instead of dynamic modeling. Comparative statics arises from questions like these: What happens to the price of a good if the technology to produce it improves? What effect does a reduction in import duties of competing foreign goods have on local production? Comparative statics is the transition of one economic outcome to another due to

---

6. For a historical summary, see John Taylor, "How the Rational Expectations Revolution Has Changed Macroeconomic Policy Research," in *Advances in Macroeconomic Theory*, ed. Jacques Drèze, 79–96 (London: Palgrave Macmillan, 2001).

changes in exogenous variables. It is the only technical knowledge necessary for understanding this book. In some parts of the book, equations are presented, but they usually are not essential and are included for the more mathematically inclined readers. Feel free to skip these sections knowing that you lose only some rigor in the process. A primer course in comparative statics is built in the next chapter, but the mechanics are relatively simple. It is the comparison between two different equilibria, before and after some change. Such changes come from what economists refer to as shocks to economic systems. Left undisturbed, economic systems would remain stable and in equilibrium. A cup of coffee would always cost the same, and people would consume the same amount of coffee every day, on average. Markets would be static and balanced, with recurring prices and quantities. Of course, that situation never happens in real life.

Comparative statics is about discrete changes. A balanced market is disturbed. It moves toward a new equilibrium. Maybe people have become richer or do not like coffee as much as they used to. The price of coffee would change until the coffee market reached a new equilibrium. And then something else changes, such as allowing for imported coffee. There would be a new balance and then stability again until some further shock. Comparative statics allow for a precise definition of macroeconomic effects, the direction of causality, and explicit tradeoffs in terms of economic policy.

Examples of comparative statics in macroeconomics and international economics occur in questions like these: What happens to the interest rate when the central bank increases the money supply? What is the effect in terms of employment if the government reduces taxes permanently? Answering these questions requires discrete and clear steps that link international markets and generate clear costs and benefits of economic policy. (Steps for using comparative statics are presented in section 2.2.)

Differently from comparative statics, dynamics trace economic effects over time. In dynamic models there are countless actions and reactions, and the behavior of agents changes over time.

Comparative statics is the main teaching tool used in this book, the instrument for explaining the tradeoffs of economic policy. It also requires another necessary condition—that market forces lead to equilibrium between quantities demanded and supplied. In this kind of framework, the changes are discrete, and markets jump from one equilibrium to another while the background stays constant. Because the reality is dynamic, it is hard to disentangle unique effects from a multitude of distinct changes. Nevertheless, the underlying premise of piecemeal analysis still holds. Conditional forecasts are the bread and butter of macroeconomics, and it is relatively straightforward to establish the tradeoffs using comparative statics. The more sophisticated models tend to introduce different levels of dynamics.

1.4 Shocks and Perturbations

Much of policy making is about the reaction to shocks to economic systems. Markets are interconnected, and shocks propagate through different markets. The structure of this book follows a simple logic. Analysis is done for a single market, shocks affect the market's variables (either demand or supply) and move it to new equilibrium, the shocks then propagate to different markets, and policy responses try to bring the markets to a path that is desired by the policymakers.

Comparative statics is the starting tool. The next step is a partial equilibrium analysis, which is the analysis of one market in isolation. Its counterpart is general equilibrium, which, as the name implies, is the study of changes in all markets simultaneously. Partial equilibrium is more tractable and straightforward than general equilibrium, but in the economics of global business, it is not enough. Economic policies are tools that act in specific markets and that affect the whole economy. For instance, the central bank can increase the money supply, thus lowering the interest rate (determined in the money market), with the ultimate goal of increasing employment (the labor market) and GDP (the market for goods and services). The present framework introduces comparative statics in a partial equilibrium scenario and build the links among macroeconomic markets, leaving the development of a semigeneral equilibrium framework for the final chapters. The general equilibrium framework is suitable for analyzing the effects of shocks on particular markets and their propagation to different ones.

Economics is complex. National economies are dynamic, general, complex adaptive systems characterized by hypersensitivity to initial conditions, which makes it impossible to model them perfectly. As in any other scientific discipline, in a textbook model there is a tradeoff between simplification and faithfulness to reality. In macroeconomics and international economics, one additional issue arises: there is no paradigmatic model commonly used. Although in physics the standard model is the framework to describe reality, no similar thing exists in economics. Worse, different models yield incompatible predictions with distressing consequences. The austerity debate in Europe in the early 2010s shows that many conflicting prescriptions were put forward by economic advisers. In the present text, the underlying framework is atheoretical, in the sense that it does not follow a single economic theory or model. Instead, there is a spotlight on the mental models of policymakers, which differ somewhat from economic theory. They face dilemmas directly, without the benefit of hindsight, and their decisions have immense consequences. The first tradeoff is between action and inaction. As political decisions have their consequences, any decision may bring harm as well as benefits to society.

The present general model has limited dynamics. Dynamics are complicated because of the interlinkage among international markets and because the effects are compounded over time. For instance, one fact on which most macroeconomic models agree is that there is a neutral relationship between money supply and unemployment (or more generally, national income) over time. This means that in the long run, when central banks change the money supply and thus the interest rate, the level of employment remains constant. In other words, variations in the interest rate might affect the national economy in the short run but not the long run. Changes to the money supply, in the short run, affect different markets and bring distinct effects that engender even more changes, depending on how the rest of the economy performs. Moreover, variables do not move in a discrete way, and most markets are beset by countless simultaneous fluctuations. The labor market, for instance, is directly affected by the strength of the economy and indirectly by many other variables, such as the world demand for local products, demographics, immigration, productivity, and technological advances. We simply cannot visualize all the effects of a simple decision like increasing the target interest rate by 25 basis points. It may deflate an asset bubble in an overheating economy, plunge a nation into recession, or have no effect at all.

This book works with the general dimensions of economic models but with a focus on graphical analysis instead of formal modeling. Graphic analysis based on comparative statics requires a compromise. Intergenerational or multistage models are brushed aside in favor of a clear and a straightforward exposition.

1.5   Tradeoffs and the Free-Lunch Conundrum

Economists usually analyze their subject on two levels—micro and macro. The former level is about the decisions of individual economic agents, and the latter deals with economy-wide totals. The underlying equilibrium mechanisms are identical but make different assumptions regarding the behavior of national and international economics aggregates. More important, different equilibria result in different consequences for societies.

The main lesson of economics of global business is that economic policies are costly. A situation in which the course of action is clear is the exception, not the rule. Generally, public authorities have a tendency to act, and although not every decision they make brings the expected benefits, they all come at a cost to society.

One example of this are the "too big to fail" policies. In the great financial crisis of 2008, the bankruptcy of Lehman Brothers, one of the largest banks in the United

States, brought the global financial system to the brink of total collapse. Central banks in the US and Europe intervened with hefty loans to commercial banks in trouble. Less than three weeks after Lehman's fall, the US president at the time, George W. Bush, signed the Troubled Asset Relief Program (TARP) into law. It made available $700 billion for programs meant to bailout US banks. Many observers were harshly critical of TARP.[7] This book argues repeatedly that no policy is without its faults or benefits. TARP, like most economic programs, comes with costs and benefits to society. Just as there is no free lunch, there are no perfect policies that generate nothing but prosperity. Chapter 5 discusses the tradeoffs between bailing out banks and letting them fail, but they are never crystal clear. The most interesting issues in the economics of global business require subjective judgments.

Austerity measures in Europe illustrate another area of contention. Even Nobel laureates criticize the actions of governments that prescribe restraint in countries with excessive public spending but are mired in recessions. Joseph Stiglitz and Paul Krugman, recipients of the memorial prize in economics, are critical of austerity measures in European countries.[8] Other eminent economists have taken more nuanced views or are against profligacy.[9] Here, every view is right—and wrong. Austerity brings benefits (credibility and lower interest rates on public debt) and costs (lower economic output). The goal is to build a framework in which policy prescriptions are context-dependent, and it is up to the reader to balance the costs and benefits and decide on the best course of action. There is no single macroeconomic model and universal policy prescription. Sometimes the two-handed economist frustrates those looking for easy and palatable answers. There are none. Macroeconomics and international economics are social sciences at its best.

1.6   Context-Dependent Economics

The main feature that makes this book different from other textbooks is its emphasis throughout on context dependency. Economics is a social science. Whenever

---

7. For instance, see Halah Touryalai, "Don't Be Fooled, There's No Profit in Bank Bailouts: TARP Watchdog," *Forbes*, April 25, 2012, https://www.forbes.com/sites/halahtouryalai/2012/04/25/dont-be -fooled-theres-no-profit-in-bank-bailouts-tarp-watchdog; and John Maggs, "Criticism of TARP Persists," *Politico*, October 1, 2010, http://www.politico.com/story/2010/10/criticism-of-tarp-persists -042995.

8. Reuters Staff, "Nobel Laureate Stiglitz Sees Italy, Others Leaving Euro Zone in Coming Years," Reuters, October 5, 2016, http://www.reuters.com/article/us-eu-euro-economist-idUSKCN1252GM; and Paul Krugman, "The Austerity Delusion," *The Guardian*, April 29, 015, https://www.theguardian .com/business/ng-interactive/2015/apr/29/the-austerity-delusion.

9. Giancarlo Corsetti, ed., "Austerity: Too Much of a Good Thing?," Centre for Economic Policy Research (CEPR), London, 2012, available at http://voxeu.org/sites/default/files/file/austerity _ecollection.pdf.

economists state that there are universal truths, they are probably wrong. The focus on the social aspect almost guarantees that there cannot be a unique economic theory. Let theoretical physicists continue on their quest for a unifying grand theory. This is not going to happen in economics. Nevertheless, there is method in the madness.

Economic advice is context-dependent but is built on a solid understanding of international economic processes. Government officials face constraints, and although one policy might be effective in a developing country, it might destroy social welfare in a rich one. Even for the same country, the best course of action may change over time: although infrastructure building had helped lift the US economy in the 1950s, it is not a panacea for what ails the United States today.

Economic theories in the economics of global business inform decision makers of the costs and benefits of policies. Expected social outcomes are stated clearly. They can be anticipated. There are policy options that bring many more costs than benefits. Not everything goes. But there is space for a healthy debate. Here is how a student should state her policy advice after finishing the book: "Although I recognize that my advice comes with some costs, I find a compelling argument based on the conditions of the economy today for advocating this particular economic policy. I realize that enacting such a policy comes with some risks, but this is the best way for us to approach (choose one: full employment, better income distribution, higher economic growth, or a lower rate of inflation)." The job of students is to delineate all possible costs, risks, and potential benefits of the policy options. To do that, their subjacent knowledge needs to be comprised of the functioning of economic markets, their connections to each other and to the rest of the world, the expectations and possible reactions of households and companies, and the constraints to policy actions. Let's begin.

I The Management of National Economies

2 Building Blocks: The Market for Goods and Services and Comparative Statics

In this chapter,

- Comparative statics as our main analytical building block
- Why unemployment is higher in France than in the US
- Business cycles and the nonlinear growth path of national economies
- Leading indicators and the importance of forward-looking analyses
- The introduction of countercyclical policies

2.1 The Market for Goods and Services

In this chapter, the main goal is to present the details for the graphical analyses that make the bulk of the economic theory in the book. The priority is to observe actual market dynamics in a simply stylized manner and not to come up with a set of rigorous theoretical models. Here is the first main tradeoff in the book—clarity of exposition versus theoretical rigor. Given that public authorities usually make decisions with simpler mental models than the elaborate ones that economists develop, the macroeconomic models here are simplified, and their essence is distilled in a graphical form.

By using mostly what is called comparative statics, the chapter shows how changing a specific parameter affects the economic outcomes. By proceeding stepwise, considering one external change or internal shock at a time, it takes an economy from one equilibrium to another. An external shock is an outside event that can leave the economy in better or worse shape. For instance, if the Chinese economy slows down significantly, the path of a country that exports to China—such as Mexico—will change. If nothing else changes, the Mexican economy should slow down as well. In this simple example, the Bank of Mexico (the Mexican central bank) may lower interest rates to make loans cheaper and try to jumpstart an economic recovery as the answer to the Chinese slowdown. In the end, there are two steps: first, an external shock moves the economy from point A to B, and second, an economic policy response is made that (if it works) takes the economy from point B to C.

Most macroeconomics books begin by looking at national accounts. Their introductory parts delve into issues such as the techniques used to estimate GDP, unemployment, and inflation. Here, unlike in a pure macroeconomics textbook, the logic is flipped. The book first discusses the inner workings of markets in a national context and then looks at technical aspects of national accounts at the end of the book.

A good understanding of the general principles behind the mechanics of economic processes is more important at this point than a more precise understanding of every term used. All the models used throughout the book are demand and supply models. The variables of interest, like interest rates and GDP, are introduced without lengthy definitions or detailed clarifications. It may seem somewhat daunting at first, but at this stage, deeper technical knowledge is not required.

Let's start with the most important national market—the market for goods and services. Understanding its dynamics is crucial to the economics of global business. A note on jargon: the terms *GDP*, *national income*, and *national output* are almost synonyms. The same applies to the terms *changes in price level* and *inflation*. Economists are supposed to use as little jargon as possible. Sometimes (critics would say usually) we fail. Other than some basic jargon, the only required knowledge of national accounts (for now) is that GDP growth generates prosperity and that rising inflation and unemployment destroy social welfare. For a poor nation, growth is important because it helps take people out of poverty, and inflation is undesirable because people value the predictability of prices. Precise definitions of what is meant by inflation are not necessary at this point, as long as it is understood that inflation is bad and growth is good. Hyperinflation is even worse: prices may double in weeks or even days when countries experience such rapid inflation. Later, the suitability of GDP as a measure of well-being is questioned, but for now it is assumed that we live in a world where infinite growth is possible.

In the market for goods and services, two of the most important economic variables—GDP growth and the rate of inflation—are determined. The market for goods and services is a representation of consumption and production of all goods and services in a country. It also presents the main tradeoff that policymakers face—that between economic growth and inflation.

The tradeoff between growth and inflation informs most of the economic policies in developing and rich countries alike. Whenever a country is mired in a recession, governments try to rekindle economic growth but are always afraid of increasing the rate of inflation. If prices are rising fast, authorities try to keep them in check but are mindful of the potential effects on economic growth. The ideal scenario would be that of an economy that expands continuously with an inflation rate of around 2% a year, leading to increased and sustained material prosperity. Unfortunately, this rarely happens. The main model of the economy in this book is the aggregate demand and aggregate supply (AD/AS) framework that is developed in chapter 4. The dynamics of aggregate demand and supply allow us to represent growth gaps, persistent inflation, stagflation, high unemployment, and many other possible scenarios that happen all around the world. In the mid-2010s, most countries in Western Europe were facing stagnation with deflation. Meanwhile, stagflation was occurring in Russia, and inflationary pressures in India. The AD/AS framework can illustrate all of these and many more. Understanding the dynamics of the market of goods and services is our main building block.

In economics, graphical representations follow a market-clearing process. Markets clear when there is no excess demand or supply. If there is excess supply, the price of a good falls until every unit is consumed. Conversely, prices rise when there is excess demand until everybody willing to buy is able to do so. Going to a supermarket, we can see the market-clearing process in action. In strawberry season, strawberries are cheap; otherwise, people would not be willing to buy the entire production of strawberries. In economics, prices move up and down, regulating the decisions of consumers and producers. Excess supply today leads firms to produce fewer goods tomorrow, and excess demand incentivizes companies to supply more goods and services—more demand, more profits. Market clearing is a dance between consumers and producers in which agents try to maximize their own welfare by either buying low or selling high. Eventually, a price is "agreed" on, and an equilibrium is reached whereby each produced unit finds its consumer.

The market-clearing process in a microeconomics setting yields the market equilibrium that determines the price and quantity (demanded and supplied) of a single good or service. In the case of the whole market for goods and services, the result is the quantity of all goods and services produced and consumed (the gross domestic product) and the price level of the economy (the inflation index). In a simple representation, aggregate demand and aggregate supply meet at the point where current price level meets current real GDP (figure 2.1).

Shifts in aggregate demand and aggregate supply change a country's GDP and price level. Micro- and macromarkets are similar. Nevertheless, even though the mechanics of supply and demand shifts are the same, the underlying supply and demand functions are quite different.

In microeconomics, demand functions describe the response of people to changes in prices of the goods that they consume. The main components for con-

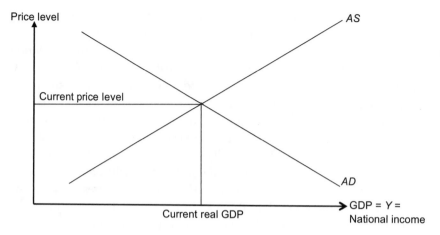

Figure 2.1

sumers' demand of any good are their preferences, their income, and the prices of other goods. People consume more if they like a good, if they are rich, and if the relative price of the good is not too high. If a component changes, decisions also change. For instance, if a new scientific study highlights the health benefits of tomatoes, the demand for tomatoes increases. On the supply side, firms produce more depending on their costs, the technology of production, and the number of competitors. If it is easier to produce something, the supply increases.

One of the main differences between micro- and macromarkets is in the composition of demand and supply. In micromodels, demand functions depend on preferences, income, and the prices of other goods, and in the basic macromodel, aggregate demand is a function of the behavior of consumers, government, and businesses. In its most simple form, for the closed economy,

$$AD = C + I + G,$$

where AD is aggregate demand, C is the aggregate consumption of all households; I is investment in expanded capacity by companies; and G is government expenditure (which is different from government outlays, but more about that later). At this stage, there is no need to delve into the specifics of aggregate supply and demand and the clearing mechanism of the market for goods and services. The only thing that matters is that the market for goods and services is a representation of the decisions of all economic agents regarding consumption and production of goods and services. Figure 2.1 is insufficient to explain the dynamics of the market for goods and services over time. Regardless of how simple or complex the actual dynamic is, inflation (price level) and GDP (national income) are the result of the equilibrium between aggregate supply and demand in the market for goods and services.

2.2   Comparative Statics

Understanding economic policy requires understanding how markets change over time. It is one thing to grasp that aggregate supply and demand determine growth and inflation but another to visualize how they evolve over time and how governments intervene in the pursuit of economic and social objectives. The analysis in this book is based on a few simple steps:

1. Describe the initial equilibrium.
2. Apply an economic shock that leads to a new equilibrium.
3. Show how government and other agents react.
4. Arrive at the final equilibrium, which will depend on the size of the shock, the correct identification of the issue, and an appropriate (or not) response.

These four steps comprise what economists call comparative statics. This kind of analysis usually compares two economic outcomes—the one before the economic shock and the one after the shock. For instance, for step 1, let's assume that our simple framework has a simple negative shock on aggregate demand (see figure 2.2).

In step 2, the economic shock leads to a new equilibrium, and the lower aggregate demand (*AD* moves to *AD'*) results in lower real GDP and inflation. This is

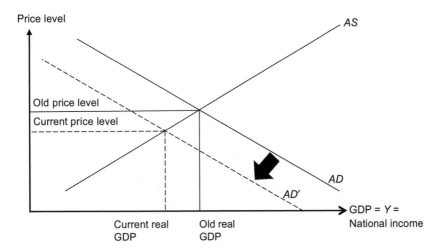

Figure 2.2

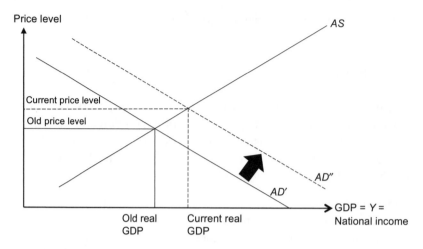

Figure 2.3

comparative statics in action. The old equilibrium ceases to exist as the economy moves toward a new balanced state.

In step 3, we usually go further and assume that the government is going to react. Let's assume that the government is competent, efficient, and accurate in identifying and designing a proper economic response. Further, let's assume that the government wants real GDP to go up to a level closer to what it was before the economic shock. Public authorities will then use the tools at their disposal (fiscal, monetary, or currency policy) to stimulate aggregate demand (figure 2.3). The government reaction moves demand from *AD'* to *AD"*. GDP goes up, as does inflation. Comparative statics can be done only when we let one or very few variables change at one time while the rest of the background is kept constant. The economics jargon is from Latin—*ceteris paribus* (in English, other things being equal). This means that in the example above, we let only *AD* fluctuate at first. The new equilibrium, step 4, is then the result of the economic shock and the timely and efficient response by officials.

Comparative statics is the fundamental building block, and things get more complicated later. Markets can be interconnected, the identification of an economic shock may be difficult, policies come at a cost, and agents amplify or restrict the efficacy of economic policy. Economic shocks can be internal or external. Wars, trade barriers, a slowdown in other countries, and the global financial crisis of 2008 are among many examples of external economic shocks. This book is called *Economics of Global Business* because countries cannot be managed as if the rest of the world does not matter. We live in a globalized world where policymaking is a frighteningly difficult balancing act, even if one shock and reaction are taken at a time.

Even in its simpler essence, the economics of global business is about tradeoffs. In the example above, the government is able to get the economy back to its original equilibrium, but its actions lead to higher price levels in step 4 when compared with step 2, the intermediate step in which the economy adjusted to the shock in aggregate demand. Something is gained (income), and something is lost (inflation).

2.3   The Labor Market

We can use the comparative statics framework to analyze another important economic market—the labor market. The rate of unemployment is determined in this market, which is a representation of the negotiation between individuals and companies regarding employment and wages. People may choose to offer themselves for employment (or not), and wages balance the demand and supply for labor. In a perfectly competitive labor market that requires only one skill from the population, unemployment would not exist (figure 2.4).

In a perfectly competitive market, the demanded quantity of labor (Q_{DL}) is equal to the quantity supplied (Q_{SL}) at the prevailing average nominal wage (w) (figure 2.5). Everybody who wants a job at the market wage is able to get one. There is no involuntary unemployment. Some people might choose not to work, but economists are concerned mostly with people who are not able to find employment. The welfare of a society is lower if an individual cannot find a job at the market

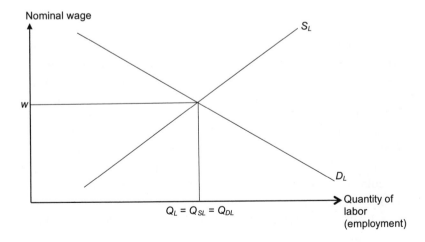

Figure 2.4

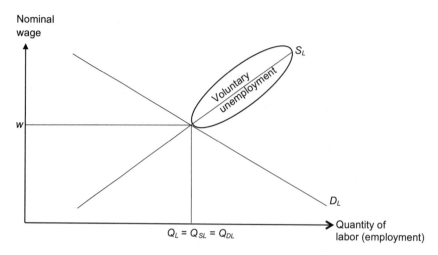

Figure 2.5

wage but not necessarily if people choose not to enter the job market. People who are unwilling to work at the market wage are voluntarily unemployed (figure 2.5).

In real life, people have many reasons for being involuntarily unemployed (from now on, simply unemployed). The main one, long recognized in micro- and macroeconomic models, is that nominal wages are not fully flexible, as a perfectly competitive market would require. Because of labor laws, trade unions, and the minimum wage (for different categories of labor), nominal wages cannot rise and fall freely. For instance, in many countries, it is illegal to reduce nominal wages. Because of that, many businesses have a lower incentive to increase wages during a boom. In a recession, companies face a tough choice—to lay off their workers or to accept lower productivity.

Let's imagine a situation in which an economy enjoying full employment suffers an external shock to its labor demand—for instance, in the shape of a confidence crisis that changes the expectations of future profits (figure 2.6). If the labor market were fully competitive, then a decrease in demand for labor (from D_L to D'_L) would result in lower wages ($w' < w$) and lower employment ($Q'_L < Q_L$). Voluntary unemployment would increase because some people would not be willing to work at a lower wage, but unemployment would still be zero.

However, with a rigid nominal wage (let's assume that it cannot be lowered at all), the result would look like figure 2.7. Because wages cannot decrease, the nominal wage w is unchanged, as is the quantity supplied of labor. As the demand for labor decreases (from D_L to D'_L), the quantity of labor demanded at wage w is now Q_{LD}, and involuntary unemployment ($Q_{LS} - Q_{LD}$) emerges.

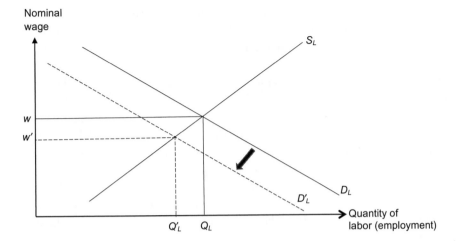

Figure 2.6

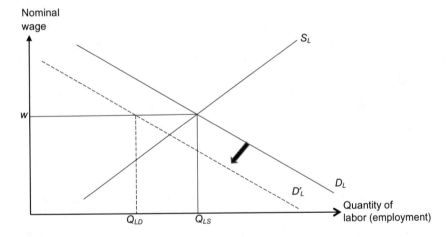

Figure 2.7

This model is a stylized way to explain how unemployment can exist even in a competitive market for labor. More sophisticated models incorporate other factors that can create unemployment. For instance, the costs for asymmetric information, indivisible contracting, and searching and matching generate unemployment even if wages are fully flexible. Given that it is costly to match the skills of people with the jobs requiring such skills and that individuals usually have more information about their skills than companies do, we cannot expect the labor market to clear immediately after any supply or demand shock. Additionally, labor contracts are not fully renegotiable at every single moment in time, resulting in frictions that delay market clearing. More important, if it is costly to hire (and lay off) people, then businesses delay hiring (and firing), leading to more unemployment. Another way to look at this is that companies keep the same number of employees because the quantity of labor in a company cannot be freely adjusted after economic shocks.

People are not goods or services. They have unique skill sets. Companies employ dozens, hundreds, or thousands of workers who have different abilities and motivations to work and who choose to work with more or less effort at any given time. Compounding this complex issue is the nontransference of skills in the short run as people who are trained in one task may find that businesses need other skills. In addition, people may not want to move to places where their skills are more in demand. Not every engineer is willing to work in a mine in the middle of an Australian desert. In reality, regional, national, and international labor markets are extremely fragmented and do not clear easily, which is seen in the large variations in unemployment around the world (figure 2.8).

Labor Laws, Structural Unemployment, and the Differences between France and the United States

In the United States, many people are concerned about the working poor—people who make the minimum wage but need to rely on the welfare system to supplement their income. Many Americans have part- or full-time jobs but still receive food stamps and other kinds of help from the federal and local governments. In Denmark, new parents divide one year of paid leave, with companies and the state footing the bill. In France, the minimum wage is around $12. It appears that the US is lagging behind the rest of the world, right? In fact, in most of Western Europe, people face much longer spells of joblessness than they do in the United States (figure 2.9).

As shown in the figure, after the great financial crisis of 2008, unemployment in the United States reached 10% and crawled back to less than 5% by the end of 2016. In the eurozone, however, unemployment remained above the 10% threshold by the end of 2017. Here is what matters: neither the US system nor the Euro-

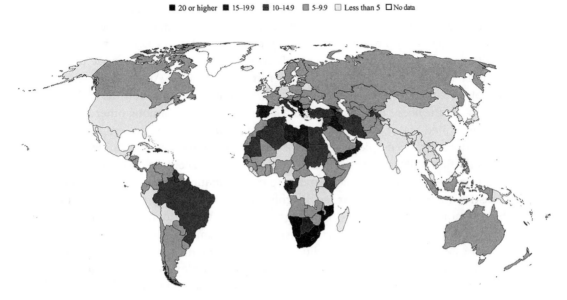

Figure 2.8
Unemployment around the world as a percentage of the total labor force, 2016
Source: World Bank, 2017, https://data.worldbank.org/indicator/SL.UEM.TOTL.ZS.

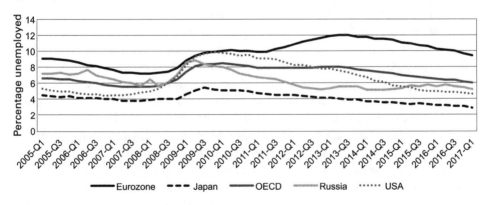

Figure 2.9
Evolution of unemployment, 2005 to 2017
Source: OECD, 2017, https://data.oecd.org/unemp/unemployment-rate.htm.

pean one is better than the other. Although the US economy is considered to be at full employment when the unemployment rate is around 4%, the French economy is considered to be at full employment when it is at 6%. One reason for the difference in full employment rates between the US and France is the difference in labor laws, which are much stricter in France than in America. Structural unemployment can be a result of labor laws, a mismatch between the skills of workers and the needs of companies, or a lack of job mobility, among other factors.

In the United States, one of the major tenets of labor laws is the "employment at will" doctrine. US employees work at the will of companies that can lay them off at any time without justification. There are some exceptions. Businesses are barred from terminating employees due to discrimination based on certain characteristics, the exercise of their legal rights, or whistleblowing, for example. But US companies and employees can negotiate most terms in their employment contracts, and this kind of flexibility leads to a dynamic labor market in which businesses are relatively free to adjust their employment policy to the business cycle. The US labor market is not as free as a pure employment-at-will doctrine would entail, and many states restrict this doctrine in some fashion. Even so, the US labor market is one of the most flexible in the world.

Companies in France operate in quite a different context. They are not free to terminate employees. Labor contracts can be either fixed-term or indefinite. After a probationary period, most fixed-term contracts cannot be terminated. With indefinite-term employment contracts, companies can terminate the contract at any time, but they must be able to justify the termination with a real and serious cause ("cause réelle et sérieuse"), and they must comply with the applicable dismissal procedure (which varies depending on the type of dismissal).[1] The two major categories of dismissals are based on real and serious cause—dismissals based on the employee's behavior ("dismissals for personal/professional reasons," such as a poor performance, the employee's negligence, or the employee's inability to work) and dismissals based on economic grounds ("dismissals for economic reasons"). Dismissals for economic reasons can be either individual or collective, depending on whether one or more positions are to be eliminated or significantly modified. The French Supreme Court has taken a restrictive approach in its interpretation of acceptable economic reasons. Judges can easily reverse firings, both individual and collective, if the court does not find the economic arguments strong enough. Indefinite contracts practically guarantee tenure to French employees who have them, generating strong incentives for companies to be cautious about hiring new staff, even during economic booms.

1. Baker & McKenzie, *The Global Employer: Focus on Termination, Employment Discrimination, and Workplace Harassment Laws*, 164–166, Key Workplace Documents (Ithaca, NY: Cornell University ILR School, 2012).

There are many consequences of the differences in the structure of labor markets in the United States and France. In the US, workers are more mobile, highly skilled workers earn more, and unemployment is structurally lower than in France. It does not mean that the American system is preferable, however. French workers enjoy more stability, their quality-of-life indicators are better, and French companies tend to pay higher wages, on average, to low-skilled workers, at the cost of higher unemployment. In France, unemployment is a major issue, but the existence of working poor much less so than in the United States.

Wage flexibility is an important factor in the distinct dynamics of the US and French labor markets, but different labor laws also play a major role in creating specific patterns of structural unemployment. The academic literature shows that labor markets with strong labor protections are sclerotic. The hiring and firing flows are anemic, and both individual unemployment and the proportion of the long-term unemployed increase. There are many reasons for this, and one model, by Thomas Sargent, a Nobel laureate, and Lars Ljungqvist try to explain the rise in structural unemployment in Europe in the 1970s by assuming that people build up their human capital while they are working on a job and that the capital decreases when they lose their jobs [2]. The result is a representation of the European labor market in which structural unemployment exists because of the adverse incentives brought about by a generous social safety net when it interacts with the unique dynamics of human capital. Wage rigidities alone cannot explain the existence of structural unemployment, and labor dynamics are much more complex than economists previously thought.

Because of its dynamic nature, the US labor market is more resilient to recessions than the European one, which is why it was able to recover much faster after the great financial crisis. After 2008, the behavior of the unemployment rate among developed economies experienced the following changes. In the United States, unemployment quickly reached 10% due to the severity of the crisis, started to decrease after that, and continued to drop until the economy was back at full employment eight years after the onset of the crisis. In 2016, it finally recovered to 4.5% and stayed low throughout 2017. Meanwhile, unemployment in the eurozone countries continued to be higher than in the period before the crisis. Although there were many other shocks during that period that can explain the rising unemployment in Europe, labor markets in Europe are relatively much more rigid than in the rest of the world. This leads to a degree of persistence in the unemployment rate that is absent elsewhere. The labor markets are just different. In fact, in 2017 the French government passed a labor reform to tackle high

2. Lars Ljungqvist and Thomas J. Sargent, "The European Unemployment Dilemma," *Journal of Political Economy* 106, no. 3 (1998): 514–550.

unemployment, but many critics thought that this would lead to more precarious working arrangements.[3]

This chapter introduces the tools that readers need to analyze how labor markets behave. The lesson is that nuance is our friend. There are no simple answers to complex human interactions.

2.4   Dynamics, Business Cycles, and Active or Passive Economic Policy

One appealing and incorrect way to predict the path of national economies is based on an inappropriate mental model of forecasting the future. Many people (and analysts who should know better) assume that whatever trend the economy is displaying now is going to continue in the future. If things are going well, prosperity is guaranteed, and during bad times, pessimism is unassailable. In 2007, for example, many people were convinced that a US$100 barrel of oil was the new norm and that companies should prepare for oil prices to double in the next few years. In January 2015, when oil prices bottomed out at US$24, many forecasted that they would drop below US$20, but they more than doubled in the ensuing two years. What some analysts failed to take into account is the business cycle. Economies move in cycles. Recessions are followed by expansions that eventually are replaced by contraction. The technical jargon for this process is the business cycle.

In introductory books, the spotlight is usually on simple representations and comparative statics. Real-life dynamics are much more complicated than simple textbook models, but dynamics is a fundamental building block of the economics of global business. Without it, it is impossible to analyze possible courses for political action. National economies (and the world economy as a whole) follow business cycles.

There are many reasons for booms and busts in economic activity. One driver is the way economic agents adjust their decisions to expectations of future market situations. Let's assume that, for one reason or another, entrepreneurs and consumers expect the economy to do worse in the future. When consumers delay consumption and companies delay investments, these actions start pushing up the unemployment rate. Rising unemployment reduces consumer purchasing power, reduces economic activity even more, and culminates in a contracting economy. As the economy shrinks, the workers lose bargaining power, and the price of capital goods (necessary for investment) decreases. Businesses that think

---

3. Heather Connolly, "Macron's Labour Reforms Are a Major Test for France's Trade Unions," speri. comment, November 3, 2017, http://speri.dept.shef.ac.uk/2017/11/13/macrons-labour-reforms-are-a -major-test-for-frances-trade-unions.

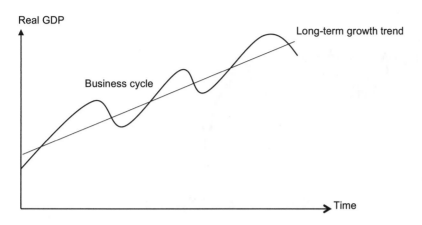

Figure 2.10
Leading index for the United States, 1982 to 2017
Source: Federal Reserve Bank of St. Louis, 2017, https://fred.stlouisfed.org/series/USSLIND.

the economy is at rock bottom use this opportunity to contract cheaper investment, and the economy eventually rebounds.

The world economy is composed of trillions of individual transactions, and the
aggregate patterns of these transactions determine whether the economy grows
or contracts. There is no linear path to prosperity. No economy ever grows constantly over time, like clockwork. World income has increased thirtyfold since
1800, but that growth has not been smooth. Instead, national economies grow
over periods of expansion and recessions. For simplicity, let's assume that the
really long-term growth trend is linear. Over time, economies grow, but this
takes place in fits of booms and busts in the business cycle (figure 2.10). Another
way to explain the behavior that generates business cycles is to use a quote
from Warren Buffet: "Be fearful when others are greedy and greedy when others
are fearful."

The growth pattern for most economies is not as clear-cut as it appears in figure
2.10, however. For instance, real GDP grows exponentially and not linearly over
time. During periods of industrialization, economic growth accelerates, and as
countries become richer, the rate of growth declines. Additionally, expansion
periods are longer than recessions, and because of globalization, changes in
growth rates reverberate throughout the world economy, synchronizing the business cycles across the world, to some extent. Figure 2.11 illustrates the pattern of
expansion and recession in the US economy. The figure has data that was taken
from the leading index by the Federal Reserve Bank of Philadelphia and that
incorporates information to help researchers forecast the growth rate of the US
economy for the next six months.

Figure 2.11
Evolution of real GDP growth in the United States, 1982 to 2017
Source: Federal Reserve of St. Louis, 2017, https://fred.stlouisfed.org/series/A191RL1A225NBEA.

Economists differentiate between leading and lagging indicators. Leading indicators are those in which changes help signal future economic activity, and lagging indicators are mainly the result of past economic activity and therefore hold little predictive power. For instance, the unemployment rate is a lagging indicator, whereas the flow of unemployment insurance claims is a leading one. If significant numbers of workers are claiming unemployment benefits, this probably means that economic activity is slowing down and companies are firing a large number of people. This shows up in employment figures later.

Data on economic growth show the pattern of business cycles. Similar patterns apply to data for unemployment. Figure 2.12 shows how the US labor market reacts to business cycles. For workers, two recessions—the first in the 1980s and the second following the financial crisis of 2008—were particularly severe, with the unemployment rate breaching the 10% barrier.

Business cycles are extremely important for the well-being of a great swathe of the population (table 2.1). The baby-boomer generation in the United States enjoyed a significant increase in living standards due to rapid economic growth in the 1950s and 1960s: GDP per capita grew strongly, and middle-class incomes rose disproportionately fast. However, workers entering the job market right after financial crises (for example, in the 1930s and the late 2000s) faced uncertain prospects, with comparatively lower indicators of living standard satisfaction.[4]

---

4. Many theoretical models generate business cycles. Some academics thought that real business cycle (RBC) theory, introduced in the early 1980s by Finn Kydland and Edward Prescott, would explain the

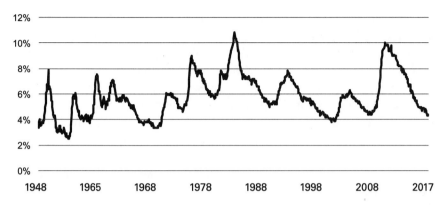

Figure 2.12
Monthly (seasonally adjusted) civilian unemployment rate for the United States, 1948 to 2017
Source: Federal Reserve Bank of St. Louis, 2017, https://fred.stlouisfed.org/series/UNRATE.

Table 2.1
Average length of business-cycle phases in the United States, 1886 to 2000

	Average length (months)		
	1886–1916	1920–1940	1948–2000
Recessions	9.7	14.0	10.7
Expansions	34.0	31.6	55.9

Source: J. Bradford DeLong, "Growth Accounting," http://j-bradford-delong.net/macro_online/growth_accounting.pdf.

major features of macroeconomic data. Two such features are volatility (aggregate investment is more volatile than GDP, and the consumption of nondurable goods is less volatile than GDP) and persistence (high growth tends to follow high growth, and low growth tends to follow low growth). RBC models are dynamic general equilibrium models in which economic agents with rational expectations optimize their decisions and key parameters generate fluctuations in economic activity. Even though the results were underwhelming, RBC models helped economists understand better how exogenous shocks reverberate through different markets and affect the whole economy.

More recently, dynamic stochastic general equilibrium (DSGE) models have become even more ambitious in building mathematical representations of the national economy. DSGE models try to encompass clearing of all macromarkets. They build hypotheses about the behavior of economic agents that are subject to random shocks. Then they proceed to the dynamics of each market and their integration. This integration generates fluctuations of GDP, inflation, and unemployment.

DSGE models have not been as successful as their creators hoped. Even if DSGE models cannot predict the world at large, however, they still have the benefit of improving our understanding of the interrelations among different markets and the tradeoffs of economic policies, among other things. Many central banks use them and they are part of the regular toolbox of policymakers around the world.

Nowadays, it is common to see headlines about millennials who are afraid that they will earn less than their parents and about unaffordable housing in many cities in the rich world. Such headlines will quickly disappear if the world economy fully recovers from the great financial crisis of 2008. We all suffer from forecasting bias—a tendency to forecast the future as a linear continuation of the present. If a country is mired in a recession, it is hard to see the light at the end of the tunnel, whereas during prosperous times, people tend to become overly optimistic. In the United States, as in most of the world, expansions last longer than recessions.

No period of growth lasts forever and calmer times eventually follow a storm. This kind of dynamic thinking is paramount to understanding the evolution of national economies.

2.5   An Introduction to Economic Policy

The basic argument for active economic policy and the main goals of governments are introduced in this section and are examined more comprehensively in later chapters. In general, government officials have at their disposal monetary (interest rate determination), fiscal (taxes and outlays), and currency (interventions in the foreign exchange market) policies. Their main goal is the smoothing of business cycles, particularly by shortening recessions. These economic policies would be countercyclical. Ideally, governments would like the economy to grow with low volatility, relatively stable prices, and full employment. The canonical economic goals are growth, full employment, and price stability. So the direct goals of economic policy are the smoothing of the business cycle and the increasing of long-term trends (figure 2.13).

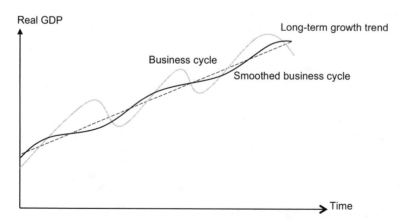

Figure 2.13
Evolution of real GDP over time

The smoothing out would prevent the formation of bubbles in real and financial markets when the economy is overheating and prevent hard recessions that have a significant impact on the quality of life of the population. Unfortunately, trade-offs are inevitable. Because of the myriad of possible economic indicators, both lagging and leading, a policymaker is always dealing with uncertainty about the future path of the economy. Currently, models are simply not powerful enough to generate predictions that accurately forecast peaks and valleys in economic activity. Every time that a government acts, there is a risk it is going to do more harm than good. What is clear is that the political system creates strong incentives for governments to take action. In most countries, policymakers are active in the pursuit of the main economic goals of full employment and price stability.

Government interventions are never free, however, and officials face restrictions in the implementation of economic policy. Additionally, tradeoffs are context dependent. For example, governments with large budget deficits have less power to try to counter a recession by spending government funds to rekindle economic activity.

Another dimension of economic policy is the choice of currency regimes. Some countries favor fixed exchange rate regimes and as a consequence face speculative attacks, and others prefer floating exchange rate regimes but have to deal with exchange rate volatility. Some countries, like the ones in the eurozone, abdicated their monetary policy in favor of a currency union. They can only try to influence the European Central Bank.

There are many examples of countercyclical policies in action, as when the Federal Reserve announces that the target interest rate in the United States will rise by 0.25%, the European Central Bank decides to extend quantitative easing, or the Chinese government increases public spending. Nevertheless, nobody can map all the possible effects of each government policy and identify how they interact over time. There are no counterfactuals, no second chances for economists and policymakers to rewrite history to weed out misguided government interventions. Economic models are useful to make conditional forecasts—that is, to determine what the more likely effect of one policy would be. Even though they cannot predict all the consequences of government action, models still yield a good understanding of how the markets interact, with current knowledge expanding daily as the models evolve.

3   Growth in the Long Run

In this chapter,

- Economic growth across history
- The Solow model and how countries can achieve economic prosperity
- China and Vietnam success stories
- Endogenous growth theory and the role of ideas

Following the conclusion of the Eighteenth National Congress of the Communist Party in 2012, Xi Jinping, general secretary of the Communist Party of China, announced an organized and enduring antigraft campaign. We know that most rich countries have low levels of corruption. Singapore, culturally similar to China, is one of the richest countries in the world and is almost devoid of corruption. The questions are whether the antigraft campaign in China will help the country turn into a rich country and what the conditions are for true economic and social development. We need an economic framework to determine such conditions. China and many other countries—like Turkey, Thailand, Uruguay, and Botswana—have left poverty behind and are now middle-income societies. What barriers are still in their way to development? At the other end of the development spectrum, will rich societies take the opposite path and become poorer? What guarantees that Italy or Canada will continue to be rich, even if there is economic stagnation?

The goal of this chapter is to establish the conditions for prosperity—what economists call long-run analysis. Prosperity does not arrive overnight but is the outcome of complex social processes. Here, as in most textbooks, macroeconomic analysis is divided into the short run and the long run. We begin with the latter.

3.1 Growth through the Centuries

Economic growth is an important piece of the prosperity puzzle, even though it started to play a significant role only in the last two hundred years. Here are three important observations related to growth:

• True long-term prosperity hinges on a country's institutions and its political stability. They are the necessary conditions for countries to become rich.
• Long-run growth stems from potential growth or the efficient use of resources. The supply side of the economy is more important. Innovation, new industries, and human capital are the key drivers.
• Short-run growth is determined mostly by demand factors, which shape the GDP growth of the current year. The path of the economy in the next few quarters is influenced by the behavior of consumers and companies, government spending, and the foreign demand for the country's goods and services.

Modern capitalist economies did not start to grow at a fast rate until the 1800s. Before then, standards of living tended to increase very slowly. In 1820 in Italy, GDP per capita was only 30% higher than it was in 1 AD, and Italians in the 1700s, after the Renaissance, were barely richer than Romans were in 1 AD. For poorer economies in Europe, standards of living merely doubled in eighteen hundred years, according to the estimates by historian Angus Maddison.[1] This pattern was no different for the rest of the world. From 1 AD to 1820, GDP per capita increased by 30% in China and by less than 20% in India. Between 1 AD and 1750, the world population grew on average 0.1% per year,[2] more than the rate of economic growth. During the first millennium, the average growth rate of GDP per capita was 0% in Western Europe and India, and between 1000 and 1820 the rate was roughly 0.14% in Western Europe and 0.02% in India.[3] Since then, income per capita has increased at least twentyfold in every major country in the world and between fifty and two hundred times in Western Europe. The world economy continues to grow at an average rate that is forty times higher than that of the pre-1800 world.

Figure 3.1 shows the growth pattern for major economies since the 1800s. We can see that significant economic growth is a recent phenomenon. For most of the last two thousand years, economies grew little, if at all. However, beginning with the industrial revolution, the world changed dramatically.

1. Angus Maddison, *The World Economy: A Millennial Perspective* (Paris: OECD, 2001).
2. Charles Jones, "The Facts of Economic Growth," *Handbook of Macroeconomics* 2 (2016): 3–69.
3. Maddison, *The World Economy*.

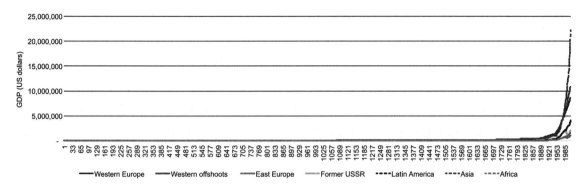

Figure 3.1
Real GDP by world region, AD 1 to 1985
Source: Max Roser, "Economic Growth," *Our World in Data*, 2017, https://ourworldindata.org/economic-growth.

Since 1800, real GDP per capita has increased over fourteen times. But economic growth has been unequal. Average Africans have five times more income than they did in the 1800s, but the average Australian is eighty times richer. In 1800, the Australian economy created US$500 of income per resident in today's dollars, and in 2015 GDP per capita was more than US$40,000. In 1800, average people living in Latin America or Asia were richer than the typical Australian, and they are now poorer. Many factors explain the rates of economic growth between countries. Australia converged to the rest of the rich world in the mid-1900s and is now a rich country. Australian growth also displays the difference between economic growth and economic development. Although the country is rich today, it came at a cost to the environment and the native peoples, who are still much poorer than the average Australian. Efforts have been made to alleviate abject poverty, but there is still a way to go in closing the gap between aboriginal Australians and the rest of the population. True development takes into account income inequality, the environment, and other measures of prosperity that go beyond mere GDP growth.

The convergence of Asian and Latin American countries is more recent. Singapore, Japan, and South Korea are examples of Asian countries that became rich in a relatively short period, and Chile in Latin America is approaching their levels (figure 3.2). Meanwhile, many other countries diverged. Argentina is the main lesson in divergence. In 1900, it was the fourth-richest country, as measured through GDP per capita, and now it is deeply entrenched in the middle-income trap (countries that are able to escape poverty but fail to improve further). In 2017, inflation was at 40% per year and cannot be compared to previous years because for a while the Argentinian government published erroneous inflation data and

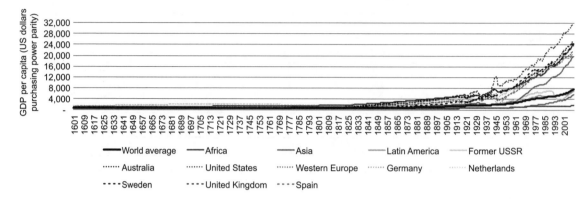

Figure 3.2
Real GDP per capita around the world, purchasing power parity (PPP) adjusted, 1601 to 2001
Source: Max Roser, "Economic Growth," *Our World in Data,* 2017, https://ourworldindata.org/economic-growth.

prosecuted any institution that tried to publish correct data. In the 2000s, the country defaulted on its sovereign debt, and its social indicators have not budged much in the last ten years. Some countries—like Australia, South Korea, and Japan—were able to climb all the way from poverty to developed status. Others, like Mexico and Russia, have not been poor for decades but stopped climbing the income ladder.

There are many explanations for the exponential growth of modern capitalist economies and how they turned economic activity into true development. We already cited two: a country's institutions and political stability and also its efficient use of resources. Daron Acemoglu and James A. Robinson (following other great economists, like Douglass North, historians, and social scientists) identify inclusive institutions as the main catalyst for sustained prosperity.[4] Inclusive institutions are those that allow companies to expand production with a time horizon in which they can be sure that other agents, such as governments, cannot extract their profits. The quality of government, secure property rights, and the rule of law allow a mobility of people, capital, and ideas that leads people to innovate and create businesses. Deirdre McCloskey argues that modern standards of living can be explained by the rise in bourgeois ethics and the spread of bourgeois values through capitalism.[5] Growth through the centuries is clearly multidimensional, and no single explanation is able to account for the patterns shown in figure 3.2.

4. Daron Acemoglu and James A. Robinson, "Paths to Inclusive Political Institutions," January 19, 2016, https://economics.mit.edu/files/11338.
5. Deirdre McCloskey, *The Bourgeois Virtues: Ethics for an Age of Commerce* (Chicago: University of Chicago Press, 2006).

Over the past two hundred years, economic growth has exploded and spread around the world, but economies have never experienced predictably sustained activity. Every modern economy goes through business cycles. Economic growth is not linear. In business cycles, the difference between the short run and the long run is not based on the time dimension, as one would expect.[6] It is related to the nature of the production of goods and services. The short run is the period when some production factors are fixed. In the long run, all production factors can be renegotiated and thus are variable. When economists talk about long-run growth, they mean a process by which the economy returns to its natural path and when the actual production of goods and services of a country meets its potential. In technical terms, it is the convergence of actual output to potential output. Actual output is measured by the current GDP. It shows how much a country is actually producing. Potential output is the amount of goods and services that the economy would be producing if it were using all its resources (capital, labor, and natural resources). In France in the early 2010s, for example, the rate of unemployment averaged 11%. France's use of labor was well behind its potential (it would have full employment when the rate of unemployment is around 6%). In the short run, French GDP lagged behind potential output because many people could not find jobs. But the French economy would be expected to reach its potential output eventually.

We can dispel some myths regarding market economies. The most common one is that economics is a zero-sum game: for some countries to prosper, others have to fail. It is understandable that many people might feel this way because Western imperialism in the nineteenth and early twentieth centuries molded the modern world. The Opium War helped keep China poor, and the apartheid regime in South Africa was tied directly to the country's colonial roots. Fortunately, the world has changed and is now interdependent. It can provide space for every

6. The term *long run* is not precise. Some historians and economists argue that there are other, longer, cycles than the business cycle. Fernand Braudel analyzes a secular cycle, with peaks in 1350, 1650, 1817 and 1974. Fernand Braudel, *Capitalism and Material Life, 1400–1800*, 3 vols., trans. Sian Reynolds (New York: Harper & Row, 1982–1992). His work is full of insights about the development of the modern nation-state, the speed of globalization, the slow adoption of capitalist institutions, and much more. Another example of different economic cycles is the kind put forward by Nikolai Kondratieff. In his work, cycles are shorter (only fifty years on average) but are still much longer than typical business cycles. Nikolai Kondratieff, *Long-Wave Cycle*, trans. Guy Daniels (New York: Dutton, 1984). For economists, the long run is different from periods of decades or centuries. The long run is the time it takes for all factors of production to be variable; it is not growth over time. In the short run, companies face fixed factors of productions that limit their actions. For instance, a company that operates an industrial plant cannot easily build another one. In the long run, the company can choose the number of industrial plants that would maximize its profits, but in the short run, it has to contend with the number of plants that it already operates. If the company takes four years to build an industrial plant, then the short run is roughly four years, and the long run is any period over four years.

country to grow and prosper. The major constraint is the impact on the environ-ment, not on another country's income status. China has risen, and India will surely follow. The world has benefited from Chinese growth, and China has bene-fited from the world's growth. Contemporary globalization provides win-win sce-narios for countries, although not always for all their citizens because constraints tend to be national in scope. Countries often fail to prosper because of internal dynamics.

Another myth is that economic growth is unsustainable. Countries can grow forever, although perhaps at lower rates. Demography is one reason that the pattern likely changes: it is harder for nations to grow when their populations shrink. Here is the main issue in political economy today: the tacit agreement between a government and its citizens is to provide material wealth. This is espe-cially true in developing countries. Vietnamese, Hondurans, Congolese, almost everybody in the developing world, and most people in the rich world, are looking for pure economic prosperity, which translates to higher GDP per capita. Escaping poverty is the main economic dream in most corners of the globe. Every-thing is easier when economies are growing. Poor countries want to converge, and rich countries look for sustained prosperity.

Consider Japan, South Korea, and Singapore in the context of true long-term prosperity, long-run growth and short-run dynamics. All these countries left abject poverty behind relatively quickly: they rapidly went from poverty in the 1940s to developed status. They now face first-world problems like aging populations, soaring healthcare costs, and short-run obstacles to more accumulation of income and wealth. Why have they been able to make the jump but other countries—like Congo, Bolivia, and Indonesia—have not?

Here is a condensed version of the virtuous cycle that led to industrial and economic development in these three Asian countries. Improved institutions allowed investment that made their economies grow. This bolstered educational opportunities outcomes that further improved institutions and created incentives for further investment. Social norms evolved, and corruption declined from endemic to exceptional.

Any form of social organization that generates efficient use of resources and creates incentives for innovation can work. Capitalism is not required (although it's the devil we know). Economic shocks—such as aging populations, global financial meltdowns, and international conflicts—can create obstacles to sustained prosperity. The main lesson is that it is relatively easy to point to the conditions of a successful economic environment and much harder to implement policies that make a country improve its institutions persistently.

John Maynard Keynes may have not been entirely correct when he stated that "In the long run we are all dead," which became a manifesto for economists to concentrate their efforts on short-run dynamics instead of long-run equilibria. The long run matters and not only for our children and grandchildren.

3.2   The Solow Model and Growth in the Long Run

Throughout the centuries, jumps in the level of development come from political and judicial stability and the quality of a country's institutions. There is no easy path for prosperity. No lottery ticket can take a country from poverty to development. The dynamics of economic growth arise from interactions between the aggregate supply and the aggregate demand in the market for goods and services. And decades of economic modeling in the subject of long-run growth have shown that for the economy to grow in the long run, aggregate supply factors are more important than aggregate demand. Conversely, short-run fluctuations are the consequence of changes in aggregate demand. To put it simply, long-run economic growth is a supply story, and short-run growth is a demand feature.

The Solow model is a powerful model of how countries prosper in the long run. Robert Solow, a Nobel laureate, developed the basis for all growth models in the mid-1950s (Trevor Swan independently advanced a similar model around the same time). Most modern growth models, from simple partial equilibrium to dynamic stochastic general equilibrium (DSGE), are sophisticated variations of the growth equation introduced by Solow and Swan. Here we use an extended version of the Solow model to incorporate natural resources in the growth function (which comes from the supply side of the economy), something that Solow himself worked out in 1974[7] and 1986:[8]

$$Y = f(K, AL, AN),$$

where Y is the output, f is function, K is capital, A is an index of productivity (technology), L is labor, and N is natural resources. In the long run, economic prosperity comes from these four simple factors. So why is the world getting richer today, and why do many countries expect to grow year after year after year, when economic output per person in 1800 was almost the same as it was when Rome was the center of the Western world? The quick answer is that this improved economic performance began with the industrial revolution and continues to this day thanks to successful waves of innovations like electricity, Fordism and its

7. Robert M. Solow, "Intergenerational Equity and Exhaustible Resources," *Review of Economic Studies* 41, no. 5 (1974): 29–45.
8. Robert M. Solow, "On the Intergenerational Allocation of Natural Resources," *Scandinavian Journal of Economics* 88, no. 1 (1986): 141–149.

economies of scale, penicillin and modern medicine, and the World Wide Web. Innovation and its diffusion allowed companies and nations to accumulate K and L, exploit N, improve A, and unlock an unparalleled economic growth engine that has been churning out economic prosperity ever since, sometimes slower and sometimes faster, depending on the position of the country in the business cycle.

Our version of the Solow model determines a country's potential level of GDP (at which the economy uses all its production factors efficiently) and not the actual level of GDP over time. Economic growth in the long run is about potential. The more potential a country accumulates, the faster prosperity can come. Think of education and human capital. It is hard for a country with uneducated people to truly prosper over time. People who are educated are more productive, on average, than those who are illiterate. Yet public investment in education does not generate early returns. Human capital accrues over time.

Solving for the Solow model analytically is beyond the scope of this book. Here we need only a basic understanding of the model to develop important implications for how countries develop over time. The essence of the model is that long-run aggregate supply (LRAS) grows over time because of the accumulation of capital and labor and the exploitation of natural resources. Yet all factors of productions (K, L, N) result in diminishing returns, so technological improvements are the only way to increase GDP per capita because they allow for better combinations of these factors of production.

Imagine automobile production, which is important in many countries, including the United States. The US economy is bigger today than it was in the past because the country produces more cars, it produces them more efficiently, and it makes better cars. The way we combine capital, labor, and natural resources to produce cars is more important than just the absolute number of cars we produce. Technological innovations allow us to produce more with the same factors of production. A poor country can grow by making more things until it uses all its resources, and from then on, only technological advances can bring more prosperity.

Let's imagine a small country that sells only textiles. To produce 1 ton, it requires capital, cotton, and the effort of 100 workers. Using all of the country's available labor of 1 million people, it could produce a maximum of 10,000 tons of textiles. Now, let's imagine a leap forward in textile technology that allows 100 workers to produce 3 tons. The potential output level increases threefold, and actual output can also increase to 30,000 tons. This is the essence of the Solow model and the reason that potential output is important but does not determine growth by itself. After all, without demand for 30,000 tons of textiles, the economy would not produce this amount. The model is about the potential and unlocking the path for growth—and after this is done, demand comes into play.

Our version of the Solow model shows a wide range of other interesting results, but its main one is that because of diminishing marginal returns, economic output cannot increase forever based solely on the accumulation of capital and labor and the exploitation of natural resources. Without growth in technology, there can be no growth in prosperity.[9]

Industrialization, China, and the Solow Model
Industrialization is a feature of emerging-market economies that allows rapid growth over a significant period. In China, GDP grew at more than 10% a year from 1979 to 2015, reaching US$10.87 trillion and making China the second-largest economy in the world (figure 3.3).

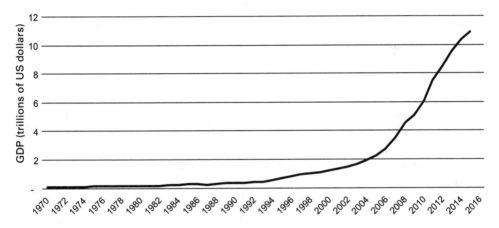

Figure 3.3
Chinese GDP at market prices, 1970 to 2016
Source: World Bank, 2017, https://data.worldbank.org/country/china.

9. The Solow model was developed in the 1950s, but most contemporary growth models also predict that aggregate supply is the main determinant of long-run growth, even though they do not use the same specifications as the one presented in this section. Current models use total factor productivity as one of the main restrictions on growth in long-run economic output. Diego Comin defines *total factor productivity* as the portion of output not explained by the amount of inputs used in production. Diego Comin, "Total Factor Productivity," *The New Palgrave Dictionary of Economics*, ed. Steven Derlauf and Larry Blume (Hampshire, UK: Palgrave Macmillan, 2008). As such, its level is determined by how efficiently and intensely the inputs are utilized in production, and it plays a critical role in economic fluctuations, economic growth, and cross-country per capita income differences. Much of the literature on real business cycles is based on the role played by total factor productivity in disseminating economic shocks to the underlying market for goods and services. Growth in the long run is still mostly a supply-side story (more on that below), and changes in the long-run aggregate supply affect potential output and the path of the economy over long periods.

There is no single explanation for the Chinese success. It was the result of a combination of several factors, including market reforms, rising labor productivity, opening up its economy to trading with the world, capital deepening (the accumulation of capital over time), and regional competition. Even though Chinese growth is multifaceted, the long-run model described in this section can explain what happened in China and other countries that experienced the industrialization and postindustrialization phases of economic development. The impressive Chinese story is far from unique. Industrialization transformed the economies of Japan and South Korea from destruction after World War II to the developed economies they are today. Industrialization also lifted Mexico and Russia from poverty to their middle-income status, and one of the main reasons that these economies are stuck in the middle-income trap today is the absence of postindustrialization technological improvements.

Part of the impressive Chinese growth over the last thirty years comes from changing the nature of working life in the country. Before the market reforms, most people lived in rural areas and worked in subsistence farming. Since 1980, however, hundreds of millions of people have moved to urban areas looking for work, and by 2030 another 250 million people are expected to migrate from rural to urban areas. The median urban worker is three times as productive as the average rural worker in the country. Using the language of the Solow model, migration increased the amount of labor (L) and its productivity (l). Growth in L and l explains 2% to 2.5% of the annual rate of growth in the Chinese GDP but does not explain all of it.

In an industrialization period, growth is due mainly to capital deepening and the increase in productivity from a sudden change in the ratio of labor to capital. Even though hundreds of millions of people moved to cities, the growth in capital in China was even higher. Aggregate investment was more than 50% of GDP for every year from 1980 to 2015 and generated strong patterns of capital deepening. Another example is the transformation of Japan and South Korea from agrarian societies to manufacturing powerhouses. Capital was shallow in these countries in the early 1900s, and now it is deep. China is going through the same process. In other parts of the world, capital deepening may be important in the future. Looking at most African countries today, their capital is shallow, with a significant part of their GDP coming from manual agriculture.

After the benefits of capital deepening end, the economy reaches its steady state, and aggregate supply grows, in real terms, at the rate of technological progress. In China, industrialization was a long process and may not be over yet. As the Chinese government prepares its new five-year plan, the main concern is how to maintain growth in a situation of diminishing marginal returns to capital. Reaching steady-state growth explains the deceleration of the Chinese economy, which was growing at 10% until 2008 and reached "only" 8% in 2013, 7% in 2015, and 6.5% in 2016. Because of this decline, the Chinese central government is signaling that innovation is the only way to keep the economy growing, a conclusion that is confirmed by the Solow long-run growth model. The pattern of capital accumulation and technological advances also explains growth in Japan and South Korea in the period between 1950 and the 1990s. Nevertheless, true prosperity will come only if China absorbs or develops new technologies to complement the capital-deepening process from industrialization.

The United States: Escaping the Middle-Income Trap

Poor countries can take two main economic paths—to middle-income status and then, overcoming the middle-income trap, they can achieve sustained prosperity. In the mid-nineteenth century, the United States started on a path similar to the one that China is traveling today. In 1800, the United States was mostly an agrarian economy. It was not poor but was far from achieving upper-middle-income status. In the early nineteenth century, the first industrial revolution spread machine-based manufacturing, and beginning in the 1830s, American industrialization was fueled by railroad construction, a capital-intensive activity (figure 3.4). By 1860, when the Civil War began, the North was more industrialized than the South but still was not an industrial economy. Only 26% of the population lived in urban centers. After the American Civil War, however, the country strengthened its institutions and made market reforms that generated a wave of prosperity that continues to this day. By the final third of the century, a second industrial revolution saw the rapid development of technologies that further expanded the

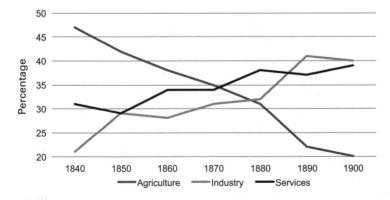

Figure 3.4
Contribution of economic sectors to total output in the United States, 1840 to 1900
Source: Joel Mokyr, *The Lever of Riches: Technological Creativity and Economic Progress* (Oxford: Oxford University Press, 1992).

economy. Immigration helped increase the labor supply, and people flocked to urban centers. Many modern US institutions, such as antitrust agencies and the Federal Reserve Bank, emerged in the late 1800s and early 1900s.

By the end of the 1920s, farmers were only 12% of the US population. Electricity, oil, and coal became the major power sources of the economy. If not for the Great Depression of the 1930s, the United States would have been a rich nation throughout the 1920s, 1930s, and 1940s. Nevertheless, by the time that World War II ended in 1945, the US had developed an industrial economy complemented by a labor-intensive service sector—the same structure that it has today.

Until 1800, most US economic growth came from agriculture. As industrialization took place, capital went from being almost zero to being the major driver for economic growth. Another phase of development started in the early 1900s, and since the mid-twentieth century, economic prosperity has come from technological advancements.

In the United States, institutions have been working relatively well for over a century. The rule of law is followed, even when parties feel that it is unjust, and property rights are respected. The country's system of checks and balances has worked reasonably well. Both the judiciary and the media are independent, especially compared with other countries.

The US has a dynamic economy because companies expect to take home future profits if they invest and develop technologies there. The system is not overly corrupt. New products turn into more profits. New technologies become even more gain.

The middle-income trap is caused by instability of norms, justice, institutions, and rights. These are the main obstacles facing countries like Russia and Turkey. And because the United States has succeeded in achieving stability in these areas, it is the richest country in the planet and still has its most dynamic economy. This is easily illustrated with data.

One way to analyze the evolution of growth over time is through growth accounting, a simpler framework than a formal model of economic growth. In growth accounting, the main idea is to isolate the sources of long-run growth by looking at their individual contributions to economic output. Bradford J. DeLong does it for US growth in the 1948 to 2000 period.[10] Table 3.1 shows US economic growth in total output or GDP (Y), GDP per capita (Y/L), technology evolution (A), and capital deepening (K/L).

As shown in this table, the economic history of America in the second half of the twentieth century can be easily divided into two periods of significant growth (1948 to 1973 and 1995 to 2000) and one period when the economy was relatively

10. Bradford J. DeLong, "Growth Accounting," May 17, 2002, delong.typepad.com/delong_long _form/2002/brad-delong-growth-accounting.html.

Table 3.1
Decomposition of growth in the United States, 1948 to 2000

Period	Annual growth rate of			
	GDP (Y)	GDP per capita (Y/L)	Technology (A)	Capital deepening (K/L)
1948 to 1973	4.0%	3.0%	1.8%	1.2%
1973 to 1995	2.7%	0.9%	0.1%	0.8%
1995 to 2000	4.2%	3.0%	1.9%	1.1%

Source: Bradford J. DeLong, "Growth Accounting," http://www.j-bradford-delong.net/macro_online/growth_accounting.pdf, 2002.

sluggish (1973 to 1995), one reason being the oil crises of the 1970s. Capital accumulation does not change much, but the technological productivity factor does. From 1995 to 2000, most of the growth in the US economy was due to the Internet revolution, which drastically improved productivity. Nevertheless, A is a measure of overall productivity that is broader than just innovation. A is technology in the broadest sense, a measure of improved combinations of production factors. Such improvements do not come only from innovation. For instance, imagine one person who is good at math and another who is a good writer. Because of a misallocation of labor, the math-inclined person is writing reports, and the one who has a way with words is working in accounting. Reassigning them makes both people more productive. The number and quality of products and services increase. Improving regulations, constraining monopoly power, reducing the costs of doing business, and spreading new ideas can all result in an improved use of other production factors.

The US example illustrates the conditions necessary for long-term prosperity and the ways that countries grow in the long run. Without improved technology, the American economy may face a secular stagnation that is akin to the middle-income trap but, in this case, for rich countries.[11] Although the United States has left the middle-income trap, its political system is becoming more dysfunctional, which can have profound consequences on the potential growth of the country's economy. Continuing dynamism, economic activity, and even the American dream hinge on the strength of its fully functioning institutions.

Human Capital and the Asian Success
What role does education play in a country's progress? So far, the model for long-run growth has included labor (L) as a variable in the aggregate supply. Human

11. Lawrence Summers, a former secretary of the US Treasury Department, has resurrected the concept of secular stagnation, a term first coined by Alvin Hansen in the 1930s.

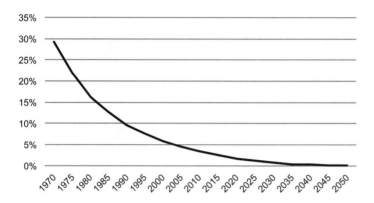

Figure 3.5
Population without access to primary and secondary education in South Korea, 1970 to 2050
Source: Max Roser and Esteban Ortiz-Ospina, "Primary and Secondary Education," *Our World in Data*,
2017, https://ourworldindata.org/primary-and-secondary-education.

capital includes the many human dimensions that translate into the production
of economic value. It might seem obvious today that a population with more
creativity, social abilities, and education generates more economic output, but the
concept, in its contemporary formulation, was introduced to the economic literature only in the late 1950s by the Nobel laureate Gary Becker and his coauthors.

Human capital helps explain the success of some Asian countries in moving
from poverty to development in the span of a few generations. In the early 1950s,
for instance, Japan was poor, with a GDP per capita that was lower than that of
most countries in South America. Nevertheless, it had one of the most educated
populations in the world, with virtually every Japanese finishing primary and
secondary education. At that time, more than 20% of Italians had no access to
basic schooling. In the 1950s, South Korea was more like Italy than Japan in
terms of school access, but the country quickly moved toward universal access
(figure 3.5).

Today, South Korea and Japan have the highest rates in the world of tertiary
education attainment by their young population (twenty-five- to thirty-four-year-
olds). Among countries in the Organisation for Economic Co-operation and Development (OECD), the lowest levels for tertiary education are in Mexico (21%), Italy
(25%), and Turkey (28%) (figure 3.6). Not coincidentally, Mexico and Turkey are the
two least developed of the OECD countries. In Japan and South Korea, most
young people have college degrees. In fact, no other country comes close to South
Korea, where 69% of people between age twenty-five and thirty-four have a tertiary degree.

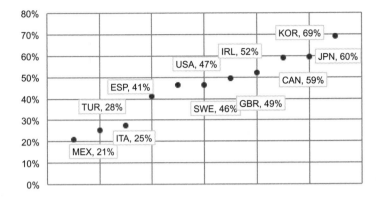

Figure 3.6
Adults twenty-five to thirty-four years old with a completed tertiary degree, OECD sample, 2017, from lowest to highest
Source: OECD, "Population with Tertiary Education," 2017, https://data.oecd.org/eduatt/population
-with-tertiary-education.htm.

Higher human capital results in more innovation, higher productivity, and a lower probability of rent-seeking (manipulating public policies and economic conditions as a strategy to increase profits). Rent-seeking is common in poor countries, where it is typified by elites who extract resources from the rest of society, limiting economic growth and social justice.[12] Improving primary and secondary education would help many countries catch up with richer nations, but such investments take time, and many governments are too short-term oriented. Over the past fifty years, two major factors in the economic development of Asian countries are that states have invested in education and families have motivated their children to study more. We also know that in poor countries, investments in early education have a higher social return than investments in later stages. James Heckman, an American Nobel laureate, has measured the costs and benefits of investments in human capital and concluded that it is more expensive to try to improve human-capital outcomes later in life (figure 3.7). Even though early education investments pay off more, human capital is so important that even moderate investments in improving education always have a positive rate of return to society.

3.3   Beyond the Solow Model

Textbook frameworks are useful narratives, but usually they do not reflect frontier academic research. The present narrative is simple: long-term prosperity in

---

12. Dani Rodrik, "Getting Interventions Right: How South Korea and Taiwan Grew Rich," *Economic Policy* 10, no. 20 (1995): 53–107.

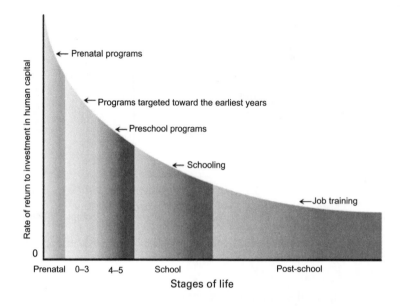

Figure 3.7
Rate of return to investment in human capital
Source: James J. Heckman and Dimitriy V. Masterov, "The Productivity Argument for Investing in Young Children," *Review of Agricultural Economics* 29, no. 3 (2007): 446–493; James J. Heckman, "Return on Investments: Cost vs. Benefits," 2017, https://childandfamilypolicy.duke.edu/pdfs/10yranniversary_Heckmanhandout.pdf.

developed countries hinges on gains in aggregate productivity, the accumulation of capital and labor, and the exploitation of natural resources. Nevertheless, many factors come into play in different countries with distinct development paths. In theory, poor countries should converge, but that does not necessarily happen. Countries like Spain, Portugal, and Greece closed much of the gap that separated them from the richer countries on the continent until the great financial crisis stopped that process. Since the crisis, European countries have been converging at distinct rates or not at all. Austria is now as rich as Germany, with some former Soviet satellite countries, such as the Czech Republic and Slovakia, not far behind. Greece, however, has been diverging and has become poorer than it was before the crisis, in both absolute and relative terms. Other former Soviet satellites, such as Romania and Bulgaria, also are diverging instead of experiencing fast growth.

Countries accumulate human capital at different rates. In Asia, the quality of education is high, and families invest significant amounts of time and money in it, but in Latin America, the quality of the education systems is low, and hyperbolic discounting leads poor families to invest relatively little in learning.[13] Governments around the world allocate resources to "strategic sectors" with varying degrees of success. Some countries spend more on R&D than others at the same stage of development. In Africa, most countries have high birth rates and are entering a demographic boom. If the countries are able to improve their institutions to provide stable political systems, they could harness private investments to benefit from increasing the productivity of their young population. In Western Europe, on the other hand, healthcare costs are soaring as the population ages. No single model can explain all the various paths toward development.

Our version of the Solow model is still a good representation of how market economies grow. They accumulate factors of production that eventually suffer diminishing returns, so they pursue sustained growth by increasing total factor productivity—that is, by implementing technological advancements. Although countries may take different paths to growth, we still can describe them using the language of the Solow model and building more sophisticated analyses after the foundations are laid. China has accumulated capital and labor at astounding rates in the last thirty years, which have sustained its growth so far, but it will need its productivity to increase in order to maintain the growth path. Authorities in emerging countries share similar concerns. For each country, the patterns of accumulation and productivity gains are different, but the present model is still an effective descriptor of economic-growth processes in the long run.

3.4   What Sustains Productivity and Long-Run Growth?

Long-run growth comes from the accumulation of factors of production, exploitation of natural resources, and increased productivity in the form of technological advancements. But what drives the pursuit of accumulation and innovation? Long-run growth comes only when somebody benefits from all these aggrandizements. Somebody needs to invest a lot and keep doing it. Prosperity comes only if agents—companies, governments, or entrepreneurs—invest, keep investing, and keep getting better at it. In every rich country, companies are the main source of investment, and their shareholders benefit from it. Even state-owned companies can provide investors with the incentives to keep going for more.

---

13. The term *hyperbolic discounting* refers to a strong preference for the near future in comparison with a more distant future. In the case of education, investment in human capital generates income in the long run: children who enter primary school at age six complete high school after twelve years. Under hyperbolic discounting, families invest little in education because they cannot or are not willing to wait for the investments in education to vest. Hyperbolic discounting also makes families save less in their old age. Families in Latin America save a much lower proportion of their income than South Asian families do, even if they are, on average, richer.

What truly matters is that organizations keep looking for new ways to improve production and inventing new things. Some countries are really good at this, and some are not. Most get better at doing this over time and catch up with the rich countries. Yet many remain oppressively poor, and no amount of foreign aid, technical assistance (from organizations like the World Bank or the International Monetary Fund), or successful neighbors can bring prosperity to some corners of the world. What makes some countries good at the economic game and others not?

Answering this question takes us away from pure economic models and into the realm of history, sociology, and political and law studies. Society creates a cultural and legal environment that allows investment that guarantees sustained prosperity. Even religion needs to be taken into account. Max Weber, a founder of sociology, argued that Protestants had a moral obligation to fulfill their duties in worldly affairs, which included maintaining a frugal lifestyle and pursuing material wealth.

The legal environment contributes much to prosperity. The first law that allowed the modern form of limited liability corporations originated in New York in 1811.[14] Before the emergence of limited liability companies, shareholders risked losing everything when their companies failed. When limited liability companies go bankrupt, however, their shareholders are not responsible for their debts beyond their stake in the company. Their investors are cushioned from the risks incurred by the companies. Because the cost of failure is lower, companies can innovate more. Limited liability allows for more creative destruction.[15]

Strong institutions are a necessary condition for countries to create prosperity. A particularly good insight comes from dividing governments into extractive and nonextractive.[16] Extractive governments extract resources of society to serve only the elite. Many dictators held on to power by massacring their people, have died rich and left their own countries poorer than they were before they came into power. But extractivism happens in both authoritarian and democratic regimes. In many democratic countries, authorities design policies to benefit themselves first and foremost. Throughout the twentieth century, Latin Americans elected many governments that destroyed social value for their own benefit.

14. "The Key to Industrial Capitalism: Limited Liability," *The Economist*, December 23, 1999, http://www.economist.com/node/347323.
15. The term *creative destruction* was coined by Joseph Schumpeter and refers to the process of less productive companies being displaced by new rivals. Capitalism is at its best when companies can emerge freely, forcing incumbents to be ever more productive.
16. The relevance of institutions for long-term growth has a long tradition in economics. See, for instance, Douglass C. North, "Institutions," *Journal of Economic Perspectives* 5, no. 1 (1991): 97–112; and Oliver E. Williamson, "The New Institutional Economics: Taking Stock, Looking Ahead," *Journal of Economic Literature* 38 (2000): 595–613.

Corruption is a major obstacle for development because it impedes the efficient allocation of resources by limiting innovation and taking away resources that could be used to increase production. A corrupt environment also creates moral hazard. For instance, if most public employees are promoted because of personal contacts instead of merit, others are discouraged and do not give their best efforts. A local government can misuse an antigraft campaign to eliminate political opposition, but if it really changes the social contract, it can boost productivity. People who have worked in Brazil or China and then live, even briefly, in Denmark are amazed by the country's high ethical standards. This Scandinavian country constantly ranks as one of the least corrupt countries in the world. Not coincidently, Danish society is rich, and its citizens enjoy a very high standard of living.

There is no single narrative that explains why some countries are better than others at fostering long-run economic growth. No two countries follow the same path to prosperity, but their long-run growth always comes from technological advances that allow for the improved use of capital and labor, exploitation of natural resources, and well-functioning institutions and political systems.

Vietnam toward Development

Vietnam's economic success has been almost as spectacular as that of China. It was a poor country before the Vietnam War (1955 to 1975) between North Vietnam (supported by China, the Soviet Union, and other communist allies) and South Vietnam (supported by the United States and other anticommunist allies). Poverty increased in its aftermath, given the level of destruction from the long war. Economic and political reforms that began in the mid-1980s, however, allowed the country to move away from a centrally planned economy and back to a market-oriented one, and by the early 2010s, it was classified as a lower middle-income country by the World Bank.[17] Average annual income rose from US$100 in 1986 to more than US$2,000 in 2016.

One path for growth was through trade. In the early 2010s, trade in goods and services represented on average 150% of GDP.[18] Most growth has come through the accumulation of capital and human capital, coupled with a demographic bonus: the country had over 90 million residents in the 2010s, most of whom were under twenty-five years of age.

17. Brett Davis, "Vietnam: The Quiet Economic Success Story of Asia," *Forbes*, February 2, 2016, https://www.forbes.com/sites/davisbrett/2016/02/02/vietnam-the-quiet-economic-success-story -of-asia.
18. "The Other Asian Tiger: Vietnam's Success Merits a Closer Look," *The Economist*, August 4, 2016, https://www.economist.com/news/leaders/21703368-vietnams-success-merits-closer-look-other -asian-tiger.

Table 3.2
Variables of the dynamic stochastic general equilibrium (DSGE) estimation for Vietnam

A. Variables that are endogenous under decomposition closure and exogenous and shocked in forecast closure	B. Corresponding variables that are exogenous under decomposition closure and endogenous in forecast closure
Real GDP	Economy-wide primary-factor productivity
Terms of trade	Shifts in export demand schedules
Wage relativities	Qualification composition of aggregate training

C. Shocked variables that are exogenous in both forecast and decomposition

Primary factor technology, by industry

Intermediate input-using technology, by commodity

Occupation-specific input requirements

Consumer preferences, by commodity

Economy-wide shifts in import and domestic preferences

Consumer price index

Number of households and population

Import prices in foreign currency

Tariff rates, value-added tax rates, and export tax rates

Land use by industry

D. Variables that are endogenous in both forecast and decomposition

Wage rates by industry, occupation, and qualification

Employment by industry, occupation, and qualification

Capital stock by industry

Investment by industry

Demand for source-specific commodities for production, investment, and private and public consumption

Export volumes by commodity

Commodity prices used in production, investment, consumption, and exports

Demand for margin m by agent k to facilitate purchase of commodity c from source s

Source: James Andrew Giesecke, Nhi Hoang Tran, Gerald Anthony Meagher,ad Felicity Pan, "A Decomposition Approach to Labour Market Forecasting," *Journal of the Asia Pacific Economy* 20, no. 2 (2015): 243–270.

Vietnam's growth, like that of China and other South Asian economies, came at first from rapid industrialization in labor-intensive industries. James Giesecke and coauthors[19] put forward a forecast based on dynamic modeling to estimate the growth and decomposition of the Vietnamese economy up to 2020. Their work highlights the complexity of dynamic stochastic general equilibrium models. The variables for their model are shown in table 3.2.

19. James Andrew Giesecke, Nhi Hoang Tran, Gerald Anthony Meagher, and Felicity Pang, "A Decomposition Approach to Labour Market Forecasting," *Journal of the Asia Pacific Economy* 20, no. 2 (2015): 243–270.

Most of the forecasted growth for Vietnam comes from total factor productivity. The model predicts that between 2010 and 2020, GDP should grow at 7.3% per year, a rate that would move Vietnam to middle-income status by the end of the decade. Of the total rise in income, 60% would come from technical change, 20% from labor accumulation, and the rest from capital accumulation from local and foreign firms. Growth from natural resources exploitation over the period would be negligible.

Many emerging countries are stuck in the middle-income trap. When industrialization and growth in potential output take economies from poverty to middle-class status, the population benefits tremendously. But after attaining that level of income, countries create further growth through strong institutions and increasing productivity as a result of technical advances. Japan and South Korea in Asia, Ireland in Europe, and New Zealand and Australia in Oceania were able to escape the middle-income trap in the last few decades. It remains to be seen if Vietnam will follow suit.

Guinea and the Plight of Poor Countries

Poor countries need investments and institutions. Nothing illustrates this better than the case of Guinea (formerly French Guinea), which is one of the world's poorest countries and yet sits on one of the largest iron ore reserves in the world. In 2015, the country had around 13 million people and a GDP of US$7 billion. In the same year, the metropolitan area of Jacksonville in Florida, had a population ten times smaller (1.3 million people) and produced ten times more economic output (around US$70 billion). GDP per capita in Guinea stood at US$540. Poverty is usually correlated with other social issues. Although life expectancy almost doubled in Guinea from 1960 to 2015, it was below sixty years for the average Guinean in 2015.

One thing that poor countries have going for them is opportunity. Reasonably competent governments can lead economies out of abject poverty relatively easily. Companies have trillions of dollars put aside waiting for good opportunities to put their cash to work. Being part of a start-up economic engine in a poor country is a good opportunity because the prices of financial and real assets are low and the few production factors that a poor country uses are misallocated. When poor countries build competent institutions, they can quickly benefit from economic gains, but opportunities usually are wasted in the developing world.

Guinea's iron ore reserves, for instance, go untapped, even though some of the biggest mining companies in the world have tried to extract it. In 2010, Guinea held its first democratic elections, and the government of newly elected president Alpha Condé promised to keep corruption in check so that mining could begin.[20] Graft impedes economic growth by lowering everything in the aggregate supply function. Resources are allocated poorly, and technology (A) grows slowly. Most important, corruption contributes to rent-seeking behavior and helps elites entrench themselves. The result is perennially poor countries or the middle-income trap for those that leave poverty behind. In Guinea, the approval for mining never led to action, even though one of the largest mining companies in the world, Rio Tinto, had the rights to explore the resources.

There are economic implications of unused natural resources. Based on our version of the Solow model, mining the roughly 2 billion tons of iron ore would generate economic growth in Guinea, and this growth could be used to start industrialization or fund investments in human capital. Mining also should balance the needs of society with those of the environment. Exploring the resources in a sustainable way would be difficult but not impossible, but in this case, it generated only legal fights.

Poor countries have many opportunities, but missing them becomes a way of life, mainly because they lack functioning institutions. Extractivist governments do not allow prosperity to emerge and never turn sporadic short-term growth into long-run dynamics. Rarely, countries like Japan and South Korea (which were as poor in the 1940s as Guinea is today) foster a virtuous path of growth that improves institutions, which then nurture more growth. Economics cannot explain everything. If it could, then the Guinean iron reserves would be extracted in a way that did not destroy the environment and would benefit all.

3.5 Levels of Development

Economic development takes time. Japan was poor in the early 1950s and now is rich. The United States was a middle-income country in the late 1880s and now is the richest large country in the world. To compare short-run and long-run growth, we create a two-dimensional classification system. The first dimension includes the actual level of development, divided in three categories of poor, middle-income, and rich. The second dimension includes the position of the economy in the business cycle—recession, stagnant, or dynamic. Countries experiencing recessions face short-run headwinds that usually are not enough to make a country take a step down on the development ladder. Over the last two hundred years, many countries climbed up the ladder, but few dropped.

For now, we are equating income to development. A rich country, in the economic development classification used in this section, is also a developed economy,

---

20. "Africa's Largest Iron-Ore Deposit Has Tainted All Who Have Touched It," *The Economist*, January 12, 2017, http://www.economist.com/news/business/21714388-billionaires-and-big-companies-have-come-cropper-one-worlds-poorest.

but this is not always the case. By the criterion of income per capita, Equatorial Guinea (formerly Spanish Guinea) is an upper-middle-income country. But the country's GDP data is skewed by its vast oil reserves. Most of the oil money never reaches the average citizen, so it is far from developed and faces many of the social issues that befall poor countries. In this section, we ignore outliers such as Equatorial Guinea; we return to the development versus growth discussion later in the book. It is hard to find examples of developed societies that are not rich. High GDP per capita is a necessary but not a sufficient condition for development.

Today, the main obstacle that the Chinese economy faces is the middle-income trap, the barrier that makes it difficult for countries to climb from middle-income status to rich. Nevertheless, China was a dynamic economy in the first half of the 2010s after its thirty-year progress from poverty to middle-income status. Around the world, Vietnam, Botswana, and Peru jumped from poverty to a lower-middle-income status in the last forty years, but they will find it hard to continue their success in the future if the middle-income trap engulfs them. Using data for 2016, we can classify these four countries as middle-income economies at the height of the business cycle. They are the true emerging countries, but there is no guarantee that they will become rich.

Meanwhile, Brazil, Russia, and South Africa were all firmly stuck in the middle-income trap that China and other dynamic emerging countries are trying to avoid. Such dysfunctional countries are not emerging markets anymore but are at best unequal middle-class societies.

There are nine possible combinations of economic development in the classification system used here—from poor countries in a recession to dynamic rich countries and everything in between. The worst-case scenario is a poor country in a recession. This was the position of Burundi and Liberia in the mid-2010s.

Poor countries that are dynamic may be going up a development level. Rwanda and Tanzania are examples of countries that are poor but growing and that could climb the development ladder. In 2017, Rwanda's development goal was to "transform the country from a low-income agriculture-based economy to a knowledge-based, service-oriented economy with a middle-income country status by 2020."[21] The economy grew 7% a year from 2014 to 2017. But to climb the ladder of economic development, a country needs to improve its institutions. Rwanda changed dramatically after its civil war ended in 1994 and ranks fifty-sixth out of 190 countries in the World Bank's "Doing Business" report for 2017. The country's overall governance increased 8.4 points on a scale of 100 from 2006 to 2015, according to the Mo Ibrahim Foundation.[22] Rwanda's score was 62.3, ninth among

21. World Bank, "Doing Business," 2017, http://www.worldbank.org/en/country/rwanda/overview.
22. Mo Ibrahim Foundation. "Ibrahim Index of African Governance," 2017, http://mo.ibrahim .foundation/iiag/2017-key-findings.

African countries, in 2015. The combination of better institutions and a dynamic economy makes the target of attaining middle-income status by 2020 feasible for the country. One example of improved institutions is the development of financial markets. According to the World Bank in 2017, Rwanda's financial markets are the second-best in the world in providing nonfinancial companies with access to credit. But there are risks too. In 1994, Paul Kagame became the ruler of Rwanda after a bloody civil war and transformed the country into a stable and orderly nation. But its institutions are far from perfect. The country is a police state, and cronyism disenfranchises a significant slice of the population.[23] If there is a peaceful leadership transition and future governments slash cronyism and enhance trust in institutions, the country should continue to develop. Otherwise, the country might devolve economically and socially.

As the world develops, it is difficult for countries to be left behind, so it is hard to find examples of decadent economies that step down the development ladder. But there are striking exceptions. Argentina was the fourth-richest country in 1900 but now is stuck in the middle-income trap. Far worse is Venezuela, which was once an upper-middle-income country but faced famine and hyperinflation in the mid-2010s. The country provides an example of how devolving institutions can make a country poorer. Hugo Chávez was president from 1999 until his death in 2013, even against clear constitutional limits. His government concentrated political power in the executive branch, a process that Nicolas Maduro, who succeeded Chávez, continued. The rule of law was weakened, and many companies were nationalized. Some companies were forced to produce goods and services according to the central government's dictums. In November 2013, Maduro enacted a plan that limited profit margins in many industries. During the governments of Chávez and Maduro, corruption increased drastically. In 2016, Venezuela ranked 166 out of 176 countries in the Transparency International's corruption perception index. On a scale of 0 (highly corrupt) to 100 (very clean), it scored 17 (in 2001, it had scored 69). The World Bank's "Doing Business" report for 2017 ranked Venezuela as 187 out 190 countries overall. Venezuela also illustrates that changes in the levels of development happen slowly. Although Venezuela has been horribly managed since the late 1990s, it still clings to a middle-income status. If nothing changes, it should become a poor country by the 2020s. Other examples of devolution are Libya and Syria, but these cases are easier to explain: civil wars plunge countries into economic depression if they last long enough.

For rich countries, a major worry is secular stagnation, a concept first put forth by Alvin Hansen in the 1930s and resurrected more recently by Lawrence Summers,

23. "Many Africans See Kagame's Rwanda as a Model: They Are Wrong," *The Economist*, July 15, 2017, https://www.economist.com/news/leaders/21725000-its-recovery-after-genocide-has-been -impressive-land-ruled-fear-can-never-be-happy.

a former secretary of the US Treasury Department. If countries stagnate for a significant period, the dreams of an optimistic middle class turn into nightmares of soaring unemployment, stagnating income, and a collective sense of dread.

Development paths may change over time or vary within countries. Some examples from the mid-2010s include Detroit, Michigan, and Dayton, Ohio, which were examples of stagnant regions in a rich nation in the mid-2010s. Dayton's unemployment was much higher than in the rest of the United States, its economic activity barely grew, and its rates of heroin overdose were among the country's highest. Recovery could happen, though, with growth in the area improving Dayton's social outcomes. Divergence within nations is also relevant to explaining fragmentation in France, and other countries. Although Paris's economy is dynamic, in many other areas, such as Nouvelle-Aquitaine and Hauts-de-France, stagnancy is the norm, creating tension and political polarization.

The best possible path for a country is the dynamic-development path. In this trajectory, dynamic economies and evolving institutions allow countries to jump from poor to middle-income to rich status. From the early 1950s to the 1980s, Japan developed quickly. In 1950, annual per capita income in Japan was US$97 (at the prevailing exchange rate of ¥360 = $1), which amounts to less than US$1,000 in 2017. This is equivalent to the per capita income in Zimbabwe or Tanzania and lower than that in India, which just entered middle-income status. In 1950, the typical middle-class salary in Japan was the equivalent of US$6,000, and it has increased nearly tenfold since then. The dynamic journey of Japan's economy was derailed by a financial crisis in the early 1990s, but from 1950 to 1990, the country escaped poverty and the middle-income trap. Throughout the 2000s and 2010s, it had a stagnant economy, but its trajectory displays how a country can become rich in less than two generations. South Korea traveled a similar path that China and India are vying to follow.

According to the World Bank, in 2017, poor (or low-income) economies were defined as having an income per capita of US$1,025 or less; middle-income countries as having an income per capita of between US$1,026 and $12,475; and rich countries as having an income per capita higher than US$12,475.[24] The pattern of income per capita around the world is shown in figure 3.8.

In the business-cycle dimension, recession is defined as negative GDP growth, stagnation as growth that is positive but lower than 2.5%, and dynamism as growth that is higher than 2.5%. Because poor countries have a lower income base than rich countries, a growth in income of 2.5% per year is not enough to make their economies truly dynamic. For a country like Spain, which is rich and has a stable

24. World Bank Data Team, "New Country Classifications by Income Level," World Bank, https://blogs.worldbank.org/opendata/new-country-classifications-2016.

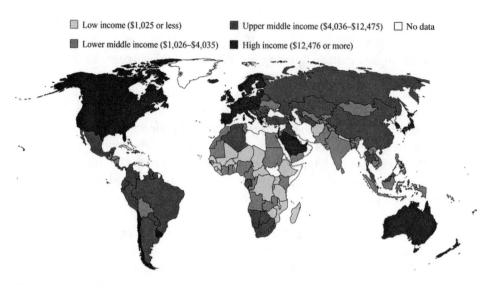

□ Low income ($1,025 or less)   ■ Upper middle income ($4,036–$12,475)   □ No data

■ Lower middle income ($1,026–$4,035)   ■ High income ($12,476 or more)

Figure 3.8
Global income per capita (Atlas method, current U$), 2016
Source: World Bank, 2017, https://data.worldbank.org/indicator/NY.GNP.PCAP.CD.

population, economic growth above this threshold means true material prosperity, but this is not so for a poor country. Furthermore, this classification system is backward looking and uses past data to identify the position of a country in the business cycle. For economic policy, expectations matter more than past data. Even with these shortcomings, the system brings forward interesting patterns (figure 3.9).

Australia has not had a recession for more than twenty-six years, from 1991 to 2017. In 2016, growth was robust, even though the country was already rich. Meanwhile, countries like Malaysia and Peru were trying to catch up to the rich world, while Mexico and Jamaica experienced middling growth.

The world continues in its prosperity path. Since the 1950s, there has been only one year in which the world's GDP receded (–1.75% in 2009). Average economic growth in the 2010s has been 3%. But prosperity is not shared equally.

Table 3.3 shows the IMF projections for the GDP per capita growth of many countries in 2022. We should still expect higher growth in the emerging world, in comparison to developed economies. Nevertheless, growth is unlikely to be well distributed. China and India are still projected to grow much faster than Nigeria, Mexico, and South Africa, while Italy should lag behind some of its European neighbors.

Some countries converge to the rich world, and others stagnate. We now have a broad framework to understand long-run growth, but it is not yet complete.

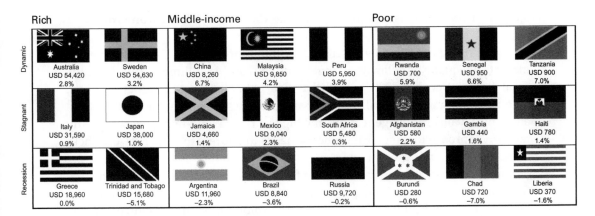

Figure 3.9
Level of development (US dollars per capita, Atlas method) and position in the business cycle (GDP growth), 2016
Source: World Bank, 2017, https://data.worldbank.org/indicator/NY.GNP.PCAP.CD and https://data.worldbank.org/indicator/NY.GDP.MKTP.KD.ZG.

Table 3.3
Projection for real per capita output in 2022 (annual percent change; purchasing power parity)

Countries	GDP growth	Countries	GDP growth
Emerging Markets	3.6%	**Advanced Economies**	1.3%
China	5.1%	Canada	0.7%
India	6.8%	France	1.4%
Mexico	1.8%	Germany	1.3%
Nigeria	−1.0%	Italy	0.9%
Pakistan	1.9%	United Kingdom	1.1%
South Africa	0.6%	United States	1.1%

Source: IMF, "World Economic Outlook, October 2017" IMF, http://www.imf.org/en/Publications/WEO/Issues/2017/09/19/~/media/Files/Publications/WEO/2017/October/pdf/main-chapter//c1.ashx.

3.6   Financial Systems, Inequality, Climate Change, and Long-Run Growth

The long-run growth model discussed in this chapter has no link to financial markets, inequality, or climate change. But the world is still recovering from the great financial crisis of 2008, which has had both short- and long-term effects. Inequality is a major political issue in many countries, including the United States and China. Climate change remains the biggest risk to long-term prosperity. Any modern approach to the global economy needs to address the link between these issues and economic growth.

Some of the underlying assumptions for this chapter's framework are that the financial markets are working properly and are not an obstacle to long-term prosperity, that growth lifts all boats, and that exploiting natural resources has no adverse environmental effects.

One barrier to long-run growth in most poor countries is that financial markets are incomplete, inefficient, and illiquid. The incompleteness of those financial markets has led to the existence of institutions like development banks. The role of this kind of institution should change over time: development banks may help unlock long-term financing for poor countries, but the need for such institutions declines as countries develop.[25]

There are many reasons that income inequality may be a significant obstacle to long-run growth. One is that it hampers institutional development. Because the poorest citizens do not have a voice in unequal societies, the elites design a political system that continuously extracts most resources from society. The economic pie never grows, and the few take the most slices. Institutions take longer to develop, if they evolve much at all. Countries become stuck, but the elites do not lose anything. William Easterly concludes that high inequality is a large and statistically significant barrier to prosperity, good-quality institutions, and high rates of schooling.[26]

Finally, there is a cap on natural resources in aggregate supply function because countries cannot extract natural resources indefinitely. We need to account for climate change and the impact of economic activity on the environment.

Without understanding financial markets, inequality, and climate change, we cannot have a complete picture of the necessary conditions for long-term prosperity. For now, however, we assume that these factors do not constrain economic activity and that all economic growth comes from capital labor, natural resources, and technology. After describing financial markets in more detail in chapter 4, in

25. Ernani Torres and Rodrigo Zeidan, "The Life-Cycle of National Development Banks: The Experience of Brazil's BNDES," *Quarterly Review of Economics and Finance* 62 (2016): 97–104.
26. William Easterly, "Inequality Does Cause Underdevelopment: Insights from a New Instrument," *Journal of Development Economics* 84, no. 2 (2007): 755–776.

chapter 5 we return to the relationship between financial markets and economic growth in the long run. We look at the importance of income inequality in chapter 12 and of climate change in chapter 13.

Economics does not hold all the answers. Institutions matter. Political scientists analyze how institutions develop. Historians bring a fresh perspective on the evolution of economic processes. Neuroscientists explain the nonlinear links between income and happiness. Physicists and climatologists provide the links between technological development and environmental impact. The economics of global business does not explain everything about the outcomes of economic activities. The model discussed in this chapter describes the most important conditions for prosperity but not all of them.

Appendix 3.A: Endogenous Growth Theory

Our version of the Solow model is not a complete description of economic growth. Other models complement its few drivers of long-run economic growth. For instance, technological diffusion[27] or globalization of ideas[28] also can contribute to sustained prosperity. Paul Romer's endogenous growth model aims to explain the exact nature of the rate of technological progress, which is the main contributor to economic growth in the long run.[29] The main departure is that the rate of technological progress (A) is not fixed or given outside the model the way that it is in the Solow model. It is endogenously determined by the creation of new products, services, or inventions.

The number of these inventions is related to how many researchers are working in R&D and how the current inventions are related to the ones before. Assume that there are L workers engaged in R&D, and this leads to the invention of new capital goods.[30] There is a production function for the change in the number of capital goods that depends on R&D activities. From Solow, the growth in output per capita depends on the increase in technology (g), which is exogenous to the model. In the endogenous growth theory, g still determines output per capita, but it is determined inside the model by

27. For a formal model, see Diego Comin and Bart Hobija, "An Exploration of Technology Diffusion," *American Economic Review* 100, no. 5 (2010): 2031–2059.

28. For a nontechnical introduction to the topic, see Paul M. Romer, "What Parts of Globalization Matter for Catch-Up Growth?," *American Economic Review* 100, no. 2 (2010): 94–98.

29. Paul H. Romer, "The Origins of Endogenous Growth," *Journal of Economic Perspectives* 8, no. 1 (1994): 3–22.

30. For a full and straightforward exposition of this model, see Karl Whelan, "Endogenous Technological Change: The Romer Model," University College Dublin, 2014, http://www.karlwhelan.com/MAMacroSem1/Notes12.pdf.

$$g = \frac{\lambda n}{1 - \phi},$$

where g is growth in technology, the parameter λ is the extent of marginal productivity as we add more researchers, n is the growth rate of the number of researchers, and Φ is the effect of past innovations on current inventions. An endogenously determined technology factor has many implications for the growth of the economy.[31]

Two types of externalities are generated by adding researchers to the economy—a positive externality due to the cumulative effect of inventions (Φ) and a negative externality resulting from the diminishing marginal return of adding researchers to the economy. The socially optimum number of researchers would balance out these effects. Empirical estimates show that the private sector usually does too little research relative to the social optimum.[32] In any case, the most important result of the endogenous growth theory is determining the variables that account for long-run growth. Implications include redesigning patent policies and providing incentives for R&D investments, and if ideas become harder to find, there may be a cap in how rich economies can grow.[33] The importance of R&D for long-run growth is clear in the thirteenth five-year Chinese plan.

Appendix 3.B: The Thirteenth Five-Year Chinese Plan

Five-year plans were designed by Soviet authorities to plan the economies of the Union of Soviet Socialist Republics (USSR) in a centralized manner, and planners in the Chinese Communist Party emulated their counterparts in the USSR. Planners in both countries used five-year plans to micromanage the Soviet and Chinese economies and allocate resources to bring to life both parties' visions of the communist dream. After the Chinese economy was opened, public authorities updated their use of five-year plans and made them more aspirational, signaling to economic agents the key areas of investment in the Chinese economy.[34] The most

---

31. For instance, an optimal number of researchers can be calculated as a share of total workers in the economy (s_r):

$$s_r = \frac{\lambda}{1 - \phi - \lambda}.$$

32. Charles I. Jones and John C. Williams, "Too Much of a Good Thing? The Economics of Investment in R&D," *Journal of Economic Growth* 5, no. 1 (2000): 65–85.
33. Nicholas Bloom, Charles I. Jones, John Van Reenen, and Michael Webb, "Are Ideas Getting Harder to Find?," NBER Working Paper No. 23782, National Bureau of Economic Research, September 2017.
34. Mark Magnier, "China's Thirteenth Five-Year Plan: Q&A with Scott Kennedy and Christopher K. Johnson," *Wall Street Journal*, blog, May 23, 2016, https://blogs.wsj.com/chinarealtime/2016/05/23/chinas-13th-five-year-plan-qa-with-scott-kennedy-and-christopher-k-johnson.

recent plan is the thirteenth five-year plan (the Soviet Union managed only twelve before the country was dissolved on December 26, 1991), and it maps out the desired path for the Chinese economy until 2020. In the early plans, the key variables for the success of the Chinese economy were almost exactly the determinants of growth in the Solow models. For instance, in the tenth five-year old plan, which ran from 2001 to 2005, some of the key tasks were to optimize and upgrade the industrial structure, strengthen China's international competitiveness, build more infrastructure facilities, and raise levels of urbanization. The plan aimed to achieve capital deepening, and physical capital (K) was the major source of growth during this period. R&D targets were modest, with authorities hoping that Chinese companies would raise the overall R&D funding to just over 1.5% of GDP.

In the thirteenth five-year plan, launched at the end of the fifth plenary session of the Communist Party of China's eighteenth Central Committee in October 2015, the spotlight is on technological development.[35] The plan's five guiding principles are innovation, coordination, green development, opening up, and sharing. The first three principles relate to technology, and the fifth relates to income distribution. According to the plan, China's future development must rest on innovation, and it sets plenty of measurable and aspirational targets regarding the technological development of companies in China, from placing significant value on "subversive technological breakthroughs" to promoting start-up incubators, crowdfunding, angel investing, and venture capital. The focus is on innovation because from the time of the initial market reforms up until the mid-2010s, most Chinese growth came from capital deepening and increased urbanization. Since then, China has been showing signs of decreasing marginal productivity in terms of capital accumulation and increased labor participation.

The thirteenth five-year plan shows an implicit use of endogenous growth theory and the Solow model. Chinese policymakers recognize that increased prosperity comes less from further urbanization and infrastructure investments and more from technology in the broad sense (A). They intend to achieve that by fostering a culture of innovation in which the country allocates resources to increase the share of researchers and the output of R&D. As always, however, the devil is in the details. If the dynamics of the economy allow for efficient use of these resources, there is a good possibility that China can escape the middle-income trap. Yet there is a chance that such an escape will require more than just attempts to increase innovation. Institutional building is important, which is why other parts of the latest five-year plan describe strategies to increase intellectual property protection and give universities and research institutes the freedom to become innovation leaders with greater powers in making decisions about research and funding.

35. PwC, "Prosperity for the Masses by 2020," PwC, 2015, https://www.pwccn.com/en/migration/pdf/prosperity-masses-2020.pdf.

4   Growth in the Short Run: The Market of Goods and Services

In this chapter,

- The main tradeoff for public authorities—inflation versus economic growth
- Aggregate demand shifts and policymakers' mistakes
- The worst economic scenario—stagflation
- Expectations and self-fulfilling prophecies
- The commodities supercycle and companies' mistakes

4.1   The Commodities Supercycle and Economic Growth in Latin America and Australia in the 2000s

In the 2000s, the rise of the Chinese economy changed the lives of its people and spread prosperity throughout many parts of the world, including Latin America. Because of a higher demand for commodities, prices skyrocketed in the mid-2000s, which led to more demand for the commodities from Latin America, a region rich in natural resources. Countries in Latin America grew extraordinarily from 2003 to 2011 (according to Bertrand Gruss, output in the region rose from 2.5% to 4% per year).[1] Prospects were so good that many companies embarked on an investment spree to increase productive capacity and service both internal and external markets.

The evolution of iron ore markets illustrates the consequences of this wave of optimism. Iron ore prices started climbing in 2004 and doubled every two years until 2010. Over the entire period, prices went from less than US$20 to US$160 per ton (figure 4.1).

1. Bertrand Gruss, "After the Boom: Commodity Prices and Economic Growth in Latin America and the Caribbean," IMF Working Paper 14/154, International Monetary Fund, August 2014, http://www.imf.org/~/media/Websites/IMF/imported-full-text-pdf/external/pubs/ft/wp/2014/_wp14154.ashx.

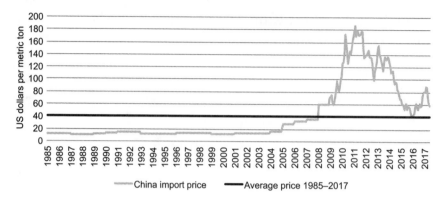

Figure 4.1
China import iron ore, 1985 to 2017
Source: IMF, 2017, https://www.imf.org/external/np/res/commod/External_Data.xls.

This explosion in iron ore prices led to the perception that higher prices were the norm, so companies accelerated investment to increase productive capacity. One example of unabashed optimism was Australia. In just over a decade, Australia tripled its iron ore production capacity. Cumulative investment exceeded US$35 billion, and capacity reached 700 million tons per annum. But the optimism was excessive. Prices crashed in 2015 and 2016, leading to a series of bankruptcies for small miners, losses for the big players, and an economic slowdown in 2015 and 2016.

Australia, Brazil, and China are responsible for approximately three-quarters of the world's iron ore production. In 2002, Australian, Brazilian, and Chinese companies mined 626 million metric tons of iron ore. By 2015, the combined output of these three countries quadrupled, reaching 2,762 million metric tons. The growth rate of iron ore production for Australia, Brazil, and China (12.1% per year) far surpassed that of the world's GDP growth in the period (around 4%) (figure 4.2).

In Latin American countries, the iron ore example was repeated across many different industries and resulted in robust growth until the early 2010s. As the supercycle ended, however, so did the contribution of these high expectations to GDP. Prospects dimmed, and agents adjusted their decisions accordingly. For some countries, aggregate demand contracted, with a corresponding fall in economic output and price levels. For others, the result was worse because it combined a reduction in demand with a currency crisis that also shifted aggregate supply to the left, an effect aggravated further by a significant political crisis.

The commodities supercycle illustrates the growth path of regular economies. Countries grow in cycles. In this chapter, we develop a model that displays the main tradeoffs that influence the decision of public authorities.

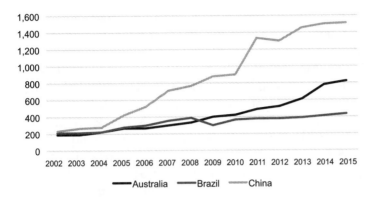

Figure 4.2
Mine production of iron ore: Australia, Brazil, and China, 2002 to 2015
Source: US Geological Survey, 2016, http://minerals.usgs.gov/minerals/pubs/commodity/iron_ore.

4.2 From Long- to Short-Run Growth

Long-run growth is a supply-side story. Aggregate supply is a function of capital, labor, natural resources, and total factor productivity (the technology component). In the short run, however, aggregate demand rules. The difference between the short run and the long run is the adjustment time that the economy takes to reach full (natural) employment of production factors. The main hypothesis for analyzing short-run fluctuations is that aggregate supply is fixed in the short run.

The history of this important hypothesis is tied to John Maynard Keynes, one of the great economists of the twentieth century. Keynes is the founder of modern macroeconomics. In *The General Theory of Employment, Interest and Money* (1936), he advances the principle of effective demand. Today's models postulate that aggregate demand changes cause short-run fluctuations instead of supply variables. They ascribe a much weaker significance to aggregate demand over long-run growth than Keynes did. Short-run growth comes from demand fluctuations, but long-run prosperity is a supply story.

In normal times, aggregate demand is the determinant of short-run economic fluctuations for two reasons. The first relates to expectations of consumers and companies. When they consume or invest more, sales increase, and this sends signals for more investment. As companies expand their capacity, they hire more people, and more wages means more consumption. The economic machine plods along.

The second reason that aggregate demand determines short-run economic fluctuations is that supply usually is fixed in the short run, and a country's productive capacity is hard to change in the short run:

1. First, changing aggregate supply variables in the short run leads to an increasing use of capital, labor, natural resources, or better technology, factors that tend to accumulate over time. In the investment process, for example, companies invest to increase production capacity in the short run. Depending on the industry profile, investment (capital expenditure) can take years or even decades to mature. Nuclear power plants take an average of four to six years to build in China or South Korea but more than ten years elsewhere, especially in Europe. In 2016, Ford announced a new factory in Mexico that would open in 2020, creating 2,800 direct jobs.[2] Investment turns into capital slowly. Technological development and increased labor supply also accrue gradually. Usually, a country's labor supply is fixed in the short run because this is related to the number of individuals of working age who are willing to work at market wages and the fact that their education level does not change dramatically in a short period.

2. Second, prices and wages are "sticky." In economic jargon, a variable is sticky if it is slow to respond to changes in other variables that should have an impact on it. Sticky wages mean that workers' remuneration does not change as often as it should to reflect variations in, for instance, labor demand or supply. In some countries, for instance, it is illegal to lower nominal wages, wages for unionized workers are renegotiated at a predetermined timeframe (such as yearly), employee contracts may stipulate that salaries are fixed for a determined period, and transaction costs make wage renegotiations costly and thus less likely to happen with a high frequency. The same thing applies to prices across different markets. N. Gregory Mankiw and Ricardo Reis developed a formal model of pervasive stickiness of prices, wages, and consumption.[3] In models of this type, supply-side variables react slowly to changes to economic policy or shocks to the economy.

When aggregate supply changes in the short run, we call it a supply shock, but such situations are the exception. For now, let's assume that changes in aggregate demand cause short-run fluctuations due to inelastic supply factors. Following price and wage stickiness and a limit on a country's productive capacity in the short run, the behavior of aggregate supply can be represented by dividing it in two parts (figure 4.3). In the first part, because of stickiness, AS is relatively flat and responds little to price and wage signals. In the second, as the actual output gets closer to potential output, supply becomes more vertical because the economy

2. Nick Bunkley, "Ford to Invest $1.6 Billion in New Mexico Small-Car Plant, Create 2,800 Jobs," *Automotive News*, April 4, 2016, http://www.autonews.com/article/20160405/OEM01/160409897/ford-to-invest-$1.6-billion-in-new-mexico-small-car-plant-create-2800.
3. N. Gregory Mankiw and Ricardo Reis, "Sticky Information in General Equilibrium," *Journal of the European Economic Association* 5, no. 2–3 (2007): 603–613.

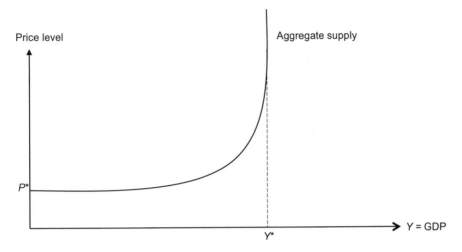

Figure 4.3

cannot produce more than potential output. If the economy is producing at potential output, it is using (almost) all its resources. Everybody willing to work at market wages is employed, and companies are using their full capacity. For a short while, if the economy is overheating, it may produce more than its capacity by a wide use of overtime, yet such instances are rare.

Most macroeconomic books divide aggregate supply into short-run aggregate supply (SRAS) and long-run aggregate supply (LRAS). A few follow the same structure as the one used in this book, which combines the hypotheses regarding the behavior of aggregate supply into a single graph that shows both short and long runs. The graph shown in figure 4.3 has the benefit of showing modifications in aggregate supply (AS) in a simple manner but the disadvantage of not accounting for the full range of possible economic paths. For instance, it is hard to represent growth superior to potential output in the current model. Y^* is the potential output, also called natural level or full employment output.[4] P^* is current price level.

---

4. Economic jargon should be relatively simple. One area where it fails is in the number of terms that can be used interchangeably. For instance, because GDP is determined in the market of goods and services by the meeting of aggregate supply and aggregate demand, various terms—output, Y, national output or income, aggregate output or income, and GDP—mean pretty much the same thing. It can be confusing when one axis on a graph is labeled GDP. Is that real or nominal GDP? The same thing happens with price levels and inflation. Technically, the change in price levels is inflation, but in textbooks, the y-axis on the market of goods and services can be labeled either price level or sometimes inflation. Given that economists usually are interested in changes in the main economic variables, there is no conflict in stating that price levels are increasing or inflation is rising. So whatever label is found on the y-axis of the market for goods and services, it represents the rate of inflation in a country. Economic growth is found on the x-axis. The differences between nominal and real GDP or between labeling economic growth by Y or GDP are mostly unimportant for the analysis of comparative statics. Nevertheless, GDP usually means real GDP, and P usually means the price level.

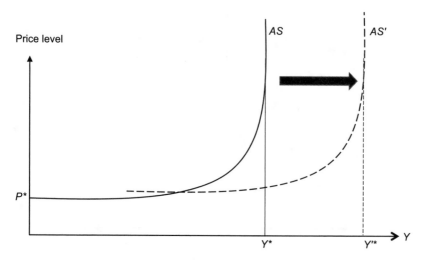

Figure 4.4

In the long run, *AS* shifts to the right as the economy accumulates capital and labor, exploit natural resources, or increases productivity (figure 4.4). Potential output expands, and the economy can grow without inflationary pressure. As aggregate supply (*AS*) moves to *AS'*, potential output goes from *Y** to *Y**. Chapter 3 described our version of the Solow model. Long-run growth is a supply-side story as is shown in figure 4.4. Aggregate supply increases only if, over time, there is an expansion on the production possibilities due to more production factors or technology.

4.3 Aggregate Demand Shifts and Short-Run Dynamics

Short-run dynamics are the domain of aggregate demand shifts. In a closed economy, aggregate demand is composed of aggregate consumption, investment, and government expenditure. Changes in these variables are mostly responsible for fluctuations in growth and inflation. More important, at any given time, the difference between actual and potential output determines the path of the economy. Our working simplified model of the tradeoff between growth and inflation depends on two things—the difference between actual and potential output and shifts in aggregate demand (*AD*). For instance, let's assume a fixed aggregate supply curve (*AS*), and a situation of growth gap, in which actual output falls short of potential output (figure 4.5). In this situation, output *Y* is below potential output *Y**, and the price level of the economy is *P*.

Let's assume that aggregate consumption rises, moving demand *AD* to the right to *AD'* (figure 4.6). As aggregate demand (*AD*) shifts to *AD'* due to more

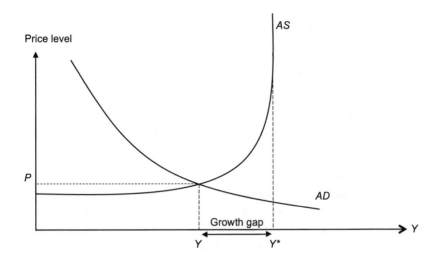

Figure 4.5

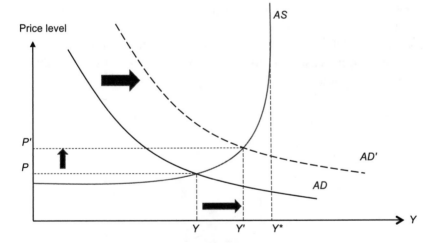

Figure 4.6

consumption, output and price levels increase. The growth gap becomes smaller. Because $AD = C + I + G$, aggregate demand likewise could shift due to an expansion in consumption, aggregate investment and/or government expenditure.

There are two main results from the interaction between shifts in aggregate demand and a fixed aggregate supply:

• In the short run, changes in output and inflation are due to aggregate demand fluctuations; and
• There is a clear tradeoff between GDP growth and inflation.

These two results inform most economic policies in developed and emerging countries. Imagine a situation of rising inflation. Combating it through government policies means weakening aggregate demand. In turn, a dwindling aggregate demand relieves inflationary pressure but at the cost of weaker economic activity. The tradeoff between short-run growth and inflation is a cornerstone of our modern understanding of economics. There is no free lunch, and any policy that is supposed to bring the economy into full employment is bound to have some adverse effect, regardless of the initial size of the growth gap.

A further example is the case of an overheated economy in which there is full employment of resources but extra demand pressure (figure 4.7). As before, AD moves to AD'. Actual GDP Y is already very close to potential output Y^*. Because of this, further demand increases lead to limited growth and expressive inflationary pressure as P moves to P'.

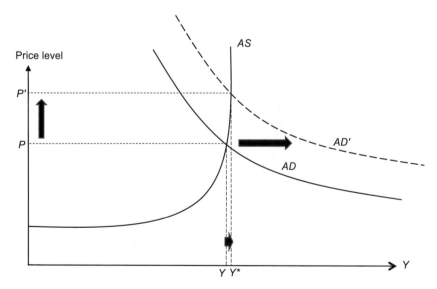

Figure 4.7

Given that short-run dynamics are a demand story, periods of growth come after recessions, and they beget expansion and so forth. This natural tendency of business-cycle dynamics points to an important argument regarding interventions in the market for goods and services: economic policies should be countercyclical. The dynamics of the market for goods and services do not necessarily require government interventions. (The arguments pro and contra active economic policies are discussed in chapter 7.) If government policies are to be useful at all, they should be countercyclical in nature. As the name implies, countercyclical policies work in the opposite direction of business cycles: in periods of rapid economic growth, public authorities should be worried about accelerating inflation; in periods of significant growth gap, the correct response should be to stimulate aggregate demand.

Given our representation of the market for goods and services, policymaking in economics of global business should be easy. There is a simple and direct tradeoff, it is clear cut, and government policies should work in a countercyclical way to smooth out GDP growth in the long run, keeping inflation under check (figure 4.8).

Unfortunately, designing economic policy is not this simple. First, policymakers must correctly identify the position of the national economy in the business cycle. To do this, officials rely on the available data about current economic activity. Leading indicators are particularly useful for this purpose because they point to future market dynamics, in contrast to lagging indicators, which are the result of past economic activity. One example of a leading indicator is the Consumer Confidence Index (CCI), which surveys consumers about their perceptions and

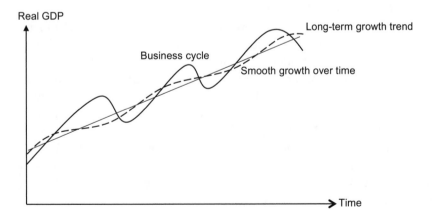

Figure 4.8
Evolution of real GDP over time

attitudes regarding present and future consumption. A declining CCI indicates potential weakness in economic activity and thus the possibility of a present or future growth gap. Conversely, one example of a lagging indicator is the rate of unemployment, which is highly dependent on previous decisions by companies and individuals in the labor market. The unemployment rate is slow to adjust to economic conditions.

A second reason that designing economic policy is difficult is that data for economic indicators, both lagging and leading ones, are not clear-cut. Some may point to weaker economic activity, and others hint at strong performance. In addition, they are not measured continuously. Some (like nominal GDP) are measured quarterly, and others (such as inflation forecasts) are measured monthly or even weekly. Economic data are built by surveyed samples and are subject to respondent biases or revisions after more accurate information is incorporated. The Bureau of Economic Analysis of the US Department of Commerce announces the current value of the US GDP quarterly, subject to many revisions. In short, economic data are not granular enough for perfect forecasts of the economic cycle, and authorities can never be certain at which point of the business cycle the national economy happens to be.

Finally, it's hard to come up with the exact dosage for what ails the economy. Policymakers face constraints imposed by different economic policies and even uncertainty in case they actually work. The main takeaway is that even though our aggregate demand and aggregate supply framework makes explicit what the tradeoff between growth and inflation is, we need more to understand the actions of public authorities.

The European Central Bank Interest Rate Hike of 2011

The success of economic policies hinges on the effectiveness of policy instruments and the correct identification of the issue at hand. In 2011, the European Central Bank (ECB) made a mistake by identifying increased inflation as the major economic threat facing Europe. As a result, the eurozone monetary authority decided to increase interest rates. It was a mistake. The effect was the opposite of what it intended and pushed Europe back into recession, at least according to Paul Krugman, who uses that 2011 ECB decision to highlight the dangers of incorrectly diagnosing macroeconomic ailments: "What happened in spring 2011? The ECB raised rates even though there was no sign of underlying inflationary pressure beyond a commodity blip, and even though the needed price adjustment in the periphery clearly needed a reasonably high inflation target."[5]

---

5. Paul Krugman, "The ECB's Reverse FDR," *New York Times*, November 29, 2011, https://krugman .blogs.nytimes.com/2011/11/29/the-ecbs-reverse-fdr.

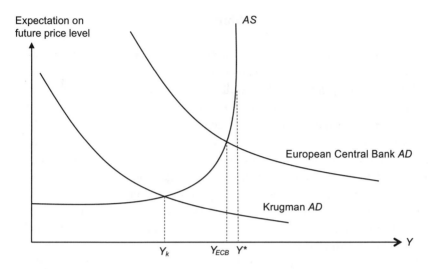

Figure 4.9

Figure 4.9 uses our aggregate supply (*AS*) and aggregate demand (*AD*) framework to visualize the differences in the views of Krugman and the ECB regarding the path of the European economy in 2011. Both Krugman and the ECB had the same information available to them, but they differed in their expectations of the position of the aggregate demand and hence the possible path of future inflation. The ECB concluded that inflation was a problem because aggregate demand was close to potential output. Krugman saw a significant growth gap ($Y^* - Y_k$), but the ECB concluded that actual output was close to potential output ($Y^* - Y_{ECB}$). For Krugman, the lack of growth was the main malady, and reducing demand through an interest rate hike would result in a recession, without any benefits in terms of inflation, which was low and unlikely to increase. For the ECB, the identification of inflationary pressure justified increasing the interest rate.

In hindsight, Krugman's diagnosis seems to have been correct because European growth in subsequent years was anemic, and inflation turned into deflation by 2014. For economic policies to work, governments have to identify the behavior of the market for goods and services accurately, choose the correct policy response, and use the right amount of policy response. Misidentification leads to the wrong response and may exacerbate the business cycle instead of smoothing it over. Business cycles are natural to market economies. Making them more pronounced would mean steeper or longer recessions during downturns and higher inflation during expansion times. Policy mistakes destroy social welfare, but when public authorities get it right, shorter recessions and longer expansion periods without price hikes benefit everybody.

4.4   Stagflation and Aggregate Supply Shifts

Stagflation is recession accompanied by high inflation. It cannot be modeled through shifts in aggregate demand because those shifts lead to positively related growth and inflation. Stagflation is the result of adverse short-run supply shocks. Such shocks are rare, but when they happen, they plunge national economies into the worst possible macroeconomic scenario, one in which policymakers are faced with rising inflation amid weak economic activity. For simplicity's sake, let's assume that for some unknown reason there is a decrease in aggregate supply, portrayed, in the aggregate supply and aggregate demand framework, as a shift of AS to the left (figure 4.10). In the beginning, the economy is at its full-employment equilibrium, with actual output at its potential level (Y) and inflation at P. As the supply shock unfolds, AS moves to AS', output falls to Y', and the price level increases from P to P'.

Stagflation is a rare phenomenon. For instance, the labor force—the people of working age who are willing to work—does not grow or shrink quickly. The same applies to the size of industries. Total productive capacity gradually changes over time. For stagflation to exist, supply shocks need to be strong enough to affect the productive capacity of the economy in a very short period.

One example of a significant supply shock is the first oil crisis of the 1970s. In October 1973, members of the Organization of Petroleum Exporting Countries (OPEC) declared an oil embargo, and by early 1974, the oil price had risen from

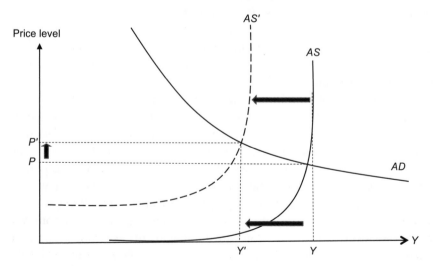

Figure 4.10

US$3 to US$12 per barrel. The price increase was swift, unexpected, and lasting. At that time, oil was one of the main production factors in many countries around the world. For many industries in importing countries, energy prices rose in tandem with the oil prices, curtailing productive capacity. Aggregate supply is a function of natural resources, labor, and capital, and we assume that these factors are relatively fixed, in aggregate, in the short run. But assume that a country imports oil to use it as an input for different industries. As oil prices quadrupled, many companies started losing money and subsequently reduced their production or went out of business. Oil was such an important input in many developed countries that the price increase had an industry-wise effect, reducing the productive capacity of the whole economy.

Assume that a plastic manufacturer uses naphtha, a by-product of crude oil, as its main variable input. If the price of naphtha quadruples, then the company will find it extremely hard to transfer its increased costs to the final price of the product. It might decrease production and even might close down loss-making facilities. Even though the productivity of companies retrenches, the prices of their goods and services go up when some of the new costs are passed on to consumers. This is not a single-industry effect but fuels price increases across different sectors.

Usually, a supply shock effect is temporary. As the economy adjusts, aggregate supply should go back to normal, leading to higher growth and lower inflation. After the 1973 oil embargo, both growth and price levels eventually should have returned to their previous paths. But there was another supply shock—a second oil crisis in 1979. Oil prices reached US$39.50, a tenfold increase over the pre-1973 level. Stagflation came roaring back in many countries.

For the United States, the years just before and around the oil crises can be divided into periods of stagflation and regular short-run dynamics. Table 4.1 has data on GDP growth and inflation, as measured by the Consumer Price Index (CPI), for the US economy in the 1970s and early 1980s. (Details about the CPI are presented in chapter 14.)

In the years preceding the first oil crisis, the American economy was doing well. In 1972, it experienced robust growth (6.9%) and low inflation (3.4%). In 1973, however, stagflation started as economic activity slowed down (4%) and prices rose (8.5%). In 1974, the full effect of the oil crisis was felt with a deep recession. GDP contracted by almost 2%, and inflation reached 12.1% by the end of the year. But that stagflation did not last. As the aggregate supply returned to normal, the period between 1975 and 1978 showed a typical pattern of short-run dynamics. The year 1978 is a good example of how aggregate demand shifts change growth and inflation, with an increase in demand resulting in significant growth but also higher inflation than in previous years. When a second oil crisis hit the US economy in 1979, a shift in aggregate supply again resulted in stagflation, with the growth

Table 4.1
Data on the US GDP and Consumer Price Index (inflation), 1971 to 1982

Year	GDP growth (percentage)	Inflation (percentage)
1971	4.4%	3.5%
1972	6.9	3.4
1973	4.0	8.5
1974	−1.9	12.1
1975	2.6	7.3
1976	4.3	5.0
1977	5.0	6.6
1978	6.7	8.9
1979	1.3	12.8
1980	0.0	12.6
1981	1.3	9.3
1982	−1.4	4.5

Source: Federal Reserve Bank of St. Louis, 2017, https://fred.stlouisfed.org/series/A191RL1Q225SBEA and https://fred.stlouisfed.org/series/FPCPITOTLZGUSA.

rate declining to 1.3% and inflation skyrocketing to 12.8%. Stagflation persisted in 1980. In 1981, aggregate supply started to return to its precrisis level. In 1981 and 1982, aggregate demand dynamics explain the reduction in inflation and growth.

Figure 4.11 represents the impact of the first oil crisis, with its effects in 1973 and 1974. For simplicity, instead of showing price and growth levels, the graph uses inflation and growth rates and assumes that aggregate demand does not change during the period.

In the short run, a decreasing aggregate supply curve led to stagflation. In 1974, the American economy shrunk, and prices increased by double digits. The memory of the stagflation grounded by the oil crisis in the 1970s is one reason that some analysts fear the possible combination of recession and inflationary pressure every time oil prices increase sharply, as they did in the mid-2000s. But that fear is misplaced. Nowadays, there is little chance that an oil crisis will cause stagflation because most importing countries are not as dependent on oil as they were in the past. Such a crisis would generate inflationary pressure worldwide, but it would not plunge the world into a recession as it did in the 1970s.

Oil is not the only determinant of a supply shock. Quick and massive currency devaluations also can shrink aggregate supply. Countries usually import a significant share of inputs and capital goods, and currency devaluations make imports more expensive. This stokes inflation. Export goods also become more expensive in the local economy as opportunity costs fuel increases in the prices of export

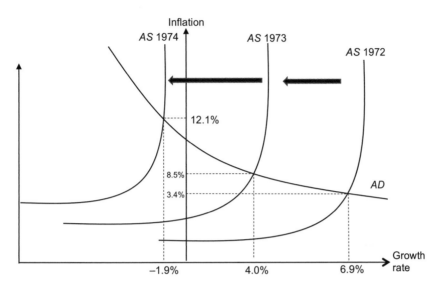

Figure 4.11

goods on local markets. Examples of currency crises that plunged countries into stagflation abound. In 2015, for instance, Russia experienced negative growth and higher inflation as a result of a significant drop in the price of natural gas and crude oil, two of its major exports, combined with a large currency depreciation, and economic sanctions imposed by the European Union.

Supply shocks, while infrequent, generate large welfare losses. They also handcuff public authorities because, at best, economic policies act on aggregate demand. For government officials, trying to prevent the economic slowdown could engender even higher inflation. If they choose to fight pressures on prices, economic activity would weaken further.

Just as negative supply shocks precipitate welfare losses, positive shocks spawn significant gains. One such example for the US economy is the rapid increase in productivity in the mid-1990s, a consequence of the Internet revolution. Small, medium, and large companies quickly benefited from shrinking information technology costs, boosting their productive capacity and generating a period of vigorous economic growth and low inflation that lasted until the dotcom bubble burst in 2001 (figure 4.12).

As before, the example assumes that the economy is close to potential output Y at price level P and that aggregate demand remains unchanged. A shift to the right takes aggregate supply from AS to AS'. Output expands (from Y to Y'), and there is less pressure on prices (from P to P').

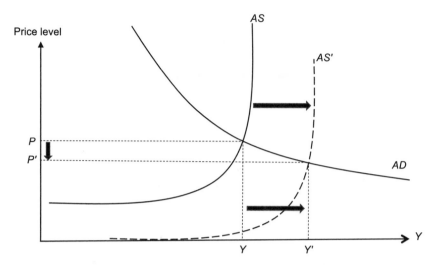

Figure 4.12

Table 4.2 presents data on GDP growth and inflation for the US economy, here for the years 1994 to 2001. From 1997 to 2000, the economy experienced vigorous GDP growth, at an average of 4.5% per year, while inflation stayed modest, picking up a bit in 2000. But it is very hard for economies to grow constantly without inflationary pressure. Strong growth leads to full employment and puts pressure on wages and prices. Prosperity like that in the 1997 to 2000 period is rare. Aggregate supply needs to grow fast if an economy is to experience sustained economic growth without concerns about inflation.

4.5 The Components of Aggregate Demand: Consumption and Investment

The dynamics of the market for goods and services is highly dependent on the behavior of aggregate demand in the short run. Here we concentrate on consumption and investment dynamics to look at how national and international economic policies influence the ways that people consume and companies invest.

In microeconomics, consumers buy a good or service based on its price, the prices of substitutes, and their preferences, expectations, and disposable income. Aggregating personal outcomes yields a macroeconomic behavior that is built on hypotheses concerning how people make decisions. More sophisticated models of aggregate consumption are outside the scope of this book, so here current aggregate consumption is

$$C = a + b(Y - T),$$

Table 4.2
Data on the US GDP and Consumer Price Index (inflation), 1994 to 2001

Year	GDP growth (percentage)	Inflation (percentage)
1994	3.4%	2.3%
1995	3.5	3.0
1996	2.6	2.7
1997	4.6	2.9
1998	4.6	1.2
1999	4.8	1.7
2000	4.2	3.4
2001	2.3	3.3

Source: Federal Reserve Bank of St. Louis, 2017, https://fred.stlouisfed.org/series/A191RL1Q225SBEA and https://fred.stlouisfed.org/series/FPCPITOTLZGUSA.

where C is aggregate consumption, people consume a fixed amount (a) plus a proportion (b) of their disposable income ($Y - T$), Y is economic output, and T is total income taxes. In this simplified equation, individuals use their income less taxes (disposable income) to buy goods and services, and they save the rest of it. Families divide their income between consumption and saving, and thus the proportion of income used for purchases is the propensity to consume (b), and the saving part leads to the propensity to save (s):

$$b + s = 1.$$

People can either consume or save their disposable income. If all people were entirely rational, they would follow the permanent income hypothesis, which posits that consumption today should be based on current and future incomes. Purely rational people would save the exact amount necessary for their old age. Individuals would accumulate only the wealth that could later be used for consumption. In this case, every country in the world would present similar patterns of b and s that would differ only with the demographics. In real life, however, many factors affect how people decide whether to buy things or put aside money for a rainy day. Culture, for instance, plays a role. Families in many Asian countries save a higher proportion of their income than people in the United States do. Inequality is also relevant because poor people tend to consume a higher proportion of their income than rich people do. Additionally, expectations on future income and wealth changes how people shop, and richer individuals can consume more than their current income by borrowing against their wealth, and young people can borrow to invest in education, counting on an increase in income.

For our purposes, a simple consumption function is enough. Household consumption is usually the largest part of GDP for most countries (table 4.3).

Table 4.3
Household final consumption expenditure by income level, 2016

Region	Percentage of GDP
High income	60.2%
Upper middle income	50.3
Middle income	53.3
Lower middle income	64.8
Low income	75.6
United States	68.4
Euro area	55.7
China	37.4

Source: World Bank, 2017, https://data.worldbank.org/indicator/NE.CON.PETC.ZS.

Consumption in poor countries tends to be higher in relative terms than it is in richer economies because the latter usually have more public and private investment. One exception is China, whose fast growth is the result of, among other things, large capital expenditure in manufacturing industries. Even after thirty years of spectacular growth, consumption in China is much lower, as a percentage of GDP, than it is in the rest of the world. This should change in the future, and household consumption should contribute more to economic output than it did in the rapid industrialization phase of the Chinese development.

Private investment (*I*) usually makes up a smaller share of GDP than consumption (*C*), but its role is particularly relevant for economic prosperity. Given that investment turns into capital and is relevant for long-run growth, increasing productive capacity is an integral part of international economic dynamics. Theories of investment, like those of consumption, begin with microeconomic foundations. Companies decide how much to invest depending on their production costs, the relative price of the goods or services that they produce, their productivity, and the cost of capital. For economic-wide modeling, one of the most important variables to affect a company's behavior is the interest rate, which influences companies' cost of capital.

As with many other concepts in economics, *interest rate* is a flexible term. The risk-free interest rate in capital asset pricing models (CAPM) is different from the one that agents refer to when describing decisions by central banks, as in "The market expects the Fed to increase the interest rate by 50 basis points." There are three important concepts to bear in mind:

• Central banks can affect, through money market operations, the target interest rate.

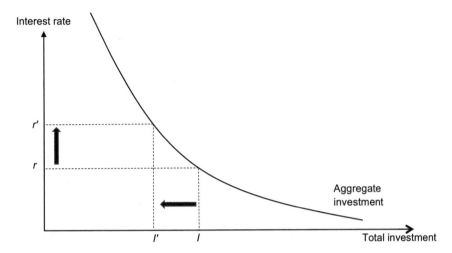

Figure 4.13

- The target interest rate is closely related to the risk-free interest rate in capital asset pricing models.
- Changes in the target interest rate may affect the price of money in the national economy.

In most macroeconomics books, interest rate is broadly speaking the cost of borrowing (or lending) money. The actual borrowing cost is different for distinct agents; a large corporation borrows more cheaply than a household. For investment or capital expenditure, what is relevant is that the interest rate of the economy influences the overall cost of expanding productive capacity. If the interest rate rises, there is a disincentive for investment, and conversely lower rates should generate spending on the expansion of productive capacity—namely, $I = I(r)$, where r is the real interest rate.

In more sophisticated models, the private aggregate investment function involves more variables, but here the main concern is to relate the decision of companies to monetary policy. This is done through an investment function that is inversely related to the real interest rate of the economy (figure 4.13). Again, as the cost of capital rises, companies invest less, and vice versa.

If the interest rate increases from r to r', then investment decreases from I to I'. The investment function captures the direct relationship between the real side and the financial side of a capitalist economy.

The New Development Bank: Investing in BRICS
The New Development Bank (formerly the BRICS Development Bank) was established in 2014 to encourage investment in Brazil, Russia, India, China, and South

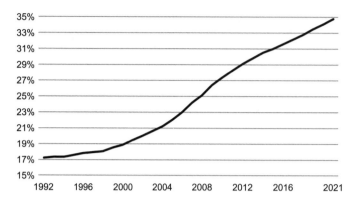

Figure 4.14
Share of world GDP in purchasing power parity: Total BRICS, 1992 to 2021 (projected)
Source: IMF, 2017, http://www.imf.org/external/datamapper/NGDP_RPCH@WEO/OEMDC/
ADVEC/WEOWORLD.

Africa (BRICS). The term *BRIC* was coined by Goldman Sachs chief economist Jim
O'Neill in 2001 and later was enlarged to include South Africa. O'Neill also predicted "that by 2041 (later revised to 2039, then 2032) the BRICS would overtake
the six largest western economies in terms of economic might" (figure 4.14).[6]

But the growth in importance of the BRICS comes solely from China and India.
In fact, the share of world's GDP held by Brazil, Russia, and South Africa might
be lower 2021 than it was in the early 1990s (figure 4.15). Bad institutions are the
main reason that the three stagnant BRICS countries are stuck in the middle-
income trap. But complementary to that, aggregate investment in these countries
has not grown, as a share of economic activity, for quite some time.

The idea behind the New Development Bank is to increase aggregate investment in these economies by subsidizing investment through interest rates that are
lower than those offered by financial markets. The tradeoff between interest rate
and investment is at the core of the bank, and one of the major outcomes it pursues
is infrastructure investment. The repressed demand for more infrastructure in
developing countries is shown in table 4.4.

Only time will tell if the New Development Bank, where bureaucrats instead
of pure markets forces allocate resources, will succeed. But the present framework
allows us to understand why it was set up—to promote investment through lower
interest rates.

6. Gillian Tett, "The Story of the Brics," *Financial Times*, January 15, 2010, https://www.ft.com/
content/112ca932-00ab-11df-ae8d-00144feabdc0.

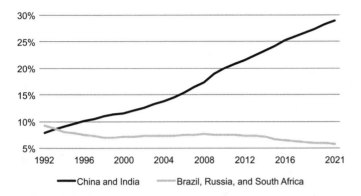

Figure 4.15
Share of world GDP in purchasing power parity: China and India versus Brazil, Russia, and South
Africa, 1992 to 2021 (projected)
Source: IMF, 2017, http://www.imf.org/external/datamapper/NGDP_RPCH@WEO/OEMDC/
ADVEC/WEOWORLD.

Table 4.4
Infrastructure in selected countries

Mode and unit	United States	Germany	Brazil	Russia	India	Mexico	China
Railways (km)	293,564	43,468	28,538	87,157	68,525	15,389	191,270
Roadways (km)	6,586,610	645,000	1,580,964	1,283,387	4,699,024	377,660	4,106,387
Waterways (km)	41,009	7,467	50,000	102,000	14,500	2,900	110,000
Pipelines (km)	2,225,032	34,335	27,468	259,913	35,676	37,008	86,921
Airports (paved runways)	5,054	318	698	594	253	243	463
Airports (national or international)	189	14	7	54	22	12	71
Land area (millions of square km)	9.161	0.348	8.459	16.377	2.973	1.943	9.569

Source: CIA, 2017, https://www.cia.gov/library/publications/the-world-factbook/rankorder/2085
rank.html.

4.6   On the Role of Expectations

Short-run dynamics are an aggregate demand story. So far, we have defined consumption and investment and established the variables that affect the demand
components. Now another component can be added to the behavior of consumers
and companies in determining economy-wide dynamics—expectations. Individuals and businesses do not make decisions based solely on their past income or the
interest rate. Economic agents are forward looking. Expectations are one of the
most important factors in the dynamics of macroeconomic markets, and modeling
them in the 1970s led to a revolution in economic models.

Investment is mostly a function of the real interest rate. Nevertheless, a change
in expectations may affect capital expenditure by influencing a company's behavior. For instance, a political crisis deadlocks the economy, and agents believe that
the crisis will take a long time to abate. In this case, both consumers and businesses may postpone spending on consumer and capital goods and services. The
result is less consumption and investment at the same price level. Because people
are forward looking, they know that due to the persistent political crisis, their
employment is less secure. The rational response is to hold back on some level of
consumption and save more. Similarly, companies tend to invest less. The result
is that expectations can create self-fulfilling prophecies: what economic agents
think will happen moves their decisions, exacerbating the actual likelihood of
that event happening. In the case of a political crisis, contractions in consumption and investment affect aggregate demand and lower economic output and
price levels (figure 4.16). After economic agents adjust their decisions due to an
expectations shock, aggregate demand (AD) moves to AD', and GDP decreases
from Y to Y'. Expectations of weaker economic activity actually contribute to its
reduction, and the country enters a recession partly because people and companies have forecast it. In the same vein, positive expectations shocks beget economic
expansion.

But even a positive expectations shock may have a dark side. One example from
the 1990s is irrational exuberance, a term coined in 1996 by Alan Greenspan, chair
of the Federal Reserve from 1987 to 2006. Irrational exuberance refers to investor
enthusiasm that is unsupported by the underlying fundamentals of the economy,
which may bring an asset bubble instead of prosperity. Its flip side is a depression (like in the 1930s), which happens when people continue to expect extremely
weak economic activity when it may not be justified. When the economy is
tanking, prices decrease, and it is cheaper to invest. During regular recessions,
expectations shift, and output starts to recover. In an economic depression, firms
do not invest because they do not believe that even cheap investment could

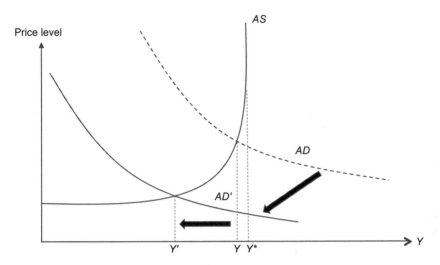

Figure 4.16

generate profits. These self-reinforcing expectations play a major role in economic cycles in both lean and buoyant periods.

The main reason that macroeconomics and international economics is context dependent is due to expectations. Public authorities cannot be certain of how firms and households will react to changes in economic policies. After the great financial crisis of the late 2000s, governments tried to lift national economies but mostly failed. Most developed countries cut interest rates to 0% in the hope that companies would use the opportunity to spend on added productive capacity. This did not happen, and ten years after the crisis, European GDP was not much higher than it was in the precrisis period. Even after authorities tried countless measures to prop up economic activity, households and companies did not behave as policymakers on the continent hoped they would. How people react to economic shocks and changes in economic policies is crucial to understanding the path of the economy. The main lesson is that the success of any economic policy hinges on the reaction of economic agents. This is why credibility is important to public authorities. When their actions are credible, the likelihood that people react in the way predicted by the public authorities is higher.

Rousseff's Impeachment: From Political Crisis to Economic Crisis

The deep political crisis of Brazil in 2015 and 2016 is an example of how changing expectations can bring economic paralysis and lead a country from middling prospects to a deep recession. The main characteristic of the Brazilian political

Table 4.5
Comparison of expected and actual outcomes of the Brazilian economy, 2015 to 2017

	Expectations for 2015			2015	Expectations for 2016			2016	Expectations for 2017	
	Jan. 2014	Jan. 2015	July 2015	Actual	Jan. 2015	Jan. 2016	July 2016	Actual	Jan. 2016	July 2016
CPI (%)	5.7	6.6	9.3	10.7	5.7	6.9	7.3	6.3	5.2	5.4
PPI (%)	5.5	5.7	7.6	10.8	5.5	6.6	8.6	6.8	5.3	5.6
Exchange rate – average (R$/US$)	2.4	2.7	3.2	3.4	2.8	4.1	3.5	3.4	4.1	3.6
Interest rate – average (%p.a.)	11.6	12.5	13.6	13.6	11.7	15.4	14.1		13.2	11.7
Net public debt (%/GDP)	34.8	35.9	37.0	35.5	37.8	39.3	43.9	45.2	41.4	48.3
GDP (%)	2.2	0.5	–1.8	–3.7	1.8	–3.0	–3.4	–3.5	0.9	1.0
Industrial output (%)	3.0	–2.5	–5.0	–7.8	2.7	–3.5	–5.9	–6.6	2.0	0.9
Current account (US$ billion)	–69.9	–77.0	–78.6	–63.3	–70.0	–38.0	–15.0	–20.3	–32.0	–12.5
Balance of trade (US$ billion)	13.0	5.0	6.4	15.0	10.0	35.0	51.1	44.5	35.0	50.0
Inbound FDI (US$ billion)	60.0	60.0	66.0	63.7	60.0	55.0	64.0	69.0	60.0	60.0

Note: CPI = Consumer Price Index; PPI = Producer Price Index; R$ = Brazilian real; p.a. = per year; GDP = gross domestic product; FDI = foreign direct investment.
Source: Brazilian Central Bank, 2017, http://www.bcb.gov.br/pec/GCI/PORT/readout/readout.asp.

debacle is that it unfolded slowly, starting in early 2015 and pretty much paralyzing the nation from January until August 2016,[7] when the impeachment process of president Dilma Rousseff finally came to its conclusion.

The Central Bank of Brazil publishes a summary of forecasts on important macroeconomic indicators by financial industry experts for the current and subsequent years. By looking at the evolution of these indicators, we can see the unfolding crisis and its impact on growth and inflation.

In January 2014, industry experts forecast a 2.2% growth in GDP and inflation of 5.7% in 2015 (table 4.5). One year later, expectations were of almost zero expansion (0.5%) and a higher CPI at 6.6%. Economic activity continued to decline, and six months later professionals were predicting a recession of –1.8% with a corresponding inflation of 9.3%. The actual growth rate was even lower at –3.7%, and

7. Juliana Barbassa, "Dismal Days for Brazilian Democracy," *New York Times*, September 2, 2016, https://www.nytimes.com/2016/09/02/opinion/dismal-days-for-brazilian-democracy.html.

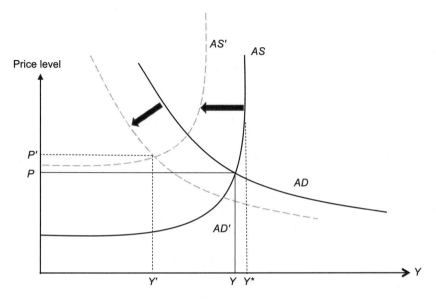

Figure 4.17

inflation reached 10.7%. The country lost almost 6% of GDP when the expected growth (2.2%) for 2015 that experts forecast in January 2014 is compared to the actual growth (–3.7%) in 2015. As the political crisis deepened, consumers retrenched, and companies stopped investing. Unemployment started to rise, and households felt an even stronger pressure to reduce spending in a vicious cycle that paralyzed the economy. Brazil experienced a severe stagflation in 2015, and a corresponding deterioration of expectations is visible in the data for 2016. In January 2015, finance professionals forecast an economic recovery for 2016, with GDP growing at 2.7% and inflation close to the central bank target of 4.5%. As households and businesses started to react to the political crisis, the economic activity slowed to a crawl, and by January 2016, experts predicted a contraction of 3%. In the end, GDP contracted by 3.4%.

There are two main ways in which the crisis affected the economy, which for simplicity's sake are shown as simultaneous (figure 4.17). Aggregate demand decreases from AD to AD' because households and companies spend less money due to the political uncertainty. Cost pressures from a currency devaluation (its reasons are explored in chapter 11) shift aggregate supply from AS to AS', causing inflationary pressure. The result is a profound stagflation in which growth is negative (represented by the extreme shift in output from Y to Y') and prices rise. At the end of 2014, Brazil was in a recession, growing a paltry 0.1% as CPI increased by 6.4%. The 2015 stagflation is the result of a 3.7% contraction and the increased inflation of 10.7%, something that continued in 2016. Inflation finally abated in 2017, but there was no recovery in aggregate demand. The depressed state of the Brazilian economy shows the importance of expectations in generating economic activity. When households and firms start to believe that the economy will collapse, their collective actions effectively ensure it.

The Faroe Islands, Croatia, and the Link between Expectations, Business Cycles, and Political Decisions

Business cycles can be a major hurdle because expectations can constrain or enable anticyclical policies. In the Faroe Islands, for example, fish prices may provide the impetus for independence from Denmark. In Croatia, the supposedly seamless process of joining the eurozone has turned into an existential dilemma.

The Faroe Islands form an archipelago in the North Atlantic and are under the administrative control of Denmark. The country's 50,000 inhabitants are outnumbered by its sheep (the etymology of the word *Faroe* is related to the word for *sheep* in Old Norse). Usually, tiny countries have volatile business cycles because any external economic shock is potentially amplified by a small economy. In the case of the Faroe Islands, the two main economic activities are fishing and tourism. Fish prices have a large impact on social welfare, and the GDP rises and falls in line with the world demand for the Islands' exports. When catches sagged in the 1990s, government debt soared and GDP shrank by 40%.[8] In the mid-2010s, the fishing industry was booming. This would create favorable conditions in which competent local politicians could take advantage of not relying on Denmark's financial support and set up new institutions to replace the Danish rule. If the country experienced any economic downturn (for instance, one caused by overfishing), increased demand for exports, or floundering tourism, however, the same politicians could regret ever embracing the cause of more independence.

Croatia faces a similar dilemma, but instead of independence, the decision is about adopting the euro as a replacement for the Croatian kuna. One of the conditions for Croatia to enter the European Union in 2013 was the eventual adoption of the euro. Although businesses and individuals expected the move toward the euro to be quick and swift, it has stalled because of the prolonged European recession following the financial crisis. What seemed to be an easy choice turned into a dilemma.[9] When the region is at the bottom of a business cycle, joining the

8. "Why the Faroe Islands Want Independence from Denmark," *The Economist*, August 12, 2017, https://www.economist.com/news/europe/21726032-and-what-it-has-do-price-fish-why-faroe-islands-want-independence-denmark.
9. Jan Mus, "Join or Not to Join: The Eurozone Dilemma in Croatia," *Central European Financial Observer*, February 22, 2017, http://financialobserver.eu/cse-and-cis/croatia/join-or-not-to-join-the-eurozone-dilemma-in-croatia.

monetary union suddenly does not seem like a great idea. These doubts illustrate the relevance of expectations for economic and political decision making. If Croatians expected Europe to enter a period of economic growth, politicians would find it easier to adopt the European currency, but the continuing slump makes the idea a much harder sell. After all, stronger ties to Europe make Croatia more susceptible to external shocks to its aggregate demand.

4.7 Summing Up and Preparing for Economic Policy

Our model of short-run dynamics is relatively simple, with shifts in aggregate demand and supply creating changes in economic output and price levels. It represents most possible scenarios of economic activity, from periods of rapid growth without inflation to growth gaps and stagflations. It incorporates the reactions of people and households that may amplify or impede economic policies. Applying such a simple model to a complex adaptive system that is a functioning closed economy has its obvious shortcomings, but they are the inevitable tradeoffs of simplicity.

The main shortcoming of any economic model is identification. Billions of agents are making transactions at any single moment, and the main goal of the present framework is to reduce all of them into a few components that represent the evolving state of the economy. Even with sophisticated models full of leading indicators, experts still disagree about the current environment that affects firms and households. There is now a consensus that the European Central Bank misjudged the risk of inflationary pressures in the early 2010s, for example. The bank increased interest rates and in doing so killed the recovery. No central bank or any other expert model can predict with perfect accuracy the current or future state of the economy.

The present model also works best with discrete shifts in aggregate demand or supply. There are important assumptions regarding the behavior of these curves, especially the stability of aggregate supply in the short run. Sticky prices and wages and a cap on production factors are not features of all economic models. The present configuration does not incorporate some features of state-of-the-art economics. The way that the model factors in expectations is particularly ad hoc, as are the effects of interest rate changes on investment and consumption.

In this working model of the national economy, there is an explicit tradeoff between economic growth and inflation, and this reflects the reality of many countries around the world. In the mid-2010s growth gap, low growth and deflationary pressure were the reality in Europe, and currency crises in Turkey and Russia led to stagflation. In China, a slowdown in the growth of aggregate supply also slowed the benefits of expanded productive capacity in the short run that allow a country to grow significantly without inflation. Now that a working model has been introduced, we are almost ready to start analyzing the effects of economic policy. But first, we need to integrate the financial sector into the real side of the economy.

Appendix 4.A: Phillips Curve, Okun's Law, Unemployment, and GDP Growth

The aggregate demand and aggregate supply framework allows us to display the tradeoff between GDP growth and inflation in terms of the dynamics of the market for goods and services. An alternative approach to this tradeoff is the Phillips curve, named after William Phillips, who gave the best-known modern formulation of the relationship between inflation and unemployment.[10] The Phillips curve is a complement to the present framework and is not required to understand the main tradeoffs that authorities face. Nevertheless, it provides interesting insights into the relationship between social outcomes, such as between unemployment and economic growth and between unemployment and inflation.

Growth and inflation and also unemployment and inflation are two sides of the same coin. As long as short-run dynamics are generated by aggregate demand shifts and as long as GDP growth and unemployment are strongly correlated, the tradeoff between inflation and GDP growth in the market for goods and services is equivalent to the one expressed by the Phillips curve.

Usually, there is an inverse relationship between GDP growth and the unemployment rate. The rationale for this is simple: as the economy grows, demand for labor expands, and regardless of the assumptions regarding sticky or flexible wages, hiring accelerates, and unemployment goes down. An explicit formula for the relationship between economic growth and unemployment is Okun's law.

Okun's law, named after Arthur Okun, is more of a rule of thumb than a proper economic law. In its original formulation, Okun's law stated that

Change in unemployment rate = −½(change in real output / potential output).

Unemployment would decrease only if real output is higher than potential output. For instance, if potential output is increasing by 1% a year (as it does in many developed economies), real output would need to increase by 2% a year so that the unemployment rate would shrink by 1%. Only economic growth that is higher than the natural course of the economy could decrease unemployment.

---

10. Robert J. Gordon, "The History of the Phillips Curve: Consensus and Bifurcation," *Economica* 78, no. 309 (2011): 10–50.

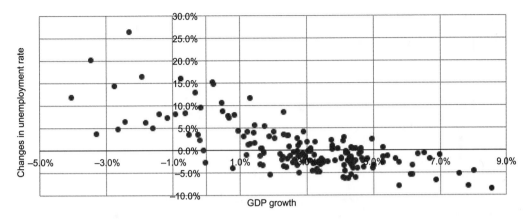

Figure 4.18
GDP growth and change in unemployment rate, United States, 1970 to 2015
Source: Federal Reserve Bank of St. Louis, 2017, https://fred.stlouisfed.org/series/CPGDPAI and
https://fred.stlouisfed.org/series/UNRATE.

Figure 4.18 shows data for the US economy for every quarter from 1970 to 2014.
On the horizontal axis is real GDP growth, and on the vertical one, changes in the
unemployment rate. The figure shows the inverse relationship between GDP
growth and the rate of change in unemployment. For the quarters with higher
growth, unemployment rate falls, and vice versa. The main result is that growth
in economic activity spreads to labor markets, and weaker activity induces higher
unemployment.

Using data for the American economy from 1949 to 2006, Edward S. Knotek II[11]
estimates that

Change in the unemployment rate = 1.20 − 0.35 ∗ (real output growth).

For this period, whenever the economy did not grow at all, unemployment
increased by 1.2 percentage points. If the economy grew at 4%, then unemployment decreased by 0.2 percentage points.

If Okun's law holds, we can choose between the supply and demand framework and the Phillips curve to evaluate the main short-run tradeoff between
economic activity and inflation faced by public authorities. The contemporary
Phillips curve is

$$\pi_t = \pi_e + (\mu + z) - \alpha u_t,$$

11. Edward S. Knotek II, "How Useful Is Okun's Law?," *Economic Review Federal Reserve Bank of Kansas
City* 92, no. 4 (2007): 73.

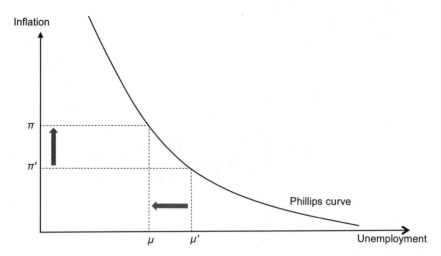

Figure 4.19
The Phillips curve

where π_t is the inflation rate at time t, π_e is the expected inflation at time t, μ is the mark-up of firms (a measure of excess profits related to their market power), z is a catch-all variable referring to idiosyncrasies in the labor market that affect the rate of unemployment (such as trade union power and employment legislation), and α is the elasticity of inflation to unemployment (figure 4.19).

Current inflation is a function of expected inflation, pricing mark-up, conditions in the labor market, and rate of unemployment. The main advantage is that the tradeoff between inflation and economic activity is explicit instead of the implied relationship that is assumed when we consider aggregate demand dynamics in the market for goods and services.

It also allows us a better insight into the mechanisms that tie the labor market to other macroeconomic markets.[12] For instance, changes in labor-market regulations (like making it harder for companies to fire employees) may shift the Phillips curve to the right and engender choices that are more difficult for policymakers battling inflation.

---

12. The mechanism behind the relationship between inflation and unemployment is captured by the so-called wage-price spiral. Low unemployment leads to higher nominal wages, and these higher costs of production prompt companies to jack up prices. Because of higher prices, workers ask for higher nominal wages the next time wages are set. The price level therefore increases again, and workers ask for another increase in nominal wages. In this way, the race between prices and wages results in relentless increases in wages and prices.

5   The Financial Side of the Economy

In this chapter,
- The link between the real and financial sides of the economy
- Why we need money and how its price—the interest rate—is determined
- How banks provide liquidity, transfer maturity, and reallocate risks
- The regulation of financial systems and the emergence of financial crises
- Are some banks too big to fail?
- How central banks operate monetary policy
- The quantity theory of money
- Quantitative easing and the rise of unorthodox policies

5.1   Quantitative Easing and the Financial Crisis

The great financial crisis of 2008 continues to send shockwaves throughout the world. It has generated the longest downturn in economic activity since the Great Depression of the 1930s, and Europe still has not fully recovered from the crisis and ensuing stagnation.

This global economy cannot be understood without a solid grasp of financial markets. So far in the book, these markets have been examined through aggregate investment, which is a function of the interest rate. This chapter establishes how the interest rate is determined and affects the real side of the economy beyond investment.

The 2010s have seen some innovations in economic policy. After the crisis, public authorities in many developed countries reduced interest rates to zero and even into negative territory and also enacted unorthodox policies such as quantitative easing.

Central banks invented quantitative easing (buying securities to lower interest rates and increase the money supply) to increase the money supply and foster economic activity. Quantitative easing is unconventional because its aim is to jumpstart a sluggish financial system when the traditional transmission mechanisms of monetary policy fail. The first example of quantitative easing comes from Japan. When the Japanese economy did not recover fully from its financial crisis of 1991, zombie banks emerged. Such banks present negative net worth and would go bankrupt in a free-market banking system. Nevertheless, usually due to their very large size, they continued to operate thanks to bailouts from the government. Given their precarious balance-sheet positions, zombie banks tend to create little credit.[1] In the early 2000s, the Japanese financial system had not fully recovered, so the federal government tried quantitative easing in order to jumpstart back to life the transmission mechanisms of monetary policy.

The practice gained traction and volume after the global crisis, affecting both the financial and real sides of the economy in emerging and developed countries. One important effect was the subsequent freezing of capital markets around the world. After Lehman Brothers failed, panic ensued, and bank runs spread from the United States to the rest of the world.

In this chapter, we develop concepts and an integrated model to explain such important issues like the advent of negative interest rates, quantitative easing, and the too-big-to-fail phenomenon.

5.2   Money and Its Role

An interest rate is the price of money. In that sense, money is a good like any other. Supply and demand determine its price and total amount. Yet it retains a special property. Money can be any good used as a universal mean to conduct transactions. In the past, the currencies used in different countries included commodities (such as salt and rice), animals (such as water buffalos and cows), and metals (such as copper, gold, and silver). In the twentieth century, most countries employed gold or dollar reserves as guarantees so that they could issue the local currency. After the end of the Bretton Woods agreement in 1971, when the United States terminated convertibility of the US dollar to gold, nations had to move to fiat currencies. Countries, usually through their central banks, have a monopoly on emitting the national currency. Money is called *fiat* (from the Latin "let it become"), and it becomes money because a law makes it compulsory to accept it as payment in trades.

Money has other properties. It helps communicate prices (becoming the unit of account) and is a financial asset that stores value. Because money is the univer-

1. For more on zombie banks and their effects on the economy, see Ricardo J. Caballero, Takeo Hoshi, and Anil K. Kashyap, "Zombie Lending and Depressed Restructuring in Japan," *American Economic Review* 98, no. 5 (2008): 1943–1977.

sal medium of exchange, it has maximum liquidity, which is defined as the ease of transforming an asset into goods and services. Of its three functions—as a medium of exchange, as a store of value, and as a unit of account—the most important one, and the one that defines it as money, is the medium of exchange. In fact, under hyperinflation,[2] money may lose its properties of unit of account and store of value, but as long as it remains legal tender, the currency issued by the government remains the nation's money.

I grew up in Brazil at a time when the country experienced a ten-year hyperinflationary period that lasted from 1985 to 1994. From 1987 to 1990, for example, inflation averaged 1,233% a year, and the country changed its currency three times, from cruzeiro to cruzado, to cruzado novo, and then back to cruzeiro. The country managed to have yet another currency (cruzeiro real) before hyperinflation was finally vanquished in 1994, when the real became the official Brazilian currency.

During the hyperinflation period, prices changed every day, and the US dollar was used as the unit of account. Every day, the first piece of information that people looked for was the exchange rate between Brazil's currency and the greenback, and the only way to determine affordability was to convert the price of a commodity from the local currency into dollars. If a pound of beans was supposed to cost roughly US$1 and if one dollar was worth 3,000 cruzeiros on that day, then the correct price for a pound of beans was roughly 3,000 cruzeiros. Computing prices like this opened the door for many instances of arbitrage,[3] and many people stocked groceries to avoid price discrepancies, a behavior common in a system in which prices change daily.

In addition to losing its role as a unit of account, the Brazilian currency also lost its place as a store of value. No rational person would keep money as a financial asset when the inflation rate typically reached 15% a month. In fact, hyperinflation increased the velocity of money,[4] and people tried to spend money as soon as they got it because any unspent currency could lose 1% of its value in a single

2. Full definitions for *inflation* and *hyperinflation* are provide in chapter 15. At this point in the book, it is enough to understand that inflation is bad and hyperinflation is truly horrible.
3. The word *arbitrage* is a technical term for a riskless trade in which one buys low and sells high. Markets are efficient when arbitrage opportunities are rare. The key word with arbitrage trades is *riskless*. All companies try to buy low and sell high, but those transactions have risks (for instance, a supermarket may fail to sell its products, or competitors can undercut it). Consider an example of a transaction with no risks. Assume that one car dealer announces that it will buy any 2007 Ford Fusion for at least US$10,000 and another dealer has a Ford Fusion 2007 for sale at US$8,000. The arbitrage opportunity is buying the car from one dealer for US$8,000 and selling it to the second dealer for US$10,000—a deal with no risk. Arbitrage opportunities do not arise often because markets tend to self-correct, erasing them.
4. As the name implies, the velocity of money is the speed at which money changes hands.

day. Foreign currency, especially the US dollar, acted as a store of value (many Brazilians to this day keep foreign currency at home as a precaution). In fact, many larger transactions (such as auto, art, and even real estate purchases) were carried out in foreign currency, which was technically illegal.

Regardless of the role played by the US dollar as a unit of account and store of value in Brazil, the cruzeiro, cruzado, and other denominations kept their role as local money because all transactions were supposed to be done in the local currency. Brazilians could use dollars to calculate equitable prices and keep them at home as liquid assets, but everyday transactions were still carried out in whatever the current currency was.

Because money is the legal tender, it has two unique characteristics as a financial asset: it is the most liquid asset, and it does not generate any cash flow. Other financial assets generate cash flows. For instance, stocks have dividends, and bonds have coupons. The money market defines the price of money, which is the interest rate. In the money market, a demand for money represents the reasons that people borrow or acquire money (their precautionary, transaction, and speculative motives). A country's central bank has a monopoly on the money supply. But understanding the money market requires understanding the banking system.

5.3   The Money Market

Money matters. Economists use a precise definition for the word *money*: it is a medium of exchange for goods and services. More precise definitions can wait, but in the US money market, people buy and sell dollars, and in China, renminbi (yuan). The money market seems quite abstract at first because it is hard to visualize people buying and selling their own national currency. There are three main characteristics of money markets:

• The price of money is the interest rate (in the representation below, it is the nominal interest rate).
• Economic agents demand money to make transactions, in a broad sense.
• The central bank (such as the Federal Reserve in the United States and the People's Bank of China in China) is a monopolist supplier of money.

In real life, there are many different interest rates. Large corporations can borrow at a lower rate than small companies, for instance. But for now, assuming that there is only one interest rate results in a straightforward money market model in which the central bank, given its monopoly power in the supply of money, can determine either the quantity of money (QM) or the interest rate (r) (figure 5.1).

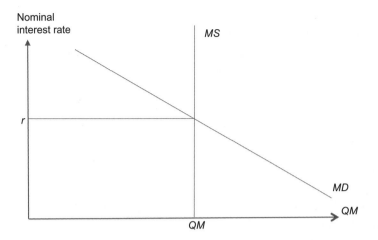

Figure 5.1

The central bank determines the supply of money, and the demand for money comes from society. There are three motives for demanding money. The precaution motive leads people to have cash on hand to pay for unexpected expenses (such as medical bills and car repair bills). The transaction motive (the largest one) leads people to have money to buy stuff. Finally, the speculative motive leads people to use cash to buy financial assets that bring more money in the future (such as shares in a listed company, gold, or any other financial product).

In the 1960s, some economists (called monetarists), like Milton Friedman, proposed that central banks should be concerned with the predictable rules of monetary expansion. If the economy is supposed to grow at 3% a year (the growth of potential output), then the Federal Reserve should increase the money supply by 3%. Modern central banks, however, choose to determine the nominal interest rate and normally adjust the money supply to changes in the demand for money or the target interest rate. Why does the market equilibrium generate a nominal (instead of real) interest rate? The real interest rate is the difference between the nominal interest rate and the rate of inflation. For instance, if one borrows at 10% a year but prices are increasing at the same rate, the effective price of this loan is zero. Nowadays, central banks operate by targeting the interest rate to influence inflation and economic growth.

The behavior of the central bank is essentially the same as that of a monopolist in a microeconomics textbook. Monopolists can choose either the quantity they sell or the price of their products. There is one exception in the case of central banks: there are no other possible entrants in the money market because the monetary authority loses its monopoly power only if it chooses to cede sovereignty to another institution. This happened, for example, when some European countries formed the euro, a common currency that went in effect in 1999. Countries in the eurozone renounced power over local money supply in favor of a central authority, the European Central Bank. Not all European Union members chose to be part of the eurozone, however. Great Britain and Denmark kept their own currencies— the pound and the krone.

The central bank's action as a monopolist requires that if it wants to maintain its control over the target interest rate, it has to react to any changes in the money demand. For instance, if South Korea's central bank, the Bank of Korea (BOK), wants to keep the interest rate at 1.25% a year, any change in demand for the won would mean an instant reaction by the BOK. Let us assume that at this interest rate, more people flock to commercial banks to borrow money. In a free market, higher demand leads to higher prices. To keep the interest rate stable, the BOK would have to increase the money supply to meet the increase in demand. In the end, the central bank would supply any quantity of money to maintain the targeted level of the interest rate.

Figure 5.2 provides a graphical analysis of this example. Assume an increase in the demand for money from MD to MD'. This would generate an upward pressure on the nominal interest rate (r).

The central bank can increase the money supply from MS to MS' (figure 5.3). It would accommodate the change in demand and keep the interest rate unchanged.

The result would be an increase in the quantity of money from QM to QM' that clears the market. There would be no excess supply or demand of money.

Today, central banks announce an interest rate target range and pursue it by making countless market interventions to adjust money supply to any changes in demand. Interest rates then should remain in the target interval. For instance, in December 2015, the US Federal Reserve announced that, for the first time in nine years, it would raise its key interest rate from a range of 0% to 0.25% to an interval of 0.25% to 0.5% per year. Later in the chapter, we explore the mechanisms through which a central bank can intervene in the money market and the reasons that it does so.

If a central bank chooses to maintain predictable levels of money supply, then the interest rate is determined by shifts in the demand for money. Most central banks prioritize the level of the interest rate. In the late 2000s and early 2010s, the US Federal Reserve, the European Central Bank, and the Bank of Japan kept interest rates at approximately 0% for long periods and then developed programs of quantitative easing.

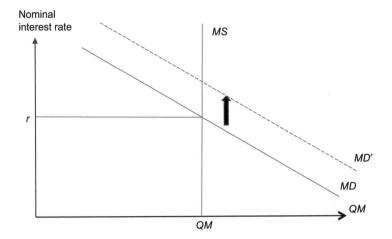

Figure 5.2

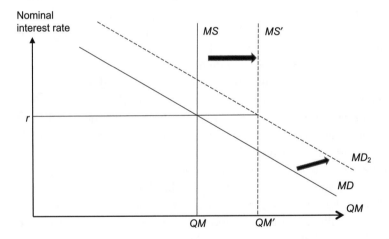

Figure 5.3

5.4   A Simple Banking System

Money has three functions in a market economy: it is a medium of exchange (payments), a unit of account, and a store of value. The financial system, when behaving well, is an elementary block of a capitalist economy. It acts as an intermediary between savers and borrowers and provides liquidity by means of processing payments, guaranteeing that economic agents can execute transactions quickly and cheaply. Financial institutions transform the maturity[5] of financial assets and reallocate risks throughout the economic system. They create the fundamental grease in the well-oiled machine of a market economy—credit. Without the financial system, a company looking for a loan for the period of two years, for instance, would have to find an economic agent willing to lend money for the same period and then would negotiate the price of such a loan—the interest rate. Commercial banks, through pooling resources from different savers, can borrow from and lend to businesses and households with completely different needs.

Banks are divided into three categories. Commercial banks take deposits from and make loans to companies and households. Investment banks provide households, corporations, and governments with advice and assistance in raising financial capital or investing in financial assets. Finally, universal banks combine commercial and investment banking in a single institution. For most of the twentieth century, the Glass-Steagall Act (enacted in 1933 and repealed in 1999) separated commercial and investment banking in the United States. After 1999, however, the five largest US banks became universal banks and increased their share of assets in the financial system, enjoying economies of scale from their commercial and investment sides (figure 5.4).

Even though investment banking is relevant to economic development, commercial banking is by far the most important side of banking for the working of a capitalist economy. By transforming the maturity of financial assets and essentially creating credit, banks provide an important service that helps generate capital investment. Let's look at a simple example of how commercial banks (1) create money and (2) turn time deposits into longer-maturity loans, generating credit that is a fundamental part of economic activity.

Suppose that there is only one commercial bank in the economy. It holds all deposits and is the only lender in the country. Assume now that a person deposits US$100 into her account. Using a simple framework with assets and liabilities, this deposit is registered as an increase in the bank's liabilities of 100 (figure 5.5).

---

5. Maturity relates to the period of a loan. For instance, if a company borrows from a bank and agrees to repay the institution in six months, six months is maturity of the loan. People with deposit accounts have immediate access to their money, but banks lend some of these deposits to companies. That is an example of how commercial banks transform the maturity of financial assets.

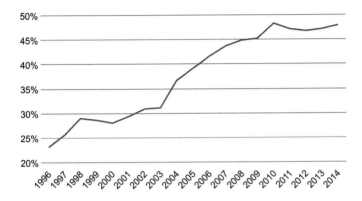

Figure 5.4
Assets of five largest banks as share of total commercial banking assets in the United States, 1996 to 2014
Source: Federal Reserve Bank of St. Louis, 2017, https://fred.stlouisfed.org/series/DDOI06USA156 NWDB.

Figure 5.5

A liability is an obligation, in this case to depositors. Assets generate future economic benefits. Banks lend and receive interest as well as the original capital, and that is why loans are put on the asset side of the balance sheet. Finally, net worth is the accounting value of a company. It is the difference between assets and liabilities in our example.

The bank proceeds to lend all or part of its deposits. In the example shown in figure 5.6, the central bank requires that the bank set aside 20% of any deposit to cover liquidity risk. We also assume that the bank has no voluntary reserves and lends all its available funds. Therefore, the bank lends 80 out of the 100 that was first deposited. In turn, the borrower uses it to buy goods and services (say, to expand a factory), and because there is only one bank in the economy, the money flows back to the bank in the form of time deposits.

The bank proceeds to lend US$64, keeping US$16 (20%) as required reserves with the central bank (figure 5.7). This amount circulates in the economy, making its way to the financial system, which proceeds to lend 80% of the amount *ad infinitum*.

Assets	Liabilities
Loans: 80	100
Reserves: 20	80

Figure 5.6

Assets	Liabilities
	100
Loans: 144	80
Reserves: 36	64

Figure 5.7

Assets	Liabilities
Loans: 400	
Reserves: 100	500

Figure 5.8

In the end, this process generates US$500 of time deposits (liabilities), distributed in terms of assets as US$400 for loans and US$100 as reserves in the central bank (figure 5.8).

In this illustration, the initial US$100 deposit is turned into US$500. Here is the important definition: because money is all means of payment, time deposits in the banking system are also considered money, and hence, in the example, the total amount of money in the economy is equal to US$500.

Commercial banks multiply the currency that circulates in the economy by taking time deposits and lending those deposits to businesses and households. In a way, commercial banks create money, dependent on two variables—the amount of currency in circulation and the required reserves ratio. Both variables are decided by the central bank, and even if commercial banks are the institutions that ultimately create money, the monopoly of money supply remains in the hands of government officials.

Economists classify money in different categories—M0, M1, M2, M3, and M4. The main difference between the categories is the liquidity of financial assets. M0 is the most liquid category and includes physical currency in the shape of notes and coins. In the context of economic policy, money is defined as M1, which includes all coins and notes as well as short-term deposits. M2, M3, and M4 (also called *broad money*) include progressively fewer liquid assets, such as long-term time deposits and money market funds. Economists use the terms *M1* and *money* interchangeably.

Another useful term is *money multiplier*—the amount of money that banks generate with each dollar of reserves. If banks behave efficiently (and, to keep it simple, hold no voluntary reserves), the total amount of money (Q_m) in a financial system is a function of only two variables—the currency base (*CB*) (all the notes and coins) and the required reserve ratio (*rr*). In countries without required reserve ratios, commercial banks hold voluntary reserves. In the simple case when banks hold no voluntary reserve, the quantity of money is:

$$Q_m = \frac{CB}{rr}.$$

For an economy with the required reserves ratio of 5% and a currency base of US$50 billion, the quantity of money would be US$1 trillion.[6]

5.5 Bank Runs, "Too Big to Fail," and Financial Crises

In a simple model of the financial system, all bank reserves are deposited in the central bank, and there are no voluntary reserves. In real life, the balance sheet of a bank is much more complicated. Commercial banks leverage their own capital to make profits on lending. For instance, for a financial institution with US$5 million in net worth and US$105 million in total assets, the leverage is 21 (105/5), which means that the bank is leveraging its net worth of US$5 million into assets of US$105 million (table 5.1).

Because of leverage and the mismatch in maturity between assets and liabilities, commercial banks need to hold capital buffers against episodes of liquidity squeeze. The Bank of International Settlements publishes standards for banking regulations through the Basel Committee on Banking Supervision. Central banks

---

6. This framework does not necessarily agree with empirical data and is simply a didactic tool. For detailed evidence on how banks create money, see recent research by Michael McLeay, Amar Radia, and Ryland Thomas, "Money Creation in the Modern Economy," *Bank of England Quarterly Bulletin* 54, no. 1 (2014): 14–27, http://www.bankofengland.co.uk/publications/Documents/quarterlybulletin/2014/qb14q1prereleasemoneycreation.pdf.

Table 5.1
Simplest balance sheet for a commercial bank (in US dollars)

Assets		Liabilities	
Property and buildings	$5 million	Demand deposits	$100 million
Government and corporate bonds	25 million	Net worth	5 million
Loans	65 million		
Cash in vault	2 million		
In accounts with the Federal Reserve	8 million		
Total assets	$105 million	Liabilities + net worth	$105 million

use these standards to regulate the behavior of managers of commercial banks in three areas:[7]

- To improve the banking sector's ability to absorb shocks arising from financial and economic stress, whatever the source;
- To improve risk management and governance; and
- To strengthen banks' transparency and increase information disclosure.

Our extremely simplified version of a banking system is useful for describing some of the important features of modern financial systems, such as financial crises, bank runs, and the emergence of banks that are "too big to fail." Because the financial system is made of interconnected institutions, when a commercial bank goes bankrupt, its competitors may face increased risks of going under themselves. One important linkage is that commercial banks rely on the stability of time deposits over time to be able to change their maturity and lend money. Banks also extend credit to each other on the interbank lending market. Essentially, banks operate without ever having enough holdings to cover their short-term liabilities because maturity transformation is a fundamental part of their activities.

When a bank fails, uninsured depositors may recover only a small fraction of their holdings. Uninsured households and companies find out that commercial banks cannot guarantee all their deposits at any point in time. In addition, they know that to recover their money, depositors would have to be the first to withdraw their resources from the banking system. For a currency base of 100 and required and voluntary reserves of 20%, the banking system has 100 in reserves to cover short-term liabilities of 500, which means that only the first agents to withdraw 100 get their money back. What is more, this is common knowledge.

---

7. Bank for International Settlements, "Basel III: International Regulatory Framework for Banks," Bank for International Settlements, 2011–2014, http://www.bis.org/bcbs/basel3.htm.

Because people are able to reclaim only a fraction of a bank's short-term liabilities (provided that they move fast), the rational action for those who are worried about their bank's health is to withdraw all their savings. This causes a bank run, in which agents move as quickly as they can to recover their funds. Because commercial banks are interconnected and the probability of other institutions failing increases when one fails, some banks are considered too big to fail by virtue of their relative size in the financial system. When a small bank fails, the reliability of the large banks is not compromised. When a large bank goes under, depositors in all institutions pay attention, increasing the possibility of a bank run.

The great financial crisis illustrates the interconnectedness of national and international financial systems. It began in the United States and quickly spread throughout the world. Banks failed or were rescued in Europe and Asia, and growth stalled all over the world.

Bank runs and financial crises are painful events for banks, depositors, and society at large. From our simple model, we know that banks "create" money by transforming maturity; this arises from their roles as financial intermediaries. Imagine a system in which the commercial banks are paralyzed, either because their deposits have caused bank runs or because they fear lending and prefer to preserve their capital as buffers against the looming crisis. In this scenario, financial transactions come to a halt, and economic activity suffers when neither households nor corporations have access to credit. Investment plummets, as does consumption. Growth and inflation slow. Financial crises cause a severe downturn by simply turning off components of aggregate demand. More important, activity cannot recover unless the financial system starts behaving efficiently again because without access to credit, companies with good investment opportunities might not be able to finance them. Given how traumatic a financial crisis can be, governments try to prevent it from happening and even resort to bailouts at the expense of the taxpayer.

The case against bailouts is simple and compelling: they cost taxpayers money (even if only in the short run) and incentivize moral hazard.[8] If banks realize they are going to be bailed out, they tend to take more risks and increase the probability that the banking system fails. In this way, bailouts reward bad behavior. This argument was central to the decision by the Federal Reserve to stop lending money to Lehman Brothers in September 2008, which led the bank to file for

8. Moral hazard is the incentive for agents to take actions that destroy social welfare. For example, if the government subsidizes all students to take courses in law, it would generate moral hazard for students who did not want to take these courses or did not have the skills to be competent in practicing law. Another example comes from industrial policy, which always creates some measure of moral hazard. Because industrial policy is based on giving incentives to selected industries, some companies invest more than they should.

bankruptcy. Bear Stearns, a similarly large bank, had been bailed out just a few months before, and the Fed wanted to send a strong signal to the banks to behave more responsibly. The result was widespread panic, however, as bank runs occurred and other similar financial institutions in different markets (such as mortgage securities and insurance) were exposed to bankruptcy. Collateral outstanding in the securities lending market decreased by US$737 billion.[9] There were bank runs. Investors took out their money from money market funds in large institutions such as BNY Mellon and Wachovia. The Federal Reserve had to intervene in financial markets and guarantee funds for institutions to settle funds redemptions. In 2016, many countries were still experiencing shocks from the great financial crisis.

Being too big to fail should not mean a free pass. Moral hazard incentivizes behavior that can destroy social welfare. Excessive risks need to be contained. Some countries nationalize banks that fail, insuring the depositors but not the shareholders or the bankers. Others prosecute bankers who took actions that were knowingly harmful. The great financial crisis highlights the difficulty of finding a balance between efficiency and safety. Some depositors were uninsured and lost their savings. Some shareholders met the same fate. Some bankers neither lost their jobs nor faced serious consequences because it is difficult to establish that bank employees committed improprieties. After all, engaging in risky behavior is part of banks' everyday activities. The great financial crisis destroyed social welfare on an unparalleled scale. The worldwide recession wiped out hundreds of millions of jobs, and some countries have not yet returned to their precrisis levels of growth. Still, curtailing all sorts of risk behavior would guarantee that some nations would never truly recover.

The main issue for financial authorities today is designing a financial system that reconciles efficiency, innovation, and stability. With too much regulation, the system will be safe but inefficient. With too little regulation, reckless banks may precipitate another financial crisis. Countries struggle to regulate their financial systems in a way that at the same time promotes economic development and decreases the risk of systemwide damage to the global economy.

Japan, Argentina, and the Consequences of Financial Crises

In the last hundred years, the world economy experienced two global financial crises. The financial crisis of 1929 started in the American stock market and set off the Great Depression in the United States and a steep recession in the rest of the

---

9. Manmohan Singh and James Aitken, "Deleveraging after Lehman: Evidence from Reduced Rehypothecation," Working Paper WP/09/42, International Monetary Fund, March 2009, https://www.imf.org/external/pubs/ft/wp/2009/wp0942.pdf.

world. The great financial crisis of 2008 also started in the United States, this time in the housing market, and contaminated the rest of global financial markets. The world has yet to fully recover from it. Crises are transmitted through the financial and trade channels. But not all financial crises are global in nature. The consequences of local crises are similar to those of global financial crises but in a national context.

In the last thirty years, financial crises destroyed social welfare in Argentina and Japan. In 1990 and 1991, an asset bubble in Japan burst, creating a financial crisis that turned the 1990s into a lost decade for the country. In Argentina, the financial crisis of 2001 to 2002 followed events in the foreign currency market. Since the early 1990s, both US dollars and Argentine pesos had been legal tender in Argentina at a conversion rate of 1 to 1. In December 2001, the country defaulted on its external debt,[10] and at least twenty-two people were killed[11] in riots and lootings. In January 2002, the country abandoned its dual-currency model, with a devalued peso as legal tender. The currency crisis contaminated the financial system, turning an economic recession into a depression.

Argentinian banks were in distress because their liabilities were mainly in dollars but their assets were denominated in pesos. With the devaluation, the liabilities increased without having correspondence in the assets. In fact, "the government decrees the unification of the exchange rate regime and the asymmetric pesoization of bank balance sheets (assets at Arg$1/US$1, and liabilities at Arg$1.4/US$1)."[12] Imagine a bank that has US$100 million in assets and US$80 million in liabilities, with a US$20 million net worth. With the changes in the balance sheet, the liabilities would increase by 40% without a correspondence in assets. Net worth and other reserve assets would not be enough to prevent the bank from failing.

When it became clear that some devaluation was inevitable, people rushed to withdraw their savings in hard currency, but the banks could not meet everybody's demands. Even more, the government issued a *corralito*, limiting the amount of daily withdrawals from banks (something similar happened in Greece in the 2010s), and eventually all deposits were converted to the devalued peso.

In Japan, nobody died in riots, but the financial crisis that followed the bursting of the bubble in the housing market was longer lasting than the crisis in Argentina.

---

10. RaboResearch, "The Argentine Crisis 2001/2002," Rabobank, August 23, 2013, https://economics.rabobank.com/publications/2013/august/the-argentine-crisis-20012002-.
11. "Timeline: Argentina's Economic Crisis," *The Guardian*, December 20, 2001, https://www.theguardian.com/world/2001/dec/20/argentina1.
12. This was on February 4. See the definitive history of the Argentinian crisis at IMF Policy Development and Review Department, "Lessons from the Crisis in Argentina," International Monetary Fund, October 8, 2003, https://www.imf.org/external/np/pdr/lessons/100803.pdf.

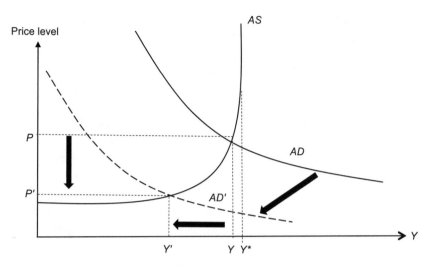

Figure 5.9

The Japanese economy still has much lower productivity, wages, and economic growth now, almost thirty years later, than it had in the precrisis period.

Financial crises spread to the real side of the economy through shifts in aggregate demand, at first. Lower consumption and investment due to lack of financing and banking services result in a recession and deflationary pressures (figure 5.9). As financial crises hit, aggregate demand shifts from *AD* to *AD'*. Price level goes down from *P* to *P'*, and output goes from *Y* to *Y'*.

In 2000, the Argentinean economy was already contracting by 0.79%, and prices were decreasing at an annual rate of 0.94% (table 5.2). There was already a growth gap. After the financial crisis, aggregate demand declined further, with GDP declining by 4.4% and inflation at around –1%. In Japan, unlike in Argentina, the economy was robust at the end of the 1980s. As the financial crisis hit, the slowdown was severe, with growth falling from 3.3% a year to 0.82% in 1992 and a corresponding decrease in inflation (prices increased only 1.7% in 1992, compared with 3.3% in the previous year).

The great financial crisis also plunged the US economy into a recession through a decrease in aggregate demand. In the years before the financial crisis, the situation in the United States was one of irrational exuberance. Both inflation and GDP growth averaged around 3.0% a year from 1990 to 2007. The financial crisis started in late 2007 but exploded with full force after the Lehman Brothers bankruptcy in September 2008. The US economy crashed in 2009. In 2008, GDP contracted by 0.29%. In 2009, it again fell, this time by –2.8%. Meanwhile, there was deflation, with prices retreating 0.4% in 2009 after increases of almost 4% in 2008.

Table 5.2
GDP growth and inflation (consumer prices): Argentina, Japan, and the United States, 1991, 2001, 2008

Country	Year of the crisis	Real GDP at t	Real GDP at t +1	CPI at t	CPI at t + 1
Argentina	2001	−4.41%	−10.0%	−0.94%	−1.07%
Japan	1991	3.32	0.82	3.30	1.71
United States	2008	−0.29	−2.78	3.84	−0.36

Note: t = year of the crisis; t + 1 = one year after the crisis.
Source: World Bank, 2017, https://data.worldbank.org/indicator/NY.GDP.MKTP.KD.ZG and https://data.worldbank.org/indicator/FP.CPI.TOTL.ZG.

Financial crises destroy wealth and income by affecting the demand side of the economy first, which means that a recession is accompanied by deflationary pressures. The effects usually last for years. Japan has not yet fully recovered from its financial crisis, and in the United States, actual output was still significantly below potential output as much as ten years after the crisis started. Argentina recovered relatively quickly, in a matter of years, but actual growth failed to keep pace with potential output for more than five years.

Systemic Risk and Losses in Commercial Banks: The Case of Sweden

A bank run squeezes the liquidity of commercial banks and, in turn, reduces credit to nonfinancial institutions. When financial troubles start, companies that need to borrow working capital or have the maturity of their debt extended cannot find financing, and their losses start to mount. To protect against such losses, banks reduce lending even more. The crisis is made worse by a negative feedback process. This was the case in Sweden.

Sweden went through a financial crisis in the early 1990s. Peter Englund, who describes the crisis in detail, notes that one of reasons for the crisis was that Swedish banks operated with only around 5% of equity, including hidden reserves.[13] The events of the crisis can be traced by following data on the banks' losses. At the peak of the crisis in the final quarter of 1992, losses were at 7.5% of lending, around twice the operating profits of the banking sector. Accumulated losses from 1990 to 1996 were approximately 20% of the total loan stock in 1990 and 12% of GDP (table 5.3).

Financial crises arise only when problems in one part of the financial system become widespread. In Sweden, losses increased sharply across the banking sector in 1991 and 1992. The macroeconomic effect was that Sweden experienced three consecutive years of negative real economic growth. Intervention by the Sveriges

13. Peter Englund, "The Swedish Banking Crisis: A Revisit in the Light of Recent Experience," Paper presented at the Riksbank Macroprudential Conference, Stockholm, June 23–24, 2015.

Table 5.3
Reported credit losses in Sweden, 1990 to 1996 (billions of Swedish kronas)

Bank	1990	1991	1992	1993	1994	1995	1996
Handelsbanken	0.7 kr	2.8 kr	7.1 kr	6.0 kr	2.5 kr	1.6 kr	1.6 kr
SEB	1.7	4.3	9.6	9.0	8.1	3.6	0.9
Nordbanken	3.6	9.8	18.2	14.3	1.7	1.1	0.6
Gota	0.9	3.7	12.5	12.0	—	—	—
Sparbanken Sv	2.8	9.8	16.6	9.6	—	—	—
Föreningsbanken	0.8	2.7	3.3	4.0	—	—	—

Source: Peter Englund, "The Swedish Banking Crisis: A Revisit in the Light of Recent Experience," Riksbank Macroprudential Conference, Stockholm, June 23–24, 2015.

Riksbank, the Swedish central bank, was untimely. Eventually, the regulatory authority nationalized the most distressed bank, Gota, and provided comprehensive guarantees to stave off the bank run.

5.6   The Instruments of Monetary Policy

Having looked at the basics of the banking system, we can now describe the money market in a more comprehensive way. The central bank has a monopoly over the money supply because it can influence the amount of currency and required reserves from commercial banks. Monetary policy is setting the desired level of interest rate or the quantity of money, with the purpose of affecting the rest of the economy. The central bank also determines the nominal interest rate (usually called the target interest rate). Central banks have five mechanisms for adjusting the target interest rate:

- Change the currency base.
- Set required reserves.
- Perform open-market operations.
- Use discount window lending.
- Use unconventional measures, such as quantitative easing.

The first of these, changing the currency base, is simple. Given their capacity to print money, governments can influence the money supply and thus interest rates by simply printing or destroying notes and coins. This is effective only in economies with simple financial systems because, for instance, there are significant transaction costs in turning on the printing presses. Second, central banks can modify the required reserves ratio to induce commercial banks to provide more or less lending to customers. As with the currency base, adjustments in

Figure 5.10

required reserves are relatively inefficient because their primary purpose is to guarantee stability for the financial system. Such changes can have potential consequences for the quality of the balance sheet and profitability of commercial banks.

Third, central banks can perform open-market operations, which are the most common instrument of monetary policy. Central banks buy and sell government bonds and by doing so influence the quantity of money available to private institutions for lending. If a central bank wants to reduce the quantity of money, it sells government bonds through the open market. Market agents buy these bonds, and central banks hold on to the cash. This way the currency base becomes smaller due to money getting out of circulation, and the target interest rate rises (figure 5.10). Conversely, if a central bank wants to increase the money supply, it buys government bonds in the open market, transferring currency to market agents and thus augmenting the currency base.

Fourth, central banks can use discount window lending to provide short-term loans to commercial banks to meet temporary shortages. Given their role as financial intermediaries, banks (unlike other businesses) have to settle receivables and payments daily. A central bank's balance sheet is composed of three parts—one in which the institution acts as the federal government bank, another in which it is the bank of banks (which parks reserves, uses discount window lending, or takes recourse on the role of central banks as the lender of last resort), and one that is related to foreign currency reserves (table 5.4). Included in the liabilities of the bank of banks are the reserves of commercial banks. A central bank also holds treasury or other government bonds with the explicit purpose of using them for monetary policy in open-market operations. The exception is the Federal Reserve balance sheet, which does not contain foreign reserves because the greenback is, for all practical purposes, the world's currency. Although central banks in emerging markets hold reserves in foreign currency, mainly the US dollar, the Federal Reserve does not need to reciprocate because it has a monopoly in the supply of the medium of exchange accepted by most economic agents in the world. The rate charged by central banks has an impact on the lending and borrowing decisions

Table 5.4
A central bank balance sheet

	Assets	Liabilities
Government's bank	Securities (such as government bonds)	Currency Government's account
Bankers' bank	Loans to banks	Required reserves of commercial banks
Foreign currency	Foreign reserves	Swaps and other derivatives in foreign currency

Source: Emily Eisner, Antoine Martin, and Ylva Søvik, "How Do Central Bank Balance Sheets Change in Times of Crisis?," *Liberty Street Economics*, February 4, 2016.

made by commercial banks. If it is high, it provides incentives for the banks to lend less and thus decrease the probability that they will need to borrow from the central bank. The discount window is then an indirect way for central banks to adjust interest rates.

Finally, central banks have a fifth mechanism for adjusting the target interest rate: they can use unusual measures, such as quantitative easing, negative interest rates and other tools for injecting liquidity into financial markets.

The most common instrument of monetary policy is the use of open-market operations. Central banks operate monetary policy by buying or selling government bonds, which in turn affects the money supply by increasing or decreasing liquidity.[14] When government bonds at large are purchased, there is an increase in the quantity of money and vice versa. Let's assume that a commercial bank has only three assets—loans to the general public, government bonds, and cash holdings. If the central bank wants to increase the interest rate, it sells the government bonds. If the commercial bank in question buys some of these bonds, then its balance sheet shows less money in its reserves account. Given that institutions offer credit based on their reserves, which went down for the whole financial system, banks' lending capacity is restricted, and the price for borrowers—that is, the interest rate—should go up.

By regulating the supply of money through open-market operations, the central bank can pursue a target interest rate. Any shock to the demand for money is met with an adjustment to the money supply to keep the interest rate constant. If the demand for loans is higher, then the interest rate should go up. Because central banks usually pursue a target interest rate, they have to increase the money supply

---

14. For a comprehensive analysis of central bank balance sheets with a focus on the United Kingdom, see Garreth Rule, "Understanding the Central Bank Balance Sheet," Centre for Central Banking Studies Handbook No. 32, Bank of England, 2015, http://www.bankofengland.co.uk/education/Documents/ccbs/handbooks/pdf/ccbshb32.pdf.

Table 5.5
The Central Bank of Brazil's holdings of government bonds by type and maturity, for use in monetary policy (in Brazilian reals), June 2016

	1 month	1–6 months	6–12 months	1–5 years	>5 years	Total
LTN	R$76,902	R$47,064,559	R$1,064,236	R$24,585,990	—	R$72,791,687
LFT	1,065,570	—	—	42,042,274	—	43,107,844
NTN-B	103,957	—	3,874,135	12,133,297	16,498,180	32,609,569
NTN-F	—	—	27,047,129	63,983,882	73,793,901	164,824,912
Total	R$1,246,429	R$47,064,559	R$31,985,500	R$142,745,443	R$90,292,081	R$313,334,012

Note: LTN = postdated bonds; PFT = zero-coupon bonds; NTN-B and NTN-F = inflation-indexed bonds.
Source: Brazilian Central Bank, "Demonstrações Financeiras," 2016, http://www.bcb.gov.br/htms/inffina/be201606/Demonstra%E7%F5esjun2016.pdf.

to meet the increased demand. As a simple example, let's assume that the interest rate in Kenya is at 6% per year and that companies want to buy more inputs. Because they need money for their purchases, the demand for money increases, and because there is more competition for money, its price should rise. If the central bank wants to keep the interest rate at 6%, however, it increases the supply of money to match the increase in demand. The price of the money—the interest rate—stays the same.

In June 2016, the Central Bank of Brazil had holdings of roughly 313 billion reals for the sole purpose of conducting monetary policy (table 5.5). The bank held four different government bonds—postdated bonds (LTN), zero-coupon bonds (LFT), and inflation-indexed bonds (NTN-B and NTN-F). Given that central banks need to intervene in money markets continuously to keep the target interest rate relatively stable, they require a reserve of bonds to do it.

In this chapter, we have examined the mechanisms by which the central bank can control money supply. It intervenes in the bond market by increasing or decreasing the currency base through open-market operations. During the 1950s and the 1960s, some economists (most prominent among them being Milton Friedman) created the monetarist theory. They claimed that the best course for monetary policy would be to set predictable targets for money supply increases over time instead of targeting interest rates.

Modeling the monetarist theory is relatively simple: central banks set targets for the growth in money supply, and movements in the demand for money function would determine the interest rate. It follows from microeconomic theory that a pure monopolist can dictate either the price of the product it sells or the quantity sold in the market. But the monetarist theory has lost favor. Nowadays, central banks set the target interest rate instead of enacting a rule for money-supply growth.

5.7   The Transmission Mechanisms of Monetary Policy

The instruments of monetary policy are the tools that central banks have for setting the nominal interest rate. But economic activity in the market for goods and services comes from changes in real variables. The difference between nominal and real variables can be explained through an example. Imagine that a senior manager earns US$100,000 in 2016 and that inflation in the country is 2% a year. When the manager receives a raise of US$2,000 in 2017, the manager's nominal salary increases to US$102,000, but the real salary stays constant. There are no real changes in purchasing power.

The transmission mechanisms of monetary policy are the conditions and links that make it possible for central banks to affect real decisions through changes in the nominal interest rate. Central to this are the credibility of the monetary authority and the trajectory of the public debt. If the government is spending recklessly, then the central bank will be less effective. The coordination between monetary and fiscal policy are addressed later in this book (chapter 7). For now, what matters is that a country has well-functioning financial markets and a credible monetary institution.

When operating efficiently, the financial system boosts economic activity by intermediating transactions and providing short- and long-term funds for both companies and households. Financial repression and incompleteness of financial markets, which are common across emerging markets, deter economic growth. Monetary policy is supposed to affect economic activity—that is, the real side of the economy—at least in the short run. For this to happen, decisions by central banks need to filter through financial systems to influence the decisions made by businesses. Changes in money supply relate to investment and consumption decisions through four major channels—credit, the balance sheet, expectations, and the exchange rate.

The first channel for changing money supply—and the most important one—is the credit channel, and it works through the interest rate. Changes in the interest rate may stimulate agents to borrow and spend more because of credit creation from open-market operations, lower required reserves, or a discount window rate. As central banks increase the quantity of money, commercial banks can use it to increase credit in the economy.

The second major channel for affecting the money supply is the balance-sheet. The balance-sheet effect is related to how lower interest rates or increases in money supply affect the price of financial assets (such as stocks and intangible assets like art, comic books, and gold). This effect boosts these assets relatively more than other prices in the economy. Thus, nominal changes may incur real modifications in the behavior of economic agents. As households become wealthier, there is a tendency to increase spending. This is commonly known as the Pigou effect, after Arthur Pigou, who first explicitly analyzed the relationship between wealth and income and the ways that people behave when their wealth changes.

The third major channel for affecting the money supply is expectations. As shown in chapter 4, if the central bank is credible, agents adjust their expectations to match the actions of the monetary authority. Expectations are so important that they may create self-fulfilling prophecies. If agents believe that something has come to pass, they will act in that direction, increasing the probability that the event will happen. If central banks announce that they are cutting interest rates to stimulate the economy, agents who believe that this will happen will start to invest more, foreshadowing the recovery. Agents react to the signals of the central banks in a way that is favorable to the monetary authority's objectives. The US Federal Reserve has credibility. Every announcement from the Fed is followed closely by the financial markets. Consumers, companies, and financial institutions change their decisions when the Fed shifts gear. Expectations matter.

Finally, the fourth transmission channel, the exchange-rate effect, is explored in the second part of this book. Mechanically, lowering the interest rate tends to depreciate the country's currency, resulting in more exports and fewer imports.

In the end, if the transmission mechanisms of monetary policy are working well, changes in money supply affect aggregate demand. During financial crises and in their aftermath, transmission mechanisms fail, and changes in the money market may not result in increased economic activity. In such situations, governments need other tools to influence aggregate demand through monetary policy.

Monetary Policy in Action: Required Reserves in Emerging Markets

Even though open-market operations are by far the most common monetary policy instrument, emerging countries also use a secondary policy instrument— the required reserve ratio. Given that in emerging countries this ratio is usually higher than in developed countries, central banks have more leeway in adjusting required reserves to make money flow into or out of the economy. The following excerpts from news articles from 2013 to 2015 discuss the use of compulsory deposits as monetary policy in emerging markets:

China Cuts Bank Reserve Requirement to Spur Growth[15]

BEIJING (Reuters) Wed., Feb. 4, 2015. China's central bank made a system-wide cut to bank reserve requirements on Wednesday, the first time it has done so in over two years. The goal is to unleash a fresh flood of liquidity to fight off economic slowdown and looming

15. Kevin Yao and Judy Hua, "China Cuts Bank Reserve Requirement to Spur Growth," Reuters, February 4, 2015, http://www.reuters.com/article/2015/02/04/us-china-economy-rrr-idUSKBN0L80 YY20150204.

deflation. The announcement cuts reserve requirements—the amount of cash banks must hold back from lending—to 19.5 percent for big banks, a reduction of 50 basis points that would free up 600 billion yuan ($96 billion) or more held in reserve at Chinese banks—which could then inject 2–3 trillion yuan into the economy after accounting for the multiplying effect of loans.

Brazil Central Bank Reduces Bank Reserve Requirements[16]

SAO PAULO (MNI) Fri., July 25, 2014. Brazil's central bank Friday issued an order reducing bank reserve requirements and expects an extra R$30 billion ($13.5 billion) to flow into the economy as a result. In addition, the central bank said it will now permit that up to 50% of certain kinds of reserves on term deposits be used for new credit operations or to buy certain kinds of loan portfolios, and it is increasing the number of banks that can use up to 20% of reserves on overnight deposits to invest in a specific kind of credit backed by the BNDES national development bank.

More Reserves[17]

Aug. 15, 2013. Indonesia last ordered banks to set aside more cash as reserves in 2010 after inflation accelerated. Lenders are currently required to set aside 8 percent of their deposits as primary reserves. Primary reserves and the secondary reserve requirement are used to determine how much commercial lenders need to place in deposits at the central bank to manage liquidity in the banking system. Today's move suggests an increase in reserve requirements of around $4 billion across the banking system, Roland Randall, a Singapore-based economist at Australia & New Zealand Banking Group Ltd, said in a note.

Required reserves are not the main instrument of monetary policy and usually are reserved to maintain a stable financial system. Yet it is a tool available to the monetary authorities.

The Independence of Central Banks

Every country faces an important decision regarding the independence of its central bank: should the central bankers be political appointees, or should the monetary institution have functional independence from the executive branch? Both choices come with benefits. A politically integrated central bank allows for better coordination between monetary and fiscal policies. An independent central bank may constrain the politically motivated efforts of the executive branch.

Central bank independence rests on the tradeoffs between discretion and constraints. Should societies prefer public authorities with discretionary power over economic decisions, or should decision makers be constrained? Moreover, which one brings credibility to the monetary authority so it can perform its duties effectively? The performances of central banks hinge on how credible these institutions are.

---

16. Daniel Horch, "Brazil Central Bank Reduces Bank Reserve Requirements," *Market News*, July 25, 2014, https://www.marketnews.com/content/brazil-central-bank-reduces-bank-reserve-requirements.
17. Novrida Manurung, "More Reserves," *Bloomberg*, August 15, 2013, http://www.bloomberg.com/news/articles/2013-08-15/indonesia-holds-rate-to-support-growth-at-slowest-in-three-years.

The main benefit of an independent central bank is related to how agents form their expectations.[18] A history of sound policies builds credibility and lowers the cost of monetary policies. The Bank of Japan, for example, has a history of pursuing price stability. Its actions are credible and consistent over time, even when unorthodox.

In most poor countries, however, economic policies are inconsistent over time because the indenpendent central banks may to try to constrain the fiscal choices of policymakers. For instance, the central bank can increase the interest rate following an announcement of excessive public spending to discourage politicians from lavishing funds on wasteful projects.

Although central bank independence is more important for emerging markets than developed countries because the likelihood for politically motivated deleterious action is higher in poor countries, the US Federal Reserve has been independent since its inception in 1914. The Federal Reserve System is composed of twelve regional Federal Reserve Banks located in major cities throughout the United States. Formal independence from the executive branch does not mean detachment from the government, however. The top central bank authority in the US is the chair of the seven-member board of governors of the Federal Reserve System. The chair is chosen by the US president from the members of the board of governors and serves four-year terms. Janet Yellen, the first woman to head the monetary authority in the United States, served from 2014 to 2018 and was replaced by Jerome Powell, who was chosen by President Donald Trump.

Even though the Fed has had formal independence since it was created, a hierarchy of policy goals was not established until the 1970s. Congress designed and passed the Federal Reserve Reform Act of 1977 during a period of surging inflation.[19] It set price stability as a national policy goal for the first time. The Full Employment and Balanced Growth Act, approved in 1978 and known informally as the Humphrey-Hawkins Act, established full employment as a secondary goal of monetary policy and obligated the Fed to report to Congress on its policies twice a year.

Since then, many analysts have questioned the independence of the Fed in setting monetary policy goals.[20] In late 2016, the Fed board voted unanimously in favor of the second increase in interest rates in ten years, setting the target interest rate on an interval of 0.5% to 0.75%. Analysts considered the raise to be an

18. How people react to governments decisions is particularly important in the economics of global business. Most of the context dependency in economic policy comes from the distinct reactions of market agents.

19. Federal Reserve Bank of San Francisco, "What Is the Fed: History," Federal Reserve Bank of San Francisco, http://www.frbsf.org/education/teacher-resources/what-is-the-fed/history.

20. Wil S. Hylton, "Greenspan Takes a Bath," *Longform Reprints*, April 2005, http://reprints.longform .org/alan-greenspan-hylton (originally published in GQ).

independent move, given that the election of Donald Trump had sent waves of uncertainty throughout the financial markets.[21]

Many economists agree that the optimal design of monetary policy entails an independent central bank. For instance, Lorenzo Bini Smaghi, member of the executive board of the European Central Bank, argues that the central bank's independence brings about lower inflation, which ensures a more stable environment for economic and employment growth.[22] Nevertheless, the definition of independence is not yet clear. In the United States, the Fed is independent, even though its board members are appointed by the president and the chair has to report to Congress twice a year. Stephen King has argued that central bankers are making decisions that are more political than economic.[23]

As with most issues in economics, the argument for the independence of central banks is nuanced. The European Central Bank is supposed to be independent, but its decision to lend money to Greece in the early 2010s was clearly politically motivated because it took place amid fears that the country would be forced to leave the eurozone. Few emerging countries have independent central banks because policymakers prefer to retain discretion, but even if countries were to build independent institutions, it would not necessarily mean that they would be shielded from pressure from the rest of the government.

We should keep two things in mind: monetary policy can be effective at stimulating growth but only temporarily, and independence is one possible way of generating credibility. A central bank's independence can help in the pursuit of credibility, but if a central bank, even in a poor country, builds a track record of responsible decisions and agents expect that it will continue to do so, then there is no need for independence. There are different paths to credibility, and independence is but one of them.

5.8   The Quantity Theory of Money

The transmission mechanisms of monetary policy connect the money market and the real side of the economy. We can now formalize it in a simple framework—the quantity theory of money (QTM). This theory first appeared in the nineteenth century and has a long and fruitful tradition in economics. There are different

---

21. Pedro Da Costa, "The Fed Just Proved It's Not Political," *Business Insider*, December 14, 2016, http://www.businessinsider.com/fed-rate-hike-proves-its-not-political-2016-12.

22. Lorenzo Bini Smaghi, "Central Bank Independence: From Theory to Practice," European Central Bank, Paper presented at the Good Government and Effective Partnership Conference, Budapest, April 19, 2007, https://www.ecb.europa.eu/press/key/date/2007/html/sp070419.en.html.

23. Stephen King, "Era of Independent Central Banks Is Over," *Financial Times*, January 10, 2013, https://www.ft.com/content/a4e41f16-5b1b-11e2-8ccc-00144feab49a.

formulations for QTM, but the standard one comes from Irving Fisher's *The Purchasing Power of Money* (1911). QTM links nominal variables to real ones. Formally, it is expressed by

$$MV = PT,$$

where M is the nominal quantity of money, V is the velocity of money (how quickly money circulates in the economy), P is the price level, and T is number of transactions (which is a proxy of output or GDP). Instead of T, we will use Y—as in $MV = PY$—because Y is used for GDP in this book's graphs.

The only variable that needs further explanation is the velocity of money. In the simplified commercial bank model used in this chapter, the single bank in the economy creates money by taking in time deposits and by lending out a part of them. The money is funneled back to the bank, which lends more *ad infinitum*. The velocity of money is the speed with which commercial banks turn their deposits into credit. Usually, economists treat velocity of money as a structural feature of banking systems and consider it fixed and of little importance.

If V is fixed, then changes in M are bound to change the value of P or Y. The QTM is more an identity than a full-blown model of the connection between the financial and real sides of the economy, but it describes the tradeoff between inflation (price level) and growth (output) in a direct manner, without the need for graphics or more complex algebraic arguments.

An important proposition that follows from most monetary economic models is that money may not be neutral in the short run but is neutral in the long run. Money neutrality refers to how changes in the quantity of money (part of the financial side of the economy) affect the real side of the economy (for instance, consumption by households or investment by corporations). Money is neutral when the financial side does not affect the real side of the economy. For instance, most people learn in school that if the government prints money at will, inflation is the main consequence. In that process, money would be neutral. It would change only nominal prices, without changing the real prices of goods and services.[24]

From the discussion of long-run growth in chapter 3, we know that prosperity is a function of production factors. The idea that money is neutral in the long run stems from the fact that changes in interest rates will not have an effect on aggregate supply. In short-run dynamics, money is not neutral if it can disturb the real decisions made by households and businesses. Most economic models allow for non-neutrality in the short run, but whether money is neutral in the long run is

---

24. The impact of the great financial crisis was so profound that this simple story does not hold anymore. When the transmission mechanisms of monetary policy fail, they may fail spectacularly.

still an open question. Robert Lucas's Nobel lecture ties expectations to arguments regarding money neutrality.[25] Guillaume Rocheteau, Pierre-Olivier Weill, and Tsz-Nga Wong provide a model of an economy in which money is neutral in the long run but not the short run.[26]

For the present framework, the description of money neutrality in the long run but not the short run fits well in the dynamics of the market for goods and services. Through the transmission mechanisms, a central bank may affect aggregate demand. The explicit nature of the tradeoff between growth and inflation is simple and elegant. In addition, by looking at the difference between money neutrality in the short run and long run, we can see a simple restriction on economic policy: no matter how the central bank intervenes in money markets, it cannot generate long-term prosperity.

Quantitative Easing and the Quantity Theory of Money

After the great financial crisis, the US Federal Reserve, the European Central Bank, and other central banks guaranteed the deposits of account holders, providing liquidity in their role of lenders of last resort and avoiding the calamity of a world without financial markets. Dodging a complete collapse was not the end of the story, though.

Fearing another crisis, commercial banks around the world simply stopped lending, imposing a credit squeeze in financial markets worldwide. Banks usually take time deposits and leverage them by lending, but after the crisis, lending fell sharply. The credit channel of the transmission mechanism of monetary policy was cut short. During a financial crisis, the banking system may suffer from a liquidity trap, where extra cash is not turned into lending because banks hoard whatever money comes their way to protect themselves against the possibility of bankruptcy.

Keynes was the first to describe the liquidity trap: "There is the possibility ... that, after the rate of interest has fallen to a certain level, liquidity-preference may become virtually absolute in the sense that almost everyone prefers cash to holding a debt which yields so low a rate of interest. In this event the monetary authority would have lost effective control over the rate of interest. But whilst this limiting case might become practically important in future, I know of no example of it hitherto."[27] In such a situation, any cash that enters the financial system will be

25. Robert E. Lucas Jr., "Nobel Lecture: Monetary Neutrality," *Journal of Political Economy* 104, no. 4 (1996): 661–682.

26. Guillaume Rocheteau, Pierre-Olivier Weill, and Tsz-Nga Wong, "Long-Run and Short-Run Effects of Money Injections," Working paper, March 2015.

27. John Maynard Keynes, *The General Theory of Employment, Interest, and Money* (London: Macmillan and Co., 1936), 187.

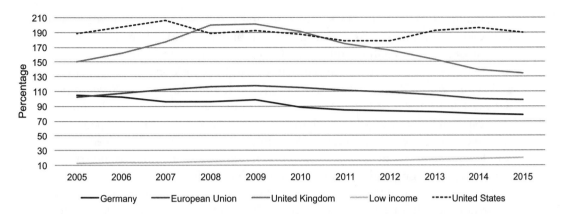

Figure 5.11
Credit as a percentage of GDP in Germany, the European Union, and the United Kingdom, 2005 to 2015
Source: World Bank, 2017, https://data.worldbank.org/indicator/FS.AST.PRVT.GD.ZS.

hoarded, and an increased money supply will not lead to credit creation. Even without a complete liquidity trap, financial fragility leads banks to create an amount of credit much below the full potential of the financial system.

During most of 2008 to 2013, regulators were concerned about the health of banks around the world. Central banks applied rounds of stress tests to verify whether banks were capable of withstanding negative events. Meanwhile, many banks reduced credit creation because of more stringent regulation, risk aversion, and streamlined operations.

Credit is strongly correlated with income per capita. Households and businesses find it much easier to borrow in developed economies with strong institutions than they do in poor countries. The evolution of credit as a percentage of GDP for selected regions is shown in figure 5.11. In lower-income countries, credit as a percentage of GDP was 13% in 2005 and reached 20% in 2015. Meanwhile, for the United States and the European Union, credit in relation to income peaked in 2007 (206%) and 2009 (118%), respectively. For the United States in 2011, deleveraging resulted in credit worth 178% of GDP, and in 2015, it was still below the precrisis level. For countries in the European Union, credit went down every year from 2009 to 2011, and this was not a result of inequality among the countries. For some of the richest countries, like the United Kingdom and Germany, the effect was even stronger than for the rest of the European Union, with credit in Germany decreasing by 20% in relative terms and in the UK, by 34%.

Between 2008 and 2014, the Federal Reserve set off three rounds of quantitative easing. The third quantitative easing program (QE3) was announced on

September 13, 2012, with the Fed announcing purchases of government bonds and agency mortgage-backed securities amounting to US$40 billion per month. In December 2012, the central bank raised the threshold to US$85 billion per month, and in December 2013, it announced that it would cut back on purchases starting in January 2014. QE3 ended on October 29, 2014, after the Federal Reserve had accumulated US$4.5 trillion. The fact that this did not engender much concern suggests that the transmission mechanisms of monetary policy in developed countries were in a precarious state. In September 2017, the Fed announced that it would start selling some of the assets it purchased during the three rounds of QE.

The Bank of England and the European Central Bank enacted quantitative easing programs in 2009. In 2015, the ECB expanded QE so it would make purchases of roughly €1.1 trillion from March 2015 to September 2016. Other countries, like Sweden and Japan, also used QE in their local markets in the years following the great financial crisis.

Why did conventional monetary policy fail? Some news commentators warned that loose monetary policy combined with quantitative easing would lead the country down a treacherous path. Paul Volcker, a former Fed chair and the inflation hawk who presided over the disinflation of the early 1980s, warned that the United States was going to create so much money that it would lead to inflation down the road.[28] A group of economists sent an open letter to the Fed warning of the dangers of inflation following QE.[29] They were clearly wrong. Eight years after the crisis, inflation was still highly irrelevant for most developed economies, and round after round of QE in the United States, Europe, and Japan failed to stoke inflation. In fact, in 2015, Japan and Europe set a goal of increasing inflation, not curbing it. What happened?

One easy way to explain this lack of inflation is through the quantity theory of money (QTM). Remember that

$$MV = PY,$$

where M is nominal quantity of money, V is velocity of money, P is price level, and Y is GDP. Roughly, changes in the quantity of money should affect either prices or output. Interest rates near zero combined with quantitative easing had no effect on prices, and after the financial crisis, most developed economies were

28. Shamim Adam and Liza Tan, "Volcker Says Quantitative Easing May Create Inflation," *Bloomberg*, November 2, 2010, https://www.bloomberg.com/news/articles/2010-11-02/fed-s-quantitative-easing -program-may-create-inflation-surge-volcker-says.

29. Cliff Asness, Michael J. Boskin, Richard X. Bove, Charles W. Calomiris, Jim Chanos, John F. Cogan, Niall Ferguson, Nicole Gelinas, James Grant, and Others, "Open Letter to Ben Bernanke," *Wall Street Journal*, November 15, 2010, https://blogs.wsj.com/economics/2010/11/15/open-letter-to-ben -bernanke.

facing the risk of deflation. We can explain this by allowing the seemingly fixed velocity of money to change and absorb all the extra liquidity in the economy.

Here is the scenario that Keynes described but could not find an example of. Commercial banks froze credit to hoard capital and reduce their bankruptcy risks, following the great financial crisis. In such a situation, the velocity of money goes down. If banks hoard cash, then credit does not flow into the real side of the economy. As M rises, there is no effect on P or Y because there is a corresponding decline in V. In normal times, quantitative easing would lead to inflation because printing money should push up prices given that real balances are unchanged. In essence, the Federal Reserve printed almost US\$4.5 trillion during the three QE phases. But if the extra liquidity does not flow into the economy (if velocity goes down), then no amount of quantitative easing could result in changes in the market for goods and services. An apocryphal quote attributed to Henry Louis Mencken sums it up: "For every complex problem, there is an answer that is clear and simple—and wrong."

6   The Loanable Funds (Credit) Market

In this chapter,

- The importance of aggregate saving and investment to economic prosperity
- How central banks affect economic activity through changes in the nominal interest rate
- The paradox of thrift: when willingness to save leads to less aggregate saving
- Negative interest rates and their economic impacts
- When governments borrow from the public
- Supply-side and trickle-down economics
- Why saving matters in poor economies and investment matters in developed countries

6.1   The Main Concepts of the Loanable Funds Market

The term *loanable funds* is another way to refer to credit. In the loanable funds markets, three variables—aggregate saving, investment, and the real interest rate—are determined. Central banks can choose to determine the nominal interest rate in the money market. In normal times, monetary institutions change the (nominal) interest rate in the money market and affect the (real) credit market—at least in the short run. In the long run, money is neutral, and prosperity comes from changes in aggregate supply (as is shown in chapter 3).

The loanable funds market congregates borrowers and lenders, savers and investors, and the government (which can compete with lenders in the case of public surplus or with borrowers in the more likely case of public deficit). Loanable funds include all forms of credit, such as commercial banks' loans, corporate and government bonds, and savings deposits. It includes private and public borrowing and lending. Supply for loanable funds comes mostly from households. Most of the demand comes from firms that need credit to invest in economic expansion, but households and governments also can demand credit (to consume part of their future income), and firms can be savers (to wait for better opportunities to use their funds). By the end of 2017, Apple had accumulated more than US\$285 billion; it waited for projects to invest in or companies to acquire.

Economists use the word *investment*, in the macroeconomic aggregate sense, to depict the expansion of companies or the creation of new businesses. In the everyday sense of the word, individuals can invest in financial assets such as stocks or bonds. Economic models distinguish between aggregate saving and investment. When people buy stocks or bonds, they are doing the opposite of investing, and such portfolio "investment" is actually saving. In this chapter, investment increases the productive capacity of the economy, and saving is the accumulation of wealth for future consumption. Investment appears on aggregate demand as investment (I) and later turns into capital (K).

The credit market is based on one of the most important economic identities: $S = I$, where S is aggregate saving, and I is aggregate investment. Saving is identical to investment. In other words, what people in the economy save is used for companies and governments to invest—the crucial variable that generates economic growth in the long run. Without loanable funds (credit), companies would not be able to invest, and there would be no economic activity because entrepreneurs would not be able to borrow in order to expand the production capacity of the economy. The investment process has a peculiar dynamic: before investment pushes up the productive capacity of an economy, it is actually a drain on its resources. To sum up, investment raises aggregate demand in the short run and adds to productive capacity (aggregate supply) in the long run.

Here we assume, for simplicity's sake, that households save but never borrow, that private companies borrow but never save, and that governments can save, invest, or be neutral (when they are neutral, there is a balanced public budget). In modern economies, governments can spend more than they earn through the emission of debt, either internal (government bonds in local currency) or external (in foreign currency, representing sovereign debt). For now, we concentrate on a closed economy in which no transactions with the rest of the world are allowed. There is no demand for local assets by foreigners, and the local government cannot accumulate foreign funds or be financed by foreign lenders. In an open economy, aggregate saving is still identical to aggregate investment, but foreigners can either supply or demand loanable funds. Many emerging countries use foreign saving as a source of funds for national investment. Instead of $S = I$, the identity becomes $S + CFA = I$, where CFA is the capital and financial account, which measures inflow (if positive) or outflow (if negative) of foreign investment in the local economy.

In a closed economy, the saving part of the loanable funds market is the amount that economic agents are willing to save at different interest rates. On the investment side, agents are willing to borrow at different costs of capital. In other words, if interest rates are high, people like to save more. At the same time, companies refrain from investing because it costs them more to repay any loans used to build new factories.

6.2   The Link between the Money Market and the Credit Market

The loanable funds market determines the amount of aggregate saving and investment in the economy. Investment affects the economy in the short run; after all, it is part of aggregate demand. Aggregate saving is important to mobilize resources for long-run projects. Investment turns into capital. Saving allows companies to borrow, produce now, and pay back the loans with the cash flow from successful operations. The lack of aggregate saving is a particularly acute problem in emerging markets. Without capital markets that allow companies to borrow so they can invest more, poor countries tend to stay poor.

The credit market is the most complicated element in our framework because it is intrinsically linked to the money market. In the money market, the central bank determines the nominal interest rate. In the loanable funds market, the interaction between savers and borrowers determines the real interest rate (figure 6.1). For the central bank to affect the economy, adjustments in the nominal interest rate must change the real interest rate. In our model, this happens in the short run but not in the long run.

Financial systems are complex. Money is moved around the world by pension and hedge funds, money market funds, managers of family offices, venture capital

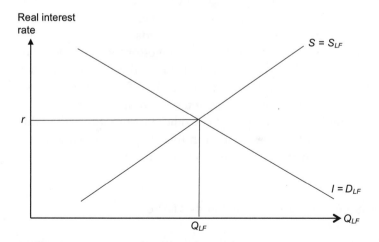

Figure 6.1

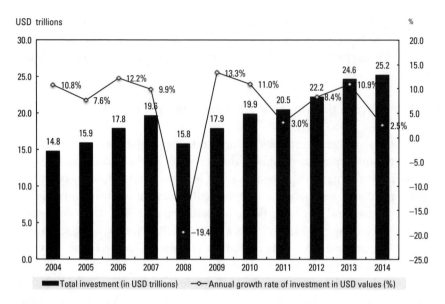

Figure 6.2
Level and annual growth rate of total assets of pension funds in the OECD, 2004 to 2014
Source: OECD, "Pension Markets in Focus," OECD, 2015.

and private equity firms, and pass-through entities. Furthermore, businesses do not borrow at the same interest rate: large and established corporations pay a smaller risk premium than small businesses do. In emerging markets, financial markets may not be complete and liquid, so some businesses are not able to borrow, and interest rates may be too high for credit to be economically feasible.

Pension funds in OECD countries, for example, managed more than US$25 trillion in the mid-2010s, and in those countries, those funds were growing much faster than the GDP (figure 6.2). Usually, institutional investors accumulate funds during the first phase of their life cycle and then disburse them to their participants when they get older. The life cycle of a pension fund is from thirty to eighty years, and they are active agents in financial systems all around the world.

Although a pension fund has a long view, some other institutions work within a shorter timeframe. The simple representation in this chapter combines all the behavior of different agents in financial markets that are complete, liquid, and efficient.

6.3   The Basic Mechanics of the Loanable Funds Market

The loanable funds model captures the changing patterns of saving and investing. For instance, let's assume that businesses see few opportunities for sales in the

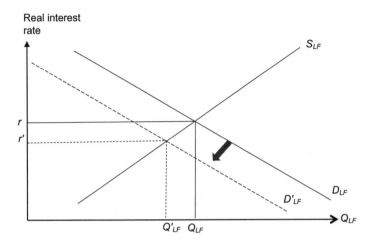

Figure 6.3

future. This depresses the demand for investment today, resulting in a lower real interest rate (figure 6.3). As business expectations go down, demand for loanable funds (D_{LF}) moves to D'_{LF}, the equilibrium quantity decreases (from Q_{LF} to Q'_{LF}), and the interest rate decreases (from r to r'). The same happens with aggregate savings and investments. Aggregate investment connects the loanable funds market and the market of goods and services. If companies foresee headwinds, they invest less, and aggregate demand falls.

The effects on the credit and the goods and services markets are simultaneous. The business environment becomes worse, contracting both the real interest rate and aggregate demand (and thus GDP and inflation) at the same time. This is when usually a central bank tries to revive the economy. Monetary policy may affect the credit market.

There are two ways to model the relationship between the money and the credit markets. In the simplest model, the central bank may affect the credit market but not vice versa, and in the more complex (and also more realistic) scenario, both markets affect each other. We choose the latter.

If companies feel that their business prospects are less favorable, they invest less, and demand for credit shrinks. Simultaneously, the demand for money for the transaction motive declines.

In the money market, a worse outlook translates to lower demand for money (from MD to MD') as companies' demand for credit falls (figure 6.4).

An important mechanism connects the money and credit markets. Assume that the central banks are all-powerful and can intervene in the money market to keep the nominal interest rate unchanged. They can do this by selling government

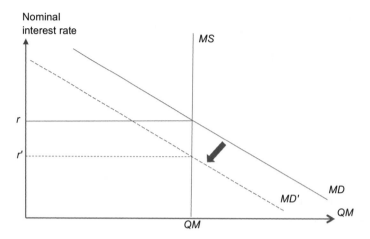

Figure 6.4

bonds, thus diminishing the money supply to match the lower demand for money (figure 6.5).

As the money supply contracts (from MS to MS'), the interest rate reverts to its target level (from r to r' to r), and the equilibrium quantity of money goes down (from QM to QM').

Returning to the market for loanable funds, an increase in the supply of government bonds decreases the supply of loanable funds, and in the new equilibrium, the interest rate comes back to its preshock level, and the quantity of loanable funds in the economy decreases (figure 6.6). An increase in the supply of government bonds decreases the supply of loanable funds because commercial banks purchase these bonds and have fewer funds to lend to private agents.

As the demand for loanable funds recedes, Q_{LF} moves to Q'_{LF}, and the interest goes down from r to r'. As the central bank intervenes in the money market, the effect on the loanable funds market is a decrease in the supply of loanable funds from S_{LF} to S'_{LF}. The interest rate goes back to its preshock level (from r' to r), and the quantity of loanable funds decreases further from Q'_{LF} to Q''_{LF}.

The connection between the money and credit market is all we need, but we can go a bit further by presenting the details of the saving and investment functions. Saving behavior depends on the wealth of individuals (W), changes in personal taxes (T), expectation of future income and prices (E), measures of risk aversion (RA), and interest rates (r). Investment is a function of aggregate costs (c), corporate taxes (T), expectation of business opportunities (E), technological change or innovation (in), subsidies (sb), and interest rates (r). Both saving and investment are related to interest rates (r), but that is already explicit in the market for loanable funds graph. Formally,

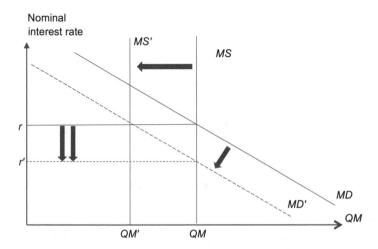

Figure 6.5

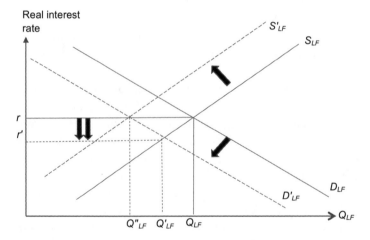

Figure 6.6

$S = f(W, T, E, RA, r)$

and

$I = f(c, T, E, in, sb, r)$.

Any changes in the variables affecting saving and investment shift the equilibrium in the market for loanable funds. However, demand for loanable funds is not equal to private investment because the government also can borrow or save money. When governments want to spend more than they earn through taxes, they act like any agent and borrow from the market at large. However, unlike private agents, governments also have another source of funds at their disposal: they can print money.

Concentrating on private investment for now, let's assume that a positive technological shock results in more productivity as a whole. In the 1990s, the dissemination of Internet use was just such a shock. In this case, the demand for loanable funds rises as companies want to invest more. If other conditions remain the same, both the interest rate and the quantity of loanable funds go up, which means higher actual investment and saving (figure 6.7).

The central bank can inject more money into the economy by purchasing government bonds and providing more loanable funds if it chooses to maintain the target interest rate constant.

The same mechanism that works for private investment also works for saving. Changes in how people save (other than those resulting from a change in the interest rate) can change the supply of loanable funds. For instance, if a demographic change occurs in which the population ages and people save less, the supply of loanable funds moves to the left, increasing interest rates to the point where the supply of and the market for loanable funds are balanced (figure 6.8).

These are the basic mechanics of the credit market. They are a bit complicated because of the link to the money market. Both markets are connected with the market for goods and services through the interest rate and aggregate investment.

If the transmission mechanisms of monetary policy are not working well, then the central bank has much less power to affect the credit market. We already saw such a situation with quantitative easing. Monetary authorities tried QE because they were not able to affect the credit market using their regular monetary policy tools. In the end, the credit market (and not the money market) affects the market for goods and services. If the transmission mechanisms of monetary policy are working well and central banks have credibility, they can influence economic growth and inflation by changing the nominal interest rate. In other words, using the quantity theory of money, the nominal quantity of money (M) may affect the price level or GDP (PY) in the short run. In the long run, M affects only the price level (P).

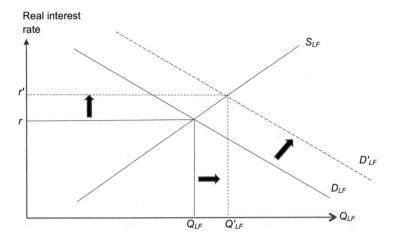

Figure 6.7

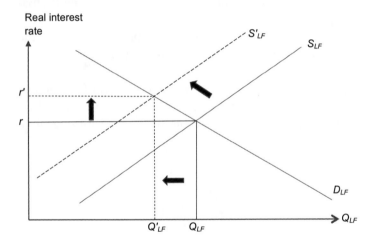

Figure 6.8

The World of Negative Interest Rates

In the wake of the great financial crisis, central banks in developed economies lowered interest rates and have kept them low for several years. In some countries, for the first time in history, government bonds had a negative yield, which means that economic agents were paying for the right to hold government debt. Can persistently low interest rates be explained within our framework?

One way to consider the effects on the loanable funds market is by analyzing the variables related to private saving and investment. After the crisis, did society experience a crisis of confidence? Did people become more risk averse? What is happening to private investment? Is it increasing?

After the crisis, the supply of loanable funds increased dramatically, both from savers and from mechanisms such as quantitative easing. At the same time, the demand shrank as businesses invested less. Although interest rates fell to zero, aggregate investment remained flat. Public investment also did not increase and has even decreased in many countries that tried to contain their ballooning debt. The result is shifts in both supply and demand for loanable funds. Even though markets became highly liquid, demand failed to respond.

For a complete picture, we would need to consider an open economy, yet the present framework of the loanable funds market can generate negative interest rates (figure 6.9).

In this highly stylized example, S_{LF} goes up to S'_{LF}, and demand for loanable funds decreases from D_{LF} to D'_{LF}. In the end, the quantity of loanable funds, borrowed and saved, is higher, but the real interest rate has moved into negative territory: from r to r'.

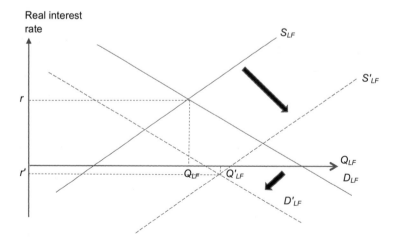

Figure 6.9

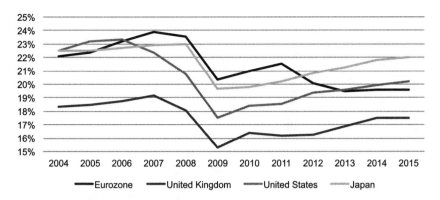

Figure 6.10
Gross capital formation (aggregate investment) as a percentage of GDP in the eurozone, the United Kingdom, the United States, and Japan, 2004 to 2015
Source: World Bank, 2017, https://data.worldbank.org/indicator/NE.GDI.TOTL.ZS.

Looking at real data shows a clear trend: private investment is lower than before the financial crisis, despite low interest rates. Even with nominal short-term interest rates at zero, gross capital formation (a measure of private investment) is much lower than it was in the period prior to the crisis.

For the four largest developed economies, gross capital formation peaked in 2008 (figure 6.10). Right after the financial crisis, central banks drove down interest rates (figure 6.11).[1]

With interest rates close to zero, private investment should have increased but did not (table 6.1). In June 2016, the *Financial Times* reported that "more than $36 bn of corporate bonds with a short-term maturity currently trade with a sub-zero yield."[2]

The only rationale for holding financial assets with negative yields is that holding cash incurs even higher transaction costs. There were 10 billion euros in outstanding bonds of BMW Finance NV, a German car company. Yields were at –0.14%. Holding 10 billion euros in paper currency would yield a return of 0% and should be preferable to buying BMW's bonds. However, a high demand for bonds with corresponding low supply can turn the yields negative, and changes in bond prices can make investors make money even if yields are already negative.

1. Even though the European Central Bank is the lender of last resort in the eurozone, there are no euro bonds, and countries inside the eurozone can still issue their own government bonds. Interest rates in figure 6.11 are three-month inter-bank market rates that follow closely the target interest rate of the central banks. For all countries, the interest rates go almost to zero during the period, showing how supply of loanable funds outstripped demand.
2. Eric Platt and Gavin Jackson, "Corporate Bonds Join Negative Yield Club," *Financial Times*, June 2, 2016, https://www.ft.com/content/e1a7dca0-285c-11e6-8ba3-cdd781d02d89.

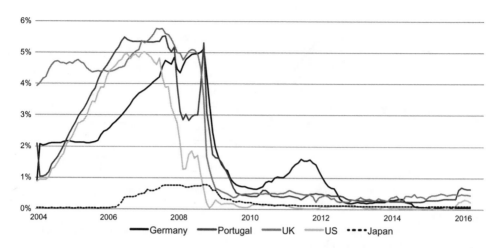

Figure 6.11
Nominal interest rate in Germany, Portugal, the United Kingdom, the United States, and Japan, 2004 to 2016.
Source: Federal Reserve of St. Louis, 2017, https://fred.stlouisfed.org/series/IR3TIB01DEM156N, https://fred.stlouisfed.org/series/IR3TIB01PTM156N, https://fred.stlouisfed.org/series/IR3TTS01 GBM156N, https://fred.stlouisfed.org/series/IR3TIB01USM156N, and https://fred.stlouisfed.org/series/IR3TIB01JPM156N.

Table 6.1
Top ten negative-yielding capital structures in the eurozone

Ticker	Issuer	Negative-yield bonds outstanding (billions of euros)	Average yield of negative bonds only (percentage)	Rating	Ultimate country of risk
BMW	BMW Financial Services	€10.0	–0.14%	A	Germany
DAIGR	Daimler	8.8	–0.09	A–	Germany
RABOBK	Rabobank	6.4	–0.05	AA–	Netherlands
ENGIFP	Engie	6.4	–0.17	A–	France
RDSALN	Shell International Finance	5.8	–0.06	AA–	Netherlands
GE	GE Capital European Funding	4.5	–0.07	AA–	US
NDASS	Nordea Bank	4.0	–0.04	AA–	Sweden
BNP	BNP Paribas	3.9	–0.03	A+	France
ORAFP	Orange	3.9	–0.09	BBB+	France
SIEGR	Siemens Financial Services	3.9	–0.15	A+	Germany

Source: Tyler Durden, "These Are the 10 Corporate Bond with the Most Negative Yields in the World," ZeroHedge, July 15, 2016, https://www.zerohedge.com/news/2016-07-15/these-are-10-corporate -bond-most-negative-yields-world.

As long as the supply of loanable funds grows at a higher rate than the demand, the yields will continue to be negative for many countries and companies.

Under secular stagnation, aggregate demand is stuck in neutral, and there is a permanent growth gap. According to Lawrence H. Summers (and his opinion is consistent with the model for the loanable funds market developed in this section): "The economies of the industrial world, in this view, suffer from an imbalance resulting from an increasing propensity to save and a decreasing propensity to invest. The result is that excessive saving acts as a drag on demand, reducing growth and inflation, and the imbalance between saving and investment pulls down real interest rates."[3]

As long as interest rates do not fall more than the transaction costs of holding cash, yields can remain negative. Before the financial crisis, many economists thought that interest rates could not remain below zero for a prolonged period of time. They have been proven wrong.

6.4 Public Debt and Its Effects on the Money Market and the Loanable Funds Market

One of the main barriers that prevent central banks from affecting the credit market is the trajectory of public debt. The main tool of monetary policy is open-market operations. Central banks sell and buy government bonds to determine the nominal interest rate. The effects of government budget decisions are discussed in chapter 8, but at this point we need to formalize the effects of new purchases or sales of government bonds in the money market and loanable funds market.

Some of the government banks in the central banks' balance sheets have the sole purpose of allowing the monetary authority to execute monetary policy. Figure 6.12 completes the process that was delineated earlier (in figure 5.10).

After the central bank decides to sell a new government bond (new because it was previously held by the monetary authority), it reduces liquidity in the money market and loanable funds market. Interest rates go up in both markets if agents react in accordance with the decision of the central bank. A similar process happens when central banks decide to purchase government bonds with the goal of lowering interest rates. The money supply and the supply of loanable funds increase because commercial banks now have more capital to lend (figure 6.13).

As the central bank sells new government bonds, market agents buy them, and the central bank keeps the money. Money supply decreases from MS to MS', and

---

3. Lawrence H. Summers, "The Age of Secular Stagnation: What It Is and What to Do about It," *Foreign Affairs* 95 (2016): 2.

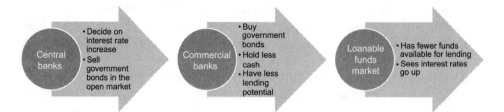

Figure 6.12

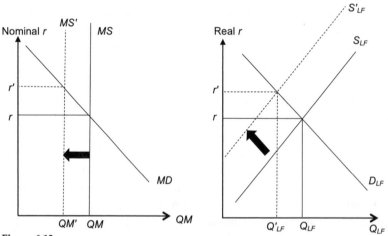

Figure 6.13
Link between money and credit markets

the interest rate goes from r to r'. In the loanable funds market, as the supply dwindles from S_{LF} to S'_{LF}, the interest rate also rises from r to r'. Open-market operations are transmitted to the market for loanable funds.

Now comes the important new mechanism. The mechanics of public budgeting and its effects on financial and real markets determine the possible impacts of public policy. If the government wants to borrow money from society, this has an impact on the loanable funds market. The more the government borrows, the higher the pressure on real interest rates. This, in itself, does not change the equilibrium in the money market. The degree of crowding-out—or the borrowing behavior of governments that affects the equilibrium in the loanable funds market—depends mostly on expectations regarding the use of this money.

6.5 Connections between Money, Credit, and Real Markets

Economic growth (GDP) and inflation come from the market of goods and services. Central banks appear on the money market, and their governors are part of the elite of policymakers. The financial press follows their moves, and changes in the stewardship of the monetary authority can rattle financial markets. Reuters, for instance, reported in June 2016 that "India's 'rock star' central bank governor Raghuram Rajan, feted by foreign investors but under pressure from political opponents at home, stunned government officials and colleagues on Saturday by announcing he would step down after just one three-year term."[4] Rarely does a society deems a public figure a rock star. Even rarer are reports on the state of loanable funds markets around the world. In national economics, the credit market unites savers and borrowers and is the grease between the cogs of economic activity. If this market is not functioning well, the economy sputters.

Based on the money market equilibrium, the central bank uniquely determines the nominal interest rate. But the bank's decisions, announced by its rock star governor, do not automatically put a check on inflation. In reality, the same interest that clears the money market is affected by the demand and supply of credit and other financial instruments. The loanable funds market represents decisions made by households and companies in relation to their lending and borrowing. It also may include foreigners investing in the local economy or borrowing from it. Things get even more complicated when moving from a partial equilibrium to a general equilibrium framework in which the local governments compete with private companies and foreign agents for funds.

Different behaviors have important real-life implications. In most emerging countries, people and companies save little, and saving depends on how high the interest rates are. In developed countries, people and businesses tend to save more, and thus there are more funds available for lending. One exception is that saving tends to be higher in Asian countries than in other countries at the same level of development. Credit constraints are a major obstacle for poor countries to climb the prosperity ladder. Here is a simple blueprint for how to integrate these markets:

- The credit market determines aggregate investment and the real interest rate.
- Aggregate investment affects economic growth and inflation in the market for goods and services.
- Central banks can try to influence aggregate investment through the nominal interest rate.
- Governments compete with businesses for savings.

---

4. Devidutta Tripathy and Suvashree Choudhury, "Indian Central Bank Chief to Step Down in Surprise Move," *Reuters*, June 18, 2016, http://www.reuters.com/article/us-india-cenbank-rajan-idUSK CN0Z40C4.

These four statements allow us to model possible contexts for economic policy. Later, we will see that governments can completely crowd out private investment. The increase in the real interest rate can negate any benefits from higher public expenditure. Or it may create a win-win situation in which the credibility of the fiscal and monetary authorities makes private agents add their own investment to existing public expenditure.

Simultaneous Clearing and the Central Bank's Reactions

The major difficulty in analyzing the market for loanable funds separately is that it is interconnected with the money market. The rationale is simple: if both markets are functioning well, interest rates behave similarly in the money market and the loanable funds market. This is because the central bank, by virtue of being the monopolist in the money market, influences saving and investment decisions. How might the central bank push the interest rate up to cool down economic activity?

1. The central bank offers new government bonds.
2. If the central bank has credibility (in other words, if investors are willing to buy these extra bonds), then as agents buy them, the money supply decreases.
3. In the loanable funds market, the supply of loanable funds also declines because agents now have fewer savings to offer to borrowers.
4. The interest rate goes up in both markets (not by the same amount because one is the nominal interest rate and the other is the real interest rate).

The same interconnection means that the central bank has to react to shocks in the loanable funds market if it wants to maintain its policy objectives. For instance, if an exogenous shock happens in the loanable funds market and demand falls, then this would lead to a decline in the nominal interest rate as well. If the central bank wants to keep the interest rate unchanged, it will have to reduce liquidity to resist the downward pressure.

In the world being described here, interest rates in both the money market and the loanable funds market move in tandem. The simultaneous clearing in this section is a shortcut that works only if the transmission mechanisms of monetary policy are working unimpeded.

Let us go through the above four steps for increasing interest rates to cool down economic activity. Assume that there is a change in the demand for loanable funds (figure 6.14). This is transmitted to the money market; there is higher demand for money (from MD to MD'). If there is no reaction from the central bank, then the result is a higher nominal interest rate (from r to r') because now more agents are competing for the same supply of money. Both markets clear, and in the money market, there is no change in terms of the actual quantity of money because the

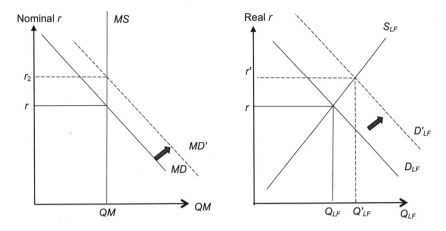

Figure 6.14
Link between money and loanable funds (credit) markets

money supply is fixed. In the loanable funds market, aggregate loanable funds go up (more demand leads to a higher volume of credit).

Partial equilibrium is not enough in the economics of global business. We need to be able to analyze changes in demand and supply functions in different markets. Changes in the interest rate related to the demand for credit affect other markets, such as the market for goods and services. This interconnectedness is at the heart of economic policy. Monetary policy is the use of the instruments in the money market to influence real decisions related to prices and output. The integration between real and financial markets is fundamental to the comprehension of economic policies, and the first step is the link between the money market and the loanable funds market.

The Paradox of Thrift

The paradox of thrift is an example of general equilibrium that is context dependent. Assume that the supply of loanable funds consists mostly of aggregate saving and that demand is mostly that of businesses looking to expand their productive capacity (investment). Governments are either passive agents or absent altogether. The paradox of thrift reveals how saving decisions impact the loanable funds and money markets. It also reverberates through the real economy by affecting decisions related to consumption, saving, and investment.

The paradox of thrift is controversial. It featured prominently in debates between two great economists, John Maynard Keynes and Jean-Baptiste Say. This paradox shows that integrating different markets is both the essence of and the main difficulty in economics and that some models can explain exceptional circumstances better than others. According to Paul Krugman,

The story behind the paradox of thrift goes like this. Suppose a large group of people decides to save more. You might think that this would necessarily mean a rise in national savings. But if falling consumption causes the economy to fall into a recession, incomes will fall, and so will savings, other things equal. This induced fall in savings can largely or completely offset the initial rise. Which way it goes depends on what happens to investment, since savings are always equal to investment. If the central bank can cut interest rates, investment and hence savings may rise. But if the central bank can't cut rates—say, because they're already zero—investment is likely to fall, not rise, because of lower capacity utilization. And this means that GDP and hence incomes have to fall so much that when people try to save more, the nation actually ends up saving less.[5]

There are two steps to the paradox of thrift as seen through the lens of loanable funds. First, when people want to save more, this should lead to lower interest rates and a higher loanable funds volume. The quantity of loanable funds is a good representation of the volume of credit in an economy. Step one is shown in figure 6.15. S_{LF} shifts to S'_{LF}, r goes down to r', and Q_{LF} increases to Q'_{LF}. In these circumstances, there is no paradox of thrift, and we simply stop at step one.

If later a decrease in consumption leads to lower aggregate investment, the paradox kicks in. A decrease in investment completely offsets the increase in the desire for saving. Step two is shown in figure 6.16.

The result is that the economy experiences lower interest rates (now r'') but the volume of credit remains constant. Aggregate saving and investment remain unchanged, and only the real interest rate falls.

The paradox of thrift is a rare occurrence. Nevertheless, it can be used as a reasonable explanation for the relative weakness of the Japanese economy after 1991. Paul Samuelson, one of the great economists of the twentieth century, used the concept to make sense of this weakness. Japan went through a devastating financial crisis that began in 1991, a result of bubbles in the real estate and financial markets. In the mid-1980s, small apartments in Tokyo changed hands for US$1 million, and that is in 1980s money. Japanese people, like many people in Asia, tend to save a high percentage of their income. When the bubbles burst in 1991, a deep financial crisis and steep recession ensued. In the mid-1990s, the Japanese economy had, simultaneously, a high proportion of saving, low level of investment, almost zero nominal interest rate, and a ballooning fiscal deficit. It is extremely hard for a country to experience increasing fiscal deficits and very low interest rates because agents require higher interest rates to hold government bonds when public authorities go on binge borrowing. Samuelson argued that the

5. Paul Krugman, "The Paradox of Thrift—for Real," *New York Times*, July 7, 2009.

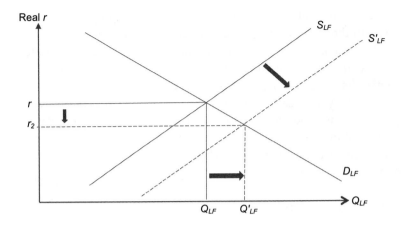

Figure 6.15

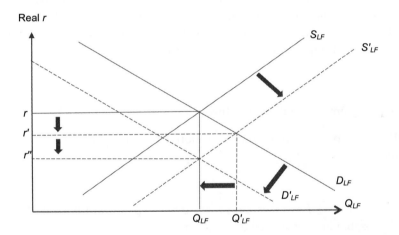

Figure 6.16

situation in Japan at that time could be explained by the paradox of thrift.[6] In 2005, Martin Wolf, the economics editor of the *Financial Times*, pointed out that the paradox could also explain another convergence of phenomena. He wrote: "strange things are happening in the world economy: falling interest rates on long-term securities, declining spreads between returns on safe and riskier assets, large fiscal deficits and huge global current account 'imbalances' should not, in normal

6. Paul A. Samuelson, "Credo of a Lucky Textbook Author," *Journal of Economic Perspectives* 11, no. 2 (1997): 153–160.

circumstances, coincide. So what is going on?"[7] In 2009, Paul Krugman again used the paradox to explain the slow recovery from the great financial crisis.[8]

One conclusion that can be drawn is that the paradox probably happens under certain circumstances but certainly not in normal times. Economics of global business is context dependent, and no model today can explain the dynamics of all national markets in a way that satisfactorily describes what happens in every country. If the paradox is assumed not to exist, then higher propensity for saving always reduces nominal interest rates and increases aggregate investment due to the integration between real and financial markets. Nevertheless, this leads to a lost opportunity to resolve some exceptional circumstances.

6.6   The Investment-Saving Identity

Is saving investment? Is investment saving? Economic models agree that investment and saving are identical. One of the most important open questions in macroeconomics regards the directional causality. Does a country need more saving to invest? Or does investment create its own saving? The saving-investment identity is easy to prove, both algebraically and conceptually, through the use of national accounts.

Let's assume that

Total output = Total income = Total expenditure = Y,

where Y is GDP or total output. Another assumption is that the government has a balanced budget, so

$G = T$,

where G is government and T is taxes. So government expenditure is equal to taxes. Because disposable income can be either saved or consumed,

$Y - T = C + S$,

where C is consumption and S is saving. So

$Y = C + S + T$.

Aggregate demand is

$Y = C + I + G$,

7. Martin Wolf, "The Paradox of Thrift: Excess Savings Are Storing Up Trouble for the World Economy," *Financial Times*, June 13, 2005, http://www.ft.com/cms/s/00b05180-dba8-11d9-913a-00000e2511c8.
8. Paul Krugman, "The Paradox of Thrift."

where I is investment. Then

$Y = C + S + T$, and $Y = C + I + G$.

Because $G = T$, then I has to be the same as S.

Later, current account is added when we consider the case of an open economy. Conceptually, private investment and saving are determined in the market for loanable funds. If there is an imbalance, then the opportunity cost of supplying or demanding funds changes until the quantity invested (borrowed) is the same as the quantity saved. On the one hand, companies need saving because this is the basis for commercial banks to create credit. On the other hand, households need investment because without business spending there would be no employment, no disposable income, and therefore no saving.

The unresolved question is which one comes first? Does investment cause saving, or is it the other way around? The Keynesian tradition favors the former option. Keynes used the term *animal spirits* as a key feature of human behavior. Entrepreneurs, because of their animal spirits (greed), want to invest, and banks create credit to accommodate such bullish behavior (figure 6.17). The wealth created by capital expenditure, in turn, generates income. A part of it is saved.

As the demand for loanable funds rises, so does the interest rate. However, the equilibrium quantity of loanable funds goes up. Because investment rises, so does aggregate demand. With higher income, both consumption and saving also rise. In the end, $I = S$.

The same process can happen if we begin with higher saving. As saving increases, interest rates fall, increasing the equilibrium quantity of loanable funds (figure 6.18). Because the quantity invested goes up as investment becomes cheaper, demand rises.

Which description is accurate? Both investment and saving may be drivers for growth, depending on the context. This epitomizes one of the main difficulties with a full understanding of economic dynamics: it is hard to disentangle the effects of a change in one variable because of its relationship to many other economic variables.

For most emerging markets, economists agree that a lack of aggregate saving is an obstacle to economic development. There are many reasons for this, such as poverty, governments with low credibility, and financial markets that are incomplete and inefficient. Let's assume that saving in Cambodia, for example, is inelastic to interest rates. Thus, improved expectations that normally would lead to higher demand for loanable funds, realized quantities, investment, and growth do not go beyond the first step, in which more demand leads to higher interest rates but no real increase in capital expenditure (figure 6.19).

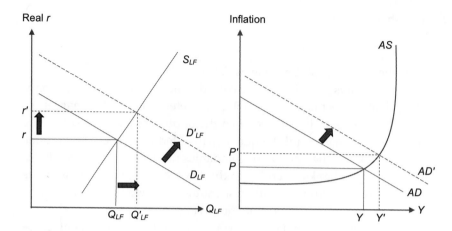

Figure 6.17

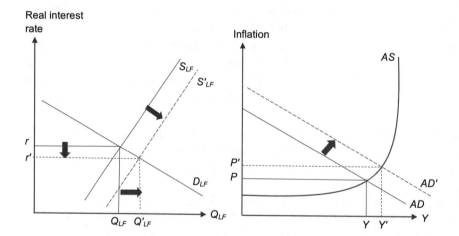

Figure 6.18

Because the supply of loanable funds is particularly inelastic, more demand pushes interest rates up but brings a comparatively small increase in the actual quantity of credit. The effect on the market of goods and services is miniscule because of the modest hike in actual investment.

Another example is Japan after the financial crisis of the early 1990s. Because demand for loanable funds was low due to a bleak outlook, higher supply of loanable funds by households or the government reduced real interest rates but brought no real economic activity (figure 6.20).

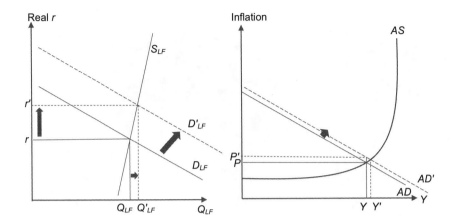

Figure 6.19

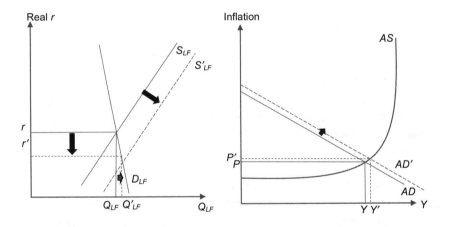

Figure 6.20

In both Cambodia and Japan, possible increases in the will to invest or save more did not have any significant effects on the real economy. This also hints at the possible heterogeneous effects of economic policy. In Cambodia, more saving would enhance social welfare much more than in the case of Japan, which suffers from a saving glut. Better business perspectives are particularly important in Japan because higher demand for credit boosts aggregate demand significantly. The patterns of national saving globally are shown in figure 6.21.

Initial conditions matter in macroeconomics, and no sweeping statements about universal rules can be made. Context is relevant, and a misjudgment of initial conditions leads to erroneous diagnostics and policies.

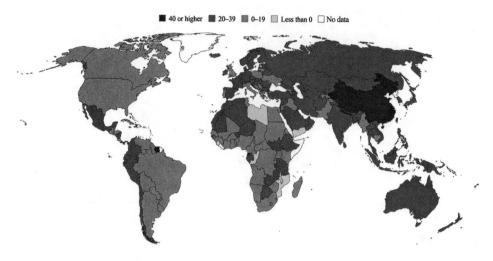

Figure 6.21
World gross national saving as a percentage of GDP
Source: Central Intelligence Agency, 2017, https://www.cia.gov/library/publications/the-world
-factbook/rankorder/2260rank.html.

Supply-Side and Trickle-Down Economics

Supply-side economics is a child of the 1980s. Its main idea is that reducing barriers and creating incentives to save and invest lead to economic prosperity. From our version of the Solow model, the supply-side argument is that when the government focuses on liberating agents to save and invest more, capital accumulates.

Supply-side economics can work. Because economics is context dependent, under the right circumstances economic policy advice can increase social welfare. But such relativism is not limitless. For example, a typical policy prescription of supply-side enthusiasts is to cut corporate tax rates. The argument goes like this: lower taxes boost companies' willingness to invest, which increases economic growth in the short run (through investment in the aggregate demand) and prosperity in the long run (through the accumulation of capital). Reducing corporate taxes can work only if (1) the elasticity of investment to profits is not zero and (2) corporations have a portfolio of good projects but their costs of capital are high, which means that some productive investment has been abandoned. In that case, tax saving would be used immediately to fund new ventures. The intuition regarding both of these two conditions is straightforward: if companies are not using their tax saving to invest, decreasing corporate taxes has no impact on long-run economic growth. If fewer taxes induce more investment, supply-side economics can work.

The case for trickle-down economics is much more tenuous as the conditions required for it to work are much stricter. The argument in favor of trickle-down economics goes like this: cutting personal income taxes on the rich generates higher aggregate demand from free saving that would be used to pay taxes. There are two conditions for trickle-down economics to induce economic activity: (1) wealthy people use the extra cash for consumption, and (2) such consumption engenders investment that is more productive than what governments could make with the forsaken tax revenue. Trickle-down economics is mostly ineffective because of the first of these conditions. Rich people usually do not spend most of their income. Karen E. Dynan, Jonathan Skinner, and Stephen P. Zeldes show that rich people tend to save more than poor people, which is intuitive.[9] Reducing personal income tax would not bring a comparable increase in consumption, and its economic impact would be concentrated on income inequality. As tax revenue contracts, income is transferred from the whole society to rich people. Income inequality gets worse with no corresponding economic benefit.

9. Karen E. Dynan, Jonathan Skinner, and Stephen P. Zeldes, "Do the Rich Save More?," *Journal of Political Economy* 112, no. 2 (2004): 397–444.

7   Monetary and Fiscal Policies

In this chapter,
- Expansionary and contractionary fiscal and monetary policies
- Preferable conditions for monetary policy
- Inside and outside lags of economic policies
- Transmission mechanisms and the efficacy of economic policies
- Discretion versus rules in emerging and rich countries

The austerity debate is always raging somewhere in the world. Following the great financial crisis, Ireland, Iceland, and Greece were as close to bankruptcy as sovereign nations can get. The spiraling American debt was a huge concern in the early 2010s. The IMF usually prescribes fiscal restraint to profligate governments in emerging markets. Should governments be fiscally responsible or act to try to spur economic growth? It depends. Both fiscal policy and monetary policy can be contractionary or expansionary. In this chapter, we explore the pros and cons of the main economic tools that are at the disposal of public authorities.

7.1   Economic Policy and Time Lags

It takes time for public authorities to design and implement monetary and fiscal policies and for the policies to affect economic activity. Inside lag is the amount of time that it takes for the decision-making process related to changing an economic policy. For a new tax, for example, it is the time necessary for designing the tax, turning it into legislation, negotiating about it, voting on it, and implementing it. Some parts of fiscal policy, like discretionary spending, have shorter inside lags. Monetary policy has a very short inside lag because most central banks in the world have autonomy in arbitrating target interest rates.

Outside lag is the amount of time that it takes for the change in policy to influence economic variables. Lowering taxes does not immediately increase spending by households and businesses. Similarly, interest rates do not impact the national (and international) economy instantaneously. How long it takes agents to act on an economic policy depends on their expectations. In rare circumstances, economic policies can have a negative outside lag. Imagine a presidential election in which the candidate viewed as the most responsible is about to win, promising certain policies to induce economic activity. Companies and consumers may start spending and investing on the prospects of the candidate's victory. Activity picks up even before the candidate secures the electoral victory.

Both monetary and fiscal policies have outside lags that depend on the situation of the economy at the time of policy change. Inside and outside lags have important implications for establishing the costs and benefits for each kind of policy. There is no a priori difference in terms of the outside lag between fiscal and monetary policies. Both influence real markets depending on how unexpected the announcements of the policy changes are and how markets adjust to the new policies. The inside lag is much shorter for monetary policy than for fiscal policy. Central banks can choose and implement policies in a matter of hours, but fiscal decisions usually take much longer. One example is the large stimulus package authorized by President Barack Obama in response to the recession generated by the great financial crisis. The federal government designed the package in late 2008, and Congress voted on it in February 2009. This was a quick turnaround for a fiscal policy. But by the end of 2008 the successive cuts by the monetary authority had reduced the target interest rate all the way down to zero.

7.2 Monetary Policy

There are two kinds of monetary policy—contractionary and expansionary. Contractionary monetary policy is the use of monetary instruments to cool down economic activity with the purpose of reducing inflation. It usually involves increasing the target interest rate to raise the cost of capital for companies and curtail credit to businesses and consumers. Central banks perform expansionary monetary policy to stimulate economic activity. The default way is by cutting interest rates to boost credit to companies and households. We have already seen how the monetary authority makes changes in target interest rates and how such modifications are transmitted through financial markets to the real side of the economy. Here we summarize all the costs and benefits of monetary policy.

Central banks ideally implement expansionary monetary policies when there is a growth gap and when the role of higher money supply is to abbreviate a recession. As the monetary authority pushes down the target interest rate, the interest rate, credit, balance-sheet, and exchange-rate channels should disturb the market for goods and services. Central banks have the autonomy and the tools to change interest rates almost immediately. If transmission mechanisms are functioning well, pared down interest rates should generate higher consumption, investment, and ultimately economic growth while simultaneously diminishing the costs of servicing the public debt. The reduction in interest payments for the public debt is important. Lower interest rates taper off the amount of the public debt service—that is, how much interest the central government should pay on its current debt.

If the debt to GDP ratio of a country is 60%, the target interest rate falls from 5% to 3% per year, and other conditions remain the same, the amount of nominal interest paid by the central government falls from 3% to 1.8% of GDP per year. From 2009 to 2016, the near zero interest rates in Germany, Japan, the United Kingdom, and the United States were paramount in limiting the growth of the public debt to GDP ratio.

Expansionary monetary policy brings potential costs, notwithstanding the possibility of a measurement error that might identify a growth gap when there is none. Because reductions in the target interest rates fuel aggregate demand, loose monetary policy may result in inflation and bubbles in asset prices. It also takes time for any change in monetary aggregates to work through financial and real markets. In other words, monetary policy has an outside lag. In addition, the central bank needs credibility for its actions to have real effects in the expected way. Because $MV = PY$ (where M is the nominal quantity of money, V is the velocity of money, P is price level, and Y is GDP or total output), if agents do not believe that the central bank can stimulate growth, then lower interest rates will only lead to inflation.

Finally, monetary policy is neutral in the long run, so changes in monetary aggregates may influence short-run decisions but will have no real impact on long-term growth (figure 7.1). For an initial growth gap ($Y^* - Y$), the goal of expansionary monetary policy is to shift aggregate demand to the right (from AD to AD') and bring output closer to its potential, even if it means that price levels can experience a moderate increase.

Because the size of the growth gap is unknown, expansionary monetary policy usually is executed in stages. Successive cuts of the target interest rate are made as the central banks monitor the transmission of the interest rate cuts to the real side of the economy (table 7.1).

For an economy that is overheating, at full employment, and with prices escalating, central banks can implement a contractionary monetary policy (table 7.2). Higher interest rates cool down aggregate demand (shifting it to the left), resulting in slower rates of growth of GDP and the price level. The main disadvantage is

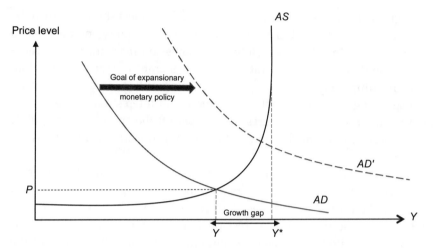

Figure 7.1

Table 7.1
Expansionary monetary policy: Potential costs and benefits

Benefits	Costs
Higher consumption	Higher inflation
Higher investment	Neutral in the long run
Higher growth	Fuels bubbles
Lower debt service	Outside lag
Central bank decides	Needs credibility

that there would be a higher fiscal cost to service the public debt. Additionally, as with all economic policies, it involves the risk of misidentification, and the effects of the policy are spread over time.

Managing Monetary Policy during Stagflation: The US Disinflation of the 1980s

Stagflation, i.e., stagnation coupled with inflation, puts public authorities in a bind. When policymakers try to fight one, the other gets worse. Stagflation arises from a decrease in aggregate supply. Given that macroeconomic policies act only on aggregate demand, government authorities face a bitter version of the tradeoff between growth and inflation. The term *stagflation* was coined in the 1960s and came to the forefront of public debate in the United States in the 1970s. The oil crises of 1973 and 1979 shrunk aggregate supply in the United States (figure 7.2). As supply AS moves to AS', output softens from the full-employment situation Y

Table 7.2
Contractionary monetary policy: Potential costs and benefits

Benefits	Costs and risks
Lower inflation	Lower consumption
Neutral in the long run	Lower investment
Prevents the formation of bubbles	Lower growth
Builds credibility	Higher debt service
Central bank decides	Outside lag

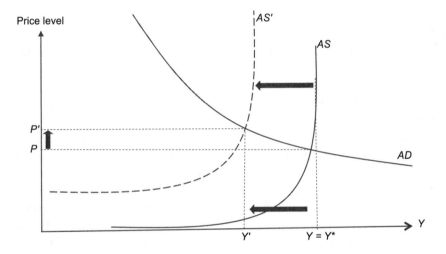

Figure 7.2

to a lower one Y'. Meanwhile, prices go up from P to P'. Usually, such a situation is also followed by a decrease in demand and the development of a growth gap. In any case, trying to reinstate growth leads to higher inflation, and keeping prices in check adds further to the recession.

In the United States, the stagflations of the 1970s generated two steep recessions, and inflation reached double digits for the first time since the 1940s. The Federal Reserve under Paul Volcker combated inflation relentlessly. In a comprehensive essay, Michael Bryan describes the disinflation process of the early 1980s: "the Volcker Fed continued to press the fight against high inflation with a combination of higher interest rates and even slower reserve growth. The economy again entered a recession in July 1981. This time, the fall in economic activity proved to be more severe and protracted, lasting until November 1982. Unemployment peaked at nearly 11 percent, but inflation continued to trend downwards and by the end of the recession year-over-year inflation was back under 5 percent. In time, as the Fed's commitment to low inflation gained credibility, unemployment retreated and the economy entered a period of sustained growth and stability. The Great Inflation was over."[1] The federal target rate reached 20%, and the prime rate 21.5% in 1981. It was the mother of all contractionary monetary policies. There was a big price to pay for the disinflation: the public debt to GDP ratio increased by 10%, and there were widespread protests against the Fed. For instance, indebted farmers drove their tractors onto C Street NW in Washington, D.C., blockading the Eccles Building. Stagflation always incurs a steep price that society must pay, regardless of authorities' actions or inaction.

Expectations and Monetary Policy: The Fed Dilemma of 2017
Economic policy is supposed to be forward-looking, which means that expectations about the future are what matters. Nothing illustrates this better than the situation of the American economy at the end of 2017. The economy was sending mixed signals: GDP and wages were not growing much, but unemployment and inflation were at historical lows.

The Federal Reserve faced a dilemma similar to what the European Central Bank faced in 2011 (which is analyzed in chapter 4). Was the economy healthy or not? If the board of the Fed were to raise the federal funds rate, it might derail a more substantial recovery or prevent future inflation. In an interview with the *Financial Times*, Loretta Mester, president of the Cleveland Federal Reserve Bank, said that taming future inflation was important and that she favored a hike in interest rates.[2] Actual inflation data did not warrant a tighter monetary policy. Inflation was well below the 2% that is the informal target of the US central bank. But the president of the Cleveland Fed was right when she stated, "I am not in the camp that we should see inflation rise to 2 percent before we take the next move."

As the Federal Reserve learned in the early 1980s, disinflation is costly, and increasing interest rates too soon also can be damaging. The Fed dilemma is much too common: public authorities seldom face a clear option.

7.3   Fiscal Policy

Previous chapters detail the transmission mechanisms of monetary policy and the ways that it is executed. Until now, we have not done the same for fiscal policy

1. Michael Bryan, "The Great Inflation: 1965–1982," Federal Reserve History, https://www.feder alreservehistory.org/essays/great_inflation.
2. Sam Fleming, "Cleveland Fed Chief Urges Rate Rise Despite Weak Inflation," *Financial Times*, August 27, 2017.

Table 7.3
Expansionary fiscal policy: Potential costs and benefits

Benefits	Costs
Higher consumption	Higher inflation
Higher investment	Higher deficit
Higher growth	Inside and outside lags

because the transmission mechanisms of fiscal policy are much more direct. Governments can try to stimulate or contract demand by reducing or increasing taxes or public spending. Spending can be either direct (for instance, when different spheres of government commission new infrastructure) or indirect (when subsidies have a clear impact on the decisions made by households and companies).

Expansionary fiscal policy has the same goal as loose monetary policy—to close growth gaps (table 7.3). The two kinds of policies differ because of the longer inside lag of fiscal policy and its impact on public debt. Expansionary monetary policy reduces the amount of net interest paid by the government on its bonds, and loose fiscal policy pushes up the deficit and hence the public debt, either because of lower taxes of higher government expenditure or transfer subsidies. Expansionary fiscal policy either decreases the primary surplus or increases the deficit (details about the government deficit are in chapter 8).

Policymakers use higher taxes and cuts in spending to reduce aggregate demand when executing contractionary fiscal policies (figure 7.3). The main benefits come from lower inflation, deficit, and public debt. It also builds credibility because the political process is usually pro-spending and a reduction in primary deficit sends a positive signal to financial markets (table 7.4). Contractionary fiscal policy also is known as austerity, and austerity measures usually are advocated for countries that have a history of fiscal profligacy.

Contractionary fiscal measures are best employed when the economy is overheating, with output at its potential and escalating prices. As governments rein in spending or lift taxes, aggregate demand cools down from AD to AD', and price level goes down from P to P'.

Contractionary fiscal policy is harder to implement than contractionary monetary policy. Not only is the inside lag longer, but the broad swathes of society affected by the spending cuts or tax hikes will always fight to stave off austerity measures.

Discretion versus Rules: Inflation Targeting and Balanced Budgets
One of the cornerstones of the economics of global business is the credibility of policymakers. Because of weak institutions and time inconsistency, fiscal and

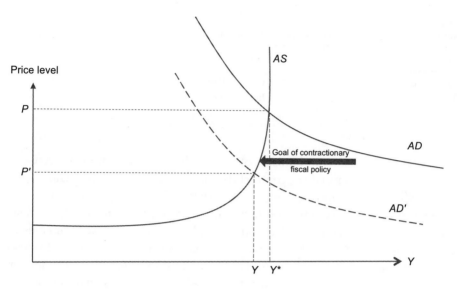

Figure 7.3

Table 7.4
Contractionary fiscal policy: Potential costs and benefits

Benefits	Costs
Lower inflation	Lower consumption
Builds credibility	Lower investment
Lower deficit	Lower growth
Lower future debt	Political process is pro-spending

monetary authorities may be constrained in the exercise of economic policy. One way of generating credibility is for society to create rules that make some instruments of economic policies passive. Taking away discretion may enhance the credibility of government officials. Rules that create automatic stabilizers take away discretion and provide *ex ante* decisions on the tradeoffs of economic policy.

Inflation targeting is an example of a rule that makes part of monetary policy fixed and minimizes discretion. The idea behind inflation targeting is simple: the central bank should pursue a predetermined value for inflation that is socially acceptable, and it should pursue it automatically. If expected inflation is above its target, then interest rates should rise until inflation is brought back down to that required level. Interest rates can fall only if the expected inflation is below the target, with some confidence interval that allows a little room for discretion.

A report by the Bank of England illustrates the mechanisms and goals of this kind of automatic rule: "inflation targeting is a framework rather than a rigid set of rules for monetary policy. Nonetheless there are a number of essential elements of an inflation-targeting regime:

1. Price stability is explicitly recognized as the main goal of monetary policy.
2. There is a public announcement of a quantitative target for inflation.
3. Monetary policy is based on a wide set of information, including an inflation forecast.
4. Transparency.
5. Accountability mechanisms."[3]

Inflation targeting is characterized as "constrained discretion" that is not entirely passive in nature but has elements that restrain the possible actions of central banks. In 1989, New Zealand became the first country to adopt it. Other developed countries followed, but today inflation targeting is used mostly in emerging markets (table 7.5). For these countries, an automatic set of rules is a path for restoring confidence in the monetary authority. In the case of developed countries that are experiencing deflation, an announcement of a positive inflation target demonstrates commitment by the monetary authority.

Inflation targeting is also a way to deal with time inconsistency. The central bank may announce that it does not accept a high rate of inflation, but if there is inflationary pressure, it may find it costly to lift interest rates and restrain aggregate demand. It is easy to imagine a situation in which the political cycle may impede interest rate hikes in election years, for example.

Balanced-budget acts usually follow the same principle of constrained discretion. Limiting government deficits by a rule is intended to bring credibility to the fiscal authorities and prevent policymakers' profligacy. Unlike inflation targeting, where central banks can pursue a precise inflation rate, balanced-budget laws are more complicated because forecasts of tax revenue and government spending are not perfect. Even so, if public authorities implement rules for primary deficits and follow them, the result is higher confidence in the government. Long-term interest rates fall, and private investment should go up.

Balanced-budget rules can be strict or can follow the business cycles. The latter form what is called a structural (or cyclically adjusted) balanced budget. A strict balanced budget posits a strict adherence to a primary surplus or deficit target. Structural budgets take into account the business cycle. Economists usually

3. Gill Hammond, "State of the Art of Inflation Targeting—2012," Centre for Central Banking Studies, Handbook No. 29, Bank of England, February 2012, http://www.bankofengland.co.uk/education/Documents/ccbs/handbooks/pdf/ccbshb29.pdf.

Table 7.5
Inflation targeting in twenty-eight countries from 1989 to 2009, as of 2016

Country	Inflation targeting adoption date	Inflation rate at adoption date (percentage)	Target inflation rate (interval)
New Zealand	1989	3.3%	1/3
Canada	1991	6.9	2 +/–1
United Kingdom	1992	4.0	2
Australia	1993	2.0	1 to 3
Sweden	1993	1.8	2
Czech Republic	1997	6.8	3 +/–1
Israel	1997	8.1	2 +/–1
Poland	1998	10.6	2.5 +/–1
Brazil	1999	3.3	4.5 +/–2
Chile	1999	3.2	3 +/–1
Colombia	1999	9.3	2 to 4
South Africa	2000	2.6	3 to 6
Thailand	2000	0.8	0.5 to 3
Hungary	2001	10.8	3 +/–1
Mexico	2001	9.0	3 +/–1
Iceland	2001	4.1	2.5 +/–1.5
South Korea	2001	2.9	3 +/–1
Norway	2001	3.6	2.5 +/–1
Peru	2002	–0.10	2 +/–1
Philippines	2002	4.5	4 +/–1
Guatemala	2005	9.2	5 +/–1
Indonesia	2005	7.4	5 +/–1
Romania	2005	9.3	3 +/–1
Serbia	2006	10.8	4 to 8
Turkey	2006	7.7	5.5 +/–2
Armenia	2006	5.2	4.5 +/–1.5
Ghana	2007	10.5	8.5 +/–2
Albania	2009	3.7	3 +/–1

Source: Sarwat Jahan, "Inflation Targeting: Holding the Line," *Finance & Development*, IMF, 2017, http://www.imf.org/external/pubs/ft/fandd/basics/target.htm.

prefer cyclically adjusted balanced budgets to strict ones. The rationale is that as recession hits the economy, tax receipts fall or increase at a lower rate of growth, and there is an incentive for expansionary fiscal policy. During a boom, more revenue comes in, and a strict balanced budget would allow the fiscal authorities to spend more, fueling inflation. A structural balanced budget would not allow public authorities to increase expenditure because of temporary growth in tax revenue.

In 2001, Chile passed a structural balanced-budget rule that was first modified in 2009 because of the great financial crisis.[4] The revised rule accommodated some countercyclical measures. In 2011, the government published a second-generation budget rule. An independent fiscal council oversees the estimations required for the budget adjustments.

In 2011, Colombia legislated its own version of a cyclically adjusted balanced budget. The plan calls for fiscal consolidation that cuts the structural deficit over time. The ceiling for the deficit was set at 1% of GDP by 2022. But there are some escape clauses. If the expected growth rate is 2 percentage points lower than the long-term growth rate, the central government can spend more. There are also some contingencies in the case of emergencies or large economic shocks.

Russia's long-term nonoil deficit target of 4.7% of GDP was suspended in April 2009 because of the crisis and formally abolished in 2012. In the same year, Italy passed a constitutional amendment that introduced the principles of a structural balanced budget.

Unlike inflation targeting, it is rare for balanced-budget laws to become institutionally entrenched. The main reason for this is that they reduce fiscal discretion, and politicians have a strong incentive to maintain control over the instruments of fiscal policy, especially the discretionary spending power. The Italian government, for instance, claimed in 2015, 2016, and 2017 that the economy was so weak that it needed some budgetary limits to be lifted.

The tradeoff between discretion and rules is clear: when rules are followed strictly, the government accumulates credibility, yet when the government has less discretion, authorities have less power to stimulate or constrain aggregate demand during the business cycle. Optimal rules are evolving: the lower the quality of institutions, the more rules need to be designed for an economy. As institutions evolve, more discretion should be in the hands of policymakers.

---

4. Details for the budget rules for Chile, Colombia, Russia, and Italy come from Victor Lledó, Sungwook Yoon, Xiangming Fang, Samba Mbaye, and Young Kim, "Fiscal Rules at a Glance," International Monetary Fund, March 2017, http://www.imf.org/external/datamapper/fiscalrules/Fiscal%20Rules%20at%20a%20Glance%20-%20Background%20Paper.pdf.

The Maastricht Treaty and the European Unraveling

The Maastricht Treaty, which was the cornerstone for the creation of the European Union, took effect on November 1, 1993. Part of the treaty deals with budget rules for the European Union member countries. Rules included limits on primary deficit (3% of GDP) and public debt (60%). Countries with debt above the ceiling were required to enact austerity measures for the purpose of making their debt converge toward the 60% threshold. Therefore, membership in the European Union came with a rule for a balanced budget. Later European authorities changed the deficit and debt limits to take into account the business cycle; in effect, rules governing spending went from a hard cap to a cyclically adjusted constrain. Deficits could be higher during recessions to allow some countercyclical spending, as long as European governments tightened their belts during periods of rapid economic growth.

It did not take long for European governments to spend more than the budgetary rules allowed. In the late 1990s, though Germany was the main proponent of fiscal discipline rules for membership access to the European Union, it was the first country to undermine the spending limits repeatedly by posting deficits higher than 3% of GDP. In fact, in the early 2000s, the annual deficits in Germany and France were higher than 5% of GDP and eroded the stability and growth pact, the part of the Maastricht Treaty that dealt with budget rules: "Its provisions were not formally abolished, but they were informally softened to such an extent that, in the future, they could be twisted at any time to benefit a government in financial trouble."[5]

Because of this softening of the balanced-budget rules, many European Union member countries had high deficits in 2008, when the great financial crisis hit Europe. Deficits ballooned in most countries in the eurozone for three reasons: resources required to bail out ailing banks, tax bases that were devastated because of the recession, and stimulus packages that tried to revive economic activity.

From 2010 to 2015, some European countries suffered successive debt crises. Five countries—Portugal, Ireland, Spain, Cyprus, and especially Greece (figure 7.4)—were particularly affected because amounts required to bail out the financial system were particularly high, in relation to GDP.

In Greece, the public deficit and debt were already high even before the crisis started. Public debt was at approximately 100% in 2007. It almost doubled by 2015, when it reached 180% of GDP. The Greek public deficit was 15% of GDP in 2009 and 11, and 11% in 2010. Moreover, a renegotiation of the country's debt led to a

5. Spiegel Staff, "How the Eurozone Ignored Its Own Rules," *Der Spiegel*, October 6, 2011, http://www.spiegel.de/international/europe/the-ticking-euro-bomb-how-the-euro-zone-ignored-its-own-rules-a-790333.html.

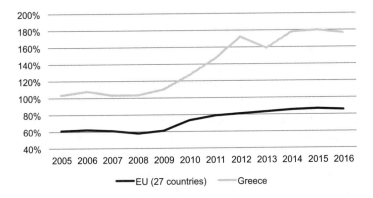

Figure 7.4
General government gross debt as percentage of GDP in twenty-seven EU countries and Greece, 2005 to 2016
Source: Eurostat, 2017, http://ec.europa.eu/eurostat/tgm/table.do?tab=table&init=1&language=en &pcode=teina225&plugin=1.

haircut (discount) of 50% of the value of government bonds in 2011. The country received bailouts in 2010, 2012, and 2015 from the International Monetary Fund, Eurogroup, and European Central Bank.

The 3% limit was supposed to build credibility in the European Union in general and the euro in particular. A monetary union like the eurozone can exist only if the countries maintain some measure of fiscal discipline. Alberto Bagnai has publicly expressed his conviction that one of the reasons that the euro is doomed to fail is that it has not reached a common fiscal agenda.[6] Balanced-budget rules are supposed to bring credibility to fiscal authorities, but European policymakers are anything but credible when it comes to reining in public spending.

7.4   Which Policy Is Better—Fiscal or Monetary?

Most of this book highlights the difficulty with finding clear-cut answers to economic dilemmas. Nevertheless, for a fundamental issue, we can provide clear-cut advice. If a government wants to act countercyclically, it should use monetary policy during a recession and fiscal policy to control inflation.

6. Alberto Bagnai, "Unhappy Families Are All Alike: Minskyan Cycles, Kaldorian Growth, and the Eurozone Peripheral Crises," in Óscar Dejuán, Eladio Febrero Paños, and Jorge Uxo Gonzalez, eds., *Post-Keynesian Views of the Great Recession and Its Remedies* (Abington, UK: Routledge, 2013); Alberto Bagnai, Brigitte Granville, and Christian A. Mongeau Ospina, "Withdrawal of Italy from the Euro Area: Stochastic Simulations of a Structural Macroeconometric Model," *Economic Modeling* 64 (2017): 524–538.

In principle, during a downturn in economic activity, government officials can choose between expansionary fiscal policy and monetary policy. Both policies should affect aggregate demand if the transmission mechanisms are performing well. Moreover, we have already seen that expansionary monetary policy is done through a reduction in interest rates and expansionary fiscal policy through higher spending or lower taxes. The preference of monetary over fiscal boils down to the effect on the debt trajectory. Decreasing nominal interest rates reduces the amount of interest paid by the government and thus the total public deficit, while more spending and lower taxes lead to higher deficits. In addition, expansionary monetary policy is easier to implement, with a shorter inside lag.

To cool down aggregate demand and prevent inflationary pressure, fiscal policy should be preferred. Tight fiscal policy results in a lower deficit, while contractionary monetary policy leads to higher interest payments on the public debt. A contractionary fiscal policy also enhances confidence in the government by showing that policymakers are willing to forego revenue to accomplish macroeconomic goals.

This is one of the rare context-independent results in economic policy: public authorities should favor expansionary monetary policy in the case of a growth gap and contractionary fiscal policy to rein in inflation.

Policymakers do not necessarily follow this script. Monetary policy is usually the default choice of public authorities because it has a short inside lag, as it can be implemented at the discretion of the monetary authority (unless constrained by inflation targeting or some other rule). Few countries have a central bank like the US Federal Reserve that is mostly independent of the other branches of government. For most nations, the central bank is a part of the executive branch. For instance, the People's Bank of China, the Central Bank of Brazil, and the Reserve Bank of India are central banks that are subordinated to the office of the president or prime minister. The Bank of Russia, like the Federal Reserve in the United States, is independent, at least nominally.

Many governments find it difficult to choose austerity measures. Even when fiscal policy should be preferred, many countries rely on monetary authorities to stave off inflationary pressure, which is understandable. Although the monetary authority is, for most people, an esoteric institution where wizards decide on interest rates by consulting old spell books, austerity has a direct, negative impact on many people's lives. Politically, it is one thing for the Turkish central bank to increase the target interest rate, but it is quite another for Greek fiscal authorities to raise taxes on pensioners or announce salary reductions for public employees.

Economic policies have limits, however. There are tradeoffs between the extant policy and the effects on public debt. In the United States after the great financial crisis, it was clear that monetary stimulus had hit a plateau. The liquidity trap meant that there had been a failure of the transmission mechanisms of monetary policy. Even when the federal fund rate was at 0%, financial markets continued to experience a credit crunch. In 2008, President George W. Bush designed a temporary stimulus using tax rebate checks. In February 2009, President Barack Obama greatly expanded fiscal policy through the American Recovery and Reinvestment Act (ARRA), a US$787 billion fiscal stimulus package that cut individual and corporate taxes, expanded unemployment benefits and other safety net provisions, and increased federal spending on education, health, physical infrastructure, and energy.

The largest part of the expansionary fiscal policy tradeoff is between growth and deficit, in addition to the usual tradeoff between growth and inflation that all economic policies experience. The Congressional Budget Office (CBO) of the United States estimated that ARRA increased budget deficits by about US$830 billion from 2009 to 2019.[7] By the CBO's estimate, close to half of that impact occurred in fiscal year 2010, and more than 90% occurred by the end of December 2012. Estimations are that ARRA did affect the economic growth trajectory. Its effects on output peaked in the first half of 2010 and have since diminished.

There is no universal rule for deciding between monetary and fiscal policies, but often there is a clear preference. Acting on it, though, is not necessarily straightforward because policymakers face various constraints regarding their possible decisions.

Managing Fiscal Policy during a Deep Recession: Austerity in Europe

Is austerity good? The eurozone situation after the great financial crisis exemplifies the limits of economic policy when public debt and credibility constrain the behavior of government officials. The effect of the crisis on the market for goods and services is easily explained by a severe contraction of aggregate demand, resulting in a deep recession with deflationary pressures. As aggregate demand AD moves to AD', economic output decreases from Y to Y', and price levels retract from P to P' (figure 7.5).

In terms of economic policy, there are two possible reactions to a deep recession: do nothing, or design expansionary policies. The European Central Bank drove interest rates close to zero, but because the transmission mechanisms of monetary policy failed, the effect on economic output was negligible. Although expansionary monetary policy failed, there was still the possibility of fiscal policy. But there was one major obstacle to using expansionary fiscal policy—the trajectory of public debt in many European countries. Because of earlier fiscal imbalances, expansionary fiscal policy would be costly. In fact, the problem of expanding debt

---

7. Congressional Budget Office, "Estimated Impact of the American Recovery and Reinvestment Act on Employment and Economic Output from October 2012 through December 2012," CBO, February 2013, https://www.cbo.gov/publication/43945.

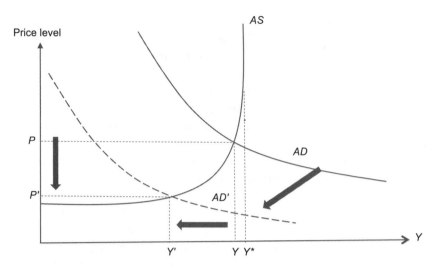

Figure 7.5

was so great that many politicians advised the opposite of more spending, calling out for austerity.

European nations were divided between two courses of action—austerity or stimulus. The rationale for austerity was that choosing contractionary fiscal policy might hurt growth in the short run but would build credibility that eventually would bring more private and public investment, strengthening a future recovery without the deleterious debt trajectory. For the bailouts of countries like Portugal, Ireland, and Greece, the international authorities suggested economic reforms and austerity to build long-term credibility.

Portugal is an example of the choices that sometimes need to be made between expansionary and contractionary measures. In November 2009, Portugal raised its 2009 forecast for the deficit from 5.9% of GDP to 8% of GDP.[8] In January 2010, consolidated data showed that the deficit in 2009 was actually 9.4%. In 2010, Portugal's deficit was supposed to be again in the neighborhood of 9% of GDP, and by then its financial system was on the brink of collapse. In March 2010, authorities announced salary freezes, new budget cuts, a privatization program, and new taxes, all austerity measures. Portuguese authorities negotiated a 78 billion euro package with the International Monetary Fund and the European Union and signed the agreement in March 2011. The bailout program lasted three years, and in June 2014, Portugal finally left it.

8. "Portugal's Debt Crisis," *Wall Street Journal*, June 10, 2011, https://www.wsj.com/articles/SB10001
424052748704904604576335101867151090.

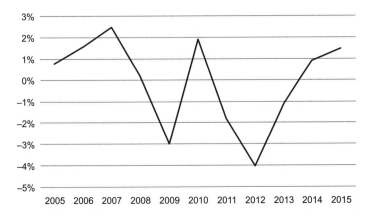

Figure 7.6
Portuguese GDP growth, 2005 to 2015
Source: World Bank, 2017, https://data.worldbank.org/indicator/NY.GDP.MKTP.KD.ZG.

The impact of these measures on growth was in line with that predicted by our framework for aggregate demand and aggregate supply. With contractionary fiscal policy on top of a growth gap, there should be lower growth and deflationary pressure. After the bailout was approved in 2011, growth turned negative and bottomed out at –4% in 2012 (figure 7.6). Meanwhile, inflation also went down, from 3.65% in 2011 to 2.77% in 2012, almost 0% in 2013, and a deflation of –0.3% in 2014.

The country experienced a severe contraction, but we cannot conclude that avoiding austerity would have improved social welfare. After all, given the size and trajectory of the public debt, inaction might have led to a confidence crisis. Another option would have been to get out of the euro and pursue expansionary fiscal policy (because Portugal is in the eurozone, the country cannot print its own money and have large fiscal deficits without access to financial markets). There is no way to establish conclusively which path was best for the Portuguese economy. As always, the goal here is to explain the tradeoffs and the decision-making process of policymakers. The austerity proponents argued that fiscal restraint was the correct path for long-term growth. On the other side of the debate, some economists like Paul Krugman[9] and Joseph Stiglitz[10] called for stimulus packages to combat the European recession and bring aggregate demand closer to potential output.

9. Paul Krugman, "The Austerity Delusion," *The Guardian*, April 29, 2015, https://www.theguardian.com/business/ng-interactive/2015/apr/29/the-austerity-delusion.
10. Joseph Stiglitz, "Adding Liquidity Is Not Enough: A Fiscal Stimulus Is Needed," *The Guardian*, October 4, 2012, https://www.theguardian.com/business/economics-blog/2012/oct/04/adding-liquidity-fiscal-stimulus.

Generalizing the European case can help us to analyze the decision-making process of public authorities. So far, we have established a model of how the real economy works, how different markets interact, and how changes in financial markets are transmitted to the market for goods and services. We established the tradeoff between growth and inflation due to fluctuations in aggregate demand. There is also a rationale for the existence of business cycles, and for models that incorporate forward-looking expectations for decision makers. Regarding financial markets, we have seen how commercial banks create credit, how this influences saving and investment, and how central banks execute monetary policy. We discussed the role of money neutrality and then focused on the public budget, which plays an important role in economic fluctuations. We also described how credibility, commitment, and the trajectories of public deficit and debt constrain the actions of public authorities.

Policy prescriptions change over business cycles, constrained by past decisions. In addition, we established the conditions in which one policy is preferred over the other. Sometimes monetary policy is the better choice, and at other times, fiscal policy should be preferred.

Nevertheless, the optimal economic policy may well be to do nothing. Sometimes the best course of action for authorities is to let the economic forces bring the economy to full employment—that is, to an equilibrium in which actual output is equal to potential output. Testing this proposition is almost impossible, however, mainly because governments do act and try, sometimes quite heavy-handedly, to affect both financial markets and the market for goods and services. It is hard to build a counterfactual that is conditional on governments sitting passively while the business cycle takes its course. Policymakers have strong incentives for pursuing active policies that try to meet society's demands. Because of such political incentives, we concentrate here on describing how public authorities adjudicate without necessarily building a strong case for their meddling.

Assuming that some action will be taken, the main implication from combining all of the earlier models of how the economy is interconnected is that economic policies should be countercyclical. In the long run, growth in productivity determines the rate of increase of potential output, and thus in our framework both fiscal and monetary policies do not necessarily affect long-run outcomes. Nevertheless, in the short run, there is a space for active policy. This follows from the dynamics of business cycles. Under recessions, the growth gap widens until prices and wages fall and prospects change so that businesses restart investing. During expansions unemployment decreases until the labor market is squeezed, and inflationary pressures can derail sustained prosperity. In both situations, economic policy could smooth the business cycle by minimizing job losses during recessions

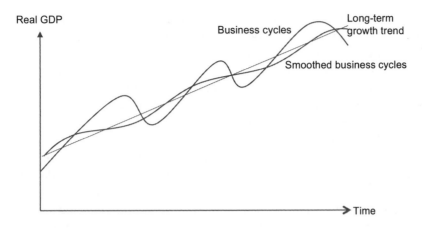

Figure 7.7

and preventing the formation of bubbles in financial and real markets as the economy overheats (figure 7.7).

7.5   Income Inequality and the Distributive Effects of Monetary and Fiscal Policies

Income inequality is a major issue in many countries. So far, the present framework says nothing about the distribution of wealth and income. In the United States, the We Are the 99 Percent movement spawned major protests in the early 2010s. In many other countries, inequality is at the forefront of the political debate. Income inequality is addressed in more detail in chapter 12, but here we have a preliminary section describing how changes in economic policy have important distributive effects.

Usually, policies to reduce inequality are not designed in tandem with the regular macroeconomic management of the economy. For instance, progressive taxation is a structural feature of modern economies. Taxes on top earners are supposed to be higher than those on poor citizens, regardless of how the economy is behaving. Nevertheless, there are plenty of examples of fiscal policies that can be regressive or progressive in nature, contributing to more or less income inequality. We illustrate this with an example from Bolivia.

Bolivia and the Tradeoffs between Growth, Income Inequality, and Basic Human Rights

Bolivia is not only one of the poorest but also one of the most unequal countries in the Americas. In 2016, income per capita was barely above US$3,000 per year, the 10% richest Bolivians held over a third of the nation's income, and 7.1% of the population lived on less than US$1.9 per day.[11] Surprisingly, this scenario comes after a strong period of growth and reduction in inequality. The situation was worse in the past. José P. Mauricio Vargas and Santiago Garriga show that inequality reduction was driven mainly by labor income growth at the bottom end of the income distribution and that this growth was concentrated in the informal, low-skilled service and manufacturing sectors.[12]

In 2017, the Bolivian government faced a dilemma. It wanted to revive a project that would build a superhighway linking the Andes with the Amazon. The purpose of this ambitious (some say excessively ambitious) project was to deliver perennial economic growth.[13] Direct distributive effects were supposed to center on two groups—indigenous people, who would be negatively affected by the project, and cocoa growers, who would benefit from better infrastructure. Both groups are poor, but the indigenous peoples are poorer in relative terms. The project also might have serious environmental impacts.

This situation illustrates the difficulties with modern policymaking. In the past, such a project would have faced very little opposition before being approved. The promise of progress (that is, economic growth) used to be the main driver for poor countries. The opportunities for graft in big projects also helped move them along. Today, we know that growth comes at a price, both to various groups and to the environment. When such a project is part of an expansionary fiscal policy, it can generate more development—but only if its deleterious effects on indigenous groups and nature are mitigated.

11. World Bank, 2017.
12. José P. Mauricio Vargas and Santiago Garriga, "Explaining Inequality and Poverty Reduction in Bolivia," IMF Working Paper WP/15/265, International Monetary Fund, December 2015, https://www.imf.org/~/media/Websites/IMF/imported-full-text-pdf/external/pubs/ft/wp/2015/_wp15265.ashx.
13. Mac Margolis, "Bolivia's Morales Goes Down an Ugly Road," *Bloomberg View*, August 17, 2017, https://www.bloomberg.com/amp/view/articles/2017-08-17/bolivia-s-morales-goes-down-an-ugly-road.

8   The Government Budget and Its Economic Impacts

In this chapter,
- Public deficit and debt
- Credibility and the commitment of public authorities
- Time inconsistency and the performance of fiscal policy
- The economic effects of public budget decisions
- How to get out of hyperinflation
- Fiscal multipliers, crowding out and in
- Austerity or profligacy?

8.1   The Public Budget and Social Welfare

Although many people like to link government and household finances ("Government spending today is a tax on our children!"), the government's budget, its trajectory, and the need to finance it are completely distinct from the budget of a typical household. After all, not many households have a central bank that sets the interest rate. Better yet, governments have at their disposal a monetary institution that can print as much money as it wants. Individuals retire, governments don't. Austerity may be recommended to reckless spenders, but it doesn't mean that the same advice applies to governments. There is one way in which households and governments are similar, however. For every family, debt is a problem if it is large relative to income and if it is growing without a cap. The same holds true for local or central governments.

Let's start with government bonds, the means through which public authorities can finance spending that is higher than tax revenue. For simplicity, assume a government that raises US$1 trillion in taxes and wants to spend US$1.2 trillion on paying its employees, providing public services, and financing a myriad of other subsidizes and transfers. Public authorities have two options—print money to cover the shortfall or issue debt that takes the form of government bonds.

Unlike families, governments can choose to roll over its debt perpetually, without ever being debt free. As long as the level of public debt is manageable, in the sense that the rest of society does not believe it will grow uncontrollably, governments do not need to balance their books.

As noted in previous chapters, understanding government bonds is central for describing how central banks operate monetary policy. Here we move on to analyze their economic impact.

The main fuel of debt is the current public deficit, which is broadly defined as the difference between tax revenue and government expenditure. Debt also grows because of the interest rate, given that government bonds pay interest to their holders. Some technical definitions are needed before we can move on to the economic impact of public deficit and debt.

Primary budget (*PB*) is the current deficit or surplus related to current government expenditure (*G*) and revenue from taxes (*T*):

$$PB = G - T.$$

The total budget deficit (*TB*) also considers interest from past debt. If the interest rate is r and total debt is D, then the total budget deficit is

$$TB = PB - rD.$$

If, as is common, there is a budget deficit, the government has two choices: it can print money or issue new debt. For now, we put aside the option of printing money. Because governments should not be in the business of printing money to plug their deficits, many incur more debt to finance their budgets, and their total debt escalates. Every year from 2010 to 2021, the US federal government either had or is expected to have a primary deficit, topping out at –8.7% of GDP in 2010 and declining to an estimated –2.4% in 2021 (table 8.1).

During the twenty-five years from 1990 to 2015, the US federal debt rose from US$3.2 trillion to US$18.1 trillion, a rate of growth of 7.2% per year (figure 8.1). During the same period, GDP also increased from US$5.9 trillion in 1990 to US$17.8 trillion in 2016 (figure 8.2). The ratio between debt and GDP doubled in the same period, with most of the growth in debt to GDP ratio coming after the great financial crisis.

In the mid-2010s, total federal debt in the United States exceeded the country's entire GDP. High levels of debt to GDP are common among developed countries, but what are the economic implications of this amount of debt? How bad is the debt trajectory of the United States? What about Europe and China? Should countries in Southeast Asia, Africa, and Latin America run large deficits or balance their budgets?

Table 8.1
Summary of US receipts, outlays, and surpluses or deficits—in current dollars, constant (2009) dollars, and as a percentage of GDP, 2010 to 2021

Fiscal year	In billions of current US dollars			In billions of constant US dollars (FY 2009)			As percentages of GDP		
	Receipts	Outlays	Deficit	Receipts	Outlays	Deficit	Receipts	Outlays	Deficit
2010	$2,162.7	$3,457.1	−$1,294.4	$2,129.3	$3,403.6	−$1,274.4	14.6%	23.4%	−8.7%
2011	2,303.5	3,603.1	−1,299.6	2,215.9	3,466.1	−1,250.2	15.0	23.4	−8.5
2012	2,450.0	3,537.0	−1,087.0	2,310.7	3,335.8	−1,025.1	15.3	22.1	−6.8
2013	2,775.1	3,454.6	−679.5	2,583.4	3,216.0	−632.6	16.8	20.9	−4.1
2014	3,021.5	3,506.1	−484.6	2,771.5	3,216.0	−444.5	17.6	20.4	−2.8
2015	3,249.9	3,688.3	−438.4	2,939.5	3,336.0	−396.5	18.3	20.7	−2.5
2016	3,335.5	3,951.3	−615.8	2,960.2	3,506.7	−546.5	18.1	21.4	−3.3
2017	3,643.7	4,147.2	−503.5	3,168.7	3,606.6	−437.8	18.9	21.5	−2.6
2018	3,898.6	4,352.2	−453.6	3,319.4	3,705.6	−386.2	19.4	21.6	−2.3
2019	4,095.1	4,644.3	−549.3	3,411.1	3,868.6	−457.5	19.5	22.1	−2.6
2020	4,345.7	4,879.8	−534.1	3,540.3	3,975.4	−435.1	19.8	22.3	−2.4
2021	4,572.0	5,124.2	−552.3	3,642.7	4,082.7	−440.0	20.0	22.4	−2.4

Note: Estimates for 2017 to 2021.
Source: White House, "Historical Tables" Office of Management and Budget, 2017.

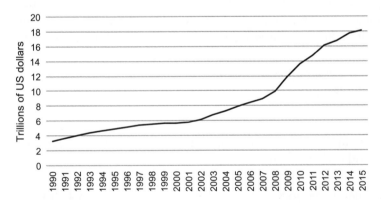

Figure 8.1
US nominal federal debt in dollars, 1990 to 2015
Source: Federal Reserve of St. Louis, 2017, https://fred.stlouisfed.org/series/FYGFD.

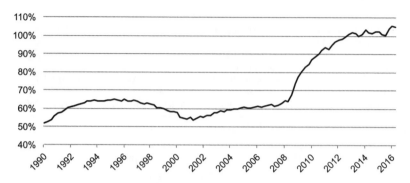

Figure 8.2
US total federal debt as a percentage of GDP, 1990 to 2016
Source: Federal Reserve of St. Louis, 2017, https://fred.stlouisfed.org/series/GFDEGDQ188S.

Governments affect social welfare through many channels, including the ways that government budgets influence the market for goods and services. Governments' decisions on taxes and expenditure affect the growth and inflation trajectories by changes in aggregate demand.

The public budget affects short-run growth in two ways—through taxes and expenditure. Higher or lower taxes affect either disposable income (if imposed on consumers) or investment (if imposed on businesses). Government expenditure (G) directly contributes to aggregate demand. Higher expenditure (such as public investment on infrastructure) increases demand. Conversely, less expenditure lowers demand.

Presently, in terms of comparative statics, there is no difference between private and public investment as a growth driver. Because

$$Y = C + I + G,$$

where Y is economic output, C is consumption, I is investment, and G is government expenditure, both $\uparrow G$ and $\uparrow I$ result in $\uparrow Y$.

The same is true in relation to personal or corporate taxes. Lowering taxes stokes aggregate demand, and increasing taxes shrinks it. This is easy to see if

$$C = a + b(Y - T),$$

where C is consumption, a is autonomous consumption (the basic things that people need to buy), b is the propensity to consume (how much we buy if income rises), Y is economic output, and T is taxes. If income taxes decrease (lower T) then disposable income ($Y - T$) increases, and hence higher consumption $\uparrow C$ leads to more aggregate demand $\uparrow Y$.

Governments also can affect aggregate demand through subsidies and income transfers. They work in the same way as expenditure. More subsidies or transfers to consumers or companies should boost demand.

If governments could spend more to induce economic activity without adverse effects, there would be no need for this book. Governments could be let loose, and everyone would enjoy the prosperity that follows. Unfortunately, the story does not stop at the simple relationship between G and Y.

8.2 Public Debt and Credibility: Crowding Out and Crowding In

The true capacity of governments to influence aggregate demand depends on the degree of crowding out between public and private funds. Crowding out happens when government expenditure displaces private investment. Crowding in is the opposite and depends on complementarity decisions by policymakers and companies.

Governments need to borrow so that they can spend. They may borrow responsibly or not. Reckless borrowing for useless projects generates few economic benefits and instead creates a burden that may restrict future spending. Companies have less funds to borrow (because the government has used them), and public displaces private investment. There is some crowding out.

Now, assume a depressed economy in which companies do not invest because income is falling. Governments step in and borrow from society to fund R&D or infrastructure investment. People are employed and use their income to consume. Prospects are revived. Higher consumption leads companies to invest more. Public spending create private investment. This is crowding in. As with everything in the economics of global business, the effects of economic policies are context dependent. Given some circumstances, there may be crowding out or crowding in, creating another layer of complexity to public authorities' decision process.

If a government wants to begin a new income transfer program, it needs to finance the program and does so by running a primary deficit and issuing debt to cover it (figure 8.3). On the market for loanable funds, the new government debt soaks up funds from the market. There is a decrease in the supply of loanable funds from S_{LF} to S'_{LF}. The interest rate goes up from r to r', and the quantity of loanable funds decreases from Q_{LF} to Q'_{LF}. This means that private businesses invest less, displaying the crowding-out effect: as government expenditure rises, it displaces private investment.

Even though crowding out is a common phenomenon in financial markets all over the world, the extent of the effect is what matters in economic dynamics and for the design of economic policies. Perfect crowding out would nullify any

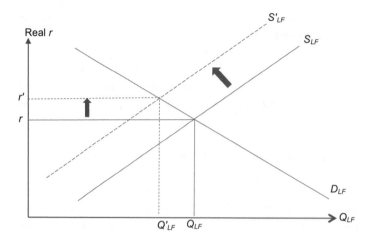

Figure 8.3
Loanable funds (credit) market

consequences of government expenditure, and fiscal policy would be completely neutral. Determining the answer to a fundamental economic question—to what extent does a public deficit crowd out private investment?—depends on a number of variables, including government credibility, Ricardian equivalence, time inconsistency, and the position of the economy in the business cycle. The pattern of budget deficits and surpluses around the world is shown in figure 8.4. High deficits destroy confidence in public authorities.

Government Credibility and Financing Public Works

In a closed economy scenario, governments issue bonds in the local currency. Because government bonds come with a guarantee by the monetary authority, they are considered the safest asset in an economy, and their interest rate is that economy's risk-free interest rate. Public authorities can offer something that no other economic agent can—a printing press that produces money that can cover all government debts. Bonds allow governments to borrow at lower costs than other economic agents. All things being equal, most lenders would rather lend to a government that issues its own currency rather than a company that can go bankrupt.

The power to issue currency gives public authorities economic and political power, but that power is not absolute. Expectations matter, and market agents need to have confidence in the capacity of public authorities to manage the long-term debt of the country adequately. When the debt is growing explosively, market agents may decide that government bonds are not the safest asset in the economy.

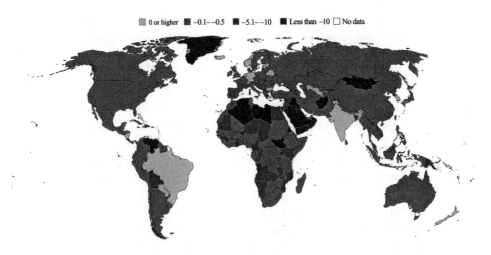

Figure 8.4
World budget surplus (+) or deficit (–) as a percentage of GDP, 2016
Source: CIA, 2017, https://www.cia.gov/library/publications/the-world-factbook/fields/2222.html.

People would refrain from financing public expenditure, interest rates would rise, and the government's only option would be to use monetary expansion (that is, print more currency) to pay for its deficit. And that, in short, is how hyperinflation is born.

In financial markets, the credibility of governments is key to establishing the responses to policy changes. Ratings agencies are responsible for presenting perceived risks related to the trajectory of the public debt. Given the rapid increase in the ratio of the US public debt to GDP, on August 5, 2011, Standard &Poor's, one of the top ratings agencies in the world, announced its first-ever downgrade to US sovereign debt, lowering the rating from AAA to AA+ with a negative outlook.

Credibility is also vital to the use of local currency as money. Because modern money is fiat (backed by the government that issues it), it relies on having private and public agents perceive that financial markets are functioning well. Credibility is transmitted along with other variables to financial markets through demand and supply for government bonds (especially long-term maturity bonds) in the secondary market. A very low interest rate on long-term bonds is a signal that market agents are willing to buy such bonds even at low yields, probably because they consider that there is a very low risk of mismanagement of public debt over time.

The central banks of emerging markets have difficulties in issuing bonds of long maturities. Most of these countries have had fiscal crises in their recent past, and market agents are not prepared to buy bonds of long maturities unless they are handsomely compensated for this extra risk. Extremely high interest rates discourage governments from issuing such long-term maturity bonds. As a result, most thirty-year bonds are emitted by developed countries.

Ricardian Equivalence

Ricardian equivalence describes a hypothetical situation in which people are almost perfectly rational. The idea behind Ricardian equivalence, named after the nineteenth-century economist David Ricardo, is relatively simple: because households and companies are forward-looking rational agents, they know that if governments are running a deficit today, they will need to run a surplus tomorrow. Thus, if officials raise public expenditure, households and businesses respond by curtailing consumption and investment, preparing themselves for a future increase in taxes to compensate for the present spending hike. Government spending would have no effect on economic activity.[1]

The equivalence does not need to be strong to neutralize the effects of government spending. Assume that public authorities announce new spending programs or lower taxes. If some market agents do not change their decisions because they believe that the government will need to compensate the newly created deficit later, the effectiveness of the policymakers' actions is decreased. A good example of a test for Ricardian equivalence is a policy enacted by President George H. W. Bush in 1992. As N. Gregory Mankiw analyzes it: "by executive order, he lowered the amount of income taxes that were being withheld from spenders' paychecks. The order did not reduce the amount of taxes that spenders owed; it merely delayed payment. The higher take-home pay that spenders received during 1992 was to be offset by higher tax payments, or smaller tax refunds, when income taxes were due in April 1993."[2] If people were perfectly rational and forward-looking, they would not change their consumption and spending patterns com-

1. Some economic models that feature Ricardian equivalence use rational expectations regarding the present and future behavior of fiscal authorities. N. Gregory Mankiw, one of the foremost experts in macroeconomics, has a model that prominently features Ricardian equivalence. See N. Gregory Mankiw, "The Savers-Spenders Theory of Fiscal Policy," *American Economic Review* 90 (2000): 120–125. In the Barro-Ramsey model of infinitely lived families, government's debt policy redistributes the tax burden among generations, but families who want to smooth their consumption over time reverse the effects of this redistribution through their bequests. Government debt is then completely neutral. In the Diamond-Samuelson model, people smooth consumption but cannot leave anything as a bequest. Public debt enriches some generations at the expense of others, crowds out capital, and reduces steady-state living standards. One of the main results from the Mankiw model is that crowding out may or may not occur, depending on how public authorities devise their tax schemes and how agents make decisions.
2. N. Gregory Mankiw, "The Savers-Spenders Theory of Fiscal Policy," *The American Economic Review* 90, no. 2 (2000): 120–125.

pared with previous years. After all, only the schedule of consumers' payments, not the overall amount of taxes they owed, changed.

President Bush claimed that his policy would provide "money people can use to help pay for clothing, college, or to get a new car."[3] He believed that consumers would spend the extra income, thereby stimulating aggregate demand and helping the economy recover from the recession. Evidence supports Bush's conjecture. Shortly after the policy was announced, Matthew Shapiro and Joel Slemrod surveyed people on what they would do with the extra income, and 57% of respondents said they would save it, use it to repay debts, or adjust their withholding in order to reverse the effect of Bush's executive order.[4] Only 43% said they would spend the extra income. This significant minority was not fully rational but was large enough for the spending to have an economy-wide effect. Ricardian equivalence, if present, limits the effects of public expenditure on aggregate demand. But there is no reason to expect that most people will behave rationally, conforming to economic models, all the time.

Time Inconsistency

Time inconsistency happens when the preference of public authorities changes over time. In 2016, for instance, the Southern Nevada Tourism Infrastructure Committee recommended raising the hotel tax in the Las Vegas area to help pay for a 65,000-seat domed venue to lure a National Football League team to the city.[5] Raising this new tax and using US$750 million of public funds were supposed to be the main draws intended to bring an NFL franchise to Las Vegas. If the NFL owners' committee approved the relocation and the team owners started building the stadium, these private owners would be locked in and could not simply abandon the construction of the new stadium. What happens if the local government reneges on the promise? If the owners finish building the stadium with their own funds (and the NFL's), then the local government has its pie and can eat it too. It has promised funds for a new stadium, has not delivered on the promise, and still gets the stadium that their constituents want.

Public authorities have incentives to change their mind about an earlier promise if the desired economic effect has already happened. A government might promise to give a tax rebate to a company to build a new factory. After the company does so, given that the factory is immobile, the government may not deliver on the tax

3. Ibid., 122.
4. Matthew Shapiro and Joel Slemrod, "Consumer Response to the Timing of Income: Evidence from a Change in Tax Withholding," *American Economic Review* 85, no. 1 (1995): 274–283.
5. "Committee Recommends $750M in Public Financing for Vegas Stadium," ESPN, September 16, 2016, http://www.espn.com/nfl/story/_/id/17555854/committee-recommends-750-million-public-money-las-vegas-stadium-raiders.

rebate. Time inconsistency happens a lot in poor countries that overpromise to twist the arm of foreign investors.

The economic effect of time inconsistency is that the higher the probability that public authorities may show time-inconsistent preferences, the smaller the likelihood that market agents will want to finance public debt. Time inconsistency and credibility are the reasons that some emerging countries try to set up rules that constrain public policies. Balanced-budget laws, for instance, require that governments should not spend more than the tax revenue. Balanced budgets require primary surpluses or, at a minimum, current revenues equal to spending. Yet in a recession, public authorities find it quite tempting to accelerate spending. Governments may squander earlier promises of austerity. That would be a classic example of time-inconsistent policymaking.

Business Cycles and Public Debt

So far we have looked at two factors that may influence public spending—the credibility of policymakers and the rationality of economic agents. It is time to add one more—the natural cycle of public deficit and debt. Governments are aware of the existence of business cycles, and in theory, it is their job to smooth them. In practice, things are rarely that simple. For example, even though the right thing to do during an economic downturn would be to increase public spending, the lower tax revenue means that doing so would significantly increase the public deficit. In the early 2010s, for instance, Greece was in the grip of a recession. One way to loosen it would be for the government to increase its spending. But the depression (and the profligacy that preceded it) meant that Greece's public finances were in a sorry state. Its ratio of debt to GDP was already the highest in Europe—and was climbing fast due to the dwindling tax revenue. There was no clear path to recovery. By spending, the debt would balloon even faster. By sticking to austerity, the economic depression would be aggravated.

The important lesson from this section is that even if no action is taken, public deficit and debt still change with the business cycle. Let's assume a fixed amount of public deficit (or surplus) and a government that simply maintains the same levels of spending over time. In a situation like this, the public deficit and the ratio of public debt to GDP might change due to tax revenues or the GDP. Tax revenues change along the business cycle. In a recession, income and corporate taxes go down as economic activity slows down; in a boom, tax revenues increase accordingly. Because tax revenue usually decreases during a recession (thus increasing the public deficit) and because GDP growth also fluctuates, the ratio of public debt to GDP tends to increase during a recession and decrease in an expansion period.

In the last twenty-five years in the United States, there has been a clear trend for the ratio of public debt to GDP to increase, but the relative size of public debt has closely tracked the business cycle. For instance, the mid-1990s was a period of robust and sustained economic growth. Tax revenues increased, and the country achieved primary surpluses for the first time since the 1970s. The ratio between debt and national output went down. After 2008, the debt exploded because of an accommodative fiscal policy that was a response to the great financial crisis. The cyclical pattern remained.

The Fiscal Multiplier

The ability of public authorities to influence economic activity relies on their credibility and commitment. We return to the concepts of crowding in and out to describe under which conditions fiscal policy may generate or destroy prosperity.

Crowding in is equivalent to stating that the fiscal multiplier is higher than 1. The fiscal multiplier measures the dynamic effect of public budget decisions on economic activity. If it is higher than 1, it means that if the governments increased spending or reduced taxes by US$1, the country's GDP would grow by more than US$1. Public authorities would be able to create prosperity simply by spending more or reducing taxes on households and companies.

A fiscal multiplier higher than 1 is a call for active policymaking. If there is a growth gap, then by investing in the economy the government increases employment. Rising income by households leads to higher consumption, which boosts profits and expectations regarding economic recovery. Companies invest to meet a surging demand, leading to more employment, consumption, and so on. This mechanism is similar to the money multiplier in the banking system, except here economic activity (not money) is created.

Algebraically, the multiplier depends on the households' propensity to consume. Its value, for a simple model, is

$$fm = \frac{1}{1-b(1-t)},$$

where fm is the fiscal multiplier, b is the propensity to consume, and t is the average income tax rate. For instance, for $b = 0.8$, and $t = 0.2$ (which means that consumers, on average, spend 80% of their increased income and have to pay 20% on extra earnings), the fiscal multiplier would be

$$fm = \frac{1}{1-0.8(1-0.2)} = 2.77.$$

In this simple case, the fiscal multiplier would be 2.77, and public authorities would be able to stimulate aggregate demand on a ratio of 2.77 per 1 unit of money spent.

Here is the catch: does the fiscal multiplier even exist? If the answer is yes, then what conditions would allow governments to step in and generate economic growth?

We began our example assuming an exogenous decision by fiscal authorities to increase public spending. Nevertheless, we know that such exogeneity does not necessarily exist and that public expenditure might crowd out private investment. The multiplier exists only if economic agents change their decisions to reflect the increase in public spending (or changes in tax). For instance, a government with debt that is already high faces more constraints to enact public spending programs than when public debt to GDP ratio is low. The same is true of governments that take time-consistent decisions. Credibility is key. Without it, there cannot be a fiscal multiplier higher than 1.[6]

Fiscal multipliers are context dependent. In an emerging market that is suffering from insufficient supply of loanable funds, more spending might crowd out private investment at a much higher rate than in the case of more developed economies with credible fiscal authorities. In some cases, public expenditure may crowd in investment. For instance, a country that is productive and has the potential to be a mighty exporter might have no ports. If public authorities build a port, it unlocks the potential of the country's industries. In this case, public infrastructure begets private investment.

The possibility of crowding out limits the action of governments. In a situation of growth gap in which financial markets provide ample liquidity and the ratio of debt to GDP is low, fiscal spending or lowering taxes may be helpful in abbreviating a recession through fiscal multipliers. But with an economy close to full employment or a government that is already highly indebted, profligacy may crowd out private investment and destroy social welfare.

8.3   Hyperinflation and Public Deficit

Hyperinflation is the result of a total loss of credibility of the fiscal authorities. Hyperinflation happens when governments finance their debt by mostly printing money. From the quantity theory of money,

---

6. The academic literature has long been preoccupied with this issue, and it gets even more complicated with an open economy. The type of exchange regime affects the size of the multiplier, according to Ethan Ilzetzki, Enrique G. Mendoza, and Carlos A. Végh, "How Big (Small?) Are Fiscal Multipliers?," *Journal of Monetary Economics* 60, no. 2 (2013): 239–254. Results in which fiscal multipliers are larger in recessions than in expansions are presented in two works—Alan J. Auerbach and Yuriy Gorodnichenko, "Fiscal Multipliers in Recession and Expansion," in *Fiscal Policy after the Financial Crisis*, ed. Alberto Alesina and Francesco Giavazzi, 63–98 (Chicago: University of Chicago Press, 2013), and Anja Baum, Marcos Poplawski-Ribeiro, and Anke Weber, "Fiscal Multipliers and the State of the Economy," IMP Working Paper No. 12/286, International Monetary Fund, December 5, 2012.

$$MV = PY,$$

where M is the nominal quantity of money, V is the velocity of money, P is the price level, and Y is the national income, so if we assume that the velocity of money V is fixed and that the public deficit has no impact on economic activity, then expanding money supply leads only to higher prices.

Inflation is more than a simple monetary phenomenon. It is the result of failed governments that cannot issue debt because they lack credibility. Overcoming inflation means acquiring credibility, usually through fiscal restraint that curtails public deficits and by signals of prudence sent to market agents.

Recently, Zimbabwe and Venezuela have experienced bouts of hyperinflation. The worst of Zimbabwean hyperinflation happened from 2000 to 2008. In 2008, the monthly inflation rate hit 3,500,000% (an egg cost 50 billion Zimbabwean dollars).[7] The Zimbabwean government continued to run a deficit to finance projects such as the country's involvement in the civil war in neighboring Congo.[8] Hyperinflation is self-reinforcing. As the government starts to lose credibility, it begins to lose its capacity to issue government debt in local currency. In quick succession, it prints money, prices rise, expectations change, and households and businesses start to adapt, with companies raising prices due to expected future inflation.

Moving out of hyperinflation requires restoring credibility. In the case of Zimbabwe, authorities chose to outsource credibility by defining foreign currencies as the means of payment in the local markets. This is similar to the process that Latin American countries used to deal with hyperinflation in the 1980s and 1990s. Almost all of them used the US dollar as a temporary anchor to local currencies. For instance, the Argentine peso was fixed at a rate of US$1 per 1 peso. By simultaneously reining in spending and rolling out good economic policies, at least for awhile, Latin American countries were able to vanquish inflation.

The Venezuelan story is similar to that of other countries that have plunged into a spiral of increasing prices. The government stopped announcing inflation rates in mid-2014, but market estimates showed that inflation surged from 63% in 2014 to 275% in 2015 and to 720% in 2016.[9] The public deficit in 2013, when prices started to accelerate, was 11.5% of GDP, but by 2015, it had grown to more than 16% of GDP. The government resorted to printing money to finance the bulging deficit.

---

7. "Zimbabwe Phases Out Local Currency at 35 Quadrillion to US$1," *RT*, June 15, 2015, https://www.rt.com/business/267244-zimbabwe-currency-compensation-hyperinflation.
8. Chris Matthews, "Hey, Can You Spare 35 Quadrillion? Zimbabwe's Crazy Exchange Rate," *Fortune*, June 12, 2015, http://fortune.com/2015/06/12/zimbabwe-hyperinflation.
9. Christopher Woody, "Venezuela's Looming Economic Catastrophe, in One Graphic," *Business Insider*, July 20, 2016, http://www.businessinsider.com/venezuela-heading-toward-hyperinflation-2016-7.

Table 8.2
Historic highest monthly inflation rates, 1923 to 2008

Country	Date	Highest monthly inflation rate (percentage)	Equivalent daily rate (percentage)	Time required for prices to double
Hungary	July 1946	$1.30 \times 10^{16}\%$	195%	15.6 hours
Zimbabwe	November 2008	79,600,000,000	98.0	24.7 hours
Yugoslavia	January 1994	313,000,000	64.6	1.4 days
Germany	October 1923	29,500	20.9	3.7 days
Greece	November 1944	11,300	17.1	4.5 days
China	May 1949	4,210	13.4	5.6 days

Source: Steve H. Hanke and Alex Kwoke, "On the Measurement of Zimbabwe's Hyperinflation," *Cato Journal* 29, no. 2 (2009).

The crisis in Venezuela was not the worst ever known (table 8.2). The worst case in modern history was in Hungary in July 1946, when prices doubled every fifteen hours. Germany in the years 1922 and 1923 was another emblematic case and had vast implications for the world order by facilitating the rise of the National Socialist German Workers' Party to power.

The Missing Inflation of the 2010s

In chapter 5, the quantity theory of money is used to explain why several economists were wrong when they predicted that hyperinflation would be triggered by quantitative easing. In their letter to the Federal Reserve chair Ben Bernanke, they stated that "we believe the Federal Reserve's large-scale asset purchase plan (so-called 'quantitative easing') should be reconsidered and discontinued. We do not believe such a plan is necessary or advisable under current circumstances. The planned asset purchases risk currency debasement and inflation, and we do not think they will achieve the Fed's objective of promoting employment."[10] During and after the three rounds of quantitative easing, inflation remained persistently low. The quantity theory of money can explain some of this result, but the explanation needs to account for the fiscal side of the story, as well.

These economists thought that quantitative easing would reinforce the fiscal authority's lack of credibility and that with increasing debt, printing money would make prices escalate. They were wrong because the rise in debt was temporary and the failed transmission mechanisms of monetary policy did not allow for the expansion in money supply to influence prices in the real economy. They also did not consider the possibility that financial markets might have been going through

10. "Open Letter to Ben Bernanke," *Wall Street Journal*, November 15, 2010.

a situation of liquidity trap. In 2009, the primary deficit was 9.8% of GDP, and in 2010, it totaled 8.6% of national income. If quantitative easing had been accompanied by accelerating fiscal deficits and a complete loss of credibility in the federal government, the United States could have gone through a period of rapid and increasing inflation. Instead, quantitative easing expanded the supply of loanable funds, and most of them did not filter to the real side of the economy. On the fiscal side, the central government did curtail the deficit, and the economy stabilized, albeit at a low growth level.

Inflation is not only a question of how much money is printed. Currency debasement follows from persistent fiscal deficits that cannot be financed by the debt-issuing government. In this situation, the US government never lost its capacity to sell its bonds in the open market, and no inflation was forthcoming.

Japan, Brazil, Credibility, and 250%

The performance of Japan's economy since the early 1990s highlights the relevance of credibility for the ability of central banks to affect financial markets and set interest rates. The size of the country's debt should have forced the Bank of Japan to face a confidence crisis at some point in the last twenty years.

Since the early 1990s, the Japanese economy has been seriously underperforming, and the public deficit has been rising steadily, mostly because of successive primary deficits used to rescue the banking system and to revive a slumping economy (figure 8.5). In 1990, gross government debt stood at 67% of GDP, and over the next twenty-five years, it climbed almost continuously. Only the period 2006 to 2008 saw a small reduction in the share of debt to GDP. After the crisis, the pace picked up, and gross debt rose from 183% in 2008 to a little more than 250% in 2016.

In recent history, no country other than Japan, developed or emerging, has shown such a relentless debt accumulation by its central government. Even if we take into account net debt, which is a better measure of true debt trajectory, Japan is still one of the most indebted advanced economies (figure 8.6).

The OECD estimates that Japan's gross debt should reach over 400% of GDP in 2040.[11] Even so, the country has had a target and effective interest rate of 0% for most of the twenty-first century, and in July 2016, the twenty-year central government bond yield turned negative, which means that investors were paying for the right to borrow from a highly leveraged government.[12]

11. Szu Ping Chan, "Japan's Huge Debt Pile Just Got Scarier," *The Telegraph*, April 15, 2015, http://www.telegraph.co.uk/finance/economics/11539776/Japans-huge-debt-pile-just-got-scarier.html.
12. Gregor Stuart Hunter, "Japan's Twenty-Year Bond Yield Turns Negative," *Wall Street Journal*, July 6, 2016, https://www.wsj.com/articles/investors-take-fright-as-havens-dwindle-1467809132.

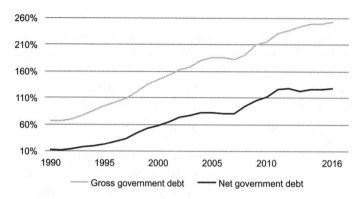

Figure 8.5
Japan government debt, gross and net, as a percentage of GDP, 1990 to 2016
Source: Federal Reserve of St. Louis, 2017, https://fred.stlouisfed.org/series/GGGDTAJPA188N.

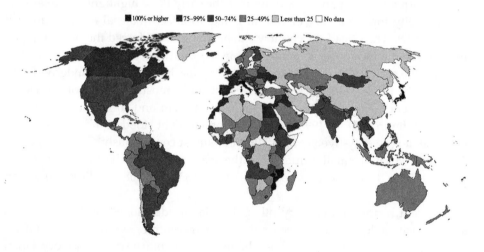

Figure 8.6
World public debt as a percentage of GDP, 2016.
Source: CIA, 2017, https://www.cia.gov/library/publications/the-world-factbook/fields/2186.html.

There is no paradox in this case, however. Most Japanese debt is held by local investors, and the Japanese government has retained confidence in its ability to manage the economy. The same does not hold true for less credible governments, where real interest rates are structurally high and the maturity of bonds short. A case in point is Brazil.

Brazil has a much lower debt to GDP ratio than Japan. In fact, in order to contain the rising yields and to create confidence in the trajectory of its public debt, Brazilian politicians designed a balanced-budget act that passed into law in 2000. At its core was the Fiscal Responsibility Law and its simple requirement that no municipal, state, or federal government entities were allowed to run a primary deficit. Given the low confidence in Brazilian politicians, such a law was supposed to rule out the possibility of time-inconsistent policies. In the mid-2000s, real interest rates fell in the country, but in the early 2010s, yields in Brazil still were 4% to 5% more than they were in developed economies, in real terms (figure 8.7).

In 2016, the average yield on government bonds was 0.25% in Japan and 6% in Brazil (both in real terms). The fiscal cost for Japan was a little over 0.6% of GDP, while for the Brazilian government it was almost 4% of GDP. Meanwhile, the maturity of the debt was an average of seven years in Japan and less than half of that in Brazil.

The underlying data for the debt trajectory over the last twenty years has been much better for Brazil than for Japan. The main difference, which results in much higher costs to Brazilian society when compared to Japan, is the confidence in the two governments and their debt management. Both countries have an aging population with pension crises looming in the near future. The uncertainty

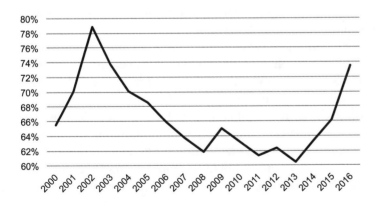

Figure 8.7
Brazil gross government debt as a percentage of GDP, 2000 to 2016
Source: Federal Reserve of St. Louis, 2017, https://fred.stlouisfed.org/series/GGGDTABRA188N.

regarding the accountability of the public authorities explains why the two governments face such different costs for refinancing their debts.

8.4   Who Sets the Interest Rate?

In the standard money market model, the interest rate is a monopoly of the central bank. The central bank can shift money supply through open-market operations or react to any shocks in the demand for money. In the aftermath of the great financial crisis, it has been hard to argue that a central bank is an all-powerful, exogenous institution that sets the interest rate by fiat.

The present model of the public budget and its relation to expectations puts constraints in the ability of central banks to determine interest rates. In normal times, when central banks do not face confidence crises, they can certainly set the nominal interest rate and affect the real one by shifting money supply. But the main lesson to take away from this book is that economics is heavily context dependent. The best way to describe the actions of central banks in financial markets is to state that central banks influence interest rates but do not unilaterally set them on a whim. Aswath Damodaran describes the mechanism of monetary authority like this: "if the Fed wants to raise (lower) interest rates, it has historically hiked (cut) the Fed Funds rate and hoped that bond markets (treasury and corporate) respond accordingly."[13] Here Damodaran is describing the world after the great financial crisis, where central banks have had to resort to heterodox monetary policies such as quantitative easing.

The all-powerful central bank setting interest rates and moving financial markets is still an adequate description of the behavior of modern monetary authorities—but not always. In some situations, like a confidence crisis or liquidity trap, central banks may not have an effect at all.

In countries with tight controls over financial markets, like China, central banks have a huge influence over the behavior of commercial banks and the market rates. But the financial markets determine the demand for money and the other variables pertaining to supply and demand for loanable funds, setting the real interest rate. It is worth keeping in mind that expectations and confidence play significant roles in the movements of financial markets. On some occasions, market agents may even completely neutralize central banks' actions if they have no confidence in them. In the present framework, central banks determine the nominal interest rate, while the real interest rate is set up in the market for loan-

13. Aswath Damodaran, "Dealing with Low Interest Rates: Investing and Corporate Finance Lessons," Musings on Markets, blog, April 3, 2015, http://aswathdamodaran.blogspot.com.br/2015/04/dealing-with-low-interest-rates.html.

able funds. In normal times, they move in tandem. That does not always need to be the case.

This also illustrates something that is crucial in relation to economic policies: confidence in public authorities is central for any policy to work in real markets. If the government has no credibility, changes in variables such as the interest rate or fiscal spending are often met by an opposite reaction, such as when agents anticipate future tax hikes.

8.5   The Instruments of Fiscal Policy and Public Debt Management

Managing public finances is one of the most important responsibilities of public authorities. Officials have to find the balance between, on the one hand, the expenses related to providing public services, running the government, deciding on subsidies and income transfers, and making public investment and, on the other hand, the taxes that the state can actually raise. How this balance is struck often is influenced by the country's level of development. Wealthier countries tend to have costlier governments as a proportion of their GDP. In most poor states, public authorities are viewed with some suspicion either because they are members of a dictatorial clique or because the democratic institutions are very fragile.

Social norms also play a role. In the United States, for example, the culture favors individuality, even if most people are happy with a quasi-socialist health care system for older people. In Denmark, however, the collective spirit prevails. Social norms in Scandinavia are captured, allegorically, in Jante's law, the rules of a town described in Aksel Sandemose's 1933 novel *En flyktning krysser sitt spor* (*A Fugitive Crosses His Tracks*). Jante's law is a collection of the townpeople's ten rules for living in social harmony. They include "You're not to think you are anything special," "You're not to convince yourself that you are better than we are," and "You're not to think you know more than we do."[14] Because of the strong collective norms in Scandinavia, the Danish government is larger than the US government as a proportion of each country's GDP.

Figure 8.8 shows the size of the government of each OECD country as a percentage of GDP. Among rich economies, Scandinavian countries and France have the largest governments, as measured by the ratio of general government spending to GDP. The United States, with a government that spends roughly 38% of GDP, is below the OECD average, which stands at 45%. Clear societal preferences are shown in the state's size. The two Asian countries in the OECD make another contrast. In these countries, the social contract is such that families are supposed to provide for family members, and being helped by the state is viewed with some

14. Aksel Sandemose, *En flyktning krysser sitt spor.* (*A Fugitive Crosses His Tracks*) Oslo: Tiden Norsk Forlag, [1933] New York: A. A. Knopf (1936), 136–137.

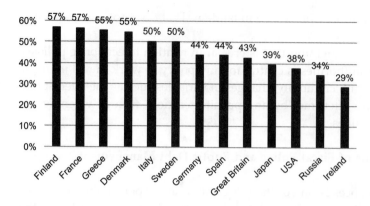

Figure 8.8
Ratio of government spending to GDP for selected OECD countries, 2015
Source: OECD, 2017, https://data.oecd.org/gga/general-government-spending.htm.

shame. The result is that Japan and South Korea have relatively smaller governments than European countries. What is undeniable is that for most countries, the size of the government has been getting bigger. The United States is a good example. In the first quarter of the twentieth century, government spending averaged 10% of GDP. This more than doubled for the period leading to 1950. From 1950 to 1975, the average went from 22% to 27%, growing to one third of national income by the end of the century. The average for the twenty-first century, so far, has been 37%.[15]

Only extremely poor countries have small governments, relative to GDP. In countries like Afghanistan, Bangladesh, Mali, and Honduras, to name a few, governments spend less than 20% of GDP. Normally, poor countries tax and spend little. Barriers to raising taxes include the lack of legitimacy, credibility, and commitment of the government. This is one of the reasons that Zimbabwe went through hyperinflation in the mid-2000s. Without legitimacy and credibility to tax its poor constituents, the Zimbabwean government resorted to printing money to finance its bulging deficit. At one point, the government was spending the equivalent of 98% of GDP but had no power (or reason) to tax as much.

The size of the government matters for economic policy. Chiefly, the capacity of the government to change taxes and decide on public spending is what makes fiscal policy possible. With its fiscal policy, the government uses its discretion over taxes and spending to try to affect economic activity. The instruments of fiscal policy can address either the revenue side or the spending side. On the revenue

15. Esteban Ortiz-Ospina and Max Roser "Public Spending," OurWorldInData.org, 2017, https://ourworldindata.org/public-spending.

side, when governments decide on the amount of taxes they want to collect, they change the disposable income of households and corporations. Raising taxes discourages economic activity, and decreasing them should favor it. On the spending side, by increasing public investment, governments can affect aggregate demand, reducing it if they decide to decrease this kind of expenditure.

Public debt management refers to the actions of governments regarding the trajectory of public debt. Policymakers affect the debt through the primary deficit and the interest rate. The higher the deficit and the amount of interest, the faster the debt rises. Context dependency kicks in through debt dynamics. The faster public debt grows, the less credible officials become, and the smaller the space for more spending. Nevertheless, a sole focus on debt reduction limits public spending to smooth out a recession. It is clear that more responsible governments are more credible and have more scope for action when needed. But public budgets are messy affairs with a plethora of interest groups fighting over the limited public resources. Some say the government should concentrate on new roads or give raises to pensioners. Corporations fight for lower taxes. Public employees feel that they deserve higher wages. Formulating and implementing economic policy is never simple. It is easy, from a distance, to proclaim that country X or Y should enact austerity measures, but it is much harder to decide where public spending should actually be cut or which new tax should be introduced.

Indonesia and the Link between Credibility and Fiscal Policy

Recessions often are self-reinforcing, sometimes because of public-debt dynamics. When a country enters a recession, its tax revenues fall, increasing the public deficit. If governments reduce spending to match the shrinking revenue, aggregate demand shifts to the left, fueling the recession. Responsible governments manage their finances anti-cyclically by saving in boom periods and spending in lean times.

Credibility is even more important for emerging countries because their institutions are usually weaker than those in developed countries. Rich countries have an advantage in terms of trust. It is easier to accept a huge deficit from the Japanese government than from the Honduran government.

An illustration comes from Indonesia. The country grew less than expected in 2015, which created a shortfall in tax revenue. The budget as a share of GDP came in at –2.5% in 2015 versus the government's initial projection of –1.9%.[16] The country has a semi-balanced-budget law that requires the public deficit to be no higher than 3% of GDP. What happens when a country like Indonesia is close to

---

16. BMI Research, "Economic Analysis: Fiscal Deterioration to Weigh on Growth—May 2016," *South East Asia* 2 (April 2016), http://www.asia-monitor.com/economic-analysis-fiscal-deterioration-weigh -growth-may-2016.

this limit? If the economy is doing badly, there is a strong incentive for the government to try to jumpstart economic activity. But a fiscal stimulus would at first make the deficit go over its constitutional limit.

This is where time inconsistency kicks in. Countries design rules to constrain governments' actions to acquire credibility. Those rules are tested in difficult times. The tradeoff for Indonesian authorities is simple: either try to reap short-term benefits and give up the constitutional limit on the size of the public deficit, or contain the growth of the deficit and ride out the economic downturn, building credibility for future government actions. What would you do?

Neutral Tax Reforms in the United States

In 2017, Donald Trump became the forty-fifth president of the United States. Both the US House of Representatives and the US Senate were under the control of his political party, the Republicans. One of the policies proposed by the new government was to enact a neutral tax reform. What would such a proposal entail, and what are the costs and benefits of tax reforms?

There are four main drivers for a tax reform: facilitating economic growth, influencing income inequality, increasing efficiency, and changing resource allocation. Tax cuts on households and corporations increase disposable income and should lead to higher aggregate demand and faster growth. Differentiating tax brackets, reducing subsidies, and simplifying the tax code have distributive effects that depend on who gets taxed more and who gets taxed less.

A neutral tax reform aims to rearrange the tax system in a way that keeps tax revenue constant. A true neutral tax reform does not have a significant effect on short-run economic growth, but it can generate prosperity if done right. For instance, the American tax system is particularly complicated. It provides many tax breaks, and people and corporations spend significant resources to reduce their tax payments. A tax reform that simplifies the tax code but does not change the total amount collected may enhance economic efficiency. American citizens spend an inordinate amount of time filling out their personal tax returns. Meanwhile, Estonian residents can complete their tax returns in mere minutes.

Corporations and people could shift resources allocated to tax avoidance to other endeavors that are more productive. There would be no short-term gains, but there possibly would be long-term benefits. But this possibility hinges on the ability of the US government to avoid the pressure from groups of interest that have tax breaks built into the existing tax code.

The design of tax systems has a significant impact on income inequality. When governments decide how much to tax rich and poor people, they end up defining the disposable income of households. One of the reasons that income distribution is different in Scandinavia than in the United States is that each country chooses distinct tax structures. For individuals, the highest marginal federal tax rate is 56% in Denmark and 37% in the United States, before deductions are taken into account. This difference is much higher when we analyze the effective tax rate. The average Americans pay around 10% to 12% of their income in federal income tax, while the average Danes fork out something like 38% to 42% of their income to fund the government. Tax reforms also influence how resources are allocated in terms of their potential impact on the environment.

From microeconomics, we know that economic activity generates positive and negative externalities. On the negative side, few results are more deleterious than the impact on the environment (whether locally in the shape of pollution or globally in the form of climate change). In 1914, for example, US greenhouse gas emissions totaled 6,870 million metric tons of carbon dioxide equivalents.[17] Markets cannot capture most of that because the direct effects on costs and prices are low. Attempts (like the Kyoto Protocol) to design global markets in prices that reflect environmental effects have failed. Taxes have an important impact on the behavior of corporations and consumers. Most countries subsidize oil production, for example, and sometimes do so quite heavily. If they moved to taxing its production or use, there would be a significant impact on fossil fuel emissions. Tax reform is an opportunity to change incentives in terms of inequality of the impact of economic activity on society in general and the environment in particular.

A proposal for a neutral tax reform may affect three social welfare variables—potential growth, income inequality, and the sustainability of economic activity as measured by its impact on the environment. It should be designed with these goals in mind. More important, public authorities should answer the following question when they propose a tax reform: what is their goal in terms of income inequality or the capture of negative externalities? This is certainly measurable, at least in terms of its short-run effects.

On December 22, 2017, President Trump signed the "Tax Cuts and Jobs Act" into law. The Congressional Budget Office estimated that the tax reform would increase the deficits over the 2018–2027 period by US$ 1.4 trillion. For the reform to be truly neutral it would need to generate enough economic growth to offset this amount.[18] Most likely, this reform will not be neutral; it also gives more tax cuts to the affluent, illustrating the distributive choices of governments.

---

17. US Environmental Protection Agency, "U.S. Greenhouse Gas Inventory Report: 1990–2014," EPA, https://www.epa.gov/ghgemissions/us-greenhouse-gas-inventory-report-1990-2014.
18. Congressional Budget Office, "Estimated Deficits and Debt under the Chairman's Amendment in the Nature of a Substitute to H.R. 1, the Tax Cuts and Jobs Act," CBO, https://www.cbo.gov/publication/53297.

II Economic Policy in a Global Context

9 The Foreign Currency Market and Macroeconomic Repercussions

In this chapter,
- The exchange rate and its economic impacts
- The balance of payments and financial flows around the world
- The mechanics of a flexible currency regime
- Brexit and the effect on currency markets
- Structural trade deficits and their consequences

China has been accused of manipulating its currency since the early 2000s, but whether directly or indirectly, every country manipulates its money to a certain degree. The US dollar rises and falls on pronouncements from the Federal Reserve about interest rates, and the same happens with the euro and the actions of the ECB. What matters is whether the manipulation negatively affects the rest of the world. Since 2014, there have been no such effects from China, and we are going to see why.

For most people who lived in Brazil in the 1980s, going abroad was a distant dream. The country suffered from successive currency crises, and the Brazilian currency (the country had five of them in eight years) held little value when compared to stronger foreign currencies. Most Brazilians wanted to hold US dollars as protection against inflation. Eventually, the country ran out of foreign reserves and defaulted on its external debt. Today, however, Brazil has free capital flows, and people can move their money in and out of the country freely. In many countries, however, capital controls are the norm. (For instance, each Chinese citizen is allowed to send only US$50,000 per year outside of the country, with some exceptions.) In terms of economic policy, what countries do locally has rippling effects around the world.

So far, this book has dealt with a closed economy in which monetary and fiscal policies have consequences over local markets and there are no links to other countries. Yet globalization matters and countries are more interconnected than ever, with spillover effects from the myriad changes in international markets. We now move to integrate national economies with the rest of the world.

9.1   Exchange Rates and Their Economic Impacts

The exchange rate is the number of units of one currency that equal a unit of another currency. There is no universal way to quote exchange rates, but when talking about two rates, people usually use as the base currency the one with the higher value. For instance, it is common to state the price of the Japanese yen in terms of the US dollar but the price of the dollar in terms of the euro. In this way, ¥110 per US$1 and US$1.13 per €1 are much more common than the equivalent US$0.009 per ¥1 and €0.88 per US$1.

Two different currencies can be thought of as two simple goods, such as coffee and tea. An exchange rate is the relative price of these two goods. Exchange-rate movements mean that the relative price of currencies is changing. Coffee can become either more expensive or cheaper than tea. A more expensive coffee is the same as stating that coffee has appreciated against tea, and a cheaper coffee is the same as saying that it has been devalued in relation to tea. Appreciation happens when one currency becomes stronger, and depreciation means that it is now weaker compared to other currencies. For instance, if the exchange rate were to change to ¥100 per US$1 instead of ¥110 per US$1, then the yen would appreciate against the dollar because one US dollar could buy less Japanese currency. If the euro were to be traded at US$1.10 per €1 as opposed to US$1.13 per €1, then the European currency would have devalued against the dollar because it would be buying less in terms of greenbacks.

Figure 9.1 shows the conventional way to display exchange-rate movements over time. The Canadian and the Australian dollar are expressed per US dollar, and the euro and the British pound are shown as an amount of US dollar per euro and per pound.

Depreciations and appreciations are important because they affect social welfare. Currency devaluations generate inflation. Depreciation results in higher price levels by changing the prices of imported final goods, imported intermediary goods, and export goods in the local market. For a company that imports final and intermediary goods, its costs are mainly in a foreign currency, and its revenues are in the local currency. As the local currency devalues, costs go up, which results in lower supply and higher prices. If a bottle of wine costs US$10 in the international market and the yen moves from ¥100 to ¥120 per US$1, for example, then the price of this bottle of wine in the Japanese market will tend to jump from ¥1,000 to ¥1,200. Because this increase is spread over all imports, inflation rises.

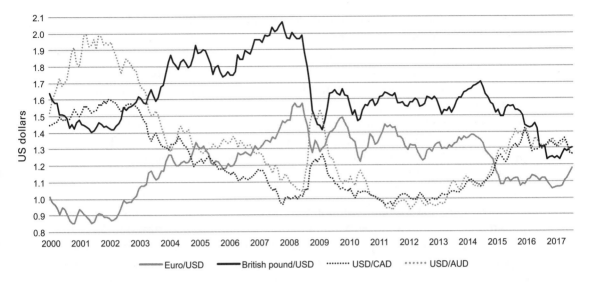

Figure 9.1
Exchange rates between the US dollar and four other currencies: Euro, British pound, Canadian dollar, and Australian dollar, 2000 to 2017
Source: Federal Reserve of St. Louis, 2017, https://fred.stlouisfed.org/categories/95.

The same rationale applies to intermediary goods: as foreign currency gets more expensive, costs of imported intermediary goods pressure the costs for the companies that use them, supply goes down, and prices soar. Finally, as the local currency devalues, exports become more attractive, the supply of tradable goods in the local market shrinks, and prices go up until there are no arbitrage opportunities. The converse also is true. Currency appreciation results in deflationary pressure. Stronger currencies make imports and the local price of export goods cheaper. This is why many countries, when faced with high inflation, try policies that would strengthen their currencies (more on this later).

The impact of currency movements on growth comes through changes in aggregate demand. Now that the economy is open,

$$Y = C + I + G + X - IM,$$

where Y is GDP or total output, C is consumption, I is investment, G is government expenditure, X is exports, and IM is imports ($X - IM$ is also referred to as Net Exports, NX, or balance of trade). Exchange-rate movements echo the total exports and imports, with devaluations jolting exports and appreciations squeezing imports.

The impact of exchange-rate depreciation on the balance of trade comes from the relation between the price of foreign currency and exporters and importers. When a currency depreciates, for example, it creates an incentive for companies to export more or enter the international market. It also makes imports more expensive in the local market. For now, the relationship between exchange-rate movements, exports, and imports is relevant for determining the path of aggregate demand over time. (Later, we allow huge currency movements to affect aggregate supply.)

Here is a simple framework for understanding the economic impacts of currency movements: when currencies become weaker (devalue or depreciate), GDP growth tends to accelerate because of rising exports, but it brings an inflationary pressure; as currencies become stronger (appreciate), growth should slow down but so should inflation.

Currency movements affect growth and inflation, but they do not happen instantaneously. The impact on inflation comes before changes on economic growth. Although imports become more expensive as soon as importers have to replenish inventories, companies cannot automatically change the amount they export. It takes some time for currency signals to affect production and marketing decisions. The difference in lag is particularly important during a currency crisis.

9.2   The Foreign Currency Market

The foreign currency market is a representation of the myriad of reasons that locals and foreigners have to conduct transactions in other currencies in a local economy. Both Chinese and foreign economic agents, for example, might demand or supply US dollars in the Chinese market. Companies may want to invest in other countries, local consumers may buy imported goods, and tourists may spend money abroad. Each transaction in a currency is recorded in a country's balance of payments (BoP). By analyzing the changes in the BoP over time, we can identify situations of external fragility, the effects of currency crises, and the mechanisms through which governments intervene in foreign exchange markets. The dynamics of the balance of payments are analyzed in section 9.3, but for now, the only necessary assumption is that all possible reasons for transactions in foreign currency in a local market are expressed by simple demand and supply functions. For the sake of simplicity, all transactions are recorded in only one foreign currency, the US dollar, in effect the world currency. For instance, the State Administration of Foreign Exchange in China presents data for the Chinese balance of payments in two currencies—the local renminbi and the US dollar. It does not represent the BoP in euros, Japanese yens, or any other currency. Most countries do not even go to the trouble of providing the BoP in local currency, publishing data only in US dollars. Figure 9.2 shows a simple representation of the Chinese foreign currency market.

In the United States, because the Federal Reserve issues the world currency, the supply and demand for foreign currency is a representation of the holdings of the

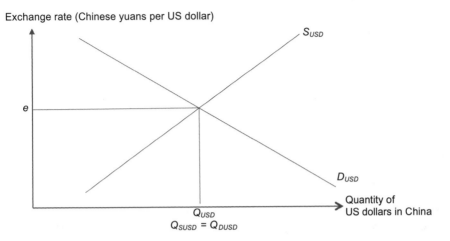

Exchange rate (Chinese yuans per US dollar)

Figure 9.2

American currency by foreigners. In that sense, the US dollar market can be thought of as being made up of two parts—the dollars floating around the US economy and the holdings of US dollars by foreigners. Nonresidents (including individuals, companies, and countries) hold US dollars as a means of carrying out trade, offshore financial transactions, tourism, or simply as a store of value. Some countries, like Ecuador, use the American legal tender as their own currency. As dollars flow into or out of the US economy, the quantity of US dollars in the world market does not change. For Ecuador, the effect is different, and capital flows determine the money supply in the country.[1]

Foreign exchange markets determine the ratio between two currencies. At first, keeping track of appreciations and depreciations in a supply and demand frame-

1. The quantity of money in a country is the total medium of exchange at the disposal of businesses and people. In countries like Ecuador, whose legal tender is the US dollar, there is a strict link between the money market and the foreign currency market. Whenever an Ecuadorian exporter sells its products, it brings US dollars into the country, and thus the money supply rises. For most countries, the money and the foreign currency markets are clearly divided. If a Saudi Arabian exporter sells its products and wants to use the proceeds to pay its employees, it needs to exchange US dollars for Saudi riyals. The company conducts this transaction in the foreign currency market. The same exporter can get a loan in the market for loanable funds. Finally, because it needs riyals so it can pay employees and suppliers, it demands money. By taking a loan to produce something for external consumption, this company demands money and funds from the money market and the loanable funds market and supplies US dollars in the foreign currency market.

In the economics of global business, markets are interconnected, which public authorities need to take into account when designing and implementing economic policies. All policies take effect in more than one market. When you read a headline stating that "The central bank increased the interest rate to contain inflationary pressure," the hike in the interest rate has a clear goal, but it also affects different markets before it brings about its intended response.

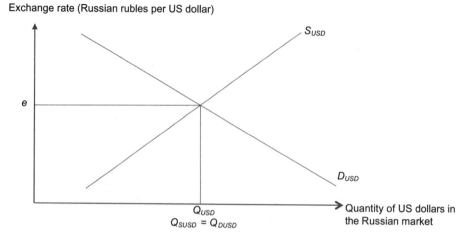

Figure 9.3

work is tricky, but it becomes easier when the way the relative prices of currencies are commonly shown is understood.

As an example, let's assume higher capital inflows (US dollars) to the Russian economy because of a strong performance of Russian exporters. What happens to the exchange rate between the US dollar and the Russian ruble? Figure 9.3 assumes a freely floating exchange rate.

Capital inflows would shift the relative supply of US dollars, moving it from S_{USD} to S'_{USD}. The result is an appreciation of the ruble (from e to e'), with more foreign currency in the local market (Q to Q') (figure 9.4).

The best resource for exchange rate data in the world is probably the Federal Reserve of St. Louis. Figure 9.5 shows the relative price of the US dollar against a basket of currencies, weighted by their trade relevance, over a twenty-two-year period (1985 to 2017).

A trade-weighted index compares a country's currency with those of its most important trade partners. For instance, the most important trade partners for the United States are Europe, Japan, China, and Mexico. A trade-weighted index puts distinct weights to an average of the euro, yen, yuan, and peso. A higher index means that the US dollar is strengthening against the currencies of its trade partners, and lower values indicate a weakening of the greenback.

The dollar strengthened from 1996 to 2002, depreciated from 2002 to 2008, and then sharply appreciated again after the great financial crisis. Even though the crisis started in the United States, economic agents still considered the American economy to be safe (relative to the rest of the world) in times of great volatility.

Exchange rate (Russian rubles per US dollar)

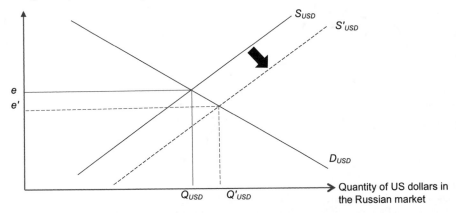

Figure 9.4

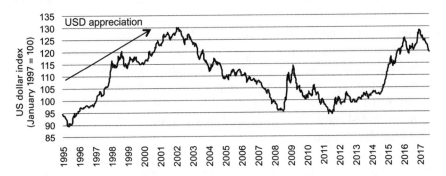

Figure 9.5
The trade-weighted US dollar index (weekly, not seasonally adjusted), 1995 to 2017
Source: Federal Reserve of St. Louis, 2017, https://fred.stlouisfed.org/series/TWEXBMTH.

This confidence led investors to park their money in the safest-possible assets, including US treasury bonds, a phenomenon called "a flight to safety." Higher capital inflows to the US economy weakened most currencies relative to the US dollar.

Brexit and the Weakening of the British Pound

Brexit (the word *British* combined with *exit*) can be considered a relatively unexpected shock to the British economy. In a referendum held on June 23, 2016, expectations were thwarted when those who voted for the United Kingdom to leave the European Union (the leavers) won over those who voted to remain (the

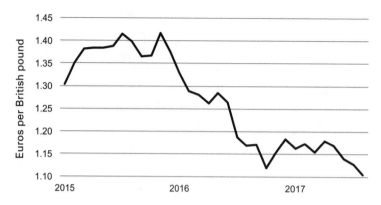

Figure 9.6
Exchange-rate, Euros per British pound, 2015 to 2017
Source: Federal Reserve of St. Louis, 2017, https://fred.stlouisfed.org/categories/95.

remainers). Given that the referendum results were a surprise, what should happen with the British pound?

Most economists, business leaders, and hedge fund managers felt that leaving the EU would be a losing proposition for the United Kingdom. One way to confirm this is by tracking the movement of the pound versus the euro from the announcement of the referendum (in January 2013) until the voting day (in June 2016) and afterward. If investors believed that leaving the EU would benefit the UK, then the pound should have become stronger after the Brexit vote. In fact, the opposite happened (figure 9.6).

The pound depreciated a bit against the rest of the world's currencies in the months before the referendum. But it dropped precipitously after the referendum's results showed that the majority of voters favored Brexit.

We can safely conclude that most investors acted on their belief that Brexit was bad for the British economy. As money flowed out of the UK, the euro strengthened. Figure 9.7 compares the value of the pound against the euro at the end of January 2016 with its value one year later.

In January 2016, 1 pound bought 1.325 euros. With the Brexit vote, the euro appreciated by over 10% against the British currency. If the leavers are right and leaving the EU will lead to future prosperity, then, all things being equal, the pound should recover its value against the euro. But it is easy to predict that it will take some time for 1 pound to buy 1.4 euros again, as it last did in November 2015.

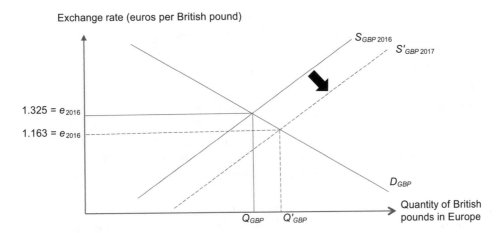

Figure 9.7

9.3   Exchange Rate Determination and the Balance of Payments

In the foreign currency market, supply and demand are affected by the various reasons that agents require or offer US dollars in the local market. For instance, US dollars are used by exporters and importers, by tourists who travel to and from the local market, by foreign companies that invest locally, and by national companies that become multinational. All these reasons are expressed in an international standard accounting system called the balance of payments (BoP).

A country's balance of payments system registers and classifies all entries and exits of foreign currency into subaccounts. Those accounts are directly related to the supply and demand for foreign currency. The BoP is the sum of all transactions between residents and nonresidents over a particular period, usually a year. For instance, when an exporter sells foreign currency from its sales to pay its employees, this transaction is registered as an entry of foreign currency (supply) due to exports, which is part of the trade account. To calculate the balance of trade, a country adds up all the entries of foreign currency from its exports and subtracts the exit of foreign currency from its imports. An exporter has costs in the local currency and revenues in foreign currency. When such a company sells goods abroad, the foreign currency received needs to be changed into the local currency. Importers, on the other hand, pay for goods in foreign currency and obtain their revenue in the local currency.[2]

2. "The balance of payments is a statistical statement that summarizes transactions between residents and nonresidents during a period. It consists of the goods and services account, the primary income account, the secondary income account, the capital account, and the financial account. Under the

The balance of payments has three main categories—current, financial, and capital accounts. The current account shows the flows of goods, services, primary income, and secondary income between residents and nonresidents. The capital account shows the credit and debit entries for nonproduced, nonfinancial assets and capital transfers between residents and nonresidents. The financial account shows net acquisition and disposal of financial assets and liabilities. The sum of the balances in the current and capital accounts represents the net lending (surplus) or net borrowing (deficit) of the economy with the rest of the world. This is conceptually equal to the net balance of the financial account. In other words, the financial account measures how the net lending to or borrowing from nonresidents is financed.

The balance of trade (exports minus imports) and all service flows—like tourism, royalties from patents, profits from foreign direct investment (FDI), and interest from international loans—are then part of the current account. When money flows in or goes out for the ownership of assets, either financial or physical, it then is part of the capital account. For instance, foreign direct investment is a capital transaction because it means that nonresidents are investing in local production.

When profits from these ventures flow back to headquarters, they are counted on the balance of services and income. All kinds of investments generate flows. An industrial plant brings profits, a loan brings interest, and technology brings royalties. The link between the initial capital expenditure (which is a measure of stock) and its later flows is called *service*. Royalties, which repay investment in technology or effort put into writing a book, are the expected flows from these kinds of investment. It is useful to separate any kind of investment into two components—the main expenditure (which is a measure of stock) and the flows that it creates. When an investment depreciates, it is worth less, suggesting that it can generate fewer flows. Loans (stock) generate interest (flow). Loans can be amortized over time, which means that the principal of the loan is being paid. After a loan is partially amortized, the amount of future interest is reduced.

Income flows and outflows are related to goods and services that are "consumed," whereas changes in stocks are perennial. Again, when a company builds a factory in another country, it changes the stock of assets in that country. Initially, there is a capital account (FDI) inflow that should later create outflows, registered in the balance of services and income (profits) (table 9.1).

---

double-entry accounting system that underlies the balance of payments, each transaction is recorded as consisting of two entries and the sum of the credit entries and the sum of the debit entries is the same. ... The different accounts within the balance of payments are distinguished according to the nature of the economic resources provided and received." International Monetary Fund, *Balance of Payments and International Investment Position Manual*, 6th ed. (Washington, DC: IMF 2009), 28.

Table 9.1
Example of a balance of payments: Current account, capital account, financial account, and errors and omissions

Account categories	Value (billions of US dollars)
Current account	
Balance on goods (net exports)	45.1
Exports	137.8
Imports	92.7
Balance on services	−9.4
Travel	−1.4
Transportation	−3.1
Operational leasing	−4.9
Other	0.0
Primary income	−27.0
Wages	0.2
Interest	−10.8
Dividends	−16.4
Secondary income	4.3
Current account balance	13.0
Capital account	
Capital account transactions balance	0.2
Financial account	
Investments, assets	35.6
Direct investment assets	28.8
Bank assets	0.9
Other assets	5.8
Investments, liabilities	53.0
Direct investment liabilities	19.4
Equity and investments fund shares	7.7
Debt securities issued in the country	11.0
Long-term loans and debt securities issued abroad	0.6
Disbursements	43.1
Debt securities, public	5.5
Debt securities, private	10.4
Direct loans	18.6
Other loans	8.7
Amortizations	42.5
Debt securities, public	18.7
Debt securities, private	6.9
Direct loans	8.8
Other loans	8.1
Short-term loans and debt securities issued abroad	−0.4
Other liabilities	14.6

Table 9.1 (continued)

Account categories	Value (billions of US dollars)
Financial derivatives, assets and liabilities	0.0
Reserve assets	30.6
Financial account balance	13.1
Errors and omissions	
Errors and omissions balance	–0.1

Exchange rate (*x* units of local currency per US dollar)

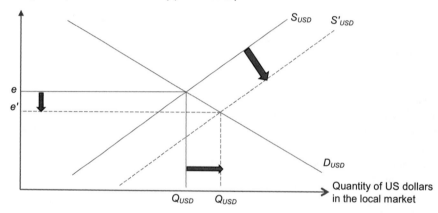

Figure 9.8

The balance of payments is by design always balanced. Analytically, if there is no statistical discrepancy (errors and omissions), then

Changes in reserve assets = Changes in current + capital + other financial accounts.

In table 9.1, there is a change in reserve assets of roughly US$30.5 billion, a result of positive current, capital, and financial accounts. We will see later that this is the result of government intervention in the foreign currency market.

In the balance of payments, we can identify all currency movements flowing into and out of the country. These movements are a representation of supply and demand and the reason that exchange rates move. If a country now exports more, the increase in exports (*X*) results in foreign capital inflow and thus a pressure on the currency to strengthen (figure 9.8). As supply goes up from S_{USD} to S'_{USD}, there is more foreign currency in the local market (from Q_{USD} to Q'_{USD}), and the local currency appreciates from *e* to *e'*.

In another example, let us assume that households and businesses have less confidence in the local government and feel that they would be better served

Exchange rate (*x* units of local currency per US dollar)

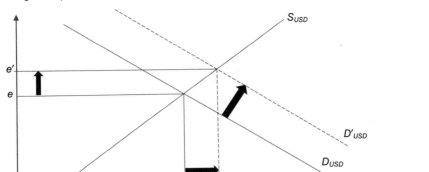

Figure 9.9

by moving their money abroad. The result would be an outflow of foreign currency through the capital account (short-term capital) and a currency devaluation (figure 9.9).

As demand goes up from D_{USD} to D'_{USD}, more foreign currency is used (from Q_{USD} to Q'_{USD}) and the local currency depreciates from e to e' until agents stop sending money abroad. Currency movements are a result of the various transactions between residents and nonresidents, all accounted for in the balance of payments.

So far, the local economy has been assumed to have a flexible exchange rate. In this kind of currency regime, the relative price of the local currency varies with supply and demand, and over time, its value reflects the strength of the national economy compared with the rest of the world. Currencies fluctuate according to the different path of their economies. There is neither an excess supply or demand for foreign currency.

Japan is a model of successful industrial, economic, and social development and illustrates how the relative prices of local currencies fluctuate according to the relative strength of the economy. From the 1950s to the early 1990s, the Japanese economy grew at an annual rate of more than 7%, an extraordinary achievement at the end of which Japan emerged as the second-largest economy in the world. The financial crisis in 1991 ushered a stagnation era, however, that has been plaguing the country ever since. From 1971 to 1991, the yen appreciated substantially against the US dollar—from ¥357 per dollar in 1971 to less than ¥120 per dollar in 1991 (figure 9.10). Since then, the yen has fluctuated within the ¥79 to ¥130 per dollar interval.

Figure 9.10
Exchange-rate, Japanese yens per US dollar, 1971 to 2016
Source: Federal Reserve of St. Louis, 2017, https://fred.stlouisfed.org/series/EXJPUS.

9.4   The Mechanics of the Balance of Payments under Flexible Exchange Rates

If the exchange rate is fully flexible—a relatively rare occurrence in the world—then the current, financial, and capital accounts balance each other out, and there are no changes in foreign reserves held by national central banks. Because the balance of payments is a representation of the foreign exchange market, under flexible prices the quantities of foreign currency demanded and supplied converge as the price fluctuates.

Throughout the business cycle, the local exchange rate devalues as recession hits and appreciates as the economy expands. In this sense, exchange rates are anticyclical. Consider foreign investment, for example. As the economy expands, more international capital flows into the country, pressuring the currency to appreciate. The converse is also true: as the economy cools, capital flows out of the country, and the currency weakens.

The present framework also allows the analysis of exogenous shocks to the local economy, transmitted through the foreign currency market. For instance, during the commodities supercycle, the demand for goods from Latin American and Australia exploded, and local currencies greatly appreciated against the major currencies of the world. Another example comes from countries that start investing abroad. In the short run, there is a devaluation pressure from capital outflows. Later, when the profits are repatriated, the currency should get stronger. If South Korea has a structural export surplus, for example, under a flexible exchange rate the South Korean won should appreciate until either the surplus is gone or there is a counterbalancing effect from the other accounts in the balance of payments.

Interactions between countries affect exchange rates. The main transmission channels of globalization are the trade and financial channels. A recession in China affects the rest of the world through the trade channel. Its trade partners suffer a decrease in the demand for their products, lose exports, and their currencies should weaken. Another example, to be explored later, is on the financial side. If the Federal Reserve raises the target interest rate in the US market, investors from around the world move part of their assets to America in search of higher yields. The dollar appreciates. The great disinflation of the early 1980s, when the Fed funds rate reached 20% per year, absorbed huge amounts of capital from the rest of the world, triggering massive devaluations in many countries. Israel, Chile, and Argentina all suffered currency crises after the US rate hike.

9.5   Structural Deficits or Surpluses in the Balance of Payments Accounts

In many countries, features of the local economy show up in the balance of payments as structural deficits or surpluses. The first means a constant outflow of foreign currency that, if not compensated by inflows in other accounts, leads to an enduring devaluation pressure. A structural surplus is associated with perennially strong currency.

Germany, South Korea, and Norway are good examples of countries with structural surpluses in their trade accounts (figure 9.11). Positive net exports are a constant source of pressure for the appreciation of the euro, the South Korean won, and the Norwegian krone. The United Kingdom and the United States have structural trade deficits and are net importers. This in itself would lead to potentially weak currencies, but capital inflows from other accounts make the British pound and the US dollar relatively strong.

Since the 2000s, Germany's trade surplus has been increasing, and in 2007, it surpassed US$200 billion per year (figure 9.12). Meanwhile, the US trade deficit has not yet been lower than US$300 billion in this century and should continue to be large as America acts as a sponge for the world's products.

Even though Germany and the United States have the highest surpluses and deficits in absolute terms among the sample of five countries shown in figure 9.12, in relative terms Norway has by far the most significant imbalance. From 2000 to 2010, Norway's trade surplus was worth approximately 14% of GDP annually. This creates a continuous pressure for a strong krone, which makes Norway one of the most expensive countries in the world.

Volodymyr Tulin and Kornélia Krajniák estimate the extent to which prices in Norway are higher than in other countries,[3] and the Big Mac Index (a lighthearted measure of relative prices that considers the McDonald's sandwich as

3. Volodymur Tulin and Kornélia Krajnyák, "How Expensive Is Norway? New International Relative Price Measures," IMF Working Paper WP/10/133, International Monetary Fund, June 2010.

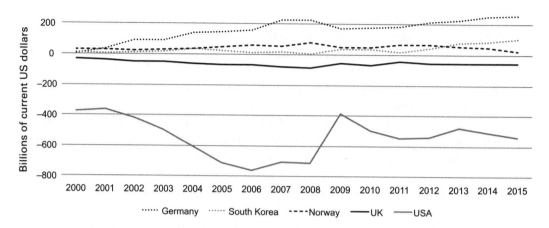

Figure 9.11
Balance of trade in Germany, South Korea, Norway, the United Kingdom, and the United States (in current US dollars), 2000 to 2015
Source: World Bank, 2017, https://data.worldbank.org/indicator/BX.GSR.GNFS.CD and https://data.worldbank.org/indicator/BM.GSR.GNFS.CD.

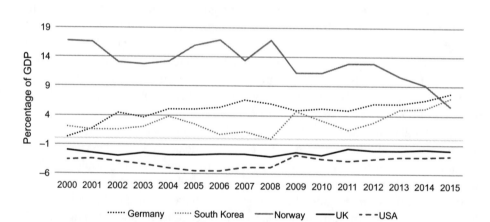

Figure 9.12
Balance of trade in Germany, South Korea, Norway, the United Kingdom, and the United States (as a percentage of GDP), 2000 to 2015
Source: World Bank, 2017, https://data.worldbank.org/indicator/NE.RSB.GNFS.ZS.

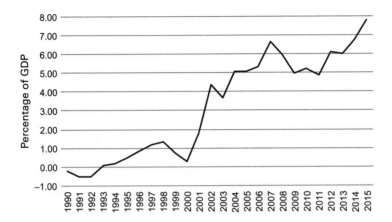

Figure 9.13
German balance of trade (as a percentage of GDP), 1990 to 2015
Source: World Bank, 2017, https://data.worldbank.org/indicator/NE.RSB.GNFS.ZS.

homogeneous among nations) constantly shows Norway as the most expensive in the world.[4] Most of Norway's structural trade surplus comes from oil, as the country boasts massive reserves. As oil prices fell in 2014 and 2015, the trade surplus declined, but it is still much higher than that of other OECD countries.

Currencies move according to the relative strength of the economies, but changes also come from sectoral imbalances. For instance, the German economy has had an increasing trade surplus since the early 1990s, which would normally strengthen the currency, as in the case of Norway (figure 9.13). Because Germany no longer has its own currency and is part of the eurozone, its surplus causes the euro to appreciate. Much of the euro's relative strength is due to Germany's structural surplus in its current account. This surplus seems nowadays to be a structural feature of the German economy. Remember that current account is the sum of the trade in goods (exports minus imports), the balance of services and income, and net transfers. For Germany, the balance of trade climbed from 1% of GDP in 1999 to almost 8% of GDP in 2015. Assuming for the sake of simplicity that net transfers are negligible, there are two options for the balancing of this surplus: either the financial and capital accounts would have to be negative in the same amount, or the country would be accumulating reserves, which, in fact, is exactly what happened.

The size of the German trade surplus affects all the countries in the eurozone. In October 2015, the US government used Germany as an example of a

4. "The Big Mac Index," *The Economist*, July 13, 2017, https://www.economist.com/blogs/graphic detail/2016/07/daily-chart-14.

potential threat to the global economy when it issued a report stating that Germany's current account surplus imposed "a deflationary bias for the eurozone as well as for the world economy."[5] Some authors, like Palvos Eleftheriadis, even consider the country to be a freeloader at the expense of other euro countries, even though the interconnection between international markets, local foreign exchange markets, and the complexity of a monetary union all come into play.[6] Germany is not a freeloader, but its large trade surpluses do pressure the euro to strengthen, which leads to fewer net exports by the other countries in the eurozone. Because the other eurozone countries have mostly performed poorly since the crisis, the German trade surplus is a barrier to the appreciation of the euro and the closing of the European growth gap.[7] If the other European countries were growing at their potential output, then they would welcome a German trade surplus because it would create a deflationary pressure in the eurozone. As it stands, this situation highlights the tradeoffs involved in building an integrated economic bloc.

In some emerging markets, structural deficits in the balance of services and income create an underlying devaluation pressure. Persistent deficits make countries vulnerable to currency crises (rapid and massive devaluations) that may contribute to rising inflation. The balance of services and income is composed of many subaccounts, but the most important ones are tourism, royalties, profits, and interest. Inflows from FDI and private and public loans later leave countries as profits, interest, and amortization. For instance, let's assume that a company issues corporate bonds in the international market worth US$1 million with an interest rate of 10% per year. After one year, the company pays US$200,000. In the balance of payments, the amount paid by the company is divided in two: US$100,000 refers to the interest paid, and the other US$100,000 amortizes the total owed by the company (now at US$900,000). The first amount is registered in the balance of services and income, and the second in the financial and capital accounts. The pattern for the royalties rubric is similar to others in the balance of services and income, with emerging markets displaying capital outflows due to imports of technology.

One example of a structural deficit in the balance of services and income is Brazil. For every year since 1947, outflows from services imports have been higher than inflows, with the amount growing as the country developed (figure 9.14).

5. Jason Lange, "US Says German Export Dependence Hurts Global Economy," Reuters, October 31, 2013.

6. Palvos Eleftheriades, "Why Germany Is the Eurozone's Biggest Free Rider," *Fortune*, October 22, 2014, http://fortune.com/2014/10/22/why-germany-is-the-eurozones-biggest-free-rider.

7. Mehreen Khan, "German Trade Surplus Swells to Fresh Record," *Financial Times*, May 9, 2016, http://www.ft.com/fastft/2016/05/10/german-current-account-surplus-swells-to-record.

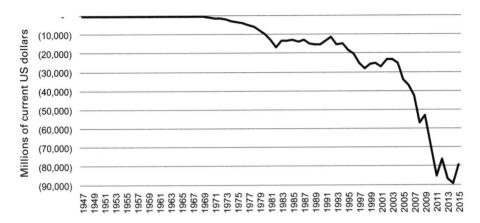

Figure 9.14
Brazil's balance of services and income (in current millions of US dollars), 1947 to 2015
Source: Brazilian Central Bank, 2017, http://www.bcb.gov.br/ftp/notaecon/balpayabpm5.zip.

From 2011 to 2016, the average annual deficit of the balance of services and income was US$75 billion.

In the 1980s, many Latin American countries went through currency crises due in part to the debt accumulated in the 1970s when borrowing was easy. The mechanism of a currency crisis is simple: as foreign money leaves, there is an upward pressure on the local currency, and devaluation leads to inflation. If money continues to leave, then further devaluations create an inflationary spiral. Compounded by the tendency of Latin American governments to run huge primary deficits, unmatched outflows to service foreign debt left the countries insolvent and led to hyperinflation in Brazil, Argentina, and Bolivia, among others. Even today, many emerging countries try to accumulate foreign reserves to use them as a cushion against sudden capital outflows. Many people in these countries believe that a country should strive to be a net exporter. In fact, countries with a structural deficit on the balance of services and income do need trade surpluses to offset capital outflows, but there is nothing inherently better about being a net exporter than a net importer (like the United States and the United Kingdom).

The dynamics of the balance of payments over time restrict the action of governments. In fact, the mismanagement of exchange-rate regimes may trigger speculative attacks, and governments sometimes face painful tradeoffs when deciding over currency policy.

10 Exchange Rate Regimes

In this chapter,

- Fixed or flexible currency regimes?
- Free or controlled capital flows?
- The US advantages of printing the world's currency
- Industrialization by import substitutions or export orientation
- Currency crises and speculative attacks

10.1 Foreign Currency Markets

Governments like the illusion of control, and nowhere is that more evident than in foreign currency (or foreign exchange, forex) markets. Very few countries allow the free trade of their currency. The main argument against such flexibility is volatility. Large inflows and outflows may result in fluctuations that would be deleterious to agents in general and exporters in particular.

Exchange rate regimes can be broadly divided into four kinds—fully flexible (or free-floating), dirty floating, fixed, and euro or dollarization. In flexible or free-floating exchange rate regimes, there is no market intervention: supply and demand in the currency market determine the exchange rate, the current account deficit or surplus approximates the capital and financial account surplus or deficit, and the exchange rate reflects the purchasing power of the residents versus non-residents. In dirty floating exchange rate regimes, central banks occasionally intervene in foreign exchange markets that otherwise fluctuate freely. In fixed exchange rate regimes, the central bank determines the nature of the peg and either the value of the local currency or an interval within which it is traded. In dollarization regimes, countries use foreign money as legal tender, abandoning their ability to print their own currency.

Central banks have to intervene constantly to keep the exchange rate stable in a fixed exchange rate regime. Sometimes, as in China, such regimes are accompanied by capital controls to improve the ability of the monetary authority to maintain the peg to other currencies.

Fixed exchange rates can be either overvalued or undervalued. When they are overvalued, as in Latin America and many Asian countries in the 1990s, the main goal is to promote price stability. In the late 1980s and early 1990s, Mexico and Argentina, two of the largest Latin American economies, experienced hyperinflation. To climb out of it, they used an overvalued peg to make imports cheaper and jumpstart a disinflation process.

Depreciated fixed exchange rate regimes, like that of China in the early 2000s, are designed to promote exports and stimulate aggregate demand, with the risk of higher inflation. Both categories of fixed exchange rate regimes have the advantage of maintaining a predictable rate of exchange between the local and foreign currencies.

Finally, countries can eschew their power over the local currency altogether and adopt a foreign currency. Additionally, a group of countries can band together and form a currency union, like the eurozone. In a currency union, a central monetary authority issues the legal tender. The European Central Bank is the central bank of the eurozone and acts as the lender of last resort in the European financial system.

In figure 10.1, nine different exchange rate systems are ranked from the one in which the monetary authority has the most autonomy (the gold standard) to the one in which it has the least autonomy (euro or dollarization). Central banks have the power to determine the local interest rate only if this is not completely offset by currency movements.

The gold standard required that the central government maintain capital controls and fix the rate between the currency and the gold reserves. The monetary base would depend solely on the gold reserves. Historically, this was the method preferred by absolutist states. In modern times, the Bretton Woods system, which lasted from shortly after the end of World War II until 1971, was a multilateral,

Figure 10.1
The relative policy autonomy of nine currency regimes

fixed exchange rate regime in which currencies were pegged to the US dollar, which in turn was pegged to the amount of gold in the reserves of the US government (this is why Fort Knox, where these gold reserves were held, was a fixture in the world's consciousness and featured in many novels and movies).

A hard peg is still the preferred option of most countries today. It requires intervention by domestic monetary authorities and a significant level of international reserves. As we move to the right on the continuum, the frequency of interventions and the required reserves tend to become lower, and they cease completely in freely floating currency systems. Some countries go even further and forsake monetary policy altogether, either by accepting more than one currency as legal tender or by abandoning the national currency altogether. Additionally, choices among these distinct regimes have implications in terms of the necessity of establishing capital controls.

10.2   Free Capital Flows and Exchange Rate Interventions

Countries can either control or allow capital movements. During the last few centuries, most countries had strict limits on the money that flowed into and out of the local economies. When the gold standard ruled and the monetary base changed with gold reserves, many countries simply forbade the export of gold.[1] At the heights of mercantilism, there were bans on the export of gold and silver, even for payments. In the twentieth century, most countries first abandoned the gold standard for the US dollar standard, and now many allow for some measure of capital movements. Usually, central banks that wish to limit capital flows establish rules about which kinds of capital are allowed to enter or leave the country. In China, for instance, most citizens can send only US$50,000 per year outside the country. In the country's balance of payments, this means that there are limits on net transfers. Furthermore, companies are not free to invest in China unless they have a local partner. Since 2014, wholly foreign-owned enterprises (WFOEs) have been allowed in China but with many restrictions. For instance, "since China still maintains foreign currency control policy, it's still advisable to choose registered capital within RMB 100,000 – RMB 500,000 as the minimum registered capital for Consulting WFOE, Service WFOE, Hi-Tech WFOE registration in Shanghai, Beijing, Shenzhen, Tianjin, Guangzhou, Hangzhou, Ningbo, Suzhou, Chengdu, Chongqing, Wuhan, Xi'an and many other cities of China. (Investor could inject the above capital within 2–10 years)."[2] The effect on the balance of payments is

1. Under a gold standard, the amount of currency in a country depends on its gold reserves, so the amount of money circulating in the economy rises and falls in line with the gold reserves.
2. "Wholly Foreign-Owned Enterprise Formation in China," *Path to China*, October 6, 2017, http://www.pathtochina.com/reg_wfoe.htm.

that foreign investment is not completely free, and the restrictions keep both the inflow and the outflow at lower levels than they would be if there were no barriers to capital movement.

In China, most foreigners cannot invest in the local stock and bond markets. Again, this means that the financial and capital accounts show less movement than they would otherwise. There are many models in which capital liberalization intensifies economic development. Verifying this relationship empirically is difficult because it is almost impossible to separate the liberalization effect from other variables to single out its effect on development. There is little consensus among economists about the optimum level of capital controls. Ross Levine, who has extensively studied the relationship between financial and economic development, favors capital-account liberalization as a precursor to long-term development.[3] Financial openness matters for economic development.[4] Yet Joseph E. Stiglitz argues that countries should have some measure of capital controls.[5] Perhaps Barry Eichengreen put it best when he wrote: "Capital liberalization, it is fair to say, remains one of the most controversial and least understood policies of our day. One reason is that different theoretical perspectives have very different implications for the desirability of liberalizing capital flows. Another is that empirical analysis has failed to yield conclusive results."[6] As with some other fundamental macroeconomic issues, economists need to plead ignorance: we simply do not know the optimal level of capital controls required to foster economic development.

What we do know is that after countries become rich, they eschew restrictions on the movement of funds. The most developed countries (the United States, the countries in the European Union, the United Kingdom, and Japan) do not limit financial flows. Some large emerging countries (like Mexico, Turkey, and Russia) liberalized their capital accounts in the 1990s. In most of the emerging world, there are barriers to the free movement of capital.

Capital controls have one important consequence. If countries establish them, there is a tradeoff in terms of the ability to intervene in the foreign exchange market and the amount of foreign capital flowing in and out of the country. If countries want to maximize the amount of foreign direct investment, then a liberalized capital account is the correct path. If their choice is the ability to influence

3. Ross Levine, "Financial Development and Economic Growth: Views and Agenda," *Journal of Economic Literature* 35, no. 2 (1997): 688–726.
4. Dennis Reinhardt, Luca Antonio Ricci, and Thierry Tressel, "International Capital Flows and Development: Financial Openness Matters," *Journal of International Economics* 91, no. 2 (2013): 235–251.
5. Joseph E. Stiglitz, "Capital Market Liberalization, Economic Growth, and Instability," *World Development* 28, no. 6 (2000): 1075–1086.
6. Barry Eichengreen, "Capital Account Liberalization: What Do Cross-Country Studies Tell Us?," *World Bank Economic Review* 15, no. 3 (2001): 341–365.

the price and the volatility of the local currency, then they are better off choosing some measures of capital restrictions.

10.3   The Mechanics of Fixed Exchange Rate Regimes

Even though there are countless types of fixed exchange rate regimes (including hard and crawling pegs and those pegged within a band), the basic mechanics are simple. Setting a predetermined amount for an exchange rate works as long as the government is willing or able to intervene in the foreign currency market. For instance, a government might determine that the local currency should appreciate against the US dollar (figure 10.2). In the case of a price ceiling that is lower than the market equilibrium, there is excess demand. Maintaining an overvalued currency is possible only as long as the monetary authority can supply foreign currency. Alternatively, it can choose to have capital controls in place that repudiate capital outflows. There are many types of controls. Here are three examples from the 1980s in Latin America: companies had to get government approval to procure foreign currency to pay for their imports, there were caps on the amount of foreign currency that residents could take while traveling abroad, and there were limits on the repatriation of profits for multinational companies.

Supplying foreign currency does not necessarily mean providing it. Future contracts, swaps, and other derivatives may also serve to provide liquidity for residents who want to hedge against the possible price movements of foreign currency. In any case, overvalued pegs last only as long as investors have confidence in the ability of the central bank to provide foreign currency.

Exchange rate (*x* units of local currency per US dollar)

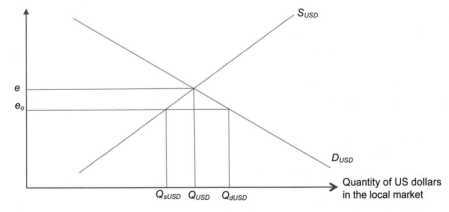

Figure 10.2

Exchange rate (*x* units of local currency per US dollar)

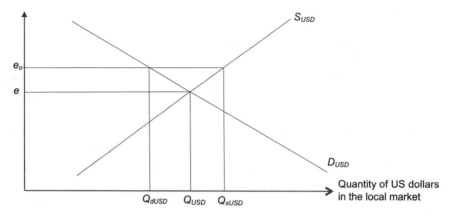

Figure 10.3

In the case of undervalued pegs, such as the Chinese renminbi (yuan) in the 2000s, central banks set the exchange rate higher than it would be kept solely by market forces (figure 10.3).

The main advantage of a depreciated peg is the incentive for export industries. Such a peg can stimulate aggregate demand through net exports at the risk of price levels going up in the domestic market (figure 10.4).

Operationally, the central bank is able to maintain a depreciated currency only if it is prepared to buy whichever quantity of foreign currency enters the local market. This, in turn, can affect the money supply because the monetary authority would pay in the local currency to acquire excess foreign currency. One way in which central banks can intervene in foreign exchange markets and have no effect on the monetary base is through the sterilization of its purchases of other currencies. The sterilization of foreign currency inflows has two steps: the central bank sells government bonds in its possession (not already in the monetary base), which decreases money supply, and the bank uses the proceeds from these sales to purchase the excess foreign currency, which expands money supply.

The sterilization of foreign currency leaves the quantity of money unchanged (figure 10.5). In the money market, the sale of government bonds by the central bank decreases money supply from MS to MS', and the interest rate rises from r to r'. As the central banks use the proceeds to buy excess foreign currency to keep the undervalued fixed exchange rate stable, money supply reverts to MS, and the interest rate returns to r.

In the end, the effects of a sterilization of capital inflows are that the reserves in foreign currency go up and the stock of public debt rises. The first effect is a

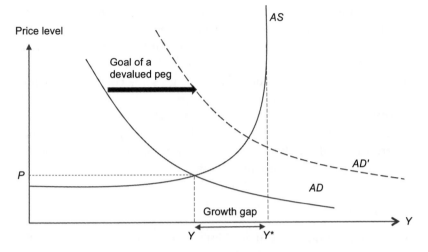

Figure 10.4

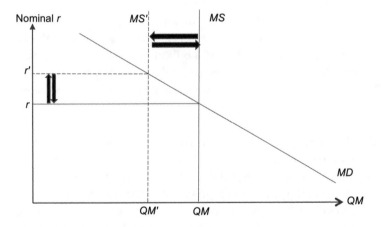

Figure 10.5

necessary condition for the stability of an undervalued fixed exchange rate regime: the central bank has to keep buying excess foreign currency. There is a cost for the sterilization policy, which is the difference between the local and international interest rates. Increases in reserves result in the central bank buying mostly US government bonds (for the sake of simplicity, although some countries also park part of their reserves in Europe or Japan, and others have built sovereign funds to lower the fiscal cost of keeping foreign reserves). The reserves earn interest based on the US interest rate. Because the central bank uses government bonds as a tool for sterilization, the public debt grows, and the financing cost of this measure is the local risk-free interest rate. In fact, the nominal fiscal cost of a sterilization policy (and in general, of keeping foreign reserves) is, annually,

$(r - r_{US})*(Reserve\ assets)$,

where r is the local interest rate, r_{US} is the US interest rate, and *Reserve assets* is the total amount of foreign reserves held by the central bank. In Brazil, for instance, foreign reserves totaled around US$370 billion in 2015. In order to finance the building of such reserves, the central bank had to issue the same amount in government bonds. The average interest rate in Brazil in 2015 was approximately 13%, and interest income for the reserves was on average 1%. The fiscal nominal cost of maintaining such reserves in 2015 was US$44.4 billion or around 2% of GDP, a high price for the country to maintain a cushion of foreign currency in the case of a currency crisis. But holding such level of reserves actually decreases the possibility of a currency crisis.

Denmark, Switzerland, and Capital Controls in Developed Countries

Denmark has its currency tied to the euro as part of its integration process with the European Union. After the great financial crisis, the Danish economy outperformed the eurozone, resulting in an average growth that was more than 1% per year higher than growth in the other eurozone countries during the 2008 to 2016 period. The result was a pressure for the appreciation of the Danish krone, in effect making the Danish peg an undervalued one (figure 10.6). If authorities had decided to abandon it, the krone would have surged against the euro and the rest of the world's currencies.

Assume that right after the crisis, the Danish peg to the euro was in equilibrium. International investors started flocking to the Danish market after 2008, given the relative strength of the Danish economy, and this expanded the supply of foreign currency (figure 10.7). As S_ϵ moves to S'_ϵ, the equilibrium exchange rate should fall from e_0 to e. Because of the peg, the price of Danish krones per euro could not fall, and the market had an oversupply of foreign currency.

Exchange rate (Danish krones per euro)

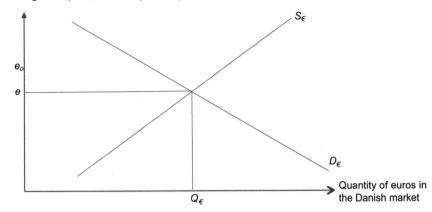

Figure 10.6

Exchange rate (Danish krones per euro)

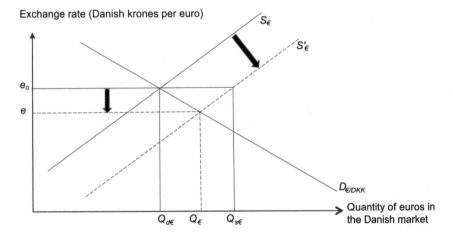

Figure 10.7

Danish authorities had four choices: decrease the interest rate to incentivize capital outflows; sterilize the entry of foreign currency; introduce capital controls; or abandon the fixed exchange rate regime, allowing the krone to fluctuate either freely or in a dirty floating system. For a while, Danish policymakers oscillated between the first two options. In 2015, Denmark had already a negative interest rate of –0.75% and large reserves of foreign currency. There was not much space for interest rates to fall further. The authorities turned to capital controls. In January 2015, Denmark suspended bond issuance to limit capital inflows.[7] Danish authorities argued that this should help reduce interest rate spreads on longer-dated bonds and limit the capital inflows, easing some of the upward pressure on the krone: "The main objective of Danmarks Nationalbank is to defend the exchange rate of the crown to the euro as a way to control inflation. It uses interest rates to make it more or less attractive to hold crowns and has a central exchange target of 7.46038 crowns to the euro, within a tolerance band of plus/minus 2.25 percent, or a rate of 7.29252 to 7.62824."[8]

Capital controls in developed markets are uncommon, but Denmark's predicament shows how difficult it is to maintain a fixed exchange rate regime in an increasingly interconnected world. Switzerland also had a peg to the euro, but public authorities grew tired of maintaining an undervalued peg. As with Denmark, given the relative strength of the Swiss economy compared with the eurozone, there was a constant influx of capital to the country. The Swiss monetary authorities dabbled with a negative nominal interest rate before turning to sterilization. Finally, the government felt that the cost of sterilizing the capital inflows and the constant pressure to decrease the interest rate further were too much to bear, and on January 15, 2015, the Swiss National Bank allowed the franc to float. In the immediate aftermath of that decision, the Swiss franc appreciated 20% against the euro.

Both Switzerland and Denmark stopped sterilizing capital inflows, and the former chose to unpeg its currency from the euro, whereas the latter imposed capital controls. These different choices are in part the result of distinct political objectives regarding integration with the rest of Europe. In a referendum in 2000, Danish citizens rejected a proposal to substitute the krone with the euro. However, Denmark is still part of the European Exchange Rate Mechanism (ERM II superseded the first ERM), which requires a peg to the euro with an interval band of 2.25% (in practice, the Danish central bank keeps the interval at which the krone

7. The announcement can be read at "Suspension of Government Bond Issuance," Dansmarks Nationalbank, January 30, 2015, http://www.nationalbanken.dk/en/pressroom/Pages/2015/01/DNN2015 21749.aspx.

8. "Denmark Raises Deposit Rate 10 bps to Minus 0.65% – Corrected," *Central Bank News*, January 7, 2016, http://www.centralbanknews.info/2016/01/denmark-raises-deposit-rate-100-bps-to.html.

can deviate from its peg to the euro to less than 1%). Denmark is also a member of the European Union. Switzerland is not a member of the EU or the ERM. Its peg to the euro was voluntary and a way to keep import and export decisions predictable for its companies when they traded with neighboring countries. When the cost of maintaining the peg became unbearable to the Swiss authorities, the decision to abandon the peg was much easier than it would have been for Danish officials.

Emerging Markets and Exchange Rate Regimes: The Case of India

In the mid-1990s, India changed its exchange rate regime. From 1947 to 1971, the Indian rupee was convertible to gold at a rate of 1 rupee per 4.15 grains of fine gold, within an interval of 1%.[9] It was de facto a gold standard, and the Royal Bank of India (RBI), the country's central bank, used the British pound to intervene in the foreign exchange market to maintain the peg between the rupee and gold. The RBI also established capital controls, enhancing its ability to maintain the peg without speculative attacks.

When Bretton Woods system of monetary management fell in 1971, the RBI pegged the rupee directly to the British pound, and this peg lasted until 1975, when the central bank replaced the pound with a broader basket of currencies. This new fixed exchange rate system lasted until 1991, when the RBI promoted a managed devaluation to contain capital outflows. It was the dawn of the age of the liberalization of capital accounts and the adoption of market-determined exchange rates, but for India it required some adjustment periods. From March 1992 to March 1993, the RBI put in place the Liberalised Exchange Rate Management System (LERMS), which consisted of a dual exchange rate system with different limits to capital outflows. Since 1996, India has had, in effect, a dirty floating system in which the RBI retains the ability to intervene in the foreign exchange market to reduce volatility (table 10.1).

As table 10.1 shows, the Reserve Bank of India intervened in foreign exchange markets every year from the beginning of the dirty floating system until the great financial crisis. During most of this period, the RBI was a net buyer of foreign currency as it tried to keep the rupee from strengthening, a sign that the Indian economy was performing better than the rest of the world. The exception was in late 2008. For the fiscal year ending in March 2009, the central bank provided extra foreign currency to keep the rupee from falling further because after the onset of the great financial crisis, money started to flow heavily from emerging markets to developed markets—a "flight to safety."

9. Pami Dua and Rajiv Ranjan, *Exchange Rate Policy and Modelling in India*, Reserve Bank of India, February 25, 2010, https://www.rbi.org.in/scripts/PublicationsView.aspx?id=12252#EXC.

Table 10.1
The Reserve Bank of India's intervention in the foreign currency market (billions of US dollars), 1995 to 2009

Year	Purchase	Sale	Net	Outstanding net forward sales or purchase (end of March)
1995–1996	$3.6	$3.9	$–0.3	—
1996–1997	11.2	3.4	7.8	—
1997–1998	15.1	11.2	3.8	$–1.8
1998–1999	28.7	26.9	1.8	–0.8
1999–2000	24.1	20.8	3.2	–0.7
2000–2001	28.2	25.8	2.4	–1.3
2001–2002	22.8	15.8	7.1	–0.4
2002–2003	30.6	14.9	15.7	2.4
2003–2004	55.4	24.9	30.5	1.4
2004–2005	31.4	10.6	20.8	0
2005–2006	15.2	7.1	8.1	0
2006–2007	26.8	0.0	26.8	0
2007–2008	79.7	1.5	78.2	14.7
2008–2009	26.6	61.5	–34.9	2.0

Source: Pami Dua and Rajiv Ranjan, *Exchange Rate Policy and Modelling in India,* Reserve Bank of India, February 25, 2010, https://www.rbi.org.in/scripts/PublicationsView.aspx?id=12252#EXC.

The dirty floating regime of Indian policymakers is one of the most common options that emerging markets choose when they abandon a pegged system. In India, the central bank feels that macroeconomic stability is more important than a freely floating currency.

10.4   Industrialization by Import Substitution versus Export-Oriented Growth

Throughout the second half of the twentieth century, countries in Asia established policies that targeted a trade surplus, and countries in Latin America, broadly speaking, developed industrialization strategies based on imports substitution. In both cases, local governments established industrial policies to foster the growth of national companies. Some were state owned, others were privately owned, and subsidies were given to some foreign-owned companies (like car-making companies in Latin America). In Asia, incentives went to export industries, like the clothing industry. In Latin America, most subsidies went to capital-intensive industries that competed with foreign imports.

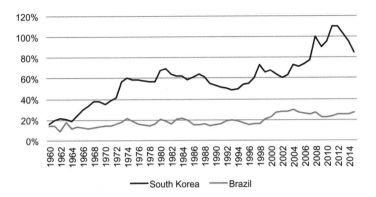

Figure 10.8
Balance of trade in Brazil and South Korea as a percentage of GDP, 1960 to 2014
Source: World Bank, 2017, https://data.worldbank.org/indicator/BN.CAB.XOKA.GD.ZS.

Industrialization by import substitution meant restricting imports in strategic sectors and subsidizing companies to build economies of scale in the absence of international competition. Export orientation was the result of subsidies to those industries that had export potential. Both approaches tried to achieve the same goals—industrialization and development.

We can see the effect of these different industrialization strategies in trade intensity data. In 1960, both South Korea and Brazil had similar patterns of trade intensity (figure 10.8). As a percentage of GDP, the sum of exports and imports of goods and services were 14.2% in Brazil and 15.7% in South Korea. The two countries were also at approximately the same level of development. In South Korea, the export-oriented industrialization process elevated the sum of exports and imports as a share of GDP to more than 100% in the 2000s, reaching an all-time high of 110% in 2012. In Brazil, trade never surpassed 30% of GDP, demonstrating how an inward industrialization strategy shows up in trade data over time.

Countries in both regions had a structural deficit in the services and income account in the balance of payments because they used foreign capital to complement local subsidies, either through FDI or by governments and companies taking loans from international banks or multilateral organizations. Remember that the services and income account is a part of the current account in the balance of payments. If there is a structural deficit, a constant outflow of foreign currency creates a pressure for the local currency to devalue. Because of this, the choice between import substitution and export-oriented growth has important implications.

Data in figure 10.9 show the cyclical patterns of the current account in Brazil and an upward trajectory that turned a deficit into surplus in South Korea. Because

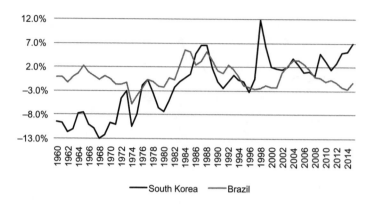

Figure 10.9
Current account balances in Brazil and South Korea as a percentage of GDP, 1960 to 2014
Source: World Bank, 2017, https://data.worldbank.org/indicator/BN.CAB.XOKA.GD.ZS.

Brazil could not rely on trade surpluses to close its deficit in the balance of services and income, there were cycles of currency crises in which the outflows were much higher than the inflows, and currency devaluations stoked inflationary processes. Debt crises were constant in Latin America, culminating in a quagmire of excessive external debt and the defaults of many countries in the 1980s.[10]

South Korea's trade surplus started to grow and eventually surpassed the deficit in the balance of services and income. Since 1997, South Korea has had continuous current-account surpluses, with the highest of them as a response to the Asian crisis of the 1990s. Countries that tried export-oriented strategies suffered less from currency crises or inflation.

10.5   The Mechanics of Foreign Reserves

Foreign reserves (reserve assets) play a major role in the macroeconomic dynamics of emerging and developed countries. China had over US$4 trillion of reserves in 2014, and in the United States, foreigners (nonresidents) held over US$6 trillion of federal debt in 2016, equivalent to 40% of its total.[11] The accumulation of reserves can be active (as in the case of countries with flexible or dirty floating regimes) or passive (as in countries with flexible exchange rates).

Active reserves can be accumulated (as in the Chinese case). With an undervalued, fixed exchange rate regime, there is a tendency to accumulate a currency

10. Jocelyn Sims and Jessie Romero, "Latin American Debt Crisis of the 1980s," *Federal Reserve History*, 2013, http://www.federalreservehistory.org/essays/latin_american_debt_crisis.
11. Marc Labonte and Jared C. Nagel, "Foreign Holdings of Federal Debt," *Congressional Research Service*, https://fas.org/sgp/crs/misc/RS22331.pdf.

Exchange rate (reals per US dollar)

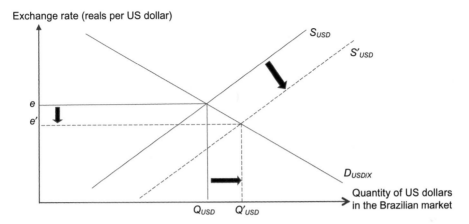

Figure 10.10

Table 10.2
Brazil's balance of payments (billions of US dollars), 2005 to 2012

Account type	2005	2006	2007	2008	2009	2010	2011	2012
Current account	13.5	13.0	0.4	−30.6	−26.3	−75.8	−77.0	−74.2
Financial and capital accounts	−9.0	17.7	87.3	33.8	73.1	125.2	135.9	93.3
Reserve assets	−4.3	−30.6	−87.5	−3.0	−46.7	−49.1	−58.6	−18.9

Source: Brazilian Central Bank, 2017, http://www.bcb.gov.br/htms/infecon/Seriehist_bpm5.asp.

surplus that can be sterilized and turned into holdings of foreign debt (mostly US treasuries in the Chinese case). Dirty floating policies can have the same result.

Brazil, for example, opened its capital and financial accounts in the mid-1990s and abandoned its overvalued, fixed exchange rate regime in early 1999, succumbing to a speculative attack. In the mid-2000s, the country experienced a boom in international demand for its products due to the commodities supercycle. The growth perspectives in different industries, the high interest rates, and the expanding stock market multiplied capital inflows. The result was an almost continuous appreciation of the Brazilian currency (figure 10.10). It fell from 3.99 reals per US dollar in 2002 to 1.54 in 2008, just before the great financial crisis. Throughout that period, the Brazilian central bank intervened hundreds of times by buying foreign currency to keep the currency from strengthening even more.

These interventions helped form the Brazilian foreign reserves, which reached over US$400 billion by the mid-2010s (table 10.2). The reserves expanded every year (a negative sign in the reserve assets category represents growth), and the

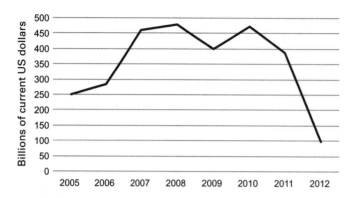

Figure 10.11
China's annual accumulation of foreign reserves (balance of payments), in billions of current US dollars, 2005 to 2012
Source: People's Bank of China, 2017, http://www.safe.gov.cn/wps/portal/english/Data/Payments.

country accumulated almost US$300 billion in reserves (the nominal sum of reserve assets from 2005 to 2012 is US$298.6 billion).

In the same period, China accumulated roughly US$2.83 trillion in reserves, averaging US$354 billion per year (figure 10.11). Reserves increased because of the sterilization of capital inflows to keep the yuan artificially weak.

A common accusation in many media outlets is that China manipulates its currency. But central bank interventions (manipulation) occur in most countries. Given the link between interest rates and exchange rates (explored further in the next chapter), any interest rate determination can be considered a form of currency manipulation. China did have an undervalued exchange rate regime for most of its postreform history, which it achieved by sterilizing capital inflows and thereby accumulating large foreign reserves. In that sense, it did manipulate its currency to foster its economic objectives. Then again, so does almost every other country in the world.

10.6 Balance of Payments Equilibrium in the United States

The United States is one of the few countries with a flexible exchange rate. In 2014, the International Monetary Fund classified all countries in terms of their exchange rate regimes and found that of the 191 countries surveyed, only 29 (15%) had freely floating currencies (table 10.3). By IMF standards, only one poor country (Somalia) and three emerging markets (Mexico, Chile, and Poland) did not intervene in their currencies.

Table 10.3
Number of countries per exchange rate regime, 2016

Exchange rate regime	Number of countries
No separate legal tender	13
Currency board	12
Conventional peg[a]	66
Crawling peg[b]	17
Other managed arrangements	18
Floating	36
Free floating	29

Notes: a. Includes stabilized arrangements; b. Incorporates both crawling and crawling-like pegs.
Source: International Monetary Fund, "Annual Report on Exchange Arrangements and Exchange Restrictions," IMF, 2016.

In free-floating regimes, the current-account balance should be equal to the capital- and financial-account balances, notwithstanding statistical discrepancies and reserve assets. Countries do not need to hold foreign reserves if their currencies are truly free to convert into foreign currency. However, the US dollar is also the world's currency in terms of trade and financial transactions, and the US financial system is considered a safe haven for financial assets. During turbulent times, the US dollar tends to appreciate as nonresidents move their money from risky countries to the United States. The result is that unlike most countries, the reserve assets of the United States represent the holding of US financial assets (mostly treasury bills) by nonresidents and not the government's reserves of foreign currency.

When the People's Bank of China sterilizes capital inflows, it acquires foreign reserves. Chinese authorities can elect to buy any asset in international markets, but the preference is usually for risk-free assets, and this means mostly US government bonds (figure 10.12). Because of its flexible exchange rate regime, the United States does not accumulate reserves in foreign currencies, but other central banks do buy US government bonds.

Given the foreign holdings of US government bonds, the US net international investment position has a negative signal (figure 10.13). In 2006, the net international investment position of the United States was negative and totaled US$1.6 trillion. Ten years later, the world had increased its holdings of US assets by almost US$7 trillion, and the total negative position of the United States was US$8.04 trillion.

The American current account is structurally in deficit, and the capital inflows from growing international holdings of American assets help keep the dollar

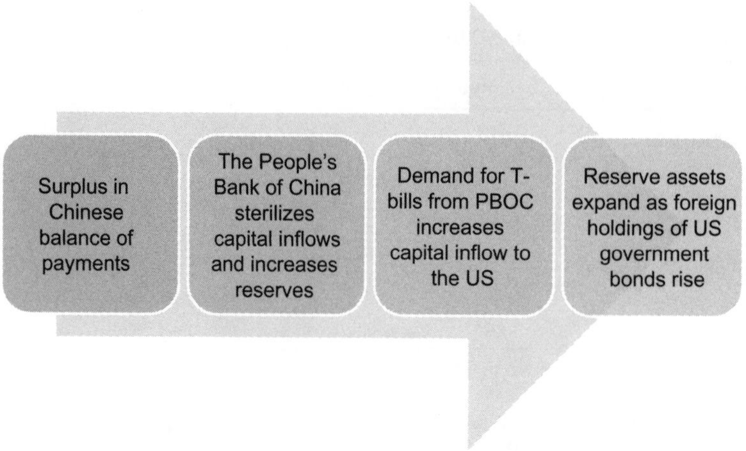

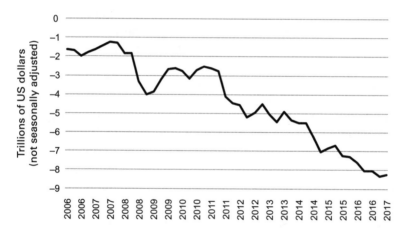

Figure 10.12

Figure 10.13
US net international investment position in trillions of US dollars (not seasonally adjusted), 2006 to 2017
Source: Federal Reserve of St. Louis, 2017, https://fred.stlouisfed.org/series/IIPUSNETIQ.

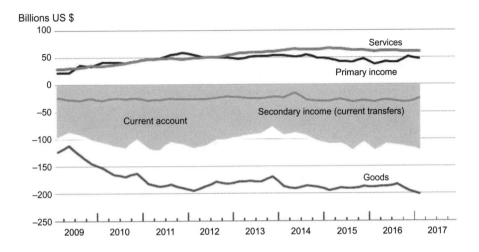

Figure 10.14
US current-account and component balances, billions of US dollars, 2009 to 2017
Source: US Bureau of Economic Analysis, 2017, https://www.bea.gov/iTable/index_ita.cfm.

relatively strong (figure 10.14).[12] The increasingly negative net international position of the United States does not necessarily mean that the US economy is exposed to political risks regarding the ownership of its assets by other countries. The deficit is the result of a larger financial and economic integration and the US economy's role of safe haven for international capital. The world is financing not the American current account deficit but the strength of the dollar.

12. Data for the US balance of payments is available at https://www.bea.gov/newsreleases/international/transactions/trans_glance.htm.

11 Economic Policies in a Globalized World

In this chapter,
- The relationship between interest rates and exchange rates
- The trilemma of economic policy
- Monetary and fiscal policies in an open world
- Currency crisis and stagflation
- The role of foreign saving

From News Australia: "An elderly man looking slumped and defeated on the footpath outside a bank has become the despairing face of the Greek financial crisis, with cash reserves in the troubled country perilously low. The sobbing pensioner was photographed sitting on the ground outside a branch of Eurobank in Thessaloniki, northern Greece, with his account book and identification discarded beside him. A security guard and staff member from the national bank were seen hauling the man to his feet as hordes of customers queued up to withdraw their money in the background."[1]

Currency policy can lead to despair, but it also can help countries escape poverty. In this chapter, the foreign exchange market is linked to other macroeconomic markets to explore the policy options that are available to public authorities.

11.1 Interest Rate Parity and Monetary Policy in an Open World

Throughout the business cycle, a local exchange rate devalues as recession hits and appreciates as the economy expands. In this sense, exchange rates are

---

1. Emma Reynolds and AFP, "Sobbing Pensioner Is Despairing Face of Greek Financial Crisis as Banks Reach Last $700m," *News.com.au*, July 5, 2015, http://www.news.com.au/finance/economy/world -economy/sobbing-pensioner-is-despairing-face-of-greek-financial-crisis-as-banks-reach-last-700m/ news-story/7fcedc95664bdf0e36ac04969c6b9496.

anticyclical: changes in relative prices are a natural consequence of variation in economic performance among nations. There also are direct links to aggregate demand through net exports and to inflation due to the pass-through of international prices to local prices.[2]

Before establishing how governments can choose between currency regimes, we need to connect the financial and foreign currency markets. This is done through the interest rate parity. The idea behind interest rate parity is simple: given that capital is mobile, changes in interest rates reverberate throughout the world through exchange rate variations. In 1981, for instance, the Federal Reserve raised the federal funds rate to 20% a year, in nominal terms. Money from all over the world flowed to the United States, triggering massive devaluations in countries vulnerable to capital outflows.

Everything else being equal, rising interest rates result in the local currency appreciation and expansionary monetary policy leads to depreciation. Changes in the money market affect economic activity through four major channels—the interest rate, the balance sheet, expectations, and the exchange rate. The link between interest rates and exchange rates is mostly through the financial account. Changes in the yields on government bonds result in different incentives for foreign investors. If countries become more attractive due to high yields on government bonds, capital flows in and the currency appreciates. Conversely, during periods of economic or financial crises, capital leaves, which may trigger rapid devaluation.

Algebraically, there are two kinds of interest rate parity—covered and uncovered. The uncovered interest rate parity establishes a relationship between local and international interest rates. Any differences between those rates affect expectations in the devaluation or appreciation of the local currency. Formally,

$$i = i_f + \frac{(e_e - e)}{e},$$

where i is the national interest rate, i_f is the foreign interest rate (for simplicity, the yield for ten-year US government bonds), e_e is the expected exchange rate, and e is the actual exchange rate.

Changes in the local interest rate affect the actual exchange rate in a way that guarantees that the parity holds. Changes in the money supply influence the price of the currency. The relationship between interest rate and exchange rate reinforces the monetary policy outcomes. Central banks change interest rates to control

---

2. Exchange rate pass-through is the movement of local-currency prices in response to changes in the exchange rate and international prices. For instance, if oil prices double, the price of gasoline in most countries rises, as does inflation.

inflation or jumpstart economic activity. To combat inflation, a central bank usually raises the interest rate, which leads to a currency appreciation that helps with inflationary pressures. The same is true if the goal is to jumpstart aggregate demand: the monetary authority cuts the target interest rate, and currency devaluation ensues. This should help net exports grow, expanding aggregate demand.

The transmission mechanism of the uncovered interest rate works through expectations regarding the future exchange rate. If capital flows are free and the financial markets work relatively well, then there is a stronger connection between interest and exchange rates through the covered interest rate parity. This linkage is not simple. The main gist is that agents can buy and sell currency establishing, today, that a transaction will take place at some point in the future through a forward or future contract. Because agents can borrow or lend using the risk-free interest rates in the local and international markets, the future price of a currency has to bear a direct relation to the difference in interest rates. Formally,

$$1 + i = \left(1 + i_f\right)\frac{e_f}{e},$$

where i is the domestic interest rate, i_f is the foreign interest rate, e_f is the forward exchange rate, and e is the spot exchange rate.

This has two main implications: changes in the local interest rate have an impact on the relative price of the currency, and the decisions of international central banks are transmitted to local markets through the interest rate or the exchange rate channels. One example is the way that market agents closely follow the Federal Reserve's decisions on monetary policy. Expectations of interest rate increases strengthen the US dollar, and a decrease in the target federal funds rate or the introduction of quantitative easing weakens the greenback.

As with everything in economics, participating in an integrated world has its costs and benefits. Although countries can access international markets to use foreign saving in order to speed up their industrialization and economic development, globalization also ties the hands of policymakers. Monetary policy influences exchange rates, and capital inflows or outflows can jumpstart policy adjustments that are interdependent, with countries increasingly experiencing common business cycles.

For instance, an increase in the interest rate from r to r' in the US market leads to a depreciation of foreign currencies against the US dollar (figure 11.1). Let's assume that the strength of the US dollar is measured in relation to a trade-weighted basket of currencies (TWB). Thus, a higher exchange rate in figure 11.1 represents an appreciation of the US dollar against the currencies from the rest of the world. Higher US federal funds rates will cause, in the foreign exchange

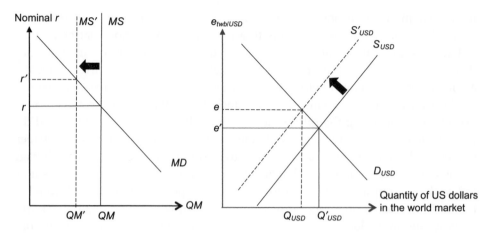

Figure 11.1

market, a surge of capital outflows to the US market (from S_{USD} to S'_{USD}) and a relative appreciation of the US dollar (from e to e'). This is what happened in December 2015, when the Federal Reserve increased the federal funds rate for the first time in almost ten years, and most currencies devalued against the dollar.

One recent development is that the covered interest parity, a staple in international finance models, seems to be weakening among the currencies of developed countries. The US dollar, British pound, euro, and Japanese yen are all free-floating currencies that suffer no direct interventions by central banks. Other actions (such as quantitative easing) do change the relative prices of currencies, but currency manipulation is not their primary intended target.

Figure 11.2 shows that since 2008, there has been a displacement in the tight relationship between the euro and the US dollar adjusted for their interest rate differentials. Some economists claim that it is time to rewrite the textbooks,[3] but past episodes of parity breakdown have simple explanations—lack of liquidity following the financial crisis in 2008 and higher sovereign risk in the European debt crisis in 2011. The covered interest rate parity misses one dimension, risk (technically, basis risk), which may explain any temporary disassociation between the prices of different currencies as expressed by interest rate covered parity.

South Africa and the Currency Crisis of 1998

The first round of globalized financial crises began in emerging countries in the 1990s. Until then, the usual pattern had been simple: viruses caused the sniffles

3. Claudio Borio, Robert McCauley, Patrick McGuire, and Vladyslav Sushko, "Bye-Bye Covered Interest Parity," *Vox*, September 28, 2016, http://voxeu.org/article/bye-bye-covered-interest-parity.

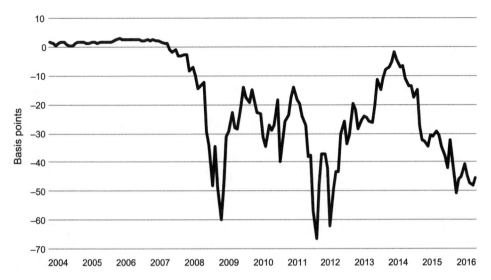

Figure 11.2
Deviation in the covered interest rate parity, US dollars per euro, 2004 to 2016
Source: Gordon Y. Liao, "Credit Migration and Covered Interest Rate Parity," Project on Behavioral Finance and Financial Stability Working Paper Series 2016-07 (2016).

in developed markets and resulted in pneumonia in the emerging world. Weak emerging countries were trapped in cycles of currency crises that were generated by their lackadaisical internal policies and the vagaries of international finance. But this changed in the 1990s. The Asian crisis of 1997 to 1998 contaminated first Russia (1998) and then Argentina (2001), and the Russian crisis led to problems in Europe. In the end, almost the whole world was affected, including South Africa.

Apartheid, a formal policy of racial segregation and discrimination, was in effect in South Africa from 1948 to 1994, when the country held its first democratic elections. The country's dual exchange rate system separated the financial market for the South African rand from the trade account, charging customers a higher rand price for foreign exchange if the purpose was to acquire assets abroad.[4] In effect, it was a dirty, floating, dual exchange rate regime.[5]

In March 1995, all of this changed. The new democratic government decided to liberalize the country's trade and capital accounts and dismantled capital

4. Jeffrey Frankel, "On the Rand: Determinants of the South African Exchange Rate," *South African Journal of Economics* 75, no. 3 (2007): 425–441.
5. Greg N. Farrell, "Capital Controls and the Volatility of South African Exchange Rates," Occasional Paper No. 15, South African Reserve Bank, July 2001, https://pdfs.semanticscholar.org/ff6b/cc110b1 bfe996cb344e9f72161eb01b919ea.pdf.

controls on the two prices of the rand. By 1997, when the Asian crisis hit world markets, South Africa was the only sub-Saharan African country truly interconnected with the global financial system and thus the only one exposed to contagion effects from crises in both emerging and developed economies.[6] Ashok Jayantilal Bhundia and Luca A. Ricci describe in detail both the 1998 and 2001 rand currency crises, but here we concentrate on the first.[7] Between late April and late August of 1998, the rand depreciated by 28% in nominal terms against the US dollar.

As always, a government can choose to let the currency depreciate or try to stem the pressure by imposing capital controls, selling reserves of foreign currency, raising the interest rate, and borrowing from nonresidents (from banks to multilateral organizations).

The interest rate parity displays the relationship between contractionary monetary policy and expected devaluation. Many emerging countries increased interest rates in 1998 to shield their local markets from the contagion from the Asian crisis. South Africa followed a similar script.

The intervention policy of the South African Reserve Bank (SARB)—via both official reserves and short-term interest rates—exacerbated the crisis and deepened its macroeconomic impact. SARB boosted the interest rate by 7% (700 basis points), and this steep surge resulted in a recession starting in the third quarter of 1998.

The example of South Africa highlights the tradeoffs inherent in its decisions on global market integration. One the one hand, the liberalization of the foreign currency market resulted in robust capital inflows, through both foreign direct and portfolio investment. One the other hand, it made the country more prone to external shocks. Financial crises propagated throughout the world in the 1990s, but with a much smaller order of magnitude than the great financial crisis of 2008.

11.2   Monetary and Fiscal Policies in a Globalized World

Capital flows and the covered and uncovered parities determine the relationship between interest rates and exchange rates. Monetary policy has an effect on the exchange rate and the market for goods and services, and exchange rate movements complement the actions of central banks. Interest rate cuts should

6. Elliott Harris, "Impact of the Asian Crisis on Sub-Saharan Africa," *Finance and Development* 36, no. 1 (1999): 14.
7. Ashok Jayantilal Bhundia and Luca A. Ricci, "The Rand Crises of 1998 and 2001: What Have We Learned?," in *Post-Apartheid South Africa: The First Ten Years*, ed. Michael Nowak and Luca Antonio Ricci, 156–173 (Washington, DC: IMF, 2005).

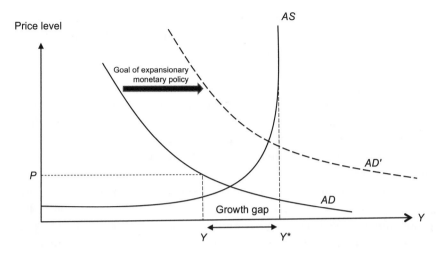

Figure 11.3

devalue currencies as well as bring changes in investment and consumption decisions.

If there is a growth gap and the transmission mechanisms are performing well, a monetary expansion should increase aggregate demand through higher investment, consumption, and net exports (the last one through the accompanying depreciation of the currency) (figure 11.3).

The relationship between fiscal and currency policies is different from the complementary role played by monetary policy and changes in the exchange rate. We simply do not know if expansionary fiscal policy causes the local currency to appreciate or depreciate. There is no theoretical underpinning of the effects of fiscal policy on currency movements. The relationship is context-dependent, with expectations playing a crucial role in how the exchange rate moves according to changes in the government budget. For instance, an expansionary fiscal policy should result in a currency devaluation if market agents view it as unsustainable. There is a chance of debt monetization, capital flees the country, and the price of the local currency spikes. A contractionary fiscal policy that is countercyclical should cause an appreciation of the currency as confidence in the policy attracts foreign investment (either productive or portfolio).

Another transmission mechanism from fiscal policy to exchange rates is through net exports. Tax cuts boost disposable income if there is no Ricardian equivalence, increasing the demand for imports and thus creating an incentive for the depreciation of the currency. The result depends on the perception of market agents regarding the tax decrease. If it is sustainable and expectations are geared toward an economic expansion, then capital inflows may offset the surge in imports. Again, this can happen only if the tax relief does not cause an unsustainable fiscal deficit. If it does, agents use their disposable income for capital outflows, and the corresponding devaluation stokes inflation instead of affecting economic output.

The relationship between fiscal policy and currency movements is empirical, and it cannot be predicted beforehand in most circumstances. Nevertheless, there is one situation in which we can make a clear prediction. Regardless of the exchange rate regime, unsustainable fiscal deficits lead to inflation and devaluation, generating an inflationary spiral.

So far, a direct relationship has been established between monetary policy and exchange rate, and an indeterminate one established between fiscal policy and currency movements. The discussion has implicitly used a country with a flexible currency. But there are limits to the discretion in the choice of currency regimes. In a fixed exchange rate regime, authorities cannot freely choose the level of interest rate or fiscal imbalances because the central bank needs to act to keep the exchange rate stable. Regardless of whether the peg is undervalued or overvalued, central banks in fixed exchange rate regimes are committed to interventions to supply liquidity in foreign currency or sterilize excess capital inflows. As such, a central bank's passive reactions to maintain a peg may neutralize the actions of other authorities in the monetary or fiscal dimensions. For instance, where there is an overvalued peg, a decrease in the interest rate will make the local bonds less attractive, should result in capital outflows as agents rebalance their portfolios, and may even trigger a speculative attack. To keep capital from fleeing the country, the central bank may need to increase the interest rate to incentivize agents to repatriate their funds.

The same process limits expansionary fiscal policy. A decrease in taxes leads to higher aggregate demand and more imports, which necessitates liquidity in foreign currency. The central bank has to raise the interest rate to increase capital inflows, negating the boost in demand.

11.3   Currency Crises

A currency crisis happens after a sudden devaluation that creates either a growth gap or an adverse supply shock. This happens for many reasons, but all currency crises share one common trait—a rapid deterioration of expectations regarding either the management of the economy or the country's economic fundamentals.

A fixed exchange regime is feasible only as long as the monetary authority has the ability to intervene in the foreign exchange market to provide or reduce liquidity in foreign currency. An overvalued regime requires the use of reserve assets or other forms to quench the excess demand for foreign currency, and an under-valued regime experiences the sterilization of capital inflows. Market agents can try to speculate on the strength of central banks by exacerbating the underlying weakness of the exchange rate regimes—for example, by borrowing in the local currency and fleeing the country to buy international assets in an overvalued currency or by betting in the opposite direction in an undervalued one. Economic weakness may cause a currency crisis by bets on the abandoning of the peg. The British debacle of 1992 is an example of a successful speculative attack. Black Wednesday, on September 16, 1992, was the day the humiliated British government was forced to withdraw the pound from the European Exchange Rate Mechanism (ERM) after it was unable to keep the pound above its agreed lower limit in the ERM. George Soros, the high-profile currency market investor, made a profit of over 1 billion pounds by short selling the pound, and he was by no means the only one. Such speculative attacks are natural responses to the mismanagement of national economies.

The macroeconomic effects of a currency crisis depend on the extent of the crisis and the possible link with a financial crisis. In the case of conjoined crises, both aggregate demand and aggregate supply fall sharply, potential output and actual output decrease, and the inflationary effect depends on the relative path of demand fall and currency devaluation. Argentina in 2001 is a good example of a currency issue that triggered a financial crisis. The country, like many others in Latin America, experienced a hyperinflation period in the 1980s and the early 1990s. Argentinian authorities went beyond overvalued pegs to restore confidence in the management of the economy and to induce the normalization of price processes. They created a currency board in which a convertible Argentine peso was tied to the US dollar (it lasted from 1992 to 2002). Every peso in circulation had to be backed by a dollar in reserve assets. In fact, dollars were accepted as legal tender because they were fully convertible into pesos. Individuals and companies could choose between dollar- and peso-denominated accounts and could borrow in either of the two currencies, with a spread making the dollar-denominated loans more expensive than the peso ones.

On a currency board with free capital flows, the interest rate is endogenous. Any period of capital outflows results in the contraction of the monetary base. In the case of Argentina, the monetary base contracted following capital outflows, a result of the one-to-one parity between the supplies of the peso and the reserve assets. Interest rates simply followed capital movements. A period of rebalancing with capital flowing from emerging to developed countries followed the series of currency crises that began in Asia in 1997. The Russian fixed exchange regime fell in 1998. In Argentina, a severe recession started in 1998, and interest rates began to climb anticyclically, reaching 16% in 2001. In December 2001, the Argentinian government defaulted on its external debt, and in January 2002, it abandoned the convertibility of dollars at the rate of 1 US dollar to 1 peso. A financial crisis followed, as banks' liabilities (mostly in US dollars) shot up in value, and the corresponding assets (in pesos) stayed the same. Financial crises normally lead to severe economic losses, and the Argentinian crisis was no exception. With a broken financial system, a sudden devaluation, and the US dollar reaching 4 pesos in 2002, a severe contraction in aggregate supply resulted in a depression that saw GDP fall over 10% and inflation shoot up to 80%. The depression of 2002 was even more severe because the economy already had been shrinking, with an average negative growth of –3% in the 1999 to 2001 period.

Sweden provides another example of the link between financial, currency, and real markets. As shown in chapter 5, the country went through a financial crisis in the early 1990s. Sweden also had a fixed exchange rate that it was forced to abandon. A shift in the exchange rate regime created uncertainty regarding the path of the currency and inflation. The country was already experiencing a GDP contraction, and fearing an additional inflationary spiral, Swedish authorities announced a formal inflation target of 2%. The target system was unsuccessful in its first year, and inflation went from 2.2% in 1992 to 4.6% in 1993. But the credibility of the monetary authority and competent reforms in the banking system were successful in containing prices, with inflation dipping below the 2% threshold in 1994 and staying around the target after that.

The Asian Crisis of 1997 to 1998

The Asian crisis started in Thailand and spread to the rest of the continent before contaminating other emerging markets. It began when Thai authorities let the baht float on July 2, 1997, abandoning its peg to the US dollar after months of fighting speculative attacks. A week later, the Philippine peso dropped significantly, while Indonesia widened the trading band of the rupiah. In August, Indonesia let its currency float, and in November the South Korean won fell below 1,000 to a US dollar for the first time. Malaysia unveiled capital controls that limited capital outflows, and Hong Kong and China managed to fend off speculative attacks.

Because Thai banks, like most in the region, had large liabilities in foreign currency, the currency crisis turned into a financial crisis, albeit a modest one, and a recession became a depression. In 1997, growth was still only –1.4% as the crisis hit the economy in the second semester. In 1998, GDP contracted by 10.5%.

The seeds of the crisis were in the current account. It averaged –8% of the GDP in the five years prior to the crisis, with capital outflows depleting Thailand's reserve assets. A similar pattern of current-account deficits was pervasive across Asia in the mid-1990s. GDP contracted in all Southeast Asian countries in 1998, when there was –13% GDP growth in Indonesia, –7.5% in Malaysia, –5.9% in Hong

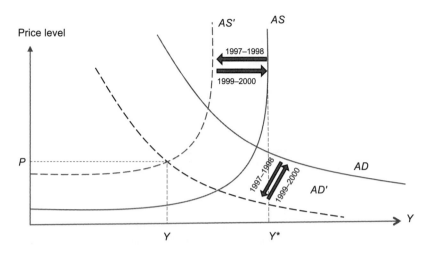

Figure 11.4

Kong, –5.7% in South Korea, and –0.5% in the Philippines. Given that the currency crises did not generate deep financial crises, however, the countries rebounded relatively fast, with growth in all affected countries coming back to more than 5% in 2000 (figure 11.4).

Debt Crises, the Lost Decade, and Hyperinflation in Latin America

During the Asian crisis of 1997 to 1998, GDPs contracted, but inflation did not explode. The same was not true for Latin America in the 1980s and early 1990s. In the 1970s, Latin American countries borrowed heavily to induce industrialization. When the US Federal Reserve hiked interest rates to 20% a year in the early 1980s, capital outflows caused massive devaluations in Latin American countries. The main differences between Latin America in the 1980s and Asian countries in the 1990s were that in the first group net exports were negative, current-account deficits were higher, and government budgets were in complete disarray. Although in Asia devaluation resulted in a significant rise in net exports and the countries increased interest rates to stem outflows, in Latin America nothing of the sort happened.

Latin American governments imposed import restrictions, tightened capital controls, and asked for funds from multilateral organizations, particularly the International Monetary Fund (IMF). In Brazil, for instance, travelers were allowed to purchase only US$2,000 for their trips abroad.

Because of the total lack of fiscal restraint, governments started to monetize the deficit, jumpstarting inflationary processes. For Argentina, Bolivia, Brazil, Mexico, and Peru, the annual consumer price index topped 3,000% at some point

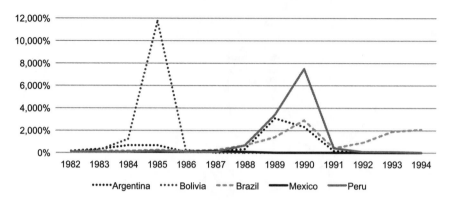

Figure 11.5
Annual inflation in Argentina, Bolivia, Brazil, Mexico, and Peru, 1982 to 1994
Source: World Bank, 2017, https://data.worldbank.org/indicator/FP.CPI.TOTL.ZG.

in the 1982 to 1994 period (figure 11.5). In all these countries, debt monetization—
because of external restrictions and escalating fiscal deficits—caused hyperinflation. Only after the countries committed to fiscal rectitude (at least temporarily)
and established overvalued pegs to anchor expectations was hyperinflation
finally quenched. Meanwhile, successive IMF loans left those countries increasingly indebted, and they all ended up defaulting on their external debt at some
point in this period.

Economic mismanagement does not get much worse than Latin America in the
1980s. Some policies failed basic tests of common sense, like the Brazilian price
control policy of 1985 to 1986. The government simply published lists with the
maximum prices that businesses could charge. Unsurprisingly, this policy resulted
in a shortage of many products, the appearance of black markets (it was probably
easier to buy cocaine than a filet mignon for a while), and inflation being stored
up—only to resurface later as prices adjusted automatically as soon as the price
controls were abandoned.

Reforms for Disinflation: The Case of Israel

Israel illustrates how short-run macroeconomic mismanagement can derail development. Today, Israel is a rich country. In 2016, GDP per capita in purchasing
power parity was US$31,715 (the OECD average was US$38,036). Poverty is the
second highest in the OECD, and income inequality a problem, but the country
boasts a well-educated population and a thriving tech industry. Things were different in the mid-1980s, however.

Israel went through a hyperinflation period in 1984, when annual inflation
was 400% and rising. This mirrored the Latin American situation: a combination

of fiscal profligacy and a massive current-account deficit created an inflationary spiral. The budget deficit was 17% of GDP, capital outflows constantly pressured the Israeli shekel to depreciate, and productivity was stagnant for over a decade.

Although Latin American countries were able to rein in inflation only in the 1990s, Israel was done with spiraling prices by 1987, when for the first time since 1972 annual inflation dipped below 20%. The country was able to do this through a combination of structural reforms and difficult contractionary measures. There were significant cuts in government expenditure and the budget deficit, and the new shekel was pegged to the US dollar. The international environment helped: oil prices, a major import, were falling, and the greenback was depreciating against the rest of the world's currencies. Also extremely important was that the country's market reforms were credible ("a crucial condition for the success of any stabilization program is that it achieves credibility in the eyes of the public").[8]

Contractionary fiscal policy and structural reforms are politically costly, and their timing matters. Israeli institutions were stronger than those of the average middle-income country, and this allowed the country to make the reforms work in the 1980s and, since then, to climb the development ladder, escaping the middle-income trap.

Rescue Packages in Developed Countries

Sovereign debt crises and rescue packages from multilateral institutions such as the International Monetary Fund do not happen only in poor and peripheral nations. Ireland and Iceland, for example, were extremely successful in the years before the great financial crisis. From 1996 to 2008, GDP growth in Ireland and Iceland outpaced the world by a comfortable margin, on average. Ireland was dubbed the Celtic Tiger and grew more than 10% a year from 1996 to 2000 and over 5% from 2001 to 2007, a trajectory that was comparable only to China in the same period (figure 11.6).

For both Ireland and Iceland, the crisis was a horrendous reality shock. It revealed real estate bubbles and financial fragility that caused a systemic failure of each country's banking system and resulted in a much stronger recession than the one that occurred in the rest of the world. Bailing out the banking system in Ireland was so costly that the country was on the verge of defaulting on its sovereign debt in 2010. Because Ireland is part of the eurozone, Irish authorities could not act as lenders of last resort and relied instead on help from abroad. Like Latin American countries in the 1980s and Asian countries in the 1990s, Ireland was able

---

8. Don Patinkin, "Israel's Stabilization Program of 1985, or Some Simple Truths of Monetary Theory," *Journal of Economic Perspectives* 7, no. 2 (1993): 103–128.

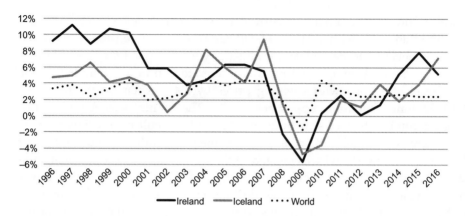

Figure 11.6
Real annual GDP growth in Ireland, Iceland, and the world, 1996 to 2016
Source: World Bank, 2017, https://data.worldbank.org/indicator/FP.CPI.TOTL.ZG.

to stave off a full default by negotiating a financial assistance program with the IMF and the European Central Bank that totaled €85 billion.

Unlike Ireland, however, Iceland allowed its banks to fail. The Icelandic banking system was much bigger, in relative terms, than in most countries, a result of the country's international profile and close access to Europe. Icelandic banks were so large that their assets were ten times the size of the island's GDP. The funding came from all over the world, but most of it had its origin in Great Britain and the Netherlands. Iceland was also a relatively indebted country, and in 2007, its sovereign debt totaled €50 billion, more than seven times the country's GDP. Icelandic authorities negotiated a rescue package of US$5.1 billion with the IMF. According to Elizabeth Matsangou,

a swift transition from an export driven-economy, with fishing, energy and aluminium smelting as its stable industries, into an international financial centre had quickly made Iceland a popular destination for foreign investment and currency trading. But the inexperienced, badly managed system was simply unsustainable and soon began buckling under the size of its own expansive growth. In tragically poetic timing, the 2008 financial crisis hit; with fiscal decline echoing around the globe, Iceland's economy had no hope of saving itself from imploding.

The authorities responded with the unthinkable: they let the country's three biggest banks collapse. It was the third-largest bankruptcy in history. Then came the implementation of strict capital controls, austerity measures and a series of reforms; Iceland thus set out to reinvent itself.[9]

9. Elizabeth Matsangou, "Failing Banks, Winning Economy: The Truth about Iceland's Recovery," *World Finance*, September 15, 2015, https://www.worldfinance.com/infrastructure-investment/government-policy/failing-banks-winning-economy-the-truth-about-icelands-recovery.

As Malaysia did in 1998, the route that Iceland chose was different than that of most countries when faced with capital flows reversal. It instituted capital controls to maintain some measure of monetary policy autonomy and prevent the currency from plunging. Letting banks fail meant that "bank bonds held by foreigners were tossed into default and turned into implicit equity claims on the collapsed lenders and bank deposits that foreign investors held in Icelandic krona were trapped in the country by capital controls."[10] There was no direct default regarding sovereign debt, but the picture is murkier if the indirect effects of the capital controls that the Icelandic authorities implemented are considered. Some US funds held sovereign bonds and claimed that Iceland committed a sovereign default by imposing haircuts in an offshore krona auction as late as 2016, eight years after the onset of the crisis.[11] The currency auction in June 2016 was designed to allow investors to replace about 319 billion kronas in securities that had been trapped behind capital controls since 2008. Debt owned by foreign funds was equivalent to about 10% of GDP, down from a peak of about 40%.[12] The auction partially failed as some funds refused to accept an almost 40% devaluation of their holdings.

The different decisions by Irish and Icelandic authorities reinforce the lack of a one-size-fits-all strategy for economic policies. Countries take distinct paths, and their choices result in different costs and benefits. Both Iceland and Ireland eventually rebounded, but they are still feeling the hangover from the bursting of the financial bubbles in 2008.

China, Sterilization, and the Holdings of US Debt

China's hard peg was in place from 1994 to 2005, and since then, the country has had a crawling peg. In 2012, the People's Bank of China announced a wider interval band for the trading of its currency. During the 2000s, a combination of growth and integration resulted in a jump in capital coming into the Chinese economy, despite capital controls. The monetary authority sterilized the entry of foreign money to keep its undervalued hard peg and later to maintain a smooth appreciation through a crawling peg.

What would happen if China were to dump all of its US assets? In China, there are two possibilities—purchases of other foreign assets or repatriation of reserve assets. In the first case, there would be no macroeconomic effects in the Chinese market, but given the size of China's reserve assets, there would be consequences

10. Tett, Gillian, "The Darker Side of Iceland's Showcase Recovery," *Financial Times*, July 17, 2014, https://www.ft.com/content/34ab12fc-0d9b-11e4-815f-00144feabdc0.

11. Omar Valdimarsson, "U.S. Funds Default Claim Hits Hurdle in Iceland's Court Process," *Bloomberg*, September 15, 2016, https://www.bloomberg.com/news/articles/2016-09-15/iceland-stalls-court-in-fight-against-u-s-funds-default-claim.

12. Richard Milne, "Iceland Poll Brings Hope of End to Capital Controls," *Financial Times*, October 24, 2016, https://www.ft.com/content/ad8a1bf4-99ef-11e6-8f9b-70e3cabccfae.

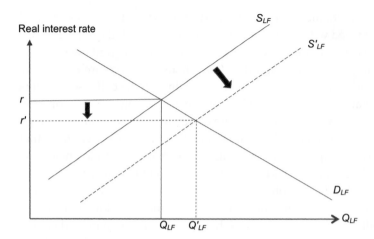

Figure 11.7

in the international public debt market, with a surge in the supply of loanable funds in whatever market the People's Bank of China decides to park its reserves (figure 11.7). For the foreign market, there is an increase in the supply of loanable funds (from S_{LF} to S'_{LF}), with a corresponding decrease in the interest rate (from r to r') and with accompanying effects on the market of goods and services—specifically, growth in the aggregate demand given the lower cost of capital.

In the United States, there would be two immediate effects. In the loanable funds market, the exit of Chinese money from the bonds market would represent a decrease in the supply of loanable funds. In the foreign exchange market, there would be higher demand for foreign currency. There would be two simultaneous effects—a devaluation of the US dollar and an increase in interest rate, which the monetary authority can decide to offset by purchasing the bonds sold by China (in effect, printing money). In the market for goods and services, net exports would go up, and the effect on the rest of aggregate demand would depend on the reaction by the US Federal Reserve. A minor currency crisis would be likely, and inflation should go up. The economy eventually, probably quickly, should rebalance, and there should be no lasting damage. The US government is not a hostage to Chinese officials who could yield power by holding trillions of dollars of US securities.

11.4   The Trilemma of Economic Policy

Currency crises maim, but financial crises kill. In some cases, such as in Argentina in 2001, a sudden devaluation prompts a financial crisis. One of the lessons learned from the many currency crises of the 1990s is that there are limits on the designs of currency policies.

In international finance, the economic theory of the trilemma requires hard choices among three fundamental options—an active monetary policy, a fixed exchange rate, and a free movement of capital. Only two of these three policies can be pursued. Pursuing all three eventually provokes a speculative attack and usually the abandoning of the fixed exchange rate regime.

Given the interest rate parity (and free capital flows), if countries try to change interest rates, there will be an impact on the currency markets. Hence, in a fixed exchange rate regime, the only way to proceed with an expansionary or contractionary monetary policy is to be able to intervene in the currency market to stem capital outflows or sterilize capital inflows. Because reserves are finite and sterilizing capital inflows has fiscal costs, countries cannot maintain fixed exchange rate regimes and at the same time maintain monetary policy autonomy if capital can move freely. Eventually, agents will start betting heavily that a country cannot maintain a peg, and the central bank will capitulate. The only way to maintain a peg with free capital movements is to have an endogenous interest rate. In essence, the central bank can have a say in either the interest rate or the exchange rate but not both (unless it has capital controls).

Hong Kong is a good example of an economy in which public authorities abandoned monetary policy in favor of a fixed exchange rate regime with free capital flows. Countries facing the trilemma are free to choose between two of the three possible actions, but changing course is always costly. In the United States, Japan, Australia, and the eurozone, the choices are for monetary autonomy and free capital flows and have been so since the end of the Bretton Woods agreement.[13] Countries like Denmark elect capital controls and fixed exchange rate regimes. In the contemporary world, there are no shortcuts. As long as countries are integrated with the international financial system, they do not have complete autonomy in their menu of possible policy decisions.

The Chinese Trilemma and the Speculative Attack on the Yuan

In 2015, China grappled with an indirect speculative attack on the yuan, even though the country had at that time trillions of US dollars in reserve. Despite that financial buffer, they should have known better. No one can mess with basic economics by ignoring the constraints of the trilemma—in China's case, by apparently assuming it could maintain tight control over its money supply and its exchange rate and, at the same time, introduce measures to free up the flow of capital.

---

13. In the eurozone, the monetary autonomy is the region as a whole. Countries in the eurozone do not have individual monetary autonomy. Instead, the euro acts as a regional fixed exchange rate regime.

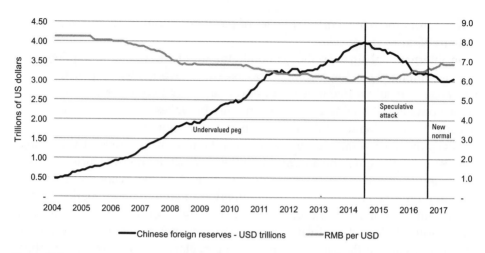

Figure 11.8
Chinese reserves and renminbis (yuans) per US dollar exchange rate, 2004 to 2017
Source: People's Bank of China, 2017, http://www.safe.gov.cn/wps/portal/english/Data/Forex.

China's situation in 2014, just before the attack, was sadly reminiscent of the missteps taken by the United Kingdom and many emerging economies in the 1990s. This time around, the global reverberations shook stock markets instead of currency markets because more countries had been keeping their exchange rates flexible. However, that provides little solace given the damage already incurred by Chinese financial policy and the continuing fallout.

As China's ill-founded attempt to test the trilemma took its toll globally, the feeble economies of Turkey and Russia were among those hit by the worst collateral damage. Both suffered massive devaluations, at least in part as a result of the worldwide movement of capital due to uncertainty surrounding the Chinese yuan. Figure 11.8 provides a snapshot of the story. A global recession and the fear of a hard landing by the Chinese economy shifted the peg from undervalued to overvalued. Because the central bank, the People's Bank of China (PBOC), kept the yuan peg relatively unchanged, it had to start selling foreign currency to investors and companies that wanted to take their money out of the country.[14]

Chinese reserves stood at about US$4 trillion in 2014, when capital started moving out of the country. This process accelerated in January 2015, a month after the US Federal Reserve increased its interest rate for the first time in almost a decade. Eventually, net outflows reached almost US$100 billion per month. A

---

14. Evelyn Cheng, "China Is Working Hard to Support Its Currency: It Sold US Government Bonds for Six Straight Months," *CNBC*, January 19, 2017, https://www.cnbc.com/2017/01/19/china-is -working-hard-to-support-its-currency--it-sold-us-government-bonds-for-six-straight-months.html.

slow-burning speculative attack on the Chinese currency was underway. In early 2016, China admitted communication flaws regarding its management of exchange rate policy.[15] Haruhiko Kuroda, Japan's central bank governor, asked Chinese officials to tighten capital controls.[16] Yu Yongding, a former central bank adviser, recommended a floating yuan.[17]

Faced with the assault, Chinese authorities had several options. They could make capital controls tighter (to impede or even prohibit different types of out-flows), raise the interest rate (to try to bring in more foreign capital), ride out the crisis (until the bank's reserves were close to exhausted), or accede to the attack. They chose the fourth option.

On two days in August 2015, the PBOC allowed the yuan to devalue by 3% and started a process of mini-devaluations until there were no more incentives for net capital outflows.[18] In doing this, China slowly brought the fixed yuan closer to its shadow price—the price of the yuan if the country had a fully flexible currency regime.

In 2016, after the equivalent of US$1 trillion was spent on thwarting the speculative attack and keeping the volatility of the yuan low, the Chinese economy stabilized. The fears of a crisis were averted, and investors stopped sending huge amounts of money abroad.[19] Things returned to normal. Capital outflows or inflows were minuscule, and confidence rebounded. In 2017, Chinese foreign holdings stood at around US$3 trillion.

The country chose a new normal. In the new normal, China continues to manipulate its currency but without real economic effects on the rest of the world. The yuan is still subject to the PBOC's control, but its value does not influence world exporters negatively because the bank keeps it close to what it would be if the currency was floating. The main reason that the PBOC does not allow the currency to float completely is to keep a hold on volatility.

Chinese authorities no doubt understood the yuan's predicament. So we can only speculate about why China delayed making the inevitable choices. Perhaps

15. Chris Giles and Gabriel Wildau, "China Admits Communication Failings on Renminbi," *Financial Times*, January 21, 2016, https://www.ft.com/content/a0690798-c01d-11e5-9fdb-87b8d15baec2.

16. Chris Giles, "Kuroda Calls for China to Tighten Capital Controls," *Financial Times*, January 23, 2016, https://www.ft.com/content/03395bdc-c1c4-11e5-808f-8231cd71622e.

17. Dhwani Mehta, "China Should Let Yuan Float to Avoid Slump, Ex-PBOC Adviser Says," *Bloomberg*, January 27, 2016, https://www.bloomberg.com/news/articles/2016-01-27/china-should-let-yuan -float-to-avoid-slump-ex-pboc-adviser-says.

18. Phillip Inman, Martin Farrer, and Fergus Ryan, "China Stuns Financial Markets by Devaluing Yuan for Second Day Running," *The Guardian*, August 12, 2015, https://www.theguardian.com/ business/2015/aug/12/china-yuan-slips-again-after-devaluation.

19. "China Ends Year of Stabilization on High as Consumers Spend," *Bloomberg*, January 20, 2017, https://www.bloomberg.com/news/articles/2017-01-20/china-ends-year-of-stabilization-on-high -note-as-consumers-spend.

there was a fear of shaking the status quo even more than it had been shaken since April 2015, especially only months after the yuan joined the International Monetary Fund's basket of currencies.

Or maybe they still hoped that the country's reserve buffer (however diminished), if accompanied by some exchange rate tinkering, could stem the tidal wave of capital outflows. In the end, public authorities tightened capital controls and were able to deter more capital outflows. Future moves toward more open capital accounts will need to be followed by the abandoning of a fully autonomous monetary policy or, more likely, the floating of the yuan.

11.5   The Role of Foreign Saving: Sectoral Imbalances

There is a long tradition in development economics to consider saving as a key variable to determining how likely poor countries are to develop. Since the 1950s, using foreign saving as a complementary source to local loanable funds has been a policy prescription. There is empirical evidence that foreign saving is relevant for development. Chung Chen, Lawrence Chang, and Yimin Zhang show how foreign direct investment was important in the 1980s and 1990s to complement incipient financial markets in China and help foster rapid capital accumulation.[20] This is the main advantage of free capital flows. With it, foreign banks and companies are more likely to commit funds to emerging markets. Ricardo J. Caballero, Emmanuel Farhi, and Pierre-Olivier Gourinchas introduce a model that takes into account new regularities (like low interest rates) in a world in which developing countries post persistent current-account deficits.[21]

As Latin American countries discovered in the 1980s, sectoral imbalances and mismanagement of the economy lead to chaos in the form of inflation and deep recessions. Sectoral balance analysis is a simple way to integrate the government budget as well as private and external saving. Algebraically,

$$(S - I) + (T - G) + (IM - X) = 0,$$

where S is saving, I is investment, T is taxes, G is government expenditure, IM is imports, and X is exports. The first part (saving minus investment) represents the balance of the private sector; the second part (taxes minus government expenditure) represents the balance of the public sector; and the third part (imports minus exports of goods and services) represents the current account, which is the external balance. In this simple analysis, government expenditure can rise without

20. Chung Chen, Lawrence Chang, and Yimin Zhang, "The Role of Foreign Direct Investment in China's Post-1978 Economic Development," *World Development* 23, no. 4 (1995): 691–703.

21. Ricardo J. Caballero, Emmanuel Farhi, and Pierre-Olivier Gourinchas, "An Equilibrium Model of 'Global Imbalances' and Low Interest Rates," *American Economic Review* 98 (2008): 358–393.

crowding out private investment as long as the country consumes foreign saving through current-account deficits.

A positive balance means that a sector has a net saving (is accumulating wealth and reimbursing debts), and a negative balance means that a sector has a net indebtedness (is accumulating debt and dissimulating wealth). The balances must add to zero: it is impossible to have a situation in which all countries enjoy a surplus or all post a deficit. Across countries, if one borrows (external or financial deficits), another is lending. Thus, the German current account and private saving surpluses from the first half of the 2010s are still financing deficits in other countries because the German government did not absorb the extra money from these markets.

We can analyze currency crises through the lens of sectoral balances: private and public debt accumulation, financed by external creditors, results in the building up of foreign debt that eventually cannot be financed anymore. A sudden stop of capital flows and a current-account reversal lead to devaluations or defaults on sovereign debt. The public sector intervenes to sustain the private-sector deleveraging, and the government deficit increases. If the deficit is financed with bonds, there is an increase in public debt; if the deficit is monetized, inflation follows.

Foreign saving can be an important tool for economic development, but reliance on capital inflows makes a country vulnerable to sudden stops and flow reversals. This external vulnerability introduces another component to business cycles—increased output volatility resulting from periodic currency crises.

One of the reasons that the world is not converging is that money tends to flow to more stable countries, and those countries tend to be rich. This can be seen in a pattern of greenfield foreign direct investment (figure 11.9). Greenfield projects are new industrial plants or venues, as opposed to a brownfield project in which existing operations are expanded or renovated. This kind of aggregate investment generates the most economic growth because it mobilizes lots of resources from the economy. In a converging world, one would expect to see more investment flowing to the poorest countries, but this does not necessarily happen. Europe is the largest recipient of FDI, most of it from intra-European investment (an Italian company investing in Portugal, for instance). Asia is also an important destination for new foreign investment. Not coincidentally, this region has been growing the most in the last thirty years. Africa, however, welcomes relatively few foreign investment. Institutional instability explains most of the aversion of investors.

Currency Crises and Stagflation

Currency crises may cause stagflation through changes in the short-term aggregate supply. External vulnerability, in terms of large current-account deficits, may

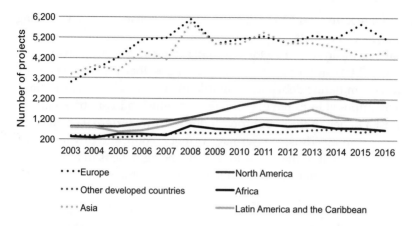

Figure 11.9
Number of announced greenfield, foreign direct investment projects by destination, 2003 to 2016
Source: United Nations Conference on Trade and Development, "World Investment Report 2017: Annex Tables," UNCTAD, 2017, http://unctad.org/en/Pages/DIAE/World%20Investment%20 Report/Annex-Tables.aspx.

trigger sudden stops of capital flows. Such sudden stops make imports more expensive. Depending on the size of external restrictions, the productive capacity of the economy falls. It is hard to predict a situation in which a currency crisis generates stagflation because changes in the exchange rate affect prices through costs and also, in normal situations, affect aggregate demand through net exports. Remember that output through the production side comes from our version of the Solow model in chapter 3 and is

$$Y(t) = f(K(t), AL(t), AN(t)),$$

where Y is output, t is time, f is a function, K is capital, A is an index of productivity (technology), L is labor, and N is natural resources. Usually, production factors are fixed in the short run. For instance, the possible labor pool is considered as simply the labor force participation corresponding to the development levels and the demographics. Extraneous events such as wars or mass migrations change the composition of the labor force rapidly, unlike the natural process of an aging population and controlled migration. The same is true of natural resources. Countries usually have a fixed amount of natural resources in the short run, and only exploration and development can increase it in the long run, often at the expense of the environment. However, sometimes countries' natural resources grow in the short run, shifting aggregate supply to the right and creating the conditions for expansion without inflationary pressures. In Australia, for example, aggregate supply increased rapidly due to Chinese demand and the relatively high elasticity of supply of the mining industry.

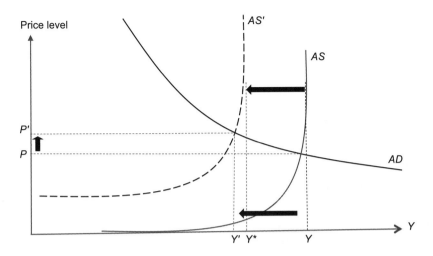

Figure 11.10

A currency crisis following a sudden stop of capital inflows usually results in a sharp decrease in imports. Although higher net exports due to rising exports lead to higher aggregate demand and reduced imports may have the same algebraic effect, the economic implication is different. Higher investment (I) in the short run leads to increased productive capacity in the long run. Similarly, imports of intermediate goods, which are either natural resources or capital goods, are tied to both short- and long-run aggregate supply through the country's production function. A sudden stop of capital flows and shrinking imports may lead to a reshuffling of production factors that pushes down aggregate productive capacity. The pass-through of massive currency devaluations to prices also reduces production (figure 11.10). In the beginning, actual output is almost at its potential level (Y), and inflation is at P. As the supply shock from the currency crisis unfolds, AS moves to AS'. Output falls to AS', and the price level increases from P to P'. Recession comes with inflation.

In the end, a currency crisis causes inflation and stagnation because relative price changes reduce productive capacity. As imports become much more expensive, the relative price of domestic inputs increases, but the marginal productivity of the economy decreases as inputs are used to substitute imports instead of their earlier more productive use. Economies usually rebound relatively quickly from currency crises because massive devaluations trigger incentives for export industries that increase the absorption of unemployed factors of production and thus higher net exports and restored productive capacity.

Turkey, for example, experienced a brief period of stagflation in 2011, when the Turkish lira plummeted against the major world currencies, falling over 20%

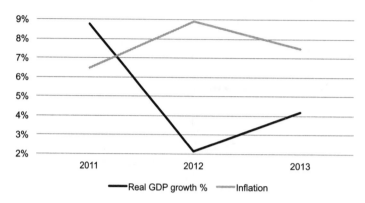

Figure 11.11
Turkish GDP growth and inflation, 2011 to 2013
Source: World Bank, 2017, https://data.worldbank.org/indicator/FP.CPI.TOTL.ZG.

against the US dollar. The two main reasons for this decline were a persistent current-account deficit and capital outflows from emerging markets due to the sovereign debt crisis of euro countries.[22] The weaker lira shrank aggregate supply, with corresponding deceleration in growth and rising prices. With the devaluation of the lira and a lower global demand for Turkish products, growth stalled, decreasing from almost 9% in 2011 to a little over 2% in 2012, and inflation increased from 6.5% to almost 9% in the same period (figure 11.11). The adjustment period was relatively short, and as aggregate supply started to return to its earlier path, growth increased in 2013 (4.2%) as the pressure on prices eased (7.5%). A shock in aggregate demand due to a sinking lira can explain the strong deceleration in growth and escalation in the inflation rate, and the easing of aggregate supply makes the economy return to an equilibrium with higher growth and lower inflation.

11.6   Dimensions of Currency Policy

The currency policies that governments can choose consist of two dimensions—the type of exchange rate regime and the operationalization of currency market interventions and reserve assets building. The options for the type of exchange rate regime are a fixed exchange rate regime, a flexible exchange rate regime, and the use of foreign currency as legal tender (figure 11.12). After the government selects the main type of exchange rate regime, it chooses from a menu of few

22. Martina Bozadzhieva, "Here's Why the Turkish Lira Is Crashing," *Business Insider*, November 5, 2011, http://www.businessinsider.com/heres-why-the-turkish-lira-is-crashing-2011-11.

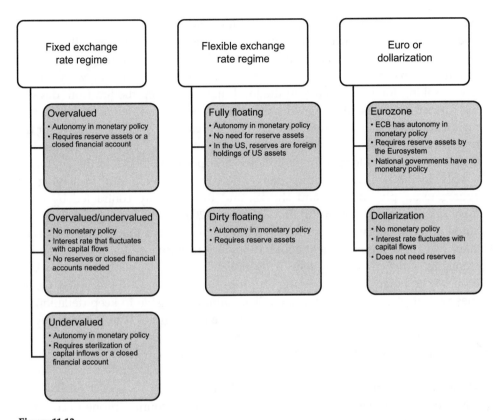

Figure 11.12

options. For instance, in the case of a fixed exchange rate regime, the secondary choices are between a depreciated or overvalued peg, a hard or crawling peg, and a free capital flow or an autonomous monetary policy.

The operationalization of each exchange rate regime depends on these choices and the external and internal economic contexts. During the great financial crisis, for example, many countries with dirty floating regimes, especially in emerging markets, had to choose between allowing rapid devaluations and using reserve assets to contain the pressure on their currencies. Although the consequences of the crisis were still unclear, in July 2008, two months before Lehman Brothers' bankruptcy, the Turkish deputy prime minister Mehmet Simsek announced that the government would not intervene to support the lira.[23] As the crisis deepened,

23. Silvia Amaro, "Turkey Is Not in a Currency Crisis: Deputy Prime Minister," *CNBC*, January 20, 2017, https://www.cnbc.com/2017/01/20/turkey-is-not-in-a-currency-crisis-deputy-prime-minister.html.

the government changed its stance and intervened to reduce currency volatility. The government was facing three options: use reserve assets, increase the interest rate, or implement a combination of the two. Given the weakening of economic activity around the world, Turkish officials chose direct intervention with reserve assets, selling foreign currency in the local market to keep the lira from devaluing further. The present framework of tradeoffs between different exchange rate regimes and the limitations of economic policy present a coherent narrative for the reversal of the Turkish government's decision to intervene in the currency market. Quick devaluations lead to more inflation and possibly shocks in the aggregate supply. In the end, the Turkish intervention was not successful in staving off aggregate supply and demand shocks, and the economy contracted by more than 13%, year on year, in the first quarter of 2009. With free capital flow and autonomous monetary policy, there is a limit to the actions that central banks can take. The Turkish government could at best try to influence the price of the lira managing a dirty floating system. Truly global capital movements left the Turkish economy and many other emerging countries subject to rapid depreciation. Countries with managed capital accounts (like China) were able to keep deflationary pressures off their currency markets. Exchange rate regimes have a major impact on the choices of economic policy. Tradeoffs determine the costs and benefits, as well as the limits of attempted interventions in foreign currency markets.

The Underperformance of the Malaysian Ringgit

Weak local currencies may benefit exports but leave a country prone to currency crises and rampant inflation. Malaysia escaped the Asian crisis of 1997 to 1998 faster than the other economies in the region. Unlike other Asian countries, the Malaysian government had established capital controls to prevent capital outflows. In the other Asian countries, flight to quality engendered currency and financial crises. Malaysia's GDP contracted by 7.5% in 1998, and Indonesia (–13%), South Korea (–6%), and Thailand (–7.6%) followed suit. Malaysia recovered quickest, with its GDP increasing by more than 7% a year in the two subsequent years, which is usually attributed to the erection of capital controls.[24]

Even though the country eased capital controls after the worst of the crisis was over, the government still tries to maintain control over currency movements. One example is the explicit policy of noninternationalization. The central bank prohibits the trading of ringgit assets outside of its jurisdiction.[25] The aim is to decrease

24. Ethan Kaplan and Dani Rodrik, "Did the Malaysian Capital Controls Work?," in *Preventing Currency Crises in Emerging Markets*, ed. Sebastian Edwards and Jeffrey A. Frankel, 393–440 (Chicago: University of Chicago Press, 2002).
25. "Malaysia's Central Bank Tries to Stem a Slide in the Ringgit," *The Economist*, November 24, 2016, https://www.economist.com/news/finance-and-economics/21710833-ringgit-underperforming -other-emerging-market-currencies-malaysias-central.

the volatility that usually accompanies free capital flows. Nevertheless, the ringgit is still a floating currency. It may be dirty floating, but it strengthens and weakens according to the path of the Malaysian economy.

In 2015 and 2016, as the world economy cooled down, so did the ringgit. The currency lost more than 20% of its value, in line with the rest of the emerging markets. Capital controls may diminish volatility but do not change the fundamental relationship between the vigor of the economy and the relative value of its currency.

The ultimate choice of national governments is about the extent of integration with the rest of the world. As long as the economy is partially or totally integrated, authorities cannot have total control over the exchange rate. They can try to peg the currency, but that always comes at some economic cost. The Malaysian case highlights the tradeoff between control and integration. Regardless of the rules about the ringgit, the exchange rate is still affected by the relative strength of the Malaysian economy compared with the rest of the world.

Dirty Floating and a Costly Lunch in Mexico

Policymakers should know that society bears the costs of every economic policy. There is no free lunch. The volatility of the Mexican peso following the election and inauguration of President Donald Trump illustrates the difficult choices facing public authorities. On the day that Donald Trump was elected, the Mexican peso devalued 7.3%, falling a further 6% in the next two days. In 2016, the Mexican currency weakened almost 20% against the US dollar (see figure 11.13).

In the wake of Mexico's currency and financial crisis in 1994, Mexican authorities opted for a dirty floating currency system. The country's central bank, the

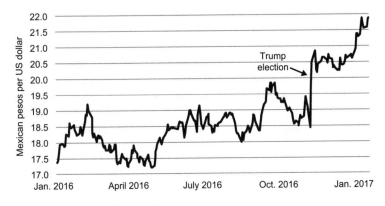

Figure 11.13
Exchange rate of Mexican pesos per US dollar
Source: Federal Reserve of St. Louis, 2017, https://fred.stlouisfed.org/series/DEXMXUS.

Bank of Mexico, officially defines the peso as a free-floating currency: "the Foreign Exchange Commission, made up of officials from the Ministry of Finance and Banco de México, is responsible for foreign exchange policy in Mexico. At the end of 1994 the Commission determined that the exchange rate would be determined by market forces (floating exchange rate / free float regime)."[26] It was never truly free, but it was mostly floating after 2013. Effective April 8, 2013, the currency auctions were suspended because volatility of the exchange rate had decreased.[27] This lasted until Donald Trump was elected, when the Bank of Mexico started to intervene in the foreign currency market again, auctioning US dollars to contain the depreciation of the peso.

Dirty floating systems have clear tradeoffs. In order to be able to intervene, central banks must first form reserves in foreign currency. Reserves come at a fiscal cost equal to the differential in the interest rates of the country and the US treasury bonds. The main benefit is reduced volatility if interventions are successful. The Mexican government decided to restart interventions after the peso plunged on the back of uncertainties regarding the trade, migration, and financial policies of President Trump. Mexican currency traders made a tongue-in-cheek suggestion that it would be cheaper for the Mexican government to buy and shut down Twitter, Inc. (President Trump's favored communication platform and valued at that time at US$12 billion) than to spend dozens of billions of dollars of the country's reserves to contain the volatility of the peso.[28]

Two-Money Systems

Emerging markets tread a delicate balance regarding currency policies. Although openness to foreign capital can bring more investment and efficiency to local markets, its sudden stop may trigger currency crises. One of the least efficient ways to control currency and money markets is through two-money systems, a fixture chosen by many countries in recent history.

Countries that use two-money systems usually face external restrictions and choose this kind of system to control capital inflows and outflows. The policy of "one country, two currencies" may seem idiosyncratic at first, but it was widespread in poor countries in the mid-twentieth century. It may be used as a result

26. "Foreign Exchange Market (Exchange Rates)," Bank of Mexico, http://www.banxico.org.mx/portal-mercado-cambiario/foreign-exchange-markets--exc.html.

27. International Monetary Fund, "Annual Report on Exchange Arrangements and Exchange Restrictions: 2014," IMF, Washington, DC, 2014, https://www.imf.org/external/pubs/nft/2014/areaers/ar2014.pdf.

28. Brendan Walsh and Isabella Cota, "Some Peso Traders Want Mexico to Buy Twitter and Shut It Down," *Bloomberg*, January 12, 2017, ttps://www.bloomberg.com/news/articles/2017-01-12/-shut-down-twitter-cry-goes-out-among-exasperated-peso-traders.

of civil war (China during the 1927 to 1950 period), closed capital accounts (Tanzania from the 1960s to 1990s), reunification (Germany in 1990), currency crises (Latin America in the 1980s), a currency board system (Argentina in the 1990s), and an artificial trade surplus (Cuba).

China had different two-money systems in the twentieth century. During the civil war period, the Communist Party issued one currency, and the Kuomintang issued another.[29] From 1978 to 1994, China again dabbled in a two-money system, but this time to ease the transition to a market-based economy. Foreigners could not hold the people's money (renminbi or yuan) and instead used foreign exchange certificates that were issued by the Bank of China and accepted at designated tourist hotels and the state-run Friendship Stores. The effect was that the renminbi (yuan) had two rates—one for trade and another for transactions inside China.

There are two main reasons for establishing a two-money system, like China's until 1994 and Cuba's until 2016. On the one hand, the home rate acts as an overvalued, fixed exchange rate that keeps prices stable and inflation in check. On the other hand, the trade exchange rate is undervalued in an effort to promote exports (overvalued fixed exchange rate regimes are good for controlling prices but act as disincentives to exports). Countries can have even more exchange rates for foreign currency, with distinct prices for things like trade and tourism. This was a feature of the 1980s in Latin America, and it created all sorts of distortions. If travelers' expenses were to be higher than the official limit, they had to buy foreign currency on the black market at exorbitant rates. Exporters were able to sell currency at the market rate, but importers faced much more expensive foreign currency. In some countries, more than six exchange rates were being used simultaneously, and agents went to great lengths to acquire foreign currency cheaply and sell it on the black market at a profit.

In mainland China, the experiment with multiple currencies ended in 1994. The government unified its two rates at the swap-market rate of 8.7 renminbis (yuans) to the US dollar—much weaker than the official rate of 5.8. At the same time, China abolished the foreign exchange certificates. The black market faded quickly, providing a simple lesson in microeconomics: if governments try to control prices without taking care of the resulting excess demand or supply, a black market will emerge; however, it dissipates as soon as the controls are eased. In 2015, for example, Nigeria, Venezuela, and Argentina set up artificially low rates for hard currency with significant restrictions regarding who could buy dollars at these

29. Andrew Browne, "Dual Exchange Rate Regime for China? An Historical View," *Wall Street Journal*, November 10, 2011, https://blogs.wsj.com/chinarealtime/2011/11/10/dual-exchange-rate-regime-for-china-an-historical-view.

low prices. Most people who wanted to buy or sell dollars simply shifted to the black market. Meanwhile, multinationals could not repatriate profits due to capital controls, and they could not bring in foreign direct investment because the official exchange rate was too low.

Venezuela maintained strict currency controls from 2003 to 2016 and had two legal exchange rates (known as the Dipro and Dicom rates) of 10 and 658 bolivars per US dollar used for priority imports.[30] On the black market, where people and businesses turn when they cannot obtain government approval to purchase dollars at the legal rates, the bolivar weakened 50% from 1,567 bolivars to 2,300 per US dollar in a single day (November 1, 2016), according to dolartoday.com, a widely watched website that tracks the exchange rate in Caracas.[31] On the border with Colombia, the rate was even weaker at 1,737.50 bolivars per US dollar, according to the website.

Tanzania is another example. After independence in 1961, the country operated a relatively open trade and payments regime supported by conservative monetary and fiscal policies.[32] These policies survived the introduction of the Tanzanian shilling in 1965, but the Arusha Declaration of 1967 generated a fundamental reorientation under the banners of self-reliance and African socialism. In the next two decades, the exchange rate on Tanzania's illegal parallel foreign exchange market rose at an average rate of nearly 2.5% per month, more than three times as rapidly as the official exchange rate. By early 1986, the parallel rate exceeded the official rate by more than 800%.

Trade and exchange rate reforms were the centerpiece of the 1986 Economic Recovery Program and its successors, with the result that over the next eight years Tanzania moved gradually toward a unified foreign exchange market. By early 1990, the premium had fallen to roughly 50%. In early 1992, the government introduced foreign exchange bureaus, allowing them to buy and sell foreign currency at freely determined exchange rates. The spread between the parallel market rate and the bureau rate quickly narrowed to below 10%. In 1993, the government liberalized nearly all remaining restrictions on foreign exchange transactions for current-account purposes, and late in that year the official and bureau markets were officially unified. The black market finally disappeared.

30. "Venezuela's Currency Is Collapsing on the Black Market Again," *Bloomberg*, November 1, 2016, https://www.bloomberg.com/news/articles/2016-11-01/venezuela-s-currency-is-collapsing-on-the -black-market-again.
31. *Dolartoday*, 2017, https://dolartoday.com/category/cotizacion.
32. Daniel Kaufmann and Stephen A. O'Connell, "Exchange Controls and the Parallel Premium in Tanzania, 1967–90," in *Parallel Exchange Rates in Developing Countries*, ed. Miguel A. Kiguel, J. Saul Lizondo, and Stephen A. O'Connell, 247–290 (Basingstoke, UK: Palgrave Macmillan, 1997).

Multiple currency regimes have little economic benefit to offer to governments not desperate for foreign currency. The costs are immense. Distortions create black markets, allocate capital inefficiently from sectors that use imported factors of production to export-oriented ones, shift the incentives of individuals to acquire foreign currency, and limit foreign direct investment inflows and outflows. Most economists would strongly advise against this kind of solution to currency woes. Nevertheless, authorities often insist on them because they provide an illusion of control.

12 Income Inequality and Economic Policy

In this chapter,
- Income versus wealth inequality
- The elephant chart and the losers from globalization
- Multidimensional poverty
- Free trade and income inequality
- Fossil fuel subsidies and social welfare
- Social mobility and justice for all

Although most macroeconomic books have paid lip service to income inequality, income inequality has been rising steadily in developed countries, and in many it has become a major economic issue. In the United States, it led to the Occupy movement (and its slogan "We are the 99%," which refers to the disproportionate wealth held by 1% of the world's population) and the US$15 minimum wage movement. This chapter integrates concerns about income inequality into our broader framework.

12.1 Income Inequality versus Wealth Inequality

Many people confuse the economic implications of wealth inequality and income inequality. Economists do not fret much about the former because it is the latter that destroys social welfare. The media often use the terms *income inequality* and *wealth inequality* interchangeably. A *Financial Times* article published in January 2016 made this mistake in the title and lead about income inequality in China: "China income inequality among world's worst. Poorest quarter of households own just 1 per cent of country's total wealth."[1] China's income inequality is not

---

1. Gabriel Wildau and Tom Mitchell, "China Income Inequality among World's Worst," *Financial Times*, January 14, 2016, https://www.ft.com/content/3c521faa-baa6-11e5-a7cc-280dfe875e28.

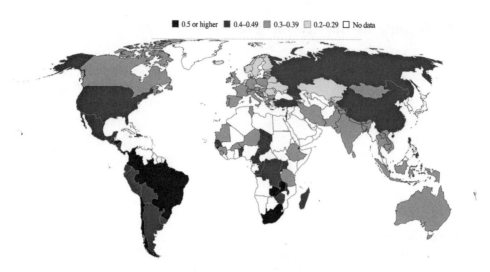

Figure 12.1
The Gini index around the world, most recent year available
Source: World Bank, 2017, https://data.worldbank.org/indicator/SI.POV.GINI.

as bad as the title of the article portrays. China's Gini coefficient (named after Corrado Gini, who first published it in a paper in 1912), which is the standard measure of income inequality, was 0.49 in the early 2010s, in line with many lower middle-income countries. China's wealth inequality, however, is very high. China has more billionaires than the United States has, and the richest 1% owns 13% of the wealth in the country.[2] Again, this is not a major issue. Income inequality is.

The Gini coefficient is the standard way to measure income inequality. It can vary from 0 to 1, with 0 being perfect income equality (every individual earns the same amount) and 1 being extreme inequality (one individual gets all income from society). Most countries fall in the 0.2 to 0.7 interval (figure 12.1).

According to the World Bank's data on income inequality for 130 countries, China is not among the world's most unequal countries. Table 12.1 shows the top ten and bottom ten countries in terms of income equality (for countries with data for at least one year in the 2010s). Although China is not among the most unequal countries, it is not far off. Nevertheless, China's widening income inequality is largely a reflection of faster income growth among the rich rather than stagnant living standards among the poor.[3]

2. Shannon Tiezzi, "Report: China's One Percent Owns One-third of Wealth," *The Diplomat*, January 15, 2016, http://thediplomat.com/2016/01/report-chinas-1-percent-owns-13-of-wealth.
3. Ian Talley, "China Is One of the Most Unequal Countries in the World, IMF Paper Says," *Wall Street Journal*, blog, March 26, 2015, https://blogs.wsj.com/economics/2015/03/26/china-is-one-of-most-unequal-countries-in-the-world-imf-paper-says.

Table 12.1
The top ten and bottom ten countries in terms of income inequality (Gini coefficient), 2010s

Country	High income equality	Country	High income unequality
Ukraine	0.25	Guinea-Bissau	0.51
Slovenia	0.25	Rwanda	0.51
Norway	0.26	Panama	0.52
Czech Republic	0.26	Brazil	0.53
Slovak Republic	0.27	Colombia	0.54
Iceland	0.27	Lesotho	0.54
Sweden	0.27	Honduras	0.55
Belarus	0.27	Zambia	0.56
Kazakhstan	0.27	Haiti	0.61
Finland	0.28	South Africa	0.63

Source: World Bank, 2017, https://data.worldbank.org/indicator/SI.POV.GINI.

Context is more important in the analysis of income inequality than it is in the case of other macroeconomic variables. Although an unemployment rate of 4% means full employment and a rate of 24% conveys a sclerotic labor market wherever the country is, comparisons between Gini coefficients cannot be disassociated from the level of the country's development and its poverty rate. Income inequality is an increasingly relevant issue in developed countries only because growth is stagnant or is benefiting some groups in lieu of others. In poor countries, income inequality causes social distress because the combination of poverty and inequality is usually the result of a continuous process in which the elites extract resources and value from the rest of society. Latin America and Africa have many examples of entrenched elites that keep countries from developing.

Wealth inequality measures differences in ownership of financial and nonfinancial assets, and income inequality assesses disparities in take-home pay. Notwithstanding the allure of owning mansions, yachts, and luxury cars, most people, including officials, have no reason to care about discrepancies in wealth. As long as rich people do not accumulate wealth through extracting resources from the rest of society, wealth accumulation has no negative effect on aggregate social welfare. The important link to social welfare comes from stable and balanced incomes that support the middle-class dream—a good education, a home, a car, a vacation once a year, and a comfortable retirement. For most people in the world, an income that supports a dignified way of life would be life changing.

Income inequality is dynamic, and its impact on social welfare changes over the development path of an economy. As countries become richer, income inequality increases at first, and if countries develop further, incomes tend to equalize up to a point over time. This process is called the Kuznets curve (named after Simon

Kuznets, who first described it in the 1960s). In the 1970s, for example, China's income inequality pattern was similar to India's today—widespread poverty and fairly equal income. Inequality increased steadily in China throughout the 1990s and 2000s, however, as the country went from a poor agrarian society to an industrial powerhouse. Rising inequality is natural when countries leave poverty and attain a lower middle-class status. Nevertheless, if inequality continues to rise as China develops, then it will become an increasingly relevant issue in Chinese society.[4]

The rise of inequality as a major economic issue in the United States follows from the country's recent economic history, the impact of the great financial crisis, and trends in trade and innovation (figure 12.2). After the early 1970s, business cycles have not followed the typical pattern where recessions lead to higher unemployment and lower growth and expansions generate inflationary pressure. Stagflation in the late 1970s posed a dilemma for policymakers: if they tried to fight inflation, recession would become steeper, and if they tried to lift income, employment will result in even higher prices. The Federal Reserve chose the first path in the grand disinflation of the 1980s. In the 1990s, a surge in productivity from the

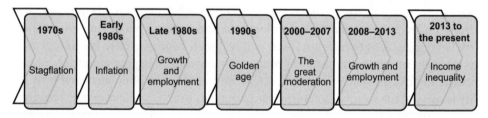

Figure 12.2
Evolution of major macroeconomic outcomes

4. In real life, people are not as rational as they are in most economic models. People are willing to forfeit some income in the search for some measure of income equality. In the Ultimatum games, one individual receives a sum and has to choose how to divide it between him- or herself and another player. The second player has only one option—either to accept the proposed division (so that both players receive a share) or reject it (so that both players go home with no income). Instrumental rationality predicts that the second player should accept any nonzero payoff division. After all, any income is better than getting nothing. Choosing the option in which no player gets anything is akin to punishing the first player for proposing an unfair arrangement. In experiments with an initial endowment of US$100, however, most people were willing to deviate from instrumental rationality by rejecting arrangements in which the first player delivered what the second player perceived as an unfair distribution. On average, people reject offers lower than 20% of the initial stake. What this experiment, many other experiments, and empirical results show is that inequality bothers people. Most individuals are willing to forfeit part of their income for a more equal society. Extreme income inequality, regardless of how prosperous a society is, reduces welfare.

Internet boom led to a rare beneficial shift in aggregate supply, generating prosperity without inflation. The expansion in trade in the early 2000s helped keep inflation low while the economy recovered from the first recession in fifteen years. The great financial crisis changed everything. The recession was sharper and the recovery much slower than in previous recessions. Recovery was two-stage: at first growth picked up, but the shock in labor markets was profound and resolved itself more slowly.

When unemployment finally started to cede, there was a sharp contrast in job creation: high-skilled workers found a welcoming labor market, but sclerosis set in for low-skilled workers. This was compounded by the effects of globalization and rapid advances in technology. It has been long recognized by international trade models that increases in international trade have important income distributional effects. Trade benefits some type of workers—in the case of developed countries, the high-skilled type. In China, this effect means that after China entered the World Trade Organization (WTO) in 2001, low-skilled workers saw their incomes rise disproportionately. This generated an economic boom in the country that benefited most people in urban areas. Meanwhile, in rich countries, globalization created a bonanza for high-skilled workers, who benefited from the lower relative prices of products made in China and from the higher demand for their services required by an increasingly integrated world. In addition, process innovation and automation shifted demand for low-skilled labor to capital expenditure. For developing countries, the golden age of trade in the early 2000s lifted all boats, but poor people benefited the most. Hundreds of millions of Chinese migrated from their farms to urban areas in search of higher wages. Inequality dropped across Latin America, one of the most unequal areas of the world. The inverse happened in rich areas of the world like Western Europe and the United States, where high-skilled workers benefited the most from the trade intensity. Prosperity across the board disguised the distributional effects. They came to the fore only as growth stalled after the financial crisis.

Distributional conflicts strain the social fabric. In the early 2000s in Europe, migration was considered the solution to an aging population. Spanish officials sponsored "move to Spain" campaigns in Latin America to attract young workers regardless of their skill level. After the crisis, however, some European countries started to move toward xenophobia. In 2016, two major political reshuffles were influenced by the fear of immigration—the United Kingdom's withdrawal from the European Union (Brexit) and the election of Donald Trump in the United States. In both cases, middle-class and low-skilled workers felt disenfranchised by globalization and the countercyclical response of European and American authorities to the recession brought about by the financial crisis.

Table 12.2
World income inequality (Gini coefficient), 1980s and 2010s

	1980s	2010s	Change
Average	0.36	0.38	+0.025
Population weighted	0.34	0.37	+0.028
GDP weighted	0.32	0.36	+0.042
Countries with worse income equality	0.30	0.36	+0.06
Countries with better income equality	0.45	0.41	−0.04

Source: Branko Milanovic and Robert Wade, "Globalisation, Migration and the Future of the Middle Classes," LSE public lecture, 2016, http://www.lse.ac.uk/assets/richmedia/channels/publicLectures AndEvents/slides/20160627_1830_globalisationMigrationAndTheFuture_sl.pdf.

Around the world, the 2010s have seen a different income distribution pattern than what was seen in the 1980s, which were a period of currency crisis in a good part of the developing world (table 12.2).

Inequality is worse in the 2010s than it was in the 1980s. But the world is also richer. Is the world following a Kuznets curve in which inequality first rises and then declines as wealth spreads? Even if that is the case, the current distributional effects in many countries have important political and economic implications. An integrated world is not a zero-sum game in which some countries can become richer only when others become poorer. Globalization can lift all boats. Nevertheless, given the dynamics of income inequality, what occurred in the late 1990s and early 2000s, when the world was becoming more prosperous and equal, is the exception and not the rule. In the same way that political cycles create incentives for anticyclical macroeconomic policies, worse income distribution corrodes welfare and increases the likelihood of populist policies that may make things worse in the long run. In addition, anticyclical policies do not benefit all people equally. Lax monetary policy has a disproportionate effect on the price of financial assets, and policymakers usually target expansionary fiscal policy in specific sectors.

12.2 Multidimensional Inequality and Poverty around the World

In macroeconomics, the important inequality dimension is income. As Angus Deaton, a Nobel laureate for his work on development economics, points out, however, inequality is multidimensional: even life itself is unequally distributed.[5] In the United States and other wealthy nations, only two to six children out of every thousand die before age one, yet in twenty-five countries, more than sixty out of a thousand do so (figure 12.3).

5. Angus Deaton, "Inevitable Inequality?," *Science* 344, no. 6186 (2014): 783–783.

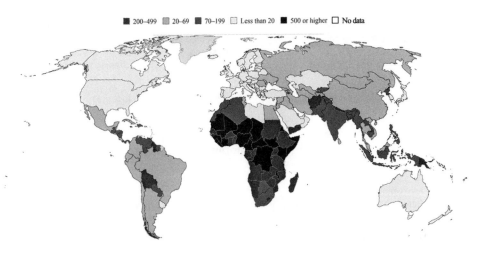

Figure 12.3
World maternal mortality ratio (modeled estimate per 100,000 live births), 2015
Source: World Bank, 2017, https://data.worldbank.org/indicator/SH.STA.MMRT.

The United Nations Development Program (UNDP) created the Human Development Index (HDI) to track more than mere income as countries develop. The HDI has only three dimensions (a long and healthy life, knowledge, and a decent standard of living) and fails to capture much of what makes a society prosperous, but it is an advance on considering only income as a proxy for well-being (figure 12.4).

The UNDP's Multidimensional Poverty Index (MPI) tries to capture the dynamics of poverty through many indicators related to three dimensions (health, education, and standard of living) (figure 12.5).

One of the most important developments in recent history was that extreme poverty was halved in the 1990 to 2010 period.[6] Bringing down poverty was one of the United Nation's eight Millennium Development Goals, and more than a billion people were lifted out of poverty in that two-decade period. Still, almost 1.5 billion people in the 101 developing countries covered by the MPI (about 29% of their population) live in multidimensional poverty—that is, with at least 33% of the indicators reflecting acute deprivation in health, education, and standard of living.[7] And close to 900 million people are vulnerable to falling into poverty if any setbacks (financial, natural, or otherwise) occur.

6. "Towards the End of Poverty," *The Economist*, June 1, 2013, http://www.economist.com/news/ leaders/21578665-nearly-1-billion-people-have-been-taken-out-extreme-poverty-20-years-world -should-aim.

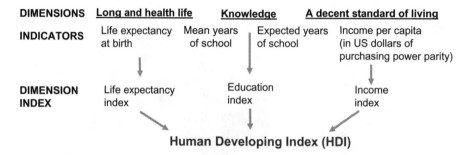

Figure 12.4
Human Development Index (HDI)
Source: United Nations Development Program, 2017, http://hdr.undp.org/en/content/human
-development-index-hdi.

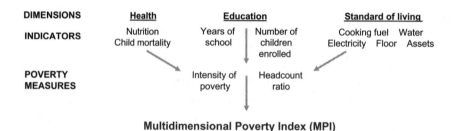

Figure 12.5
Multidimensional Poverty Index (MPI)
Source: United Nations Development Program, 2017, http://hdr.undp.org/en/content/multidi
mensional-poverty-index-mpi.

The MPI data displays a startling pattern for many countries in Africa: at least half of the population in fourteen of the countries surveyed are living in a state of deprivation with less than US$1.25 a day in purchasing power parity (PPP) (table 12.3). There are over 220 million poor people in those fourteen countries. Poverty clearly affects countries outside of Africa, too. Latin America and Southeast Asia concentrate hundreds of millions of people living in extreme poverty.

Inequality is also multidimensional. Wage inequality has increased faster than consumption inequality in the last three decades.[8] There are gender inequality and education premiums that sometimes are available only to a few wealthy students. Government redistribution through taxes and transfers can reduce the level of

7. For details on the Multidimensional Poverty Index, see http://hdr.undp.org/en/content/multidimensional-poverty-index-mpi.
8. Dirk Krueger, Fabrizio Perri, Luigi Pistaferri, and Giovanni L. Violante, "Cross-sectional Facts for Macroeconomists," *Review of Economic Dynamics* 13, no. 1 (2010): 1–14.

Table 12.3
Multidimensional poverty in Africa

Country	Survey	Population living in multidimensional poverty		Population living below the income poverty line	
		Number of people	Intensity of deprivation (percentage)	National poverty line, 2004–2014 (percentage)	US$1.25 a day PPP, 2002–2012 (percentage)
Congo	2014	50,312,000	50.8%	63.6%	87.7%
Madagascar	2009	15,774,000	54.6	75.3	87.7
Liberia	2013	3,010,000	50.8	63.8	83.8
Burundi	2010	7,553,000	54.0	66.9	81.3
Zambia	2014	8,173,000	48.6	60.5	74.3
Malawi	2010	10,012,000	49.8	50.7	72.2
Rwanda	2010	7,669,000	49.7	44.9	63.0
Central African Republic	2010	3,320,000	55.6	62.0	62.8
Nigeria	2013	88,425,000	54.8	46.0	62.0
Mozambique	2011	17,246,000	55.6	54.7	60.7
Sierra Leone	2013	4,724,000	53.0	52.9	56.6
Lesotho	2009	984,000	45.9	57.1	56.2
Togo	2014	3,394,000	49.9	58.7	52.5

Note: PPP = purchasing power parity.
Source: United Nations Development Program, "Human Development Data (1990–2015)," UNDP, 2017, http://hdr.undp.org/en/data.

income inequality, but in weak institutional settings, privileged groups can use the government as a vehicle for additional wealth and income concentration.

Around the world, the two most pressing economic issues are extreme poverty in the developing world and inequality in the rich countries. Growth is a necessary but not sufficient condition to tackle these issues. According to Angus Deaton, "When whatever growth exists is not shared, new problems arise. Those who are left behind may be patient when they are getting something, but if their incomes are flat or declining, they are unlikely to remain patient for long. Inequality becomes a political issue. Ideally, such dissatisfaction will bring political change. But if the political system is sensitive only to the needs of the wealthy— something that is arguably true of the U.S. Congress—there is a direct threat to political stability and, ultimately, to democracy itself. If the main political parties offer nothing to those who are excluded, they may turn to political remedies or candidates that threaten liberal democracy."[9] This is true in poor and rich countries alike. Good

9. Angus Deaton, "The Threat of Inequality," *Scientific American* 315, no. 3 (September 2016): 48.

economic policies and solid institutions are the necessary conditions for economic growth to generate true prosperity. Unlike with other macroeconomic variables, there is no a priori preferred income inequality coefficient for each country.

Social Mobility and Development for All

So far, we have discussed poverty as a common feature of emerging markets assuming that its effects are spread around evenly across the population. That is not so. In most countries, even rich ones, poverty and inequality are concentrated in certain groups. Aboriginal citizens are poorer than the other Australians, African Americans have the highest poverty rate in the United States and Latin America, and women face countless constraints to better income in most of the world. Sometimes, privileges are so entrenched that they become law. In 1972, the government of Hong Kong, where land is the most expensive in the world, enacted a small-house policy: male villagers have the right to build a house of up to three floors on a plot of land in their ancestral village, and if they have no land themselves, they can buy it from the government at a discount.[10] But this kind of privilege is nothing compared to the worst displays of unequal treatment in the world: family members have sanctioned at least 200 million girls and women alive today to female genital mutilation. Even though this horrendous practice has been declining, in Mali more than three in four girls between the ages of 0 and 14 years have been mutilated, and in some countries there is no law restricting the practice.[11]

Dynamically, income inequality is less of a problem when social mobility is high and people have access to education and are free to pursue their careers. But around the world, that has never been the case. Gender discrimination is real and destroys social welfare. It may be related to identity (same-sex relationships are criminalized in approximately 70 countries) or show up as subtle practices in national education or the workplace.[12]

Even though in rich countries there is no large gender disparity in access to tertiary education, social norms impact career choices and may allocate labor suboptimally. Using data from middle schools in South Korea, Jaegeum Lim and Jonathan Meer find that female students taught by a female versus a male teacher score higher on standardized tests compared to male students even five years later. They also find that having a female math teacher increases the likelihood

10. "In Hong Kong, a Row over Land Rights Reflects a Bitter Divide," *The Economist*, August 10, 2017, https://www.economist.com/news/china/21726116-why-communist-party-sides-landlords-hong -kong-row-over-land-rights-reflects.
11. "Female Genital Mutilation and Cutting," *UNICEF*, https://data.unicef.org/topic/child -protection/female-genital-mutilation-and-cutting.
12. Pamela Duncan, "Gay Relationships Are Still Criminalised in 72 Countries, Report Finds," *The Guardian*, July 27, 2017, https://www.theguardian.com/world/2017/jul/27/gay-relationships-still -criminalised-countries-report.

that female students take higher-level math courses, aspire to a STEM degree, and attend a STEM-focused high school.[13] It is unclear how these findings should shape public policy. Should countries enact affirmative action for people of less privileged backgrounds and different ethnicities? Should we have a quota for women in the boards of public companies? Much clearer is the path for reducing gender and ethnic discrimination in much of the developing world. Laws that guarantee equal rights to women, LBGT, and people from different ethnicities should be pursued by every country.

Usually, GDP per capita, Gini coefficients and other macroeconomic measures do not capture distinctions between different groups. We should keep in mind that, in formulating economic policy, people should be free to climb the income and social ladder. One cannot look at true development without considering that it should be spread out to all.

12.3   Distributional Effects of Monetary and Fiscal Policies

Conventional and unconventional economic policies have many distributional effects, although they are usually of secondary importance. Conventional monetary policy, for instance, consists largely of open-market operations to raise or lower the target interest rate, with the main goal to stabilize inflation. Changes in interest rates go beyond the market of goods and services and have important implications on both the real and financial sides of the economy. Lower interest rates cause financial assets to become more valuable. Stocks, in particular, rise when interest rates are low. Concurrently, savers of liquid assets are losing, especially savers who hold liquid, cash-like instruments such as bank deposits, certificates of deposit (CDs), and money market deposit accounts.

On the real side of the economy, interest rates affect industries asymmetrically. The real estate industry, for instance, tends to be more sensitive to interest rate movements than other industries due to the effect of rate changes on mortgages.

Research corroborates the effects that monetary policy has on income inequality.[14] Unbridled inflation affects poor people disproportionately, especially as prices rise on food and energy. The end of hyperinflation resulted in less poverty and inequality for Latin American countries in the 1980s and 1990s.[15] Furthermore,

13. Jaegeum Lim and Jonathan Meer, "Persistent Effects of Teacher-Student Gender Matches," NBER Working Paper No. 24128, National Bureau of Economic Research, 2017.
14. Karen Davtyan, "The Distributive Effect of Monetary Policy: The Top One Percent Makes the Difference," May 2017, https://researchgate.net/publications/317247731_The_distributive_effect _of_monetary_policy_The_top_one_percent_makes_the_difference.
15. Aleš Bulíř, "Income Inequality: Does Inflation Matter?," IMF Staff Papers 48, no. 1 (2001): 139–159.

economic shocks may affect different strata of society distinctly. In the inflation and postinflation periods in Latin America, there is an asymmetry in the effect of income change on poverty and inequality. The beneficial effects of a 1% growth in aggregate income are more than erased by a 1% decline in aggregate income, evidencing the high social costs of economic shocks.[16]

Even though monetary policy may have distributional effects, they are of the second order and not necessarily large. The link between income inequality and fiscal policy is stronger. Fiscal policy has by its nature strong effects on income inequality. On the side of public revenue, the way the state structures taxes defines its progressiveness and efficiency. Francesca Bastagli, David Coady, and Sanjeev Gupta from the IMF describe the ideal scenario for policymakers: "Tax and spending measures should enhance or maintain the distributive effects of fiscal policy while supporting economic efficiency. Such measures include reducing opportunities for tax evasion and avoidance, increasing the progressivity of income taxes over higher income brackets, cutting unproductive expenditure, and expanding means-tested programs. Enhancing the distributive impact of fiscal policy in developing economies will require improving their capacity to raise tax revenues and to spend those resources more efficiently and equitably. Resource mobilization should focus on broadening income and consumption tax bases and expanding corporate and personal income taxes by reducing tax exemptions and improving compliance. Expenditure reforms should focus on reducing universal price subsidies, improving the capacity to implement better targeted transfers, and gradually expanding social insurance systems."[17]

In rich countries, there is evidence that the recent austerity has had significant effects on income inequality. Laurence M. Ball, Davide Furceri, Daniel Leigh, and Prakash Loungani show that "fiscal consolidation has typically had significant distributional effects by raising inequality, decreasing wage income shares and increasing long-term unemployment. The evidence also suggests that spending-based adjustments have had, on average, larger distributional effects than tax-based adjustments."[18] There are numerous ways to do fiscal policy, from changes in taxes to public expenditure or transfers, and there is plenty of literature on

16. Alain de Janvry and Elisabeth Sadoulet, "Growth, Poverty, and Inequality in Latin America: A Causal Analysis, 1970–94," *Review of Income and Wealth* 46, no. 3 (2000): 267–287.

17. Francesca Bastagli, David Coady, and Sanjeev Gupta, "Income Inequality and Fiscal Policy," IMF Staff Discussion Note SDN/12/08, June 28, 2012, International Monetary Fund, http://www.imf .org/~/media/Websites/IMF/imported-publications/external/pubs/ft/sdn/2012/_sdn1208rev .ashx.

18. Laurence Ball, Davide Furceri, Daniel Leigh, and Prakash Loungani, "The Distributional Effects of Fiscal Consolidation," IMG Working Paper WP/13/151, June 2013, International Monetary Fund, https://www.socialjustice.ie/sites/default/files/attach/publication/3061/2013-07-16-imfausterity incomedistribution.pdf.

optimal taxation and optimal tax systems.[19] Austerity measures or expansionary fiscal policy target some industries. Taking into account potential distributive effects should be a primary concern for public authorities. The fact that the world is full of contradictory tax schemes is a testament to the political clout of vested interests.

Bringing the Poor to the Table: Bolsa Família and the Law of Big Numbers

The concept of a negative income tax is commonly discussed in economics textbooks, but it is rarely realized due to its politically controversial nature. The experience of income transfer in Brazil, however, has improved income inequality in a country with some of the worst indicators in the world.

When Bolsa Família was launched in January 2004, conditional cash transfer was not a new idea, even in Brazil. Similar programs had been used in the mid-1990s. Nevertheless, the expansion of the program and the unification of different initiatives into a coherent framework contributed to making Bolsa Família successful. By the end of 2017, the program was helping 13.6 million families by supplementing their income by an average of US$50 dollars a month (table 12.4). The main benefit of the program is invisible: the transferred amount to each family is small, but it provides a stable stream of income that helps lift families from extreme poverty. The main criticisms of the program are that it is too expensive, creates a disincentive for individuals to search for formal employment, and has some level of corruption embedded in the system. But Bolsa Família is not expensive: it costs a bit over 0.5% of Brazil's GDP. Because the amounts transferred are

Table 12.4
Bolsa Família's requirements and disbursements

Requirements:

Extreme poverty: family per capita income of US$34 per month

Poverty: per capita income of US$68 per month

Disbursements (maximum US$100 per month per family):

Basic benefit: US$33 per month with more for extreme poverty

Children age 0 to 15 and pregnant women (conditional health checks, nutritional care, and school attendance for children): US$15 to US$32 per month

Children age 16 to 17: US$15 to US$32 per month

Source: Brazilian Ministry of Social Development, "Requisitos para o Bolsa Familia," MDS, 2017, http://mds.gov.br/area-de-imprensa/noticias/2017/setembro/bolsa-familia-saiba-quais-sao-as-regras-para-participar-do-programa.

19. Joel Slemrod, "Optimal Taxation and Optimal Tax Systems," *Journal of Economic Perspectives* 4, no. 1 (1990): 157–178.

small, the disincentive to work is marginal, if it exists at all. Corruption has not been a big problem so far, either. Most cases are anecdotal, and there is no evidence that it is widespread.

There are many social programs in Brazil, but the advantages of Bolsa Família rest on its capillarity and its ability to reach the poorest families in the country. It helped to bring down income inequality in Brazil sharply (the Gini coefficient came down from 0.596 in 2001 to 0.519 in 2012), although Brazil still has one of the worst income inequalities in the world. As the country progresses, Bolsa Família should be phased out, but it will be difficult to terminate a program that generates such copious amounts of political capital. There is little doubt that Bolsa Família has played a major role in poverty reduction, especially in rural areas in Brazil. The challenge for the future will be to balance the economic efficiency of the program and the changing dynamics of the economy.

Demonetization in India

Demonetization is not part of the menu of macroeconomic policies, but it displays the important distributional effects of policymaking in action. In 2016, India tried to contain corruption and curb the growth of informal sectors and black markets by removing from circulation all banknotes of high denomination and replacing them with new ones. During an unscheduled live televised address on November 8, 2016, Prime Minister Narendra Modi announced that all 500 and 1,000 rupee notes would be terminated as legal tender as of the following day.

The unanticipated move agrees with economic theory that shows that unexpected actions have a better chance of success than those with long lead times because agents cannot counter the policy before it takes effect. Unfortunately, this measure negatively affected the lives of the ordinary and poor citizens who were the unintended targets of the demonetization process. Nearly six weeks after India abruptly scrapped high-denomination banknotes accounting for about 85% of its currency by value, the economy continued to slow.[20] Poor and middle-class Indians were still suffering from the shortage of new bills. The long-term effects of India's demonetization gambit are unclear, largely because no other major economy has attempted such an experiment except during a crisis. But with growth slowing and job losses rising, the short-term prognosis appeared grim.

In fact, India has done this before.[21] In 1946, all 1,000 and 10,000 rupee notes were recalled. In 1978, notes with face values of 1,000, 5,000, and 10,000 rupees

20. Sadanand Dhume, "India's Demonetization Debacle," *Wall Street Journal*, December 15, 2016, https://www.wsj.com/articles/indias-demonetization-debacle-1481851086.
21. Wade Shepard, "One Month in, What's the Impact of India's Demonetization Fiasco?," *Forbes*, December 12, 2016, https://www.forbes.com/sites/wadeshepard/2016/12/12/one-month-in-whats-the-impact-of-indias-demonetization-fiasco.

were demonetized. But this time, a monetary reform with the purpose of increasing taxes had the opposite effect. It disproportionately affected many poor people, who had to migrate back home as jobs were slashed in many parts of the country in which informal arrangements were key to economic growth. It also strained the credibility of the Reserve Bank of India, the country's central bank. The lack of confidence may translate in lower effectiveness of monetary policy in the future.

Carbon Taxes, Subsidies, Macroeconomics, and Income Inequality

Optimal tax design is part of microeconomics.[22] Nevertheless, given the potential impact of climate change on social welfare and the relation between fiscal policy and inequality, the tax regime on energy is particularly relevant and can have significant macroeconomic impacts. Carbon emissions could be minimized efficiently through a Pigouvian tax (a tax that tries to minimize the negative effects of economic activity by going for the agents that generate the adverse effects such as pollution, for instance), but it is almost impossible to design such a tax perfectly. Aparna Mathur and Adele C. Morris show that a carbon tax by itself is regressive, making a simple design unadvisable because it would make income inequality worse.[23] Nevertheless, "Results suggest that if policymakers direct about 11 percent of the tax revenue towards the poorest two deciles, for example through greater spending on social safety net programs than would otherwise occur, then on average those households would be no worse off after the carbon tax than they were before."

In developing countries, a major source of inequality comes from energy subsidies. Gasoline subsidies affect mostly rich individuals in these countries because most people do not own cars. There is a case for higher gasoline prices in developing countries.

For European countries, the usual arguments in favor of higher gasoline taxes include reduced carbon dioxide emissions and local air pollutants, reduced traffic congestion, and increased government revenue. In addition, gasoline taxes are efficient because they are easy to administer and fuel has a relatively low price elasticity. Increased gasoline taxes also save lives. Given that car users in emerging markets are usually richer and governments need incentives to improve infrastructure, the redistributive effect of gasoline taxes makes an even stronger argument for making them higher in developing countries than in developed countries.

The redistributive argument is simple: because most car users in emerging markets are upper middle class or rich, higher gasoline taxes would redistribute

22. A great book about the subject is Alan J. Auerbach and Kent Smetters, eds., *The Economics of Tax Policy* (Oxford: Oxford University Press, 2017).
23. Aparna Mathur and Adele C. Morris, "Distributional Effects of a Carbon Tax in Broader US Fiscal Reform," *Energy Policy* 66 (2014): 326–334.

income efficiently. Combined with all the other benefits, in particular the environmental one, higher gasoline prices make economic sense for poor and emerging countries alike (unless the social contract is one in which most transportation costs are related only to gasoline and not to other fuels, like diesel).

According to the traffic department of China's Ministry of Public Security, for instance, at the end of 2014, the country's civilian fleet amounted to over 264 million vehicles, of which 154 million were cars. The fleet had grown by 20 million cars in 2014. Thus far, infrastructure investment has increased at the same rate as car production, but that pace is bound to change, and traffic, which is already bad in cities like Beijing and Shanghai, is going to get worse. Higher gasoline prices would curb the driving of the new Chinese middle class, especially in cities with good transportation infrastructure. Analyzing a longer time horizon, however, as China develops, the number of cars per capita will rise. Today this ratio stands at 1 car per 9.05 people (in Latin America the ratio is 1 to 4.20). As urbanization increases, the number of cars in China will increase. Notwithstanding other effects, a number of cars in China equivalent to the ratio in Latin America would mean a further 330 million cars, with all the associated negative effects on the environment and traffic conditions.

Brazil has 48 million cars, with 26 million in the rich southeast region. For ten years, gasoline prices had a price cap, which has damaged the ethanol industry and made the gasoline production and distribution industry much less competitive internationally. Curiously, Petrobras has become the only monopolist company in the world that actually lost money by being a monopolist. Given that gas prices were fixed, the company had to import oil at international prices but could charge only lower prices locally.

For some countries, low gasoline prices are a structural feature of their energy markets. The most extreme examples are Venezuela (US$0.02 per liter) and Russia (US$0.60 per liter), but Mexico, Colombia, and South Africa also have cheap gasoline (figure 12.6). In many emerging countries, gasoline prices are not necessarily low, relative to income. The most interesting cases are Turkey, Uruguay, and Paraguay, where gasoline prices are in line with most developed countries, even though incomes are much lower.

Gasoline prices are particularly low in the United States, Australia, and Canada, where the social contract encourages families to own cars because distances are large and the population dispersed and where governments provide good road infrastructure but few efficient public transportation systems. In Europe, car ownership is relatively lower, public transportation is more efficient, and high gasoline taxes are used to curb consumption, improve the environment, and generate government revenue, even in oil-producing Norway.

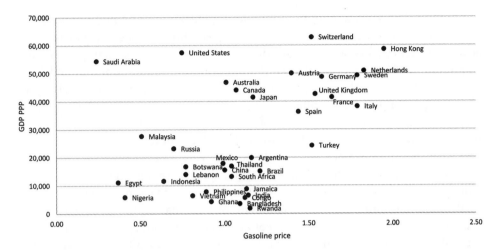

Figure 12.6
Gasoline prices (in 2017 US dollars per liter) and GDP per capita (in US dollars purchasing power parity) around the world, 2016
Source: GlobalPetrolPrices.com and World Bank, 2017, http://www.globalpetrolprices.com/gasoline_prices/ and https://data.worldbank.org/indicator/NY.GDP.PCAP.CD.

High gasoline taxes have some downsides. For some countries, the auto industry is an important component of private investment, and higher gasoline prices reduce the demand for new cars. Moreover, there would be a temporary spike in inflation. However, long-term benefits would make this a sensible policy for long-term infrastructure planning. Higher gasoline prices could even induce more urban infrastructure investment in countries with poor transport systems, like Brazil and Peru, given higher demand for public transportation after the introduction of such a tax.

Economists have long known that consumption taxes are more efficient than income taxes, and increased gasoline taxes in countries like Brazil and China would bring some market distortions but result in significant positive externalities to their economies and the rest of the world. Low gasoline prices, like the one enjoyed by consumers in many emerging markets, create many environmental and economic distortions.

12.4 Trade, Inequality, and Politics

Trade increases GDP. That is an undisputed fact. It also has an effect on income inequality, something that is compatible with most models of trade. Recently, the links between trade, technology, and politics have become even more relevant due to their macroeconomic effects.

Trade models like the one developed by Eli Heckscher and Bertil Ohlin posit that trade has a permanent effect on income inequality: it rises in countries with abundant high-skilled workers and decreases in others.[24] For example, assume that two countries have two kinds of workers (high-skilled workers and low-skilled workers) and that one country (perhaps the United States) has plenty of high-skilled workers and the other (perhaps China) has many low-skilled workers. What would happen in the absence of trade (which economists deem autarky)? In the United States, the goods that use high-skilled workers as factors of production (such as complex machines) would be relatively cheaper than they would be in China, and the goods that use low-skilled labor (such as electronics and clothes) would be more expensive in the US than they would be in China, in relative terms. As these nations trade, the US specializes in complex machines, and China specializes in electronics and clothes. Both countries benefit from specialization (in the sense that GDP is higher when trade is free instead of autarky), but not everybody benefits in both countries. In the US, as production shifts to the production of complex machines, low-skilled workers and the companies that employ them fare worse than they would fare under autarky. Trade lifts all boats, but it lifts some much more than others.

Until recently, most economists assumed that specialization would have no significant impact on other macroeconomic variables, such as employment. Companies and individuals would adjust, and low-skilled workers would move to other occupations, increasing the incentive to pursue education. In the long run, trade would create growth, and income inequality would not destroy social welfare. Recent research, however, has shown that such adjustments do not necessarily happen fast enough. David H. Autor, David Dorn, and Gordon H. Hanson have analyzed the impact of the burgeoning trade between China and the United States on the US labor markets.[25] They show that these impacts are most visible in the local labor markets in which the industries exposed to foreign competition are concentrated. Adjustment in local labor markets is remarkably slow, with wages and labor-force participation rates remaining depressed and unemployment rates remaining elevated for at least a full decade after the China trade shock commenced. Exposed workers experience greater job churning and reduced lifetime income. At the national level, employment has fallen in the US industries that are more exposed to import competition, as expected.

24. Rodrigo Zeidan, "These Two Swedish Economists Foresaw a Globalization Backlash. In the 1930s," *World Economic Forum*, May 16, 2017, https://www.weforum.org/agenda/2017/05/these-two -swedish-economists-foresaw-a-globalization-backlash-in-the-1930s.
25. David H. Autor, David Dorn, and Gordon H. Hanson, "The China Shock: Learning from Labor-Market Adjustment to Large Changes in Trade," *Annual Review of Economics* 8 (2016): 205–240.

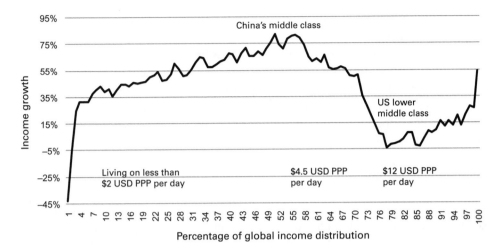

Figure 12.7
Real income growth and global income distribution (in 2005 US dollars purchasing power parity), 1988 to 2008
Source: Adam Corlett, "Examining an Elephant: Globalisation and the Lower Middle Class of the Rich World," Resolution Foundation, 2017, after Branko Milanovic, "Global Income Inequality in Numbers: In History and Now," *Global Policy* 4, no. 2 (2013): 198–208.

Branko Milanovic captures a more general trend in the evolution of inequality in his elephant figure (figure 12.7).[26] The figure decomposes income growth for individuals around the world, from the poorest (first tenth percentile) to the richest (last tenth percentile) in the period 1988 to 2008, when trade boomed and increased tenfold. The comparison between 1998 and 2008 is made in terms of purchasing power parity, a measure that adjusts income to the cost of living. For instance, an Indian earning US$12,000 a year in India is comparatively less poor than an American earning the same amount in the United States because living in India is cheaper than in the US. The figure shows that almost every individual in the world experienced a significant expansion in income in this period. The one exception was persons in the eightieth percentile, whose income stagnated during this period.

The biggest relative winners and losers over this period can be separated and shown to correspond to the average middle-class Chinese and US citizen, respectively. Trade and growth took hundreds of millions of Chinese people out of poverty, and the new middle class in China was the greatest beneficiary from the

26. Branko Milanovic, "Global Income Inequality in Numbers: In History and Now," *Global Policy* 4, no. 2 (2013): 198–208.

market reforms in the country, the speeding of globalization, and the country's membership in the World Trade Organization in 2001. At the other end of the spectrum, the income of the US middle class has been stagnant since the late 1980s because of a combination of trade and technology. As the gap in productivity between the average US worker and the world's average declined, US companies found it feasible to move operations elsewhere. This brought an end to the golden age of the baby boomers. The increasing productivity, wages, and job stability that they had enjoyed for decades cannot be brought back by protectionism because competition now is global.

The elephant figure shown in figure 12.7 helps explain the rise of middle-class discontent in the developed world. Populism is rising as the political process responds to the anxiousness of the middle class. As incomes in the middle class in the developing world start to stagnate, following the Kuznets curve (which shows that as an economy develops, market forces first increase and then decrease economic inequality), such discontent can go global. In fact, Chinese authorities are worried about income inequality and the dwindling incomes of their new middle class. China is going to produce around 200 million college graduates by 2020,[27] and many are already struggling to find work commensurate with their expectations.[28] If the Chinese economy stalls, middle-class frustrations (which now are felt in rich countries) can strain the delicate social fabric of the burgeoning nation. Getting stuck in the middle-income trap with a stagnant income is a real possibility for many emerging countries around the world, and those middle-class frustrations helped fuel the Arab spring uprising in the early 2010s.[29] It is harder for societies stuck in low-growth high-inequality situations to function well.

12.5   Inequality and Macroeconomics Redux

Growth is a necessary but not sufficient condition for prosperity. It may or may not lift all boats. Income inequality is not always bad, but it can destroy social welfare. It happens gradually but cumulatively, and the fabric of society can be strained only to a certain point before it breaks. Most of macroeconomics is usually disassociated from income inequality because governments that pursue full

27. Keith Bradsher, "Next Made-in-China Boom: College Graduates," *New York Times*, January 17, 2013, http://www.nytimes.com/2013/01/17/business/chinas-ambitious-goal-for-boom-in-college -graduates.html.
28. "Dreams Collide with China Slowdown for Job-Seeking Graduates," *Bloomberg*, July 2, 2015, https://www.bloomberg.com/news/articles/2015-07-02/dreams-collide-with-china-slowdown -for-job-seeking-graduates.
29. "Middle-Class Frustration Fueled the Arab Spring," World Bank, October 21, 2015, http://www .worldbank.org/en/news/feature/2015/10/21/middle-class-frustration-that-fueled-the-arab -spring.

employment and stable and low inflation are supposedly looking out for the greater good. Yet economic policies are not distributive neutral. Quantitative easing may bring some economic activity that benefits all, but it increases the prices of scores of financial assets. Fiscal policy done well can lift people out of poverty, but when done badly, it turns into a bystander of crony capitalism.

In the present framework, there is no explicit connection between macroeconomic markets and Gini coefficients. In fact, comprehensive models with income inequality as the main output do not exist. Income distribution is multidimensional. It arises from labor-market interactions but is affected by things like inflation, past wealth (endowments), the rate of human capital accumulation, saving profiles, taxation, demographics, the rate of innovation, and the amount of insurance against shocks. Unlike other variables, not every increase in inequality is bad for society in the same way that rising unemployment or recessions affect people. It also moves at a different timescale than other macroeconomic variables that follow the regular business cycles. Gini coefficients change almost imperceptibly in the short run. It can take decades for nations to become more or less unequal.

Giuseppe Bertola, Reto Foellmi, and Josef Zweimüller have investigated the dynamics of income distribution in macroeconomic models.[30] The most comprehensive empirical evidence comes from Thomas Piketty, who in his book *Capital in the Twenty-first Century* puts forward long-run trends in wealth and income inequality.[31] Unfortunately, inequality was not a priority in the past. Instead, growth, employment, and inflation usually have been the first-order issues, and in most countries, the old order remains. Nevertheless, for the rich world and for all countries that do not want to be stuck in the middle-income trap, inequality is now at the forefront. The main issue with inequality is that we do not know the best course of action. Some countries are experimenting with a basic universal income, and others with taxation that is more progressive. There is no easy and simple solution to this complex issue.

30. Giuseppe Bertola, Reto Foellmi, and Josef Zweimüller, *Income Distribution in Macroeconomic Models* (Princeton, NJ: Princeton University Press, 2014).
31. Thomas Piketty, *Capital in the Twenty-first Century* (Cambridge, MA: Harvard University Press, 2014).

13 Climate Change, the Environment, and Economic Policy

In this chapter,

- Climate change and economic shocks
- Water conflicts and economic growth
- Climate events and stagflation
- The tradeoff between the environment and growth
- How macroeconomic policies can improve environmental outcomes

13.1 The Great London Smog and Life in Contemporary China

Pollution is the price of progress. At least, that was the motto of public authorities when I was growing up, and it was probably the same around the developing world at that time, and probably still true today in some parts of the world. Officials disregarded the negative externalities generated by economic activities. The social contract in developing countries was a simple one: public authorities should provide people with jobs and more money. All the other consequences that came with it were considered minor side effects.

The standard of living of most of the world's citizens has improved, as long as we consider only income. More than one billion people left extreme poverty in the first fifteen years of the twenty-first century alone. In the *The Road to Wigan Pier* (1937), George Orwell wrote about the miserable conditions in which miners and their families lived in industrial England three generations ago. In one passage, a woman comments that "Teeth is just a misery." In one house where five people lived, a fifteen-year-old "boy was the only one who possessed a single tooth of his own, and his teeth were obviously not going to last long."[1]

There are virtually no extremely poor people in the United Kingdom anymore. Income inequality is still a major issue, but access to dental care and other health

---

1. George Orwell, *The Road to Wigan Pier* (London: Victor Gollancz, 2001 [1937]), 97.

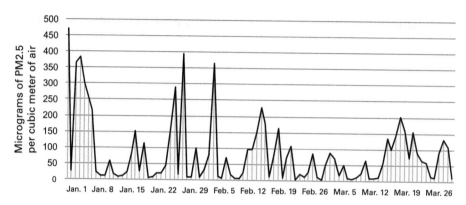

Figure 13.1
Concentration of PM2.5 air pollutants in Beijing, measured daily at 8 a.m. in the first quarter of 2017
Source: US Embassy, "Beijing: Historical Data," Mission China, Beijing, 2017, http://www.stateair.net/
web/historical/1/1.html.

care for low-income people has increased dramatically. The effects of British industrialization on the environment, however, will stay with us for a long time.

In 1952, the Great Smog of London, caused when coal particulates gathered in windless conditions, killed more than 4,000 people and made over 100,000 sick.[2] Since then, however, a major share of manufacturing has shifted from rich countries to industrializing emerging countries, and the most polluted cities in the world are in China and India.

Beijing is a good example of the plight of large urban areas in emerging markets. The World Health Organization considers that any concentration of fine air pollutants—particulate matter of a diameter of 2.5 micrometers (PM2.5)—of over 50 micrograms per cubic meter is a health hazard. In the first quarter of 2017, the pollution level in Beijing, measured at 8 a.m., was above this threshold on twenty-four occasions (figure 13.1). On eleven days, the PM2.5 concentration was above 200 micrograms per cubic meter, a level that is considered "very unhealthy" and that triggers a health alert (it may cause anyone to experience serious health effects).

The social contract in China is changing, and as people escape poverty, they are clamoring for a better quality of life. Economic policy cannot focus solely on growth, unemployment, and inflation as national outcomes. We need to incorporate the environment into our economic framework.

2. Bert Brunekreef and Stephen T. Holgate, "Air Pollution and Health," *The Lancet* 360, no. 9341 (2002): 1233–1242.

13.2   Nature and Economic Shocks

One simple and direct way to add the environment to our aggregate demand and aggregate supply framework is with an economic shock, either positive or negative. There is little doubt that the world's climate is changing and that human beings are responsible. Climate change is usually incremental, but some short-run consequences of that change (like storms and droughts) can be quite dramatic.

In the discussion in this chapter, most adverse climate events affect either aggregate supply or aggregate demand. A violent storm, for example, may destroy houses and leave people without electricity. This kind of event clearly lowers aggregate demand, at least temporarily.

Things become even more complicated with perennial climate change, like a long drought spell in a mostly agricultural country. At first, this curtails aggregate supply as production dries up (figure 13.2).

With time, if agriculture is the main economic activity of a country, this will gradually lower aggregate demand. GDP contracts, unemployment shoots up, and inflation recedes.

From a purely economic point of view, climate change should result in a series of shocks and perturbations with short- and long-run effects. Aggregate demand shifts are more important in the short run, and supply shocks are more important in the long run.

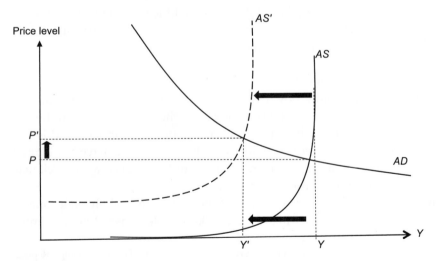

Figure 13.2
Market for goods and services

Given that

$$AD = C + I + G + X - IM,$$

where AD is aggregate demand, C is consumption, I is investment, G is government expenditure, X is exports, and IM is imports, negative shocks sap investment, and consumption and international trade create and widen a growth gap.

Climate change, natural disasters, and other environmental challenges are a major obstacle to the expansion of aggregate supply. In addition, there is a fundamental difference between a climate change shock on aggregate supply and, for example, stagflation provoked by a currency crisis. A sudden devaluation is transitory, and its effect is diluted eventually as aggregate supply recovers from the shock. Climate change, however, creates a permanent pressure on supply factors. The exploitation of natural resources creates negative externalities. Higher greenhouse emissions intensify climate variability, lowering yields in agriculture (to name one negative aftermath).

In the long run, events that increase the cost of production and limit productivity growth have the most pernicious effect: they lower potential output. This, in turn, limits economic growth and puts a cap on prosperity. William D. Nordhaus and Andrew Moffat have estimated the global economic impacts of climate change using a systematic research synthesis and found that at 3 degrees Centigrade warming the world's income would decrease by –2.04% and at 6°C warming income would decrease by –8.06 (±2.43)%. This could lead to stagflation or even an economic depression. Ignoring climate change in the name of short-run growth will cause economies to grow less in the future.[3]

Drought and Famine in Somalia

Climate change should slow down economic activity worldwide and disrupt many regions to varying degrees. Data show that the level of concentration of carbon dioxide in the atmosphere has reached 400 parts per million and is still increasing (figure 13.3). Moreover, changes in climate patterns have the biggest impact on the poor because richer areas can afford insurance against climate change as long as events are not too dramatic.

The worst-case scenario in terms of climate shocks to an extremely poor country occurred in Somalia, where in 2010 to 2011, 250,000 people perished from a famine

---

3. William D. Nordhaus and Andrew Moffat, "A Survey of Global Impacts of Climate Change: Replication, Survey Methods, and a Statistical Analysis," NBER Working Paper No. 23646, National Bureau of Economic Research, 2017.

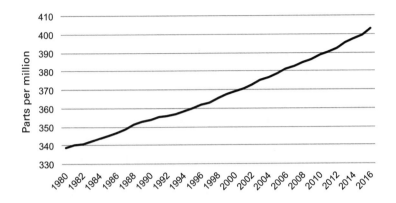

Figure 13.3
Mean carbon dioxide levels globally, 1980 to 2016
Source: Ed Dlugokencky and Pieter Tans, "Trends in Atmospheric Carbon Dioxide," NOAA/ESRL, 2017, https://www.esrl.noaa.gov/gmd/ccgg/trends/global.html.

caused by a two-year drought. The country experienced another severe drought in 2017,[4] when at least 60,000 people died.[5]

Displacement and social revolts usually follow a long drought as people try to escape famine. Aggregate supply and aggregate demand collapse. GDP goes down, and inflation ceases to be a major issue. A poor country becomes even poorer.[6] Modeling this kind of event using the tools of economics is relatively easy. Preventing large-scale starvation is harder, even in a world that is becoming richer by the day.

Water Management and the Economy

The world will never lack fresh water. The problem is not that its supply will be depleted but that some countries may not be able to guarantee a constant supply of this most precious resource. Countries need water security so that human health can be maintained and economic activity can continue unimpeded. Climate change and the production of goods and services affect water management due

4. "Prolonged Drought Drives a Food Security Emergency in Somalia and Southeastern Ethiopia," *FEWS NET*, July 6, 2017, http://www.fews.net/east-africa/alert/july-6-2017.
5. Jason Burke, "'We've Never Seen This Drought, This Disease': Somali Families Bury Their Dead," *The Guardian*, April 20, 2017, https://www.theguardian.com/world/2017/apr/20/weve-never-seen -this-drought-this-disease-famine-looms-in-somalia.
6. Ismail Akwei, "Reality of the Worst Drought since 1945 Peaking in Parts of Africa," *Africanews*, March 17, 2017, http://www.africanews.com/2017/03/17/depth-of-the-worst-drought-since-1945 -peaking-in-parts-of-africa.

to many factors, from the rate of evaporation to redistribution of rainfall to pollution of aquifers.[7]

Water is an important issue in emerging markets due to chronic underinvestment. Because governments consider it a public good, most countries subsidize the access that their citizens and companies have to water. Given that water is never (and never should be) priced according to market forces, society needs to rely on public investment, directly or through private-public partnerships. This is even more important in countries that rely on hydropower as a major source of energy. When any environmental problem, such as drought, is compounded by underinvestment, the combination can lead to macroeconomic shocks.

Modeling the economic impact of water rationing shows what can be expected. If the rationing is temporary and affects residential consumption, then an aggregate demand shock reduces economic growth and reduces inflation. If water rationing leads to industrial stoppages, however, then aggregate supply shrinks and stagflation follows. The more severe the crisis, the more serious the economic consequences.

Although access to water may lead to some geopolitical conflicts, the world probably will not experience international water wars. The world already has the technology to produce fresh water from salt water. But water prices will continue to climb as long as countries keep wasting this not completely replenishable resource.

Not all groundwater is exploitable, and calculating water resources by country is difficult. The United Nations' Food and Agricultural Organization has published many reports on water resources in various countries. In the early 2000s, the countries in the Middle East and North Africa were already withdrawing almost three-quarters of their total renewable water resources.[8] A third of the world's freshwater aquifers are already overstressed, and another third are variably stressed (figure 13.4).

In resource-rich countries, deforestation, pollution, and other factors deplete once abundant reserves. Even worse, economic shocks due to water shortages probably will become more common in the future, especially in poorer countries that can ill afford them.

Water Conflicts and Economic Growth in Africa and Asia

Even though wars for access to water are an unlikely scenario, some geopolitical crises due to water management issues may lead to a slowdown in economic activity. In Southeast Asia and Africa, two examples of complicated negotiations

7. "The Impact of Climate Change on Water Resources," Grace Communications Foundation, http://www.gracelinks.org/2380/the-impact-of-climate-change-on-water-resources.
8. "Water Resources Data," World Bank, http://siteresources.worldbank.org/INTMENA/Resources/App-all-Scarcity.pdf.

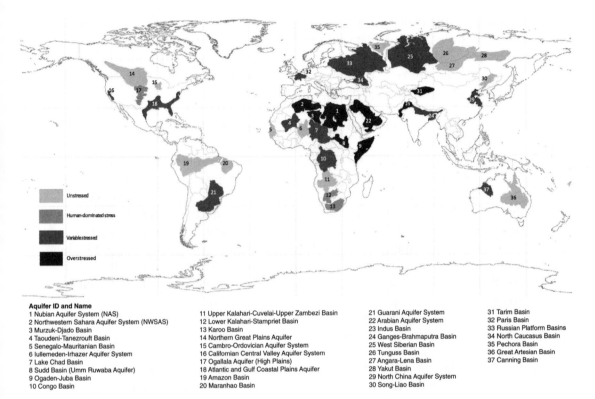

Aquifer ID and Name

1 Nubian Aquifer System (NAS)	11 Upper Kalahari-Cuvelai-Upper Zambezi Basin	21 Guarani Aquifer System	31 Tarim Basin
2 Northwestern Sahara Aquifer System (NWSAS)	12 Lower Kalahari-Stampriet Basin	22 Arabian Aquifer System	32 Paris Basin
3 Murzuk-Djado Basin	13 Karoo Basin	23 Indus Basin	33 Russian Platform Basins
4 Taoudeni-Tanezrouft Basin	14 Northern Great Plains Aquifer	24 Ganges-Brahmaputra Basin	34 North Caucasus Basin
5 Senegalo-Mauritanian Basin	15 Cambro-Ordovician Aquifer System	25 West Siberian Basin	35 Pechora Basin
6 Iullemeden-Irhazer Aquifer System	16 Californian Central Valley Aquifer System	26 Tunguss Basin	36 Great Artesian Basin
7 Lake Chad Basin	17 Ogallala Aquifer (High Plains)	27 Angara-Lena Basin	37 Canning Basin
8 Sudd Basin (Umm Ruwaba Aquifer)	18 Atlantic and Gulf Coastal Plains Aquifer	28 Yakut Basin	
9 Ogaden-Juba Basin	19 Amazon Basin	29 North China Aquifer System	
10 Congo Basin	20 Maranhao Basin	30 Song-Liao Basin	

Figure 13.4
A third of the world's big groundwater basins in distress
Source: Alexandra S. Richey, Brian F. Thomas, Min-Hui Lo, John T. Reager, James S. Famiglietti, Katalyn Voss, Sean Swenson, and Matthew Rodell, "Quantifying Renewable Groundwater Stress with GRACE," *Water Resources Research* 51, no. 7 (2015): 5217–5238.

about international access to water supply involve the building of dams on rivers that cut through more than one country.

The Grand Ethiopian Renaissance Dam on the Blue Nile River in Ethiopia was met with resistance by Egypt, which sits downstream and relies on the flow of the river for hydroelectric power and agriculture. There also has been resistance to the many dams that are being built on or proposed for the Mekong River, which originates in the Tibetan plateau and flows through China, Myanmar, Thailand, Laos, Cambodia, and Vietnam. Laos, for instance, intends to build nine dams to harness hydroelectric power. Vietnam, where many peasants depend on the river for irrigation, fears that the projects could cause ecological damage and change agricultural patterns.[9]

9. "The Political Ebb and Flow of the Mekong River," *Stratfor Worldview*, April 11, 2016, https://worldview.stratfor.com/article/political-ebb-and-flow-mekong-river.

There is little doubt that building dams may affect downstream ecosystems, which, in turn, can cause demand or supply shocks to economic activities, such as fishing and agriculture. In our long-run model, natural resources enter aggregate supply directly. Disruption in the use of resources may cause stagflation and make poor people even poorer.

Stagflation Due to Water Shortages: The Case of Brazil in 2001
In the late 1990s, the Brazilian government was looking to privatize part of the country's water and sewage system and therefore stopped investing in improving and expanding the public water system. This lack of maintenance meant that the system was ill prepared for an extended drought that the country experienced in the early 2000s. Brazil relies heavily on hydropower, which is responsible for over 70% of the total energy supply in the country. This combination of drought and underinvestment required public authorities to resort to energy rationing for both residential and industrial consumers. The result was a severe economic shock that greatly affected the market for goods and services. Economic growth floundered, and inflation picked up.

In 2000, the economy grew 4.36%, and inflation was 5.92%. In 2001, due to the rationing and other shocks, GDP real growth was only 1.51%, and prices surged by almost 8%. More important, the Brazilian government decided to incentivize the building of coal and natural gas power plants. A country that had used mostly replenishable or renewable resources turned to nonrenewables. This was more pronounced in 2007, when Petrobras, the state-owned oil company, discovered and started exploring the largest oil reserves discovered in the twenty-first century.

The Brazilian case illustrates the many risks facing countries due to climate change and the mismanagement of water supply. Potential and actual output are increasingly at risk.

California Drought and Economic Activity
The state of California, like Brazil, suffered from water shortages, but they affected mostly aggregate demand. The regional drought lasted almost three years, from 2014 to 2016. In 2015, the drought in agriculture caused losses of US$1.8 billion in direct costs and 10,100 full- and part-time jobs statewide, and in 2016, the drought caused losses of US$600 million and 4,700 full- and part-time jobs.[10] Fortunately, these losses were not enough to push the state's economy into a recession because

---

10. Josué Medellín-Azuara, Duncan MacEwan, Richard E. Howitt, Daniel Sumner, and Jay R. Lund, "Economic Analysis of the 2016 Drought for California Agriculture," Center for Watershed Sciences, University of California, Davis, CA, August 15, 2016, https://watershed.ucdavis.edu/files/Executive_Summary_Drought_Report.pdf.

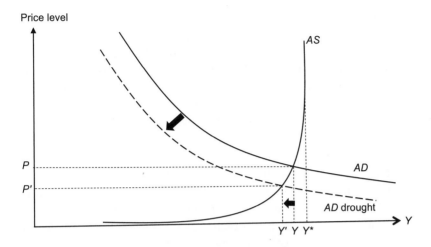

Figure 13.5
Market for goods and services

other parts of the economy were unaffected and performed well enough to cover the shortcomings in agricultural production. California's GDP went up, but the water shortage kept the economy from growing even more.

Figure 13.5 illustrates California's situation according to a comparative statics model.

A severe drought may cause aggregate supply to shrink as well, causing prices to shoot up, but here we assume that the effect is only on aggregate demand. *AD* drought displays the lower level of economic activity due to income and job losses. The Californian economy would perform better if precipitation was normal, but this relatively small effect can be amplified. In societies that rely on agriculture, concurrent shocks from climate events can short-circuit economic activity, leading to a recession or even stagflation.

13.3 Climate Change and Productivity

Climate change is one of the biggest risks for the future of humanity. It brings, however, many opportunities for both developed and developing countries. Even though there is a clear tradeoff between economic growth and the environment, this is not absolute. In the short run, a country that is looking to stop all carbon dioxide emissions will grow more slowly, but productivity can help improve national economies and the environment. As is discussed in chapter 3, technology, in a broad sense, is the major driver for long-term prosperity. Ideally, innovations would cut amount of carbon dioxide and other greenhouse gases that are generated from human activity, something that has been growing since the industrial revolution.

The Malthusian trap—Thomas Malthus's 1798 theory that population growth would outpace agricultural growth and lead to starvation—has been averted due to innovation and productivity growth. Innovation also is at the core of prosperity for rich countries. Because these countries already allocate capital, labor, and natural resources well, only advances in technology can bring them further economic growth.

The auto industry is moving toward electric car substitutes for gasoline and diesel vehicles. Norway aims to end the sale of gas and diesel cars by 2025, India aims to do this by 2030, and the United Kingdom and France have committed to a total ban by 2040.[11] Meanwhile, companies are moving toward improving electric battery technology to support a completely new infrastructure for electric vehicles. Chinese, German, and US companies have been investing heavily in huge battery factories.[12] One example is Tesla, whose lithium ion battery manufacturing facility is expected to produce 35 gigawatt hours, which could power approximately 10 million houses.

Advances in productivity are critical to growing agricultural production for a larger world population, and innovation is at the core of the decarbonization of the economy. Such efforts are driven by changes in consumer behavior, strong regulation by national government and international institutions, and market mechanisms. There is no guarantee that such investment can offset the adverse shocks of climate change and other environmental effects, but the drive for mitigating the effects of climate-related risk events can bring economic growth to many countries.

Bolivia, Borneo, and the Growth/Deforestation Dilemma

For many poor countries, the tradeoff between growth and environment is real and affects mostly its poorest citizens. Borneo, the third-largest island in the world, and Bolivia illustrate the dilemma faced by public authorities and international organizations in the fight against deforestation. These two regions host some of the most biodiverse areas in the world. Since 2011, Bolivia has deforested an average of about 865,000 acres of land annually for agriculture, and in Borneo, barely over 50% of the original forest cover remains.[13]

11. Stephen Castle, "Britain to Ban New Diesel and Gas Cars by 2040," *New York Times*, July 26, 2017, https://www.nytimes.com/2017/07/26/world/europe/uk-diesel-petrol-emissions.html.
12. Ryan Browne, "Elon Musk's Tesla Could Soon Be Overtaken in the Global 'Arms Race' for Batteries, Strategist Says," *CNBC*, August 7, 2017, https://www.cnbc.com/2017/08/07/elon-musks-tesla-could-soon-be-overtaken-in-batteries-arms-race.html.
13. Rhett A. Butler, "Borneo," *Mongabay*, https://data.mongabay.com/borneo.html.

In both instances, deforestation follows directly from export activities. In Borneo, palm oil and logging drive deforestation. In Bolivia, the main culprit is soy. According to the executive director of the Bolivian Institute of Forestry Investigation, a Bolivian nongovernmental organization that monitors and researches the country's forests, "There's a lot of pressure for economic development. When resources are flowing, production is happening and people have work. It's very hard to argue with that."[14]

In poor countries, economic growth and jobs usually win over the environment. Corrupt institutions tend to facilitate deforestation.[15] But rich countries are not completely immune to the allure of economic growth over environmental impact. Australia's economy has been robust since 1991, and part of the country's economic resilience in this period has come from capital expenditures by the mining industry, sometimes proceeding despite the objections of local communities.[16] The same drive for more investment has been true in Canada, another country with a robust fossil fuel export industry. Curbing economic activity due to environmental concerns in both rich and emerging countries comes at a significant political cost.

13.4   The Environment and Economic Policy: Moving Forward

Of the three macroeconomic tools at the disposal of public authorities—monetary, fiscal, and currency policies—fiscal policy is the most suited to tackle the environmental and social impacts of the pursuit of economic growth. By deciding on taxes, subsidies, and other measures, public authorities can directly influence the allocation of resources in different industries.

Subsidies for the fossil fuel industry, for instance, were set up because of the link between investment by oil and gas companies and direct and indirect jobs in those industries. There is very little doubt that today these are some of the world's least effective policies. As the editors of *Bloomberg* note, they are wasteful, expensive, environmentally destructive, and unnecessary.[17] In addition, many subsidies are granted by emerging countries that can ill afford them. Fossil fuel

14. Hiroko Tabuchi, Claire Rigby, and Jeremy White, "Amazon Deforestation, Once Tamed, Comes Roaring Back," *New York Times*, February 24, 2017, https://www.nytimes.com/2017/02/24/business/energy-environment/deforestation-brazil-bolivia-south-america.html.

15. Hiroko Tabuchi, "How Big Banks Are Putting Rain Forests in Peril," *New York Times*, December 3, 2016, https://www.nytimes.com/2016/12/03/business/energy-environment/how-big-banks-are-putting-rain-forests-in-peril.html.

16. Matt Siegel, "Coal Mine Fight Embodies an Economic Struggle in Rural Australia," *New York Times*, August 14, 2013, http://www.nytimes.com/2013/08/14/business/global/in-australia-signs-of-a-tilt-in-economic-equilibrium.html.

17. Editors, "Fuel Subsidies Are the World's Dumbest Policy," *Bloomberg*, September 1, 2016, https://www.bloomberg.com/view/articles/2016-09-01/fossil-fuel-subsidies-are-the-world-s-dumbest-policy-editorial.

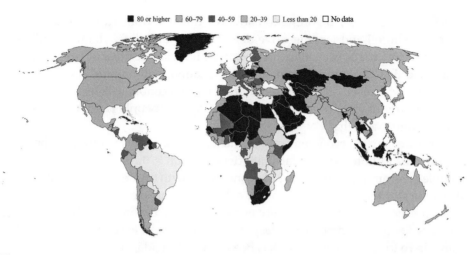

■ 80 or higher ▨ 60–79 ■ 40–59 ▨ 20–39 □ Less than 20 □ No data

Figure 13.6
World electricity from fossil fuels as a percentage of GDP
Source: CIA, 2017, https://www.cia.gov/library/publications/the-world-factbook/rankorder/2237
rank.html.

consumption subsidies totaled almost half a trillion dollars in 2014, with most of them coming from Iran, Saudi Arabia, Russia, and Venezuela.[18] Some researchers estimate that if production and consumption subsidies of fossil fuels were cut, global carbon dioxide emissions would fall by over 20%, and government revenues would increase by US$2.9 trillion or 3.6% of the world's GDP at the time of the study.[19]

This does not mean that reducing these subsidies will come at no cost. There is never a completely free lunch. Yet shifting these subsidies to renewables would potentially help maintain the same amount of economic activity and improve environmental outcomes. Such a shift would come as close to a free lunch as we can get in the economics of global business. The world needs to curb the use of fossil fuels. Unfortunately, in most of the world, a large part of electricity generation comes from fossil fuels (figure 13.6).

Most economists favor a carbon tax. John Cochrane said as a complement to an op-ed for the *Wall Street Journal*, "I favor a uniform carbon tax in place of all

18. For data on that, see the International Energy Agency website at http://www.worldenergyoutlook
.org/resources/energysubsidies.
19. David Coady, Ian Parry, Louis Sears, and Baoping Shang, "How Large Are Global Energy Subsidies?," IMF Working Paper WP/15/105, International Monetary Fund, May 2015, https://www.imf
.org/external/pubs/ft/wp/2015/wp15105.pdf.

the other direct energy regulations and subsidies."[20] Regardless of the design of good economic policies to help mitigate the risks of climate change, we need to start by scrapping the subsidies for industries that are intensive in carbon dioxide emissions.

Leading the Drive for Renewables: European Subsidies and Macroeconomic Repercussions

Climate change and other environmental consequences of economic activities are worldwide challenges. Economic growth in a country affects everybody, local people first and the rest of the world later. Pollution in Beijing makes the lives of residents harder and increases greenhouse gas emissions that affect the whole planet. Europe has been the leading region in pushing for more sustainable energy production. The European Union set a target of 20% final energy consumption from renewable sources by 2020, and 27% by 2030.[21] Unfortunately, achieving such targets is not an easy task, since badly designed incentives may distort energy markets and shrink overall productivity.

Since long-run economic growth comes from higher productivity, a careless push for renewables that make energy too expensive could generate economic harm that would dissuade the countries from achieving the targets set by the EU. That is why the European Commission has crafted detailed directives, to try to be careful in establishing the support mechanisms to make renewables more competitive with other sources of energy.

A more comprehensive agreement, although less binding, is the Paris Climate Agreement, signed in 2017 by 172 members of the United Nations. The goal is for countries to pursue efforts to contain the global temperature rise to less than 2% below preindustrial levels. In August, 2017, President Donald Trump formally told the UN that the United States was withdrawing from the Paris Agreement.[22] His argument followed the basic short-run growth/environment tradeoff: without worrying about sustainability the US economy could grow more. Of course, such a line of thinking shows a disregard for long-run effects.

But even when countries pursue more sustainable economic policies, there is no easy path to a prosperous future with limited environmental impact. On an analysis of European energy markets, researchers have shown that the income

20. See John Cochrane, "On Climate Change," *The Grumpy Economist* (blog), July 31, 2017, http://johnhcochrane.blogspot.nl/2017/07/on-climate-change.html.

21. "Renewable Energy," European Commission, 2017, https://ec.europa.eu/energy/en/topics/renewable-energy.

22. Valerie Volcovici, "US Submits Formal Notice of Withdrawal from Paris Climate Pact," *Reuters*, August 4, 2017, https://www.reuters.com/article/us-un-climate-usa-paris/u-s-submits-formal-notice-of-withdrawal-from-paris-climate-pact-idUSKBN1AK2FM.

elasticity of fossil fuel imports in the European Union is relatively high.[23] This means that one of the reasons that the countries in the region had been able to meet the environmental targets is that economic growth was lagging in the region throughout the 2010s. If GDP growth were to pick up, imports of fossil fuel should rise disproportionately. The drive for renewables, as with most economic policies, creates dilemmas for public authorities.

Ignoring long-run growth to focus on short-term benefits, like the United States is doing by withdrawing from the Paris Climate Agreement, seems unwise. But moving toward a completely sustainable economy does come with costs; it is impossible to do so in a short time and can be quite costly in terms of income.

China is another country pursuing sustainable policies. After all, its citizens breathe in the negative consequences of GDP growth. The country is adopting a new green index in a bid to pressure local governments to reduce pollution and create more sustainable economic development.[24] This is necessary in China and in many other places.

Ignoring climate change and the negative externalities of economic growth will reduce future output. We have to move toward true prosperity, limiting the environmental impacts of economic activity.

The Oil Industry in Canada: Inequality, Growth, and the Environment

Canada is one of the most developed countries in the world. Income is high, inequality relatively low, and multiculturalism thrives. In many ways, Canada illustrates the triumph of globalization: a country where people of all faiths have access to education and a path to a prosperous future. But at the same time, regional differences play a major role in internal politics and the distribution of society's gains. Case in point: the oil sector in Canada.

The country is a major producer of oil and gas (6% of GDP), with oil alone contributing 2% of GDP. The country exported 3.1 million barrels of oil per day in 2016, a growth of almost 50% in comparison with 2012 (2.3 million). The oil industry in Canada is concentrated in one region, Alberta. Of the 189.5 megatons of GHG emissions by the oil and gas industry in Canada in 2016, the province of Alberta is directly responsible for 70% of it (132.3 megatons). In fact, compared to 2000 the annual GHG emissions of all other regions in the country have gone down (figure 13.7).[25]

23. Svetlana Fedoseeva and Rodrigo Zeidan, "How (A)symmetric Is the Response of Import Demand to Changes in Its Determinants? Evidence from European Energy Imports," *Energy Economics* 69(1), (2018): 379–394.

24. Chao Deng, "China Takes Another Green Step Forward," *The Wall Street Journal*, December 26, 2017, https://www.wsj.com/articles/china-takes-another-green-step-forward-1514289286.

25. "Energy Information," National Energy Board, Government of Canada, https://www.neb-one .gc.ca/nrg/sttstc/crdlndptrlmprdct/stt/crdlsmmr/2016/smmry2016-eng.html and https://www .neb-one.gc.ca/nrg/ntgrtd/mrkt/snpsht/2017/12-05cndhstrclghgmssn-eng.html.

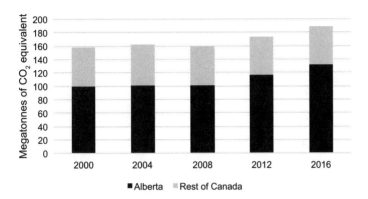

Figure 13.7
Canada's historical GHG emissions
Source: National Energy Board, 2017, https://www.neb-one.gc.ca/nrg/ntgrtd/mrkt/snpsht/2017/12
-05cndhstrclghgmssn-eng.html.

The push for a more sustainable future creates many dilemmas. In Canada, none is more visible than in the importance of the oil industry for the province of Alberta. Because of its oil sector, the province boasts the highest GDP per capita in the country. Predictably, it also has the worst income inequality, since most of the top earners work in the oil industry. That in itself is not a problem, but the economy of the region is heavily dependent on the business cycle of the oil industry. Alberta experiences higher highs and lower lows than the rest of the country.[26]

More troubling, because of the importance of the oil industry for the country, Canada pulled out of the Kyoto Protocol and implemented special subsidies for oil producers, in the form of royalty reductions and tax deductions.

A more sustainable future will most likely go through the devolution of the oil industry. Nevertheless, even developed countries are easily attracted by the siren song of oil producers, with its promises of riches and higher employment. But even if subsidies are curtailed and the there is a bigger push for renewables in Canada, there is no clear and easy answer to how the country should deal with the regional consequences of falling capital expenditure in the production of oil and gas in the country. The costs of lower investment would be concentrated in Alberta, while the benefits would be spread across the rest of the world.

26. Rebecca Graff McRae, "A Rising Tide Doesn't Lift All Boats," *Parkland Institute,* September 21, 2017, http://www.parklandinstitute.ca/a_rising_tide_doesnt_lift_all_boats.

14 National Accounts: GDP, Inflation, Inequality, and Unemployment

In this chapter,

- Definitions of gross domestic product (GDP), unemployment, inflation, and income inequality
- The limits of GDP
- Labor markets and social welfare
- Global market comparisons and interactions
- Why people perceive inflation higher than it actually is.
- Informal workers and the problems with persistent high unemployment.

What does an unemployment rate of 7% exactly mean? Is GDP an outdated measure (as *The Economist* suggested in April 2016)?[1] How do are inequality and inflation rates compared among countries? By the end of this chapter, we will have examined all the different market interactions and their macroeconomic outcomes. Then we will put everything together, establishing a final framework for the economics of global business.

14.1 Gross Domestic Product (GDP)

Economists define economic growth as the real (as opposed to nominal) rate of change in a country's gross domestic product (GDP). GDP is the market (monetary) value of all final goods and services produced by the country. This definition raises at least three questions: Why final goods? Why use market value? Why produced instead of sold?

There are three ways to calculate GDP, and they all yield the same result: the production approach (supply), the expenditure approach (demand) and the

1. "The Trouble with GDP," *The Economist*, April 30, 2016, http://www.economist.com/news/briefing/21697845-gross-domestic-product-gdp-increasingly-poor-measure-prosperity-it-not-even.

income approach (value-added). Because GDP is determined in the markets for goods and services through a clearing equilibrium following aggregate supply and demand interactions, it follows that the aggregate supply of domestic goods quantity is equal to aggregate demand of domestic goods quantity. Both need to be equal to the value-added way of calculating GDP. All three measures are actually estimations instead of calculations, and all are fraught with methodological problems. It is almost impossible to observe the production of all services and goods produced in an economy over a period. GDP has many limits and provides unsatisfactory answers to issues such as these: Should we count illegal activity? Does GDP take into account nonremunerated work (such as cooking one's own food)? Is it moral for GDP to increase following a tragedy (such the loss of life in a car accident)? GDP is flawed and should never be used as a proxy for true development. It is, at best, a good proxy about material prosperity.

GDP and GDP per capita are measures of economic output and indicate the income flow generated by countries and their population. GDP per capita shows the average income of a person in a country. GDP is not a good measure of social cohesion, life satisfaction, or anything else. It is simply a measure of how much a country produces that is measurable at market prices. Nevertheless, the spotlight is on GDP because most people want an increase in living standards, and income is a good proxy for them. In general, growing income improves living standards across the world, and an increase in income is something that most people can easily comprehend. Most governments' economic policies aim at growth because people want to become richer (or less poor). GDP measurements miss many other dimensions of life, which is why some people favor the creation of new measures. What counts in favor of GDP is the fact that we know what it measures, so we can compare it across countries and over time. The focus on GDP may cause some important unintended consequences, such as growth policies that cause significant harm to the environment. At the same time, economic growth in poor countries is relevant to alleviating poverty. GDP is not a perfect measure, but it is still the major goal of macroeconomic policy around the planet. We need to understand how it is measured.

Production (Supply of Domestic Goods)
Production (or supply of domestic goods) is one of the three ways to measure GDP. How this is done can be shown in a simple example, like the production of bread, assuming the following:

1. There are only three stages in the production chain of bread—wheat, flour, and bread.
2. The economy is closed.

3. All wheat is used to produce flour.
4. All flour is used to produce bread.
5. All production at each stage is sold (in other words, markets clear).

The market value related to the production of bread can now be calculated. In this example, farmers produce wheat and sell it for 180. Flour manufacturers buy the wheat at 180, process it into flour, and sell it for 350. Bakers buy flour and sell bread for 600. How much value is added into the economy? Each production step adds value into the economy: wheat farmers add 180, flour manufacturers add 170, and bakers add 250, for a sum of 600, which is the market value of all bread produced and sold (in this simplified case, there is no inventory). When calculating GDP, it is not necessary to consider anything other than market prices and final goods (in principle). Intermediate goods are already incorporated in the market value of final goods, so aggregating the value added of all goods and services allows us to calculate the country's GDP.

Income (Value Added)

We can decompose GDP into the different remunerations of input factors and calculate GDP through another lens. For each stage of production, flows can be divided into three segments—intermediate goods, labor, and capital. We implicitly use a supply-side function in which the production of any good or service in the economy is

$$Y = f(K, AL, AN),$$

where Y is output, f is a function that relates variables to output, K is capital, A is an index of productivity, L is labor, and N is natural resources. This is our version of Solow's growth model that is the main driver of long-run growth. The main idea of computing GDP by looking at production factors is to divide the value of goods and services in terms of who owns the factors of production. Let's assume that we can neatly divide the production of each step of production of bread into wages, intermediate goods, and profits. For instance, farmers pay 70 in wages, pay 80 in rents (machines, interest on loans, and silos), and receive 30 in profits. We assume that there are no intermediate goods for the production of wheat, a gross simplification but one of the reasons that agriculture is classified as a primary sector. If the other steps in the production of bread are similar in nature, the results are as shown in table 14.1.

Estimating GDP through the remuneration of production factors forms the basis of the way input-output (IO) models work. IO models show the interdependence of the economy by targeting how intermediate goods are transformed into final goods. For the United States, the data come from the Bureau of Economic

Table 14.1
Remuneration of production factors in the production of bread

Wheat	70	80	30	180
Flour	50	70	50	170
Bread	100	100	50	250
Total	220	250	130	600

Analysis.[2] The comprehensive version consists of 389 industries and is divided into production of commodities by industry, use of commodities by industry valued at producers' prices, and use of commodities by industry valued at purchasers' prices.

The idea behind value added, then, is to understand which processes contribute more to the GDP of a nation. Full input-output models have hundreds of different components and are both time-consuming and computationally difficult to work with. But they detail the contribution of each industry in generating economic prosperity.

Expenditure (Demand)

In addition to the production side of the economy, which looks at value-added factors and the remuneration of production, there is a demand side (where does GDP go?). The demand side can be divided into five components:

$$AD = C + I + G + X - IM,$$

where AD is aggregate demand, C is the aggregate consumption of all residents in a country, I is new private investment in capital goods (another way to say investment in expanded capacity), G is the value of government expenditure on individual and collective goods and services, X is total exports, and IM is imports from other countries. There are important differences between these concepts and the standard way most people talk about these variables. Is government investment in aggregate demand equal to government outlays? Do imports actually lower national economic output? Let's try to explain why economists define aggregate demand the way they do and try to make sense of the previous questions.

Consumption (C) is the easiest variable to understand. It is the total value of the good and services consumed by households. From a macroeconomic point of view, families have only two possible choices regarding their incomes—either consume them or save them. The propensity of consumption, which is the percentage of families' income increase that goes to consumption, is a relevant variable

2. For more, see https://www.bea.gov/industry/io_annual.htm.

for modeling the dynamics of the market for goods and services. The propensity of saving is the part of income that is saved instead of consumed. A propensity to consume of 0.75 means that, on average, consumers spend 75% of their income on goods and services and save 25% for future consumption.

Investment (I) is the expenditure of firms on the expansion of productive capacity. It is counterintuitive to find aggregate investment in the demand function instead of the supply function. In fact, we separate investment intertemporally because of its macroeconomic effects. When companies first plan expansion, they are consuming resources from society to be able to buy machinery, expand headquarters, hire workers, and so on. Supply does not increase immediately. In that sense, investment can be thought of as comprising of two phases: in the first phase, investment increases demand because companies consume resources from society (final goods and services); in the second phase, society's productive capacity goes up because of increased K (capital) in the aggregate supply function. Although the two-stage process of today's investment increasing tomorrow's production is usually clear-cut, occasionally higher investment will not actually lead to capital accumulation.

One such example is the case of ghost cities in China—the new cities built by local Chinese governments that occasionally fail.[3] Ordos, a ghost city in Inner Mongolia, was built for over a million people, but in 2016, only a few thousand (mostly public servants in care of the city's infrastructure) lived there. In the short run, building such a city certainly increases aggregate demand and GDP because resources are consumed for the lavish project. In the long run, however, a nation's productive capacity is unchanged as such projects are swept away by the rivers of history.

Building ghost cities is a failure of government planning that can happen when politicians disregard economic efficiency. Yet there are examples of private megaprojects that boost aggregate demand in the short run without generating increased capacity. Eike Batista, a Brazilian entrepreneur, was once the wealthiest man in South America, with a fortune of US$34.5 billion.[4] Most of his wealth came from many industrial projects in Brazil. All were linked to his major planned source of revenue—offshore oilfields. After investing billions of dollars in several companies (all listed with names that ended in X to signal the proposed multiplication of wealth), OGX, the cornerstone of the X empire, found only 2% of the anticipated 1.5 billion oil barrels, halted exploration, declared bankruptcy, and is now a tiny

3. Kenneth Rapoza, "What Will Become of China's Ghost Cities?," *Forbes*, July 20, 2015, https://www.forbes.com/sites/kenrapoza/2015/07/20/what-will-become-of-chinas-ghost-cities.
4. Blake Schmidt, "Batista Bounces Back From $35 Billion Loss, but He's Still Stuck in Prison" *Bloomberg*, February 13, 2017, https://www.bloomberg.com/news/articles/2017-02-13/batista-sheds-negative-billionaire-label-as-he-stews-in-prison.

company in the hands of its former debt holders. The end of the commodities supercycle expedited the demise of the other companies in the X empire, and in 2016, Batista was estimated to be worth a negative US$1 billion. He was jailed in 2017, accused of bribing local officials. Most of the billions of dollars invested by the X group had little effect on the capital accumulation, and thus long-term growth, of the Brazilian economy.

Government expenditure (consumption and investment) (G) is different from government outlay. The former is related to capital accumulation generated by local and national governments, and the latter is the total amount in government budgets. For instance, G does not include interest payments on the government debt.

Figure 14.1 shows data for government investment and gives an idea as to the relative size of the government in different countries. As measured by the ratio of government expenditure to GDP, governments in South Africa, Canada, and most of the Europe have the highest relative presence in the respective local economies. The two largest economies in the world, China and the United States, are in the intermediate group, with the US government spending only a little more, in relative terms, than the Chinese one (14.6% for the United States and 13.6% for China), in 2014. On average, governments around the world have been increasing their expenditure over time, from an average of 14.5% of GDP in the 1960s to 17.5% in the 2010s (figure 14.2).

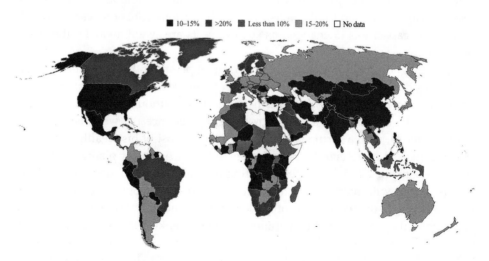

Figure 14.1
World general government final consumption expenditure as a percentage of GDP
Source: World Bank, 2017, https://data.worldbank.org/indicator/NE.CON.GOVT.ZS.

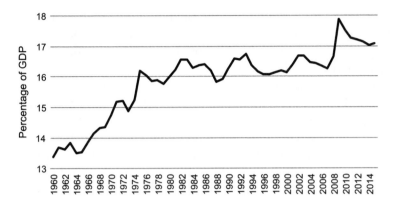

Figure 14.2
Growth in world general government final consumption expenditure as a percentage of GDP, 1960 to 2014
Source: World Bank, 2017, https://data.worldbank.org/indicator/NE.CON.GOVT.ZS.

Finally, exports (X) and imports (IM) comprise international trade. Exports represent the demand for local goods abroad, and imports represent the locals' demand for foreign goods.

The simple arithmetic of the aggregate demand equation implies that rising imports decrease a nation's GDP. At first, it may seem that higher imports are bad for the local economy. This is not true, however, and we need to take imports out of the aggregate demand to avoid conflicts in the ways that aggregate demand (AD) and value added are measured. Imports are comprised not only of final goods; international trade is also buoyant because of intermediate and capital goods. Take our example value-added bread production. We found that bread contributes 600 to GDP because it is the market value of all the sales of bread in the country. Now, let's assume that the local economy does not produce wheat and that flour manufacturers import all of this primary good from abroad. Switching from national wheat to foreign wheat does not change the value of bread on the market. Flour manufacturers still spend 180 to purchase the wheat, add 170 of value, and sell all the flour to bread manufacturers at 350. However, if the wheat is bought in the international market, the bread will add not 600 of value to the local economy but only 420, which is the value of bread sales minus the value of imported wheat. This example highlights the reason that IM has a negative sign in the aggregate demand (AD) calculation. Without it, we would overestimate GDP by counting as domestic added value the production of goods and services imported from abroad. In chapter 11, we have already seen that although many people think that it is better for a local economy to be a net exporter ($X - M > 0$), this is not necessarily true. In any case, it would be impossible for all countries to simultaneously run trade surpluses unless interplanetary trade became a reality. Imports would result in economic losses (instead of having a simple accounting impact) only if the local economy was able to provide equivalent goods and services more efficiently and could do so without lowering the economic output in general. This situation is impossible in real life because international trade shifts internal resources to industries that are more efficient. By engaging in trade, countries are able to produce more than they would be able to do in an autarky (that is, in the absence of international trade). It is easy to see that production in an autarky is less efficient than production in countries that engage in trade because a country would need to devote its resources to producing every good and service consumed in the country, losing economies of scale in some industries and productivity in others.

Bringing It All Together

Regardless of how GDP is calculated, the result is the same. It is the output that is the sum of value added from all industries, and that is consumed by society. The GDP composition of the two largest economies of the world, China and the United States can be used to answer questions about whether the US is mostly a service-based economy or whether China is the manufacturing center of the world. In figures 14.3 and 14.4, the economy is divided, on the supply side, into three major sectors—agriculture, industry, and services. The demand side is the regular composition of aggregate demand:

$C + I + G + X - IM.$

Some important differences can be identified in the ways that China and the United States produce and consume things. China is indeed a manufacturing powerhouse in which industrial output accounts for more than 40% of GDP. The US economy, however, is now comprised mostly of services, which correspond to almost four out of every five dollars produced in the country. Agriculture, which is still relevant in China, represents only 1.2% of the income generated in the United States. There also is an extreme difference in the power of consumers in the two countries. Chinese households consume only a little over one in three dollars produced in the country, whereas US households are responsible for more than two out of three dollars of the US economy. In the US, net exports $(X - IM)$ are negative, whereas for China they are positive.

The data for both countries is for 2014. In that year, the US economy generated US\$15.5 trillion of economic output, and the Chinese economy, US\$9.2 trillion. Even though the Chinese economy is probably eventually going to surpass the US economy, the average American is still much richer than the average Chinese. The main way to compare the income of people from different countries is through

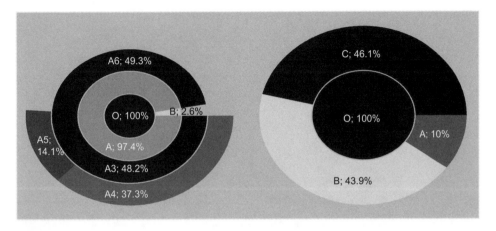

Figure 14.3
GDP composition breakdown for China, 2014
Notes for the left-hand figure: O: GDP (current) US$9,240,270,452,050; A: Gross national expenditure US$9,003,474,413,754; A3: Final consumption expenditure, etc. US$4,449,395,127,883; A4: Household final consumption expenditure US$3,446,754,675,468; A5: General government consumption expenditure US$1,299,157,066,729; A6: Gross capital formation US$4,554,079,285,871; B: External balance on goods and services US$236,796,038,296. *Notes for the right-hand figure:* O: GDP (current US$%) US$9,240,270,452,050; A: Agriculture, value added US$925,204,387,867; B: Industry, value added US$4,055,851,231,952; C: Services, etc., value added US$4,259,214,832,230. *How to read and make sense of the circloid:* Each slice of a circle is the summation of the subslices in the layer on top of it—that is O = A + B, A = A3 + A6, A3 = A4 + A5.
Source: Mecometer.com, 2017, http://mecometer.com/infographic/china/gdp-composition-break down.

GDP per capita, which is calculated by dividing the GDP of a country by the number of people living in it. In 2015, GDP per capita in China was US$7,924, and the average American earned seven times more, US$55,838, according to data from the World Bank. Yet because GDP is not a perfect measure of economic well-being, one can easily find flaws with the comparisons using GDP per capita. Distinctive patterns of income inequality in different countries make average comparisons less straightforward, even if adjustments for costs of living are taken into account. Even so, the best way to compare standards of living in different countries is by using purchasing power parity (PPP) as a methodology that takes into account the price dispersion among them.

How Is GDP Actually Measured?

As has been shown, GDP can be measured by adding the value produced by each industry in the economy, by looking at aggregate remuneration of factors, or by dividing income into its demand components. The GDP in the United States is a

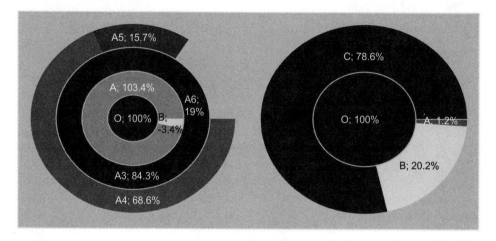

Figure 14.4

GDP composition breakdown for the United States, 2014

Notes for the left-and figure: O: GDP (current) US$16,244,600,000,000; A: Gross national expenditure US$16,791,800,000,000; A3: Final consumption expenditure, etc. US$13,697,600,000,000; A4: Household final consumption expenditure US $11,149,600,000,000; A5: General government consumption expenditure US$2,548,000,000,000; A6: Gross capital formation US$3,094,200,000,000; B: External balance on goods and services –US$547,200,000,000. *Notes for the right-hand figure:* O: GDP (current US%) US$15,533,800,000,000; A: Agriculture, value added US$193,461,490,065; B: Industry, value added US$3,130,113,406,586; C: Services, etc., value added US$12,210,225,103,367. *How to read and make sense of the circloid:* Each slice of a circle is the summation of the subslices in the layer on top of it—that is, O = A + B, A = A3 + A6, A3 = A4 + A5.

Source: Mecometer, 2017, http://mecometer.com/infographic/united-states/gdp-composition-break down.

very precise number—US$15,333,800,000,000 in 2014. But all countries do not measure GDP exactly the same way, although the results are comparable, in general. In the United Kingdom, the three main approaches to estimating GDP are combined into one number, while in the United States, GDP is estimated via the income approach by the Bureau of Economic Analysis.[5] In every country, however, GDP is estimated through surveys, and the numbers that statistical offices use are mere estimates of the true economic activity happening over billions of transactions in the economy. GDP figures are frequently revised because of the constant flow of more precise information about different economic sectors. Some market analysts find that, in some countries, GDP estimates are unreliable due to the manipulation of data by government agents or outright fraud. Argentina declared a national statistical emergency in December 2015 because its recently

5. "How Countries Calculate Their GDP," *The Economist*, March 26, 2014, https://www.eonomist. com/blogs/economist-explains/2014/03/economist-explains-26.

elected government accused INDEC, the Argentinian statistical office, of generating misleading economic indicators for years.[6]

Even though GDP is an estimate, it usually is a reliable one, comparable over time and methodologically sound, notwithstanding the cases of data manipulation by some unscrupulous governments. In the United Kingdom, the Office for National Statistics publishes its methodology and presents an accessible overview of how it calculates GDP: "It is not possible to use the production approach in the short term as value added data are not readily available. Therefore GDP is based on turnover data from monthly surveys as well as other data sources. The data used are considered the most timely and robust over a short time horizon. At the preliminary estimate, produced 25 days after the end of the quarter, approximately 44% of the output data is available and no information is available for the expenditure or income approaches."[7]

Nominal versus Real GDP

Thus far, we have looked at how to calculate GDP for one period, usually a year. In order to be used to make comparisons over time, nominal data needs to be transformed into a real GDP series. When arguing about the strength of the economy, analysts and pundits use the real GDP growth rate, and the real growth rate of economic output is the most important macroeconomic variable to track the basic standards of living in a country over time. Statistical agencies calculate it by taking away the effect of changing prices. To do that, agencies use a measure of inflation called the GDP deflator. As the name implies, this measure deinflates the nominal GDP to extract the effect of inflation on nominal GDP so that the value amount of goods and services produced can be compared in different quarters or years.

Another way to look at the nominal and real GDP distinction is to separate the changes in GDP over time into two dimensions—price and quantity. GDP is the aggregate market value of goods and services produced in a period, usually a year or a quarter. The change in the GDP deflator represents price variations. Algebraically,

$$Real\ GDP_t = \frac{Nominal\ GDP_t}{GDP\ deflator_t} 100$$

6. AFP, "Argentina Declares 'National Statistical Emergency,'" *Yahoo Finance*, December 30, 2015, https://www.yahoo.com/news/argentina-declares-national-statistical-emergency-001038414.html.
7. Office for National Statistics, "Understanding GDP and How It Is Measured," August 23, 2013, National Archives, http://webarchive.nationalarchives.gov.uk/20160107005843tf_/http://www.ons.gov.uk/ons/rel/elmr/explaining-economic-statistics/understanding-gdp-and-how-it-is-measured/sty-understanding-gdp.html.

Here is a simple example. In 2018, for example, nominal GDP is US$20 trillion, and the GDP deflator is 100. In 2019, nominal GDP is US$21 trillion, and the GDP deflator is 103. Nominal GDP is measured through a survey of goods and services and the computation of their market values. Real GDP is the result of the disassociation between the price (GDP deflator) and quantity effects. Changes in the GDP deflator over time reflect price variations and are then a measure of inflation. In the example, nominal GDP increases 5% (from US$20 trillion to $21 trillion), and inflation increases 3% (GDP deflator increases to 103 from 100). Formally,

$$Real\ GDP_{2018} = \frac{20}{100}100 = 20$$

$$Real\ GDP_{2019} = \frac{21}{103}100 = 20.388$$

Real GDP grows 1.94% from 2018 to 2019. In real terms, it means that society is producing and consuming approximately 1.94% more goods and services. Whenever the press or economists talk about long-term growth or evolving living standards, the variable they are referring to is real GDP growth.

Potential versus Actual GDP

The difference between actual and potential GDP represents an important measure—the growth gap. Potential output is the amount of goods and services that the economy should be producing at full employment. The actual GDP is the output that agents currently are producing and consuming. When the economy is overheating, actual GDP can surpass potential GDP temporarily, but it is much more common to have a gap resulting from potential GDP being higher. The difficulty in measuring the growth gap lies in modeling the potential output. The GDP growth is calculated by national statistical agencies, and there are long series of actual output data for most countries. But potential output is trickier to estimate and often requires sophisticated models.[8]

Throughout the book, potential output has been an abstract measure, and the growth gap an analytical tool. The difference between potential and actual GDP represents situations in which economies are performing at below their optimal level. This kind of economic weakness would show in real data as persistent high unemployment, for instance. After all, an economy in full employment by definition has relatively few people struggling to find a job. In that sense, potential

8. See Andrew Burns, Theo Janse Van Rensburg, Kamil Dybczak, and Trung Bui, "Estimating Potential Output in Developing Countries," *Journal of Policy Modeling* 36, no. 4 (2014): 700–716, for a model that estimates potential output for 159 countries using a production function method with many assumptions but with good results.

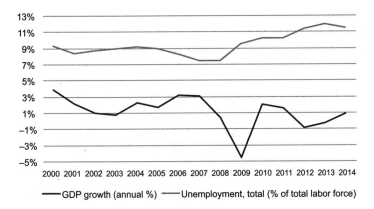

Figure 14.5
Real GDP growth and unemployment in the eurozone, 2000 to 2014
Source: World Bank, 2017, https://data.worldbank.org/indicator/SL.UEM.TOTL.ZS.

output is related to the nonaccelerating inflation rate of unemployment (NAIRU), which is a representation of an ideal job market in which most people are employed at stable real wages. If the economy is overheating, unemployment falls, and nominal wages increase rapidly as companies compete over the limited number of people willing to work. When the economy is depressed, unemployment rises, and workers compete for a fixed number of jobs in the private sector.

One example of a growth gap is Europe. Not every country in the region has done badly in the first years of the twenty-first century, but the consensus is that especially after the great financial crisis of 2008 the eurozone economy underperformed, with Germany being a notable exception (figure 14.5). NAIRU in Europe is around 5% to 7%. By the end of 2007, these countries were close to full employment, with actual growth over 3% and unemployment approaching 7%. After 2008, there was only one year in which real GDP advanced at a pace of 2%—namely, 2010. In the rest of the 2009 to 2016 period, growth was either negative or anemic. As a result, unemployment increased 2% in structural terms, going from an average of 8.5% of the labor force in the 2000 to 2008 period to 10.8% from 2009 to 2016. There was a clear growth gap between potential and actual output throughout the early 2010s. A reasonable estimate for potential growth in the eurozone should be 2% to 2.5% with a NAIRU of 6% to 7%. At the end of 2017, the eurozone countries were nowhere near that.

Limits of GDP
GDP is supposed to be a measure of prosperity, but it increasingly fails to capture it for many reasons, including methodological shortcomings and the changing

nature of the modern world. Given that a national economy is composed of a myriad of transactions, GDP cannot capture them all. This is not usually a major issue because as long as GDP measurement is consistent over time, it is still possible to compare standards of living intertemporally. The main issues are that many of the goods and services we consume today are not traded in the market, the pace of innovation is quicker than it was in the past, and there is a nonlinear relationship between income and welfare.

GDP captures transactions and disregards nontraded goods. In the past, most of value-added activity was in the production of goods and services. Manufacturing, which is easy to measure by GDP standards, accounted for 35% of GDP in the United Kingdom in the 1950s but less than 10% in the 2010s. Meanwhile, cooking and reading to kids at home are not considered economic activities. In modern life, in which opportunity costs are high, such activities—even though not measurable by value-added methodologies—are valuable and improve social welfare, in both the short and long runs. The Internet and other modern technologies have improved the global society, but their major contribution is not directly captured by economic indicators as GDP, for instance, is not readily adjusted to reflect the value of having most information at our fingertips.

For poor countries, GDP has a strong correlation to standards of living. In the developing world, growth is necessary to improve every dimension that makes life better, including health, access to education, and sanitation. For rich countries, that is not necessarily true. Money buys happiness only up to a point (it does, however, buy life satisfaction without limit).[9] Nobel recipients Angus Deaton and Daniel Kahneman studied the issue and showed that in 2015 dollars the relationship between money and short-term well-being levels off at approximately US$75,000. For most people, there is a measure of income below which the stress of providing for everyday life is high. But there is no way to develop a perfect relationship between money and well-being for most people because the amount necessary for basic quality of life varies across countries, regions, gender, age, and risk-aversion profile. After some quantity of money that satisfies basic needs, more money does not necessarily lead to satisfaction with our lives. This should inform policy in many developed countries, in which income per capita is already dozens of times higher than it was a couple of centuries ago. For many rich economies the average citizen does not necessarily benefit much from ever-increasing GDP. If that is the case, the race for accelerating output will not necessarily lead to improved life standards. It would turn into a flawed measure. For poor and

9. Ethan Wolff-Mann, "What the New Nobel Prize Winner Has to Say about Money and Happiness," *Money*, October 13, 2015, http://time.com/money/4070041/angus-deaton-nobel-winner-money -happiness.

emerging markets, GDP growth would still be a priority but one with decreasing returns over time. This raises the question of whether public authorities in developed countries should replace GDP growth with other variables (such as employment or inequality) as the priority of macroeconomic policy.

There are other criticisms of GDP based on methodological concerns, but the main ones are the insufficient link to quality of life, the increasing importance of nonmarket activities, the evolution of goods and services, and most important, the relationship between GDP and the environment. Not every unit of GDP generates environmental damage, but a large part of it does. Navigating the tradeoff between growth and environmental concerns is one of the most important issues in political economy today.

14.2   Unemployment

Escalating unemployment destroys social welfare. People feel powerless when finding work seems like a hopeless task. Nevertheless, who counts as unemployed in a society? How can countries like Spain or Greece maintain rates of unemployment of over 20% without collapsing? After all, labor markets function like any other. The invisible hands of economic folklore should move demand and supply for labor toward equilibrium and get rid of joblessness.

Most countries follow the standards set by the International Labor Organization (ILO), an agency of the United Nations. Defining the unemployment rate is trivial in essence but operationally complex. First, only a person who is in the labor force can be unemployed. Individuals who are not regarded as part of the labor force include those who are under age sixteen, students, retired, in the military, taking care of children or other family members, incarcerated, and neither working nor seeking work. An unemployed person is somebody who is part of the labor force and cannot find a job, even though he or she is actively looking for one.

In the United States, the labor force rose from approximately 150 million persons in 2016 to 160 million in 2016. By comparison, the labor force in Hong Kong totaled 4 million people at the end of 2016. Unemployment in the United States at the end of 2017 was 4.1%, which meant that 6.5 million individuals in America could not find a job (figure 14.6). In Hong Kong, unemployment stood at 3.4%, with 136,000 people without a job in the same period. Yet both countries were considered to be in full employment. The unemployment rate follows the business cycle, rising in a recession and decreasing as the output increases. After the 1950s, the two deepest recessions in the United States happened in the early 1980s and in 2009, with unemployment in both cases hovering at 10%. The first was due to the great disinflation and the second was a recoil from the great financial crisis of 2008.

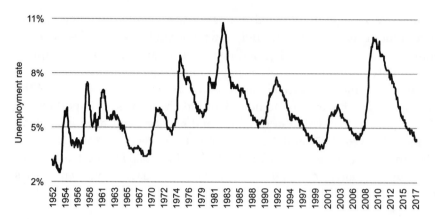

Figure 14.6
The unemployment rate in the United States, 1952 to 2017
Source: Bureau of Labor and Statistics, 2017, https://data.bls.gov/timeseries/LNS14000000.

Is the ideal unemployment rate 0%? In fact, economists consider an economy at full employment if the unemployment rate is around 4% to 5% because not every unemployed person results in social harm. This is partly due to frictional unemployment, which results mainly from people switching jobs. When people leave a job for another one, technically they remain unemployed for the period during which they receive no income, but this does not cause any social harm. Policymakers are concerned about involuntary unemployment. Being laid off without a social or family safety net can be a traumatic event. Public authorities rarely come under any more pressure than during recessions when unemployment goes through the roof.

Unemployment is defined as the ratio between persons who cannot find a job and the entire labor force. Unfortunately, as we can see from the figures for the United States, there is rarely a period in which unemployment is both low and stable. National economies are dynamic by nature, and the unemployment rate rises and falls in accordance with the business cycle.

In the United States, the Bureau for Labor Statistics (BLS) is responsible for surveying the population and estimating the unemployment rate. The Current Population Survey (CPS) has been conducted in the United States every month since 1940.[10] Today, there are about 60,000 eligible households in the sample for this survey. Similar procedures are in place for most countries in the world. The unemployment rate is not the only measure that is useful to understand labor dynamics. Researchers extrapolate the strength of the economy and general social

10. For more information on the Current Population Survey, see https://www.bls.gov/cps/cps_htgm.htm.

welfare from complementary measures such as the decline in labor force participation and the number of individuals collecting unemployment insurance.

Unemployment Dynamics

If labor markets were fully flexible, there would not be involuntary unemployment, and excess supply of labor would be only frictional. In perfectly competitive microeconomic markets, prices rise and fall with changes in demand and supply, clearing whatever amount of excess they might have. Figure 14.7 shows the analysis presented in chapter 2. Given a perfectly competitive market, the quantity demanded of labor (Q_{DL}) would be equal to the quantity supplied (Q_{SL}) at the prevailing nominal wage (w). Any worker looking for a job at the prevailing market wage would get it; there would not be structural unemployment. Some people would choose not to work at the current wage, but this would not decrease social welfare. There would also be a lot of precarious employment, with many people earning very little in bad work environments.

There is one main difference between the labor market and the market for, say, tomatoes. Tomatoes are almost homogeneous in nature, and it is much easier to match tomato supply to demand than it is to match people to jobs. Even with differentiated products (like cars), it is still much simpler to match consumers to different types of cars than it is to match employers and employees. Increasingly, job descriptions are fluid, and people accrue different skills at different rates. Although it is easier to check all features of a car, it is impossible to know beforehand all the skills and the level of effort that people will put into their jobs. Job interviews are a symptom of how difficult it is to match people to jobs efficiently. A program to hire employees requires time and money, and firms still may hire

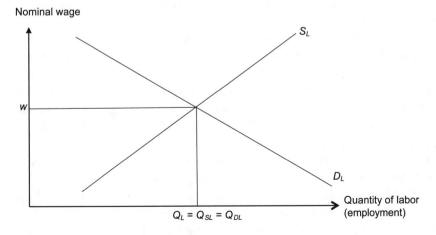

Figure 14.7

individuals who are not suitable for the job. At the same time, there are many underappreciated employees around the world who are generating far more value than they could claim if the market was operating efficiently.

Additionally, some occupations attract an excess supply of candidates, and others involve little competition. For instance, the world is facing an excess demand for computer programmers, something that shows no sign of abating anytime soon. If markets were truly efficient, the higher wages for this kind of work should attract people until the relative wage of a computer programmer fell to the national average. But this is unlikely to happen. Acquiring skills is expensive, and access to education is heterogeneous across the globe. Furthermore, people do not choose careers based solely on the monetary returns. Businesses and people are not fully mobile. There may be excess demand for some particular job in one part of the country or continent and excess supply in others. Language barriers act as deterrents in a globalized world. There are many transaction costs, and unemployment above full employment is a structural feature in most countries. In the end, true involuntary and persistent unemployment is one of the main measures of economic welfare, and most politicians promise jobs, especially during downturns in the business cycle.

As noted above, the full employment rate is also known as the nonaccelerating inflation rate of employment (NAIRU). Structural unemployment happens when the actual rate of unemployment is persistently higher than the NAIRU. For many reasons, most countries suffer from structural unemployment. Regulations, shocks, and institutions that work poorly contribute to chronic unemployment. Labor dynamics are much more complicated than a clearing market where the quantity supplied of homogeneous labor equals the quantity demanded and where freely moving nominal wages guarantee that the economy is always at full employment. In most countries, minimum wages guarantee that wages cannot move freely.

Using a very simple microeconomic framework, it is easy to see that if the minimum wage is set at a value that is "too high," then unemployment follows. The number of people willing to work at the minimum wage is higher than the supply of work available for them. The argument is similar in the case of nominal wages that are rigid. In many countries, companies cannot negotiate or impose lower nominal wages, and the result is that any shock that reduces labor demand creates structural unemployment.

Let's assume a labor market that is in complete equilibrium (figure 14.8). There is no unemployment ($Q_{SL} = Q_{DL}$) at the prevailing market wage (w). If there is nominal rigidity (for simplicity, wages are fully immobile), a shock that shrinks labor demand (from D_L to D'_L) causes structural unemployment ($Q_{SL} - Q'_{DL}$). Unless the economy recovers, real wages will be higher than they would be under

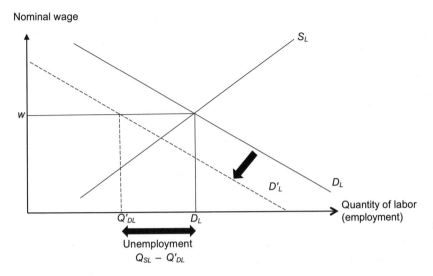

Figure 14.8

contractual flexibility, and there are going to be more people looking for work than the companies can employ. Positive economic shocks should bring the economy back to full employment, but unless that happens, structural unemployment can be persistent.

Another feature of labor-market dynamics is hysteresis. Successive recessions or persistent stagnations should be counterbalanced by periods of economic buoyancy. Economies do not grow linearly. But over time, the unemployment rate should be close to full employment. Positive economic shocks should balance out negative ones. The rate of unemployment would increase in a recession, but the economy would come back to full employment as economic activity picks up. Sadly, this rarely happens in most countries. One explanation, first devised by Olivier J. Blanchard and Lawrence H. Summers in 1986, is that if the economy does not recover quickly, many workers lose skills that are not easily recouped.[11] After the economy recovers, they do not necessarily share in the prosperity, especially if the labor market has other rigidities that create incentives for companies to screen the candidates by looking at the amount of time that a worker was unemployed. Hysteresis is one possible reason that structural unemployment can become persistent over time, and it is one of the reasons that European countries face high and persistent rates of unemployment.

11. Olivier J. Blanchard and Lawrence H. Summers, "Hysteresis and the European Unemployment Problem," in *NBER Macroeconomics Annual*, ed. Stanley Fischer, 15–90 (Cambridge, MA: MIT Press, 1986).

Labor dynamics are much more complicated in real life than they are in any stylized model. Numerous regulations, actions of trade unions, and many other factors make the labor outcomes uncertain. It is fair to assume that when comparing the United States and France, the relative lack of regulations in the US culminate in an unemployment rate that is lower than in France. At the same time, there are many more people working in bad conditions in the United States than in France.

Minimum wages are a feature of labor markets in many countries and can have employment and distributive effects. In the United States, for example, the minimum wage is relatively lower than it is in France. It is hard to make predictions of what would happen with the US economy if authorities decided to jack up the minimum wage significantly for most occupations. In every microeconomic textbook, students learn that price caps do not work. When governments try to control prices by fiat, there are two possible outcomes—rationing or the emergence of black markets. These were common features when governments decided on the prices of goods and services in the Soviet Union in the twentieth century and in Venezuela in the twenty-first century. A minimum wage is just another price cap set by policymakers to influence markets—in this case, the labor market. If the minimum wage is set below the prevailing market wage, it has no effect; if it is above it, it generates unemployment. This is basic microeconomics. But in macroeconomics, context dependency rules.

The impact of a minimum wage on employment depends on several variables, including a country's level of development, the conditions of local labor markets, and the size of informal markets. In the 2000s, for instance, increasing minimum wages was important to combat poverty in Latin American countries and China. In these countries, higher minimum wages affected income and not unemployment because of their low levels, a buyer's labor market, and enforcement capabilities.[12] For these countries and other emerging nations, raising the minimum wage affected formal and informal workers alike. In fact, informal workers— workers not affected by payroll taxes—experienced significant wage increases when the minimum wage was raised.[13]

Even for developed countries, there is evidence that minimum wages can have a significant impact on general wages but almost no discernible impact on jobs.[14]

---

12. Jinlan Ni, Guangxin Wang, and Xianguo Yao, "Impact of Minimum Wages on Employment: Evidence from China," *Chinese Economy* 44, no. 1 (2011): 18–38.

13. Melanie Khamis, "Does the Minimum Wage Have a Higher Impact on the Informal Than on the Formal Labour Market? Evidence from Quasi-Experiments," *Applied Economics* 45, no. 4 (2013): 477–495.

14. Arindrajit Dube, T. William Lester, and Michael Reich, "Minimum Wage Effects across State Borders: Estimates Using Contiguous Counties," *Review of Economics and Statistics* 92, no. 4 (2010): 945–964.

Evidence from the United Kingdom shows that there is some profitability reduction for companies but no effect on bankruptcies.[15] More important, the minimum wage is a powerful redistributive tool.[16]

Given all the evidence, surely the US federal government should mandate a US$15 minimum wage immediately? Not so fast. It is one thing to mandate rising wages in developing economies with tight labor markets and soaring aggregate demand. It is another to do so in a flexible labor market in the United States, where firms are more nimble. This does not mean that it cannot be done, but it would be difficult to model all possible and secondary effects of wage gains by decree. For a precise answer, a researcher would need short- and long-run estimates on several variables, including the elasticity of unemployment, the rate of substitution between capital and labor (in other words, the rate at which companies would replace costlier workers with investment in automation), and potential increases in productivity from higher living standards. It is easier to campaign for improved living standards by fiat when labor productivity is rising in emerging countries. It is harder to do so in developed countries where productivity is stagnant or unevenly distributed. The result can be unemployment of lower-skilled workers, exactly the group that was targeted by the policy in the first place. It is also a matter of degree. Although moderate increases will most likely have little effect on unemployment rates, a steep increase can most certainly introduce rigidities in markets that have been until now mostly free of them. The minimum wage debate of the mid-2010s in the United States became a major point in Bernie Sanders's campaign for the Democratic Party nomination in the 2016 presidential election. He was not necessarily right.

This analysis of unemployment reinforces once again our main tenet: there are no unequivocally good policies.

Labor Markets and Social Welfare

The rate of unemployment does not capture all of the labor-market dynamics that influence social welfare. The use of unemployment rate as the only macroeconomic variable related to the labor market comes down to the tradeoff between simplicity and sophistication. It is easier to point out that accelerating unemployment hurts society and that falling unemployment improves its well-being. In most instances, simply using the rate of unemployment as the main outcome of labor-market interactions would suffice. But in the United States in 2016, most of the narrative for the presidential election was based on the discontent of many

15. Mirko Draca, Stephen Machin, and John Van Reenen, "Minimum Wages and Firm Profitability," *American Economic Journal: Applied Economics* 3, no. 1 (2011): 129–151.

16. Richard B. Freeman, "The Minimum Wage as a Redistributive Tool," *Economic Journal* 106, no. 436 (1996): 639–649.

groups. When the election was held in November 2016, the unemployment rate was at 4.6%. The American economy was at or very close to full employment, and yet people felt well-being slipping through their fingers. Complaints about jobs moving to China and the death of the American dream were common. Yet the country was experiencing full employment.

Labor-market outcomes other than the official unemployment rate are relevant to economic well-being. Some of these outcomes include underemployment and discouraged workers, formal versus informal employment, temporary versus permanent employment, and regional patterns.

Underemployment, for instance, describes the situation in which the employment of an individual is incomplete, either in terms of the hours worked or his or her skills not being fully matched. Recent immigrants face many difficulties in adapting to foreign countries. Engineers, for example, might drive cabs, a job that requires skills very different from those of an engineer. The vacuum created by departing manufacturing companies may also result in underemployed workers as blue-collar individuals cannot find a similar occupation, do not move to look for better jobs, and instead are stuck in positions not matching their abilities. This pattern of underemployment creates social tension and reduces social welfare. It also drives up the value of nostalgia—the love of simpler times when underemployment affected other kinds of individuals while blue-collar workers thrived.

Another kind of underemployment is due to discouraged workers—individuals who stop looking for work and drop out of the labor force. If somebody cannot find a good enough job and simply stops looking for one, the unemployment rate is unchanged because it counts only the people who are actively looking for a job. A higher number of discouraged workers has a significant impact on social welfare, even as the unemployment rate is steady. Finally, the concept of underemployment includes those who work full-time but live below the poverty level— the working poor.[17] The numbers for the United States reveal the extent of welfare destruction generated by the great financial crisis. In the United States, the working poor are people who spent at least twenty-seven weeks in the labor force (that is, working or looking for work) but whose incomes still fell below the official poverty level. The percentage of working poor people went from approximately 5% of the working population before 2008 to over 7% after the financial crisis (a 40% increase) (figure 14.9). The number of poor people with steady work has totaled more than 10 million for every year after 2008. It was 7.5 million in 2007.

Another important labor-market outcome related to social welfare that is not captured by a single unemployment rate is the degree of informality in a national

17. Kimberly Amadeo, "What Is Underemployment? Its Causes, Effects and the Current Rate," *The Balance*, April 20, 2017, https://www.thebalance.com/underemployment-definition-causes-effects -rate-3305519.

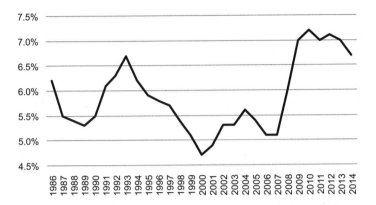

Figure 14.9
Percentage of working poor over the entire working population in the United States, 1986 to 2014
Source: Bureau of Labor and Statistics, "A Profile of the Working Poor, 2015," https://www.bls.gov/opub/reports/working-poor/2015/home.htm,2017.

economy. Informality is the scourge of emerging countries. Informal workers earn less, enjoy reduced access to public services, and suffer from instability in their employment and careers. There is a negative correlation between informality and health. For instance, researchers found that in Chile there was a positive and statistically significant association between informal employment and mental health in all genders.[18]

The size of the informal sector depends on many variables, including the relative costs of formal and informal workers and the strength of institutions meant to enforce the rule of law and curb corruption. Even constitutional reforms can influence the flow of people from and to informal sectors.[19] Yet informal working arrangements are not entirely bad for society. Many kinds of informal work arrangements increase social welfare. For example, many workers in highly paid positions in emerging countries prefer flexible contracts, especially if there are gray areas in terms of tax implications. This happens even in developed countries, and many workers in the service sector (like waiters and waitresses) have informal arrangements in which their social welfare does not necessarily decrease. Some restaurant workers are happily making six-figure salaries in New York City, but those putting up with precarious employment arrangements in the distant suburbs probably would prefer more stability.

18. Marisol E. Ruiz, Alejandra Vives, Èrica Martínez-Solanas, Mireia Julià, and Joan Benach, "How Does Informal Employment Impact Population Health? Lessons from the Chilean Employment Conditions Survey," *Safety Science* 100, pt. A (December 2017): 57–65.
19. Mariano Bosch, Edwin Goñi-Pacchioni, and William Maloney, "Trade Liberalization, Labor Reforms and Formal-Informal Employment Dynamics," *Labour Economics* 19, no. 5 (2012): 653–667.

Another example of flows from formal to informal sectors that did not decrease social welfare comes from Colombia. Adriana Camacho, Emily Conover, and Alejandro Hoyos analyzed the link between the Colombian government's expansion of social programs in the early 1990s, particularly formal employment and the publicly provided health insurance.[20] They found an increase in informal employment of 4 percentage points after the introduction of publicly provided health insurance. As in the case of the Patient Protection and Affordable Care Act (also known as Obamacare) in the United States, many individuals choose formal employment instead of flexible labor contracts due to the benefits (such as access to subsidized health care) embedded in formal labor contracts. After access to health is funded by the public purse (as in Colombia) or healthcare subsidies shift from employers to employees (as in Obamacare), individuals who were holding on to formal jobs just for access to the healthcare subsidies drop out, reducing the labor force but without any change in social welfare. If anything, social welfare goes up because some people can freely choose a different path. As with most of macroeconomics, there is no easy, simple, comprehensive, and direct explanation for a single data point. Full employment may hide underemployed workers and huge informal sectors, and flows from formal to informal sectors may not be bad for society.

Regional patterns also can make it more difficult to define the social welfare effect of labor-market outcomes. The national economy may not be at full employment and have many pockets of tight labor markets that create local labor shortages. Yet regional disparities should not affect social welfare if people are willing to move freely from areas with an excess supply of labor to those with a lack of workers. People are not goods and services that can simply be hauled from low-paying markets to better ones, however, and although some citizens are truly mobile and even global in their attitudes, others prefer being able to build a stable life with a guaranteed income. If families do not really want to move but have to follow the developments in labor markets, they are experiencing social harm. The unemployment rate is a national aggregate that does not reveal much about regional patterns. Many variables—including technology, trade, and transactions costs—affect labor-market outcomes countrywide and drive the regional markets. Detroit in the mid-2010s is a good example of a dysfunctional labor market that does not find an equilibrium in the same way as in the rest of the United States. The city has been in decline since its heyday in the mid-twentieth century, when its population hit 1.8 million (it fell to around 700,000 in the mid-2010s). In the 2010 census, the city had a 24.8% unemployment rate, which was the highest

20. Adriana Camacho, Emily Conover, and Alejandro Hoyos, "Effects of Colombia's Social Protection System on Workers' Choice between Formal and Informal Employment," *World Bank Economic Review* 28, no. 3 (2013): 446–466.

among the fifty largest US cities (and the distance between Detroit and the city with the second-highest rate, Fresno at 18%, was greater than the rate of Omaha, which was at the bottom of the ranking at 5%). Detroit filed for bankruptcy on July 18, 2013. Some people did move away to greener pastures, but it is hard to explain the lack of adjustment in the labor market. The decline in job opportunities should be matched by the number of people leaving the city, and the unemployment rate should not be different from the national average. Unfortunately, labor-market dynamics are far from clear. Regional disparities are another source of discontent, even if on average the national economy is at full employment.

Another source of social dissatisfaction is the increase in the ratio of part-time to full-time work. Social welfare is maximized when people can choose and move freely between part-time and full-time employment. When labor markets are not functioning well, however, people may be stuck in part-time occupations even when they would prefer full-time jobs. As with informal workers, many workers who can find only part-time work resent it and tend to be poorer. In 2014, the Bureau of Labor and Statistics showed that for the United States, the working poor are more likely to be part-time workers than full-time workers.[21] Among people in the labor force for twenty-seven weeks or more, the working poor included only 4.1% of those usually employed full-time but were 13.5% of part-time workers.

Although the path of the unemployment rate has a direct relationship with social welfare, other labor-market outcomes also influence the quality of life of society.

Uber Drivers, Unemployment, and Informal Contracting   Are Uber drivers employees? How are they counted in the Bureau of Labor Statistics surveys? Uber is a perfect example of the economies of scale provided by the combination of the shared economy and deep financial markets of the United States. Alongside other unicorns (recent Internet private companies with valuations of over US$1 billion), Uber has disrupted established transportation markets in many cities around the world, using a business model in which the company is the intermediary between drivers and consumers.

Although the company is ferocious in pursuing growth, cities around the world have revised their regulations regarding the competition between Uber cars and taxis (and other forms of transport) and the employment situation of Uber drivers. The company contends that all Uber drivers are independent contractors who own their cars. In late 2015, Uber drivers in California pursued a class action suit in which they claimed they should be considered regular employees instead of

21. "A Profile of the Working Poor, 2015," BLS Reports, Report 1068, April 2017, https://www.bls.gov/opub/reports/working-poor/2015/home.htm.

independent contractors. In April 2016, the company and the drivers reached a settlement, in which Uber agreed to pay US$100 million but did not recognize its drivers as regular employees.

The battle between Uber and its drivers in California is representative of the changes in labor markets around the world. Individuals are increasingly finding a fragmented labor market where occupations are fluid and skills are constantly adjusted. Labor contracts all over the world are becoming more flexible. Until the late 1980s, workers in Japan had an implicit guarantee of long-term job security in private companies, but that seems like ancient history now. Even the tenure system in high education is changing as the requirements become more stringent and more teachers compete for fewer positions. There are relevant implications of these changes for employment data. Flexible contracting reduces unemployment but also increases underemployment. As markets become more flexible, high-skilled employees are able to benefit disproportionately, which increases income inequality. Meanwhile, job security is lower, and many people are forced to work part-time in suboptimal arrangements. The unemployment rate tends to display a lower correlation with social welfare than it did in the past. Macroeconomic indicators such as GDP and unemployment rate are not as good a proxy of well-being as they used to be. The case of Uber drivers is a result of this new dynamic. Although statistically every Uber driver is employed, the question of their under-employment remains open.

Informal Workers in India   In many emerging markets, labor markets are far from perfect. Regulations designed to protect workers end up increasing the costs for businesses to hire workers formally. Weak institutions create incentives for employers to hire people informally. The result is a large informal side of the economy where contracts are more flexible but abuses are common.

India is an example of a country where most workers are employed in the informal sector. Informality has many dimensions, and Rina Agarwala and Geert De Neve capture some of them in two excellent books about informal labor in a country where almost 90% of workers toiled in the informal sector until the mid-2010s.[22]

The impact of informality on unemployment is also far from clear, and in the case of India, it varies across regions. Labor in the informal sector is casual, inse-cure, and unprotected.[23] Yet regulations that try to augment the number of formal

22. Rina Agarwala, *Informal Labor, Formal Policies, and Dignified Discontent in India* (New York: Cambridge University Press, 2013); Geert De Neve, *The Everyday Politics of Labour: Working Lives in India's Informal Economy* (New Delhi: Social Science Press, 2005).
23. Jan Breman, *At Work in the Informal Economy of India: A Perspective from the Bottom Up* (Oxford: Oxford University Press, 2016).

workers may have the opposite effect if they increase the relative cost of formal versus informal occupations. As always in economics, solutions are context-dependent. Informality that destroys social welfare in developed countries may, for a time, increase well-being in developing countries. Finding the right balance is always difficult, especially in a dynamic world.

Sclerotic Labor Markets

Although economists try to communicate efficiently and minimize their use of jargon, economic models include plenty of words with strange meanings. One instance of this is sclerotic models. The word *sclerosis* is a medical term referring to the hardening of tissue. In the disease called multiple sclerosis, tissue around the nerves hardens, slowly injuring the brain and the spinal cord. In labor markets, the word *sclerosis* refers the hardening of the unemployment rate and other labor-market outcomes.

In sclerotic labor markets, flows decrease, and both individual unemployment duration and the proportion of long-term unemployed increase. Olivier Blanchard's simple model of sclerotic labor markets helps explain persistent unemployment in Europe.[24] In his model, jobs are constantly created and destroyed. Workers who lose their jobs become unemployed and look for new jobs. Companies that create new jobs look for workers by posting vacancies. In a situation of equilibrium, there is positive unemployment, positive vacancies, and flows of workers into and out of employment. Job destruction happens for many reasons, including technological changes, shifts in demand, and changes in the quality of the match between job and worker on the job. If the shock is bad enough, companies terminate the job and lay off the worker.

The main advantage of Blanchard's model is that it shows the relationship between employment protection and the unemployment rate: higher protection leads first to sclerosis and later to hysteresis. It does not explain all structural unemployment, but it is a significant factor in the difference of unemployment rates across countries.

Employment protection is born out of the important goal of protecting workers from the whims of corporations, especially when oligopolies are the norm. But there is a delicate balance between too little and too much employment protection. Too little regulation may generate underemployment and scores of working poor, and too much regulation may lead to sclerosis and hysteresis or to flows from formal to informal markets.[25]

24. Olivier Blanchard, "Employment Protection, Sclerosis and the Effect of Shocks on Unemployment," lecture 3, Lionel Robbins Lectures, London School of Economics, London, 2000.
25. A great analysis of differences in labor market dynamics is Olivier Blanchard and Pedro Portugal, "What Hides behind an Unemployment Rate: Comparing Portuguese and US Labor Markets," *American Economic Review* 91, no. 1 (2001): 187–207.

The US recovery after the great financial crisis was slower than its recoveries after earlier recessions, something to be expected after a once-in-a-generation event. Nevertheless, the painful recovery process made some academics wonder if labor markets in the US were becoming sclerotic.[26] They were not. Sclerosis usually follows dysfunctional regulation that put an unnecessary burden on employees and employers. The United States is still a pro-business environment in which most employees work in at-will arrangements. Job stability is mostly the consequence of labor negotiations instead of being mandated by federal and state laws. After the crisis, flows of workers to the labor eventually increased, and the unemployment rate reached full employment in 2016—eight years after the peak of the crisis but still much sooner than in most countries in Europe.

Unemployment in South Africa Unemployment rates in some countries are high because of informal workers. In Spain, for example, surveys should show informal workers as employed, but sometimes the survey design falls short. In South Africa, however, unemployment is persistently high and, unlike in other countries, does not change even with adjustments for informal labor.

According to a *Statistics South Africa* report, "between 2009 and 2015 employment increased from 14.2 million to 15.7 million. This rise, however, did not keep pace with the increase in the working age population and as such the absorption rate at 43.7% in 2015 was still 2.2 percentage points below the 2008 prerecessionary high."[27] According to Kevin Lings in *BIZ News*, in 2015, 35.9 million people between ages fifteen and sixty-four lived in South Africa.[28] This group had 20.8 million people who were economically active, 15.6 million who were employed, and 5.2 million who were unemployed. If the numbers were to reflect discouraged workers, the unemployment rate would be 34.9% (not 25%), and the unemployment rate for people under age twenty-five would be 63.1%.

In 1994, South Africa had 1.8 million skilled workers, 4.2 million semi-skilled workers, and 2.9 million low-skilled workers. By 2014, the number of skilled workers had doubled to 3.8 million, increasing faster than the number of semi-skilled (7 million) and low-skilled (4.3 million) workers. Since 1991, South Africa's unemployment rate has been lower than 20% only once—in 1995 (figure 14.10). Otherwise, the rate has averaged 24%, or one in four South Africans.

26. Pedro S. Amaral, "Is the U.S. Labor Market Becoming More Sclerotic? And Does It Matter?," Federal Reserve Bank of Cleveland, July 5, 2011, https://www.clevelandfed.org/newsroom-and -events/publications/economic-trends/2011-economic-trends/et-20110705-is-the-us-market -becoming-more-sclerotic-and-does-it-matter.aspx.
27. See "Labour Market Dynamics in South Africa, 2015," Statistics South Africa, October 11, 2016, http://www.statssa.gov.za/?p=8615.
28. Kevin Lings, "In SA One in Four Still Unemployed: Youth Crisis as 63.1% Remain Jobless," *BIZ News*, July 29, 2015, http://www.biznews.com/thought-leaders/2015/07/29/sa-q2-unemployment -eases-to-25-but-63-1-of-youth-remain-jobless.

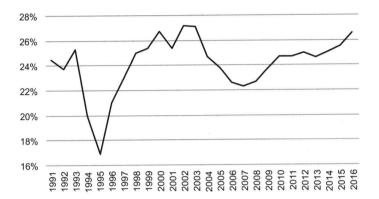

Figure 14.10
Unemployment in South Africa, 1991 to 2016
Source: World Bank, 2017, https://data.worldbank.org/indicator/SL.UEM.TOTL.ZS.

When Geeta Gandhi Kingdon and John Knight looked for the reasons for this pattern, they found that even the informal sector presents barriers to entry by job seekers. On average, participating in informal employment in South Africa leads to higher well-being than being unemployed.[29] Being unemployed is horrible, especially in developing countries. For example, Kingdon and Knight show that per capita monthly household income (expenditure) for the unemployed is only 48.2% of the corresponding figure for the informally employed. Living conditions—in terms of living space and access to drinking water, sanitation, and electricity—are also far worse for the unemployed than for the informally employed. Insofar as the unemployed take account of their own individual income rather than household income per capita, unemployment insurance is very limited in scope. The benefit lasts for only the first six months of unemployment and is received by only 1.3% of the unemployed. This pattern does not change for people in informal self-employment or in informal wage employment, such as domestic workers.

Some of the barriers to informal employment in South Africa are peculiar to that country, and others are shared by most emerging countries. Beginning in 1948, for example, the apartheid system in South Africa repressed the informal activities of black South Africans through restrictive laws (like the Group Areas Act), harsh licensing requirements, strict zoning regulations, and the effective detection and prosecution of offenders. Such barriers did not immediately collapse after the end of apartheid in 1991. But the enforcement of minimum wage laws and other labor contract stipulations is strong and applied to all companies in the region,

29. Geeta Gandhi Kingdon and John Knight, "Unemployment in South Africa: The Nature of the Beast," *World Development* 32, no. 3 (2004): 391–408.

irrespective of size. This imposes a burden of high labor costs on small firms and makes it more difficult for informal arrangements to emerge. Self-employment should ensue but is limited by restrictions on and insecurity in credit, land, and capital. In South Africa, the institutional arrangement and economic environment suppress even survival entrepreneurship, resulting in extremely high levels of unemployment in comparison with other emerging markets.

As is shown in chapter 3, long-run growth and declines in unemployment rates can be achieved only by a combination of stronger institutions and increased productivity. Like most emerging countries, South Africa brims with potential that is wasted on the search for short-term solutions to long-run issues.

14.3   Inflation

One of the few unanimities in economics is that inflation is bad. People who grow up in a country with hyperinflation usually continue to fear inflationary processes. Because hyperinflation was widespread in the developing world in the 1980s and 1990s, most people age forty and older in Latin America, Africa, and some former Soviet bloc countries have been left traumatized. Even if developed countries have not experienced hyperinflation in decades, they participated in the fight against widespread inflation in the 1970s and 1980s. The battle to tame it left the US economy reeling in the early 1980s. Germany still suffers from hyperinflation phobia, even though its last bout was almost a hundred years ago. Regardless of their backgrounds, almost all citizens in the world know that inflation is bad. But what exactly is inflation?

Inflation is an increase in the prices of goods and services. Statistical agencies measure it as the weighted average price of a basket of goods and services that is representative for the typical consumer. It is supposed to be simple: rising prices destroy social welfare, and price stability is an important element of sound governments. Nevertheless, as with other macroeconomic variables, nobody can observe the real inflation rate. Instead, statistical agencies around the world use a similar methodology to estimate the inflation rate:

1. Define the goods and services that comprise the typical basket of goods.
2. Establish the weight of each product.
3. Investigate the price changes in the marketplace.
4. Calculate the index.

There is an almost infinite combination of weights and baskets and thus of possible price indexes. For economic analyses, the two main indexes in the United States are the Consumer Price Index (CPI), which is a proxy for rising costs of living for the average household, and the Producer Price Index (PPI), which

Table 14.2
Calculating inflation (consumer price index)

Good	Weight	Year 1	Year 2
Housing	40%	5000	5500
Transportation	20%	200	240
Foodstuff	40%	2000	1900

describes the average increase in costs for the producers of goods and services. The price of imported machinery, for instance, will affect disproportionately the PPI and will result in CPI changes only if the producers are able to pass on their higher costs to consumers. The price of fruits, however, will affect consumers more than producers and thus result in a higher CPI but not necessarily a higher PPI.

The simplest way to calculate a consumer price index is as follows. Assume that a country has only three final goods—housing, transportation, and foodstuffs. In this country, people only work, eat, and come home to do it again the next day. The prices of these goods over two years are shown in table 14.2.

Here, weights are constant, and the CPI would be a weighted average of price increases:

$$CPI = \sum w_i p_i \, ,$$

where w_i is the weight of product i, and p_i is the change in price of product i. Then,

$$CPI = 0.4*0.1 + 0.2*0.2 + 0.4*(-0.05) = 0.06 = 6\%$$

A CPI of 6% a year is high for developed countries but average for emerging markets. In essence, the calculation of inflation indexes is simple, as the example demonstrates. In real life, many of the following issues complicate the matter.

Core versus Noncore Goods and Services

Most economists use core instead of general inflation indexes to estimate the strength of an economy or forecast future inflation.[30] The division between core and noncore goods and services comes from differences in volatility. The core CPI excludes some food and energy categories. The volatility of food and energy prices comes from a system in which commodities are traded globally, and their prices respond to worldwide demand and supply variables. In Great Britain in 2016, for

30. The Federal Reserve Bank of San Francisco has a series of primers on basic definitions, including "What Is 'Core Inflation,' and Why Do Economists Use It Instead of Overall or General Inflation to Track Changes in the Overall Price Level?," Federal Reserve Bank of San Francisco, October 2004, http://www.frbsf.org/education/publications/doctor-econ/2004/october/core-inflation-headline.

example, the economy was performing moderately well, but in some months, the economy experienced a deflation, which usually is associated with a weak economy. The reason for the deflation was a sharp decline in the price of oil that the country imports. As the oil prices rebounded later in the year, the overall CPI climbed back into positive territory. Excluding volatile items such as oil prices yields a more precise measure of the cost of living over time.

Technology, Quality, and Cost of Living

One dimension that CPI does not capture well is the evolution in the quality of goods and services. In the 1950s, for instance, cars were death traps that consumed huge amounts of fuel. Today they are much safer, have more computer processors than the average laptop, and are continuing to evolve. Yet in real terms, the price of a car has been constant for a long time.

The methodology of CPI and PPI changes over time to take into account some quality changes, but the updates are minimal. Given the rise in the quality for goods and services, the CPI overstates the true inflation. Over time, costs of living decrease in real terms as the quality and the technology improve. A computer's price may be the same as it was twenty years ago, but its processing power is thousands of times faster and larger.

Perceived versus Real Inflation

Whatever the official inflation index is, there is a widespread perception that the actual inflation rate is much higher. Although many media articles point out that the CPI understates the true inflation, they are wrong. People persist in perceiving inflation to be higher because the individual basket of goods is different than the one used in the CPI's calculation and a psychological bias leads us to concentrate on the goods that became expensive and ignore the goods with constant or declining prices.

Figure 14.11 illustrates the price changes of goods and services over twenty years in the United States. Education became much more expensive, relatively, but clothing became cheaper. Today it is easier to find somebody complaining about high college costs than celebrating low-cost clothes.

In our earlier simple example of CPI calculation, the CPI was 6%. Now let's assume two consumers, Etienne and Laurie. Etienne works from home (she spends 20% of her income on rent) and is a foodie (80% on food). The CPI overstates Etienne's personal inflation, which was much lower that the announced rate. Laurie likes traveling (she spends 50% of her income on travel), rents two apartments in two different cities (40% on housing), and spends relatively little on foodstuffs (10% on food). Here the perception of inflation is much higher for Laurie than Etienne, who has a much bigger incentive to complain that the CPI

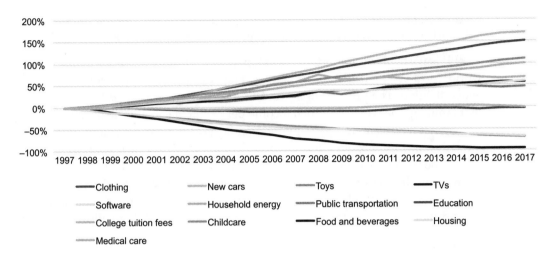

Figure 14.11
Price changes in consumer goods and services in the United States, 1997 to 2017
Source: OurWorldinData, 2017, https://ourworldindata.org/grapher/price-changes-in-consumer
-goods-and-services-in-the-usa-1997-2017.

is "wrong." In fact, because of loss aversion and other sources of psychological biases, we tend to focus our attention on the goods and services that become more expensive over time and ignore those that are relatively cheaper.[31] We tend to create a mental model of the CPI in which we ascribe a larger weight to goods and services that are more relevant and have the highest price bumps. Whenever relevancy and high price bumps coincide, we tend to complain that our costs of living are getting out of control, even if that is far from the truth.

Purchasing Power Parity
Purchasing power parity (PPP) is the main tool for economists to compare prices and income in different countries. After all, a family earning US$ 10,000 per year will be poor in the United States but middle class in Bangladesh.

Angus Deaton and Bettina Aten explain how PPP works:

Purchasing power parity exchange rates are international multilateral price indexes that measure, for the various components of GDP, the amount of local currency required to purchase the same real amount in that country relative to a numeraire, which is typically the United States. Non-traded goods are typically cheaper in poorer economies, so that PPPs are typically lower than exchange rates for poor countries, and are more so the poorer

---

31. Daniel Kahneman's major work is on prospect theory, explaining deviations from pure rational behavior. An accessible introduction is *Thinking, Fast and Slow* (New York: Farrar, Straus and Giroux, 2011).

the country: for example, in 2011 the market exchange rate for India was 46.7 rupees to the dollar, while the PPP exchange rate for consumption was 15.0 rupees to the dollar.[32]

PPP is particularly important for estimating the number of poor people in the world. Most economists rely on the World Bank poverty line to determine who is above the line. The poverty line was US\$ 1.90 PPP per day in 2017. That means that family in the world in which income per capita was higher than US\$ 1.90 per day cannot be considered poor, by the standards of the day. Of course, poverty is a relative and not absolute term: many people in rich countries consider themselves poor when they are not, in comparison with the rest of the world, and being a lower middle-class family in a poor country is probably worse than being poor in a rich one. Nevertheless, we do need a measure to compare income and prices around the world, and the purchase parity power methodology allows us to do so.

14.4   Income Inequality

Income inequality is usually measured by the Gini coefficient, although other measures give a more intuitive notion of how income is distributed within a country. The Gini coefficient varies in a 0 to 1 interval, with 0 implying complete equality (all people receive the same income) and 1 implying total inequality (one person receives all the income generated by society). The Gini coefficient is the area (calculated by taking an integral) under a Lorenz curve of ordered income from all persons, from poorest to richest. The curve represents the distribution of income in an economy. A point (x, y) on a Lorenz curve shows the percentage y of total income of the poorest $x\%$ of the population. In figure 14.12, Japan has a better income distribution than the United States. In 2014, the Gini coefficient for Japan was 0.33 and for the United States, 0.39.[33]

Another way to measure income inequality is with a simple ratio between the top $x\%$ of the richest and poorest. Some interesting findings can be made based on table 14.3's data on inequality and poverty in OECD countries for the latest available year:

• The two Latin American countries in the sample, Chile and Mexico, are the only countries in which the 20% richest individuals earn more than ten times the amount the poorest individuals earn.

32. Angus Deaton and Bettina Aten, "Trying to Understand the PPPs in ICP 2011: Why are the Results so Different?," *American Economic Journal: Macroeconomics* 9, no. 1 (2017): 243–264.
33. The OECD publishes data on Gini coefficients for its members at http://www.oecd.org/social/income-distribution-database.htm.

Table 14.3
Income inequality in OECD countries, latest year available

OECD country	Ratio between the top 20% and the bottom 20%	Percentage in poverty	Gini coefficient	Percentage in poverty, ages 18–25 ty 18–25	Percentage in poverty, ages 65+ty 65+
Australia	5.7	12.8	0.337	8	25.7
Austria	4.2	9	0.280	10.4	9.7
Belgium	4	10	0.268	11.1	9.1
Canada	5.5	12.6	0.322	17.1	6.2
Switzerland	4.4	8.6	0.295	7.1	19.7
Chile	10.6	16.8	0.465	15.3	15
Czech Republic	3.7	6	0.262	4.9	3
Germany	4.4	9.1	0.292	13.2	8.4
Denmark	3.6	5.4	0.254	21.4	3.8
Spain	6.7	15.9	0.346	20.1	5.5
Estonia	6.7	16.3	0.361	12.8	23.5
Finland	3.8	7.1	0.262	15.9	6.6
France	4.4	8	0.294	12.6	3.5
United Kingdom	6	10.4	0.358	10.5	13.5
Greece	6.3	15.1	0.343	21.5	8.6
Hungary	4.5	10.1	0.288	11.9	8.6
Ireland	4.8	8.9	0.309	16.4	7
Iceland	3.4	4.6	0.244	6.4	3
Israel	7.6	18.6	0.36	16.6	22.6
Italy	5.8	13.3	0.325	16	9.3
Japan	6.1	16.1	0.33	19.7	19
Korea	5.4	14.6	0.302	9	48.8
Lithuania	6.2	12.4	0.353	11.8	13.1
Luxembourg	4.2	8.4	0.281	8.6	3.6
Latvia	6.3	14.1	0.352	8.7	19.6
Mexico	10.4	16.7	0.459	12	25.6
Netherlands	4.2	7.9	0.28	21.7	2.1
Norway	3.8	7.8	0.252	24.4	4.3
New Zealand	5.3	9.9	0.333	10.4	8.2
Poland	4.7	10.5	0.300	12.2	7.4
Portugal	6.1	13.6	0.342	17.7	10.2
Slovak Republic	4.1	8.4	0.269	8.5	3.7
Slovenia	3.8	9.5	0.255	7.9	12.2
Sweden	4.2	8.8	0.281	17	7.6
Turkey	7.6	17.2	0.393	14.1	18.9
United States	8.6	17.2	0.394	19.2	20.6

Source: Organisation for Economic Co-operation and Development, "Income Distribution and Poverty," OECD Income Distribution Database, 2017.

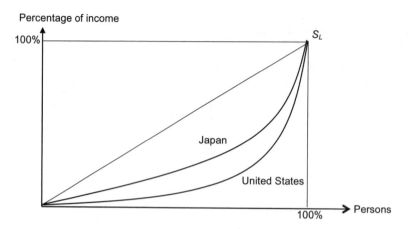

Figure 14.12
Hypothetical Gini indexes for the United States and Japan, 2014

- In most of Western Europe younger individuals are poorer than older individuals, displaying an intergenerational conflict that is at the heart of the welfare state in the region.
- The myth of the Scandinavian egalitarian society is confirmed in the data, with Denmark, Sweden, and Norway presenting relatively low Gini coefficients and fewer differences between poor and rich individuals. Nevertheless, the intergenerational conflict remains. Other countries with similar political systems, such as Iceland and Finland, are similar in terms of income equality and the differences between young and old adults.
- Inequality in the Pacific Rim countries (Japan, South Korea, Australia, and New Zealand) is relatively low but not as low as it is in the countries in Scandinavia.
- Income inequality in the United States is higher than in every other OECD country except for Chile and Mexico.

Inequality is not always bad, but extreme inequality is. Analyzing income inequality data can be far from straightforward. Some increase in inequality may be acceptable as countries develop. Some facts remain: income equality in Scandinavia and the Pacific Rim solidifies the social fabric and generates social welfare, and intergenerational inequality is likely to remain a problem for most rich countries in the near future.

15 Economics of Global Business: Integration, Limits, and Open Questions

In this chapter,

- The integration of all macro markets
- The effects of shocks on short and long run growth
- Establishing the correct context for designing economic policies
- The main constraints for sustainable prosperity and how to deal with them
- The limits of economic policy

15.1 Integrating All the Macroeconomic Markets

The main difficulty with macroeconomic analysis is the complexity of markets. Economic systems are dynamic and computationally impossible to forecast with precision. For these reasons, most macroeconomic prognoses are context-dependent and conditional. In other words, economic models are good for answering questions like "What happens to growth when the central bank increases interest rate in the United States?" and "What is the impact of the higher Federal Reserve funds rate on net exports?" In the first case, the contraction in money supply slashes growth rates, and in the second, a stronger dollar reduces net exports.

Conditional predictions are important for understanding economic policies, which is why previous chapters analyze the functioning of distinct markets and the ways that they determine the main macroeconomic variables that affect quality of life (GDP growth, inflation, unemployment, inequality, and sustainability). Integrating all markets necessitates clear transmission mechanisms among macro markets, with a clear hierarchy between start and end processes.

Macroeconomics is the science of shocks—of everything that jolts economic agents out of their placid and tranquil equilibrium. Another way to view shocks is as changes in the independent variables of a macro market, such as an increase in demand for local products or a sudden spike in energy prices.

A correct analysis often begins by asking how, for instance, government officials from a country with primary surplus and low debt to GDP ratio usually respond to a contraction in aggregate demand. Policymaking is context dependent, and the environment for decision making needs to be described appropriately. The scenario has to be clear enough to allow the correct identification of all possible choices, their respective costs and benefits, and their effects on different macro-economic markets.

Let's start with a situation of a growth gap affecting an otherwise well-functioning economy (for example, one in which the transmission mechanisms of fiscal, monetary, and currency policies work as expected in normal situations). In this relatively common case, a policy prescription based on Keynesian insights is defensible by the current models of economic processes. This means that the government could choose monetary or fiscal policies to try to bring the economy back to full employment. Given that expansionary monetary policy reduces the debt trajectory and fiscal policy increases it, the former should be the preferred option.

A typical expansionary monetary policy means a decrease in the target interest rate via an increase in the money supply. It simultaneously affects the loanable funds market, the foreign exchange market, the labor market, and the market for goods and services. Establishing all tradeoffs and possible contexts was the role of previous chapters. Connecting all macroeconomic markets means defining the context, constraints, and possible sources of measurement errors. An expansionary monetary policy in a situation of growth gap would result in the effects shown in the five graphs in figure 15.1.

This example displays the best-case scenario for economic policy because it has the desired effect of pushing the economy back into full employment. An expansion in money supply pushes down the interest rate in the money market and companies borrow to invest more. Money supply increases from MS to MS', reducing the nominal interest rate from r to r'. In the loanable funds market, the supply of loanable funds goes up from S_{LF} to S'_{LF}, which reduces the real interest rate from r to r'. This gets transmitted to the foreign currency market through either increased demand for foreign currency (as capital flows out of the country) or reduced capital inflows (via interest rate parity). The local currency devalues from e to e'. In the labor market, higher aggregate investment is followed by greater demand for labor from D_L to D'_L. Given a fixed nominal wage w^* and initial unemployment $Q_{SL} - Q_{DL}$, the change in demand for labor reduces unemployment $(Q_{SL} - Q'_{DL})$ as the expansionary monetary policy takes effect from time t to $t + 1$. Finally, in the market for goods and services, aggregate demand goes up from AD to AD' because of increases in consumption, investment, and net exports (due to the devaluation). The growth gap shrinks as output goes from Y to Y' and moves closer to full employment Y^*. Inflation picks up as prices rise from P to P'.

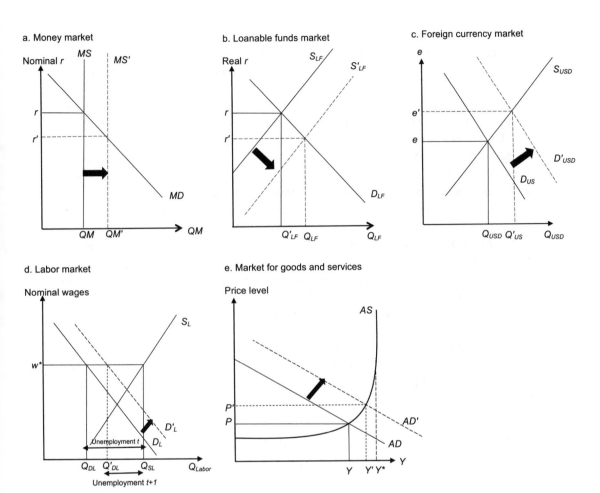

Figure 15.1
Integration of macroeconomic markets

Now we can see the complete picture of the growth/inflation dilemma. If the central bank increases money supply, then growth should follow at the expense of controlled inflation. This should be a simple process, but in the years after the great financial crisis, many central banks brought interest rates all the way down to zero triggering neither growth nor inflation. Throughout this book, the main focus has been on painstakingly building partial equilibrium models with all necessary assumptions. Regarding the breakdown in the relationship between interest rates and the real side of the economy, we have seen that it is due to failures in the transmission mechanisms of monetary policy. Lower interest rates did not lead to aggregate investment. The equilibrium in the loanable funds market did not change. Money had become neutral even in the short run. When quantitative easing followed, neither inflation nor growth ensued. One cannot find a better case for the disruption of the links between the financial and real sides of developed economies.

Given the ineffectiveness of monetary policy, the Keynesian conventional wisdom posits that a fiscal approach was the answer to all macroeconomic woes. The United States followed this logic with the American Recovery and Reinvestment Act of 2009, which consisted of a US$787 billion fiscal stimulus package and was enacted six months after the bankruptcy of Lehman Brothers in September 2008. In a best-case scenario, a fiscal stimulus works by increasing aggregate demand without deleterious effects (such as crowding out) in the credit or currency markets. If the effects on these markets are ignored, then expansionary fiscal policy would simply consist of the effects shown in the two graphs in figure 15.2.

This is the same process that occurs in the case of monetary policy with functioning transmission mechanisms, but expansionary fiscal policy bypasses the other markets to act directly on the labor market and the goods and services market. In the labor market, higher aggregate investment boosts demand for labor (from D_L to D'_L). Given a fixed nominal wage w^* and initial unemployment $Q_{SL} - Q_{DL}$, the rise in demand for labor reduces unemployment ($Q_{SL} - Q'_{DL}$) as the expansionary fiscal policy takes effect from time t to $t + 1$. Finally, in the market for goods and services, aggregate demand goes up from AD to AD' as consump-

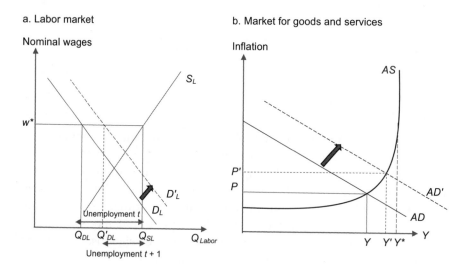

a. Labor market

Nominal wages

b. Market for goods and services

Inflation

Figure 15.2
Simultaneous changes in the labor and goods and services markets

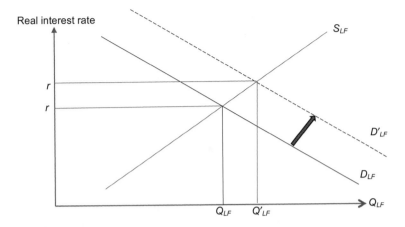

Figure 15.3
Loanable funds (credit) market

tion and investment grow. The growth gap shrinks as output moves from Y to Y' and closer to full employment Y^*. Inflation picks up as prices rise from P to P'.

The differences between expansionary fiscal and monetary policy in the present framework relate mainly to the credit and currency markets. Although expansionary monetary policy brings lower interest rates and exchange-rate devaluation, the effects are not the same as in the case of loose fiscal policy. In the latter, increased public expenditure or lower taxes may crowd out private investment depending on the expectations regarding the trajectory of public debt.

If governments spend more, there is a shift in the demand for loanable funds from D_{LF} to D'_{LF} (figure 15.3). In normal times, there is some crowding out as the interest rate rises to compensate the increase in demand. The equilibrium quantity increases from Q_{LF} to Q'_{LF} but at the cost of some marginal private projects (those that would be financed at r but not at r'). Complete crowding out, either due to lack of confidence or Ricardian equivalence, would bring demand and interest rate back to the same levels.

Demand for loanable funds would increase from D_{LF} to D'_{LF} but then return to its original position following the reduction in private demand for credit (from D'_{LF} to D_{LF}) (figure 15.4). There would be no transmitted change to any other market, and fiscal policy would be completely neutral. Aggregate demand or supply would not change at all. This is a rare case, but it could explain the ineffectiveness of many irresponsible governments in poor countries to jumpstart growth by higher spending.

The present framework is context dependent. It gives different answers to the same question depending on the path of the economy at each moment in time and

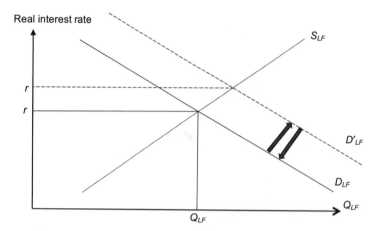

Figure 15.4
Loanable funds (credit) market

the country's level of development. Expansionary fiscal policy may engender growth in one country and inflation in another, even if both economies have indistinguishable growth gaps.

The main advantage of the model in this book is its flexibility. It can accommodate neoclassical models (which make strong assumptions about the role of money and clearing properties of macroeconomic markets) and the Keynesian insights (which posit anticyclical roles for fiscal and monetary policies in the presence of rigidities in the labor market and other markets).

Given an exogenous shock, we should follow these steps for creating conditional forecasts:

1. Determine the context of the economy. For instance, what is the currency regime—fixed or flexible exchange rate? Is the economy already in a growth gap or at full employment? What is the current level of interest rate, public deficit, and debt? Is the world growing quickly or slowly?
2. Establish the trajectory of the public debt and with it the possibility of crowding out or other effects.
3. Make assumptions about the links between the real and monetary sides. Are the transmission mechanisms of monetary policy working? If not, money may be neutral in both the short run and the long run.
4. Are any other constraints in place?
5. Form expectations about other markets that may indirectly affect the variables of interest.
6. Estimate the reaction of consumers and businesses.
7. Build scenarios and counterfactuals.

As an example, an economy suddenly experiences an adverse supply shock that drives it away from full employment. Inflation is the variable of interest. All transmission mechanisms are working, and the country has a balanced budget, flexible exchange-rate and a relatively low debt to GDP ratio. Another assumption is that Ricardian equivalence holds. What are the macroeconomic effects of such a shock? This situation generates a typical case of stagflation (figure 15.5). The aggregate supply shock plunges the economy into a recession as Y moves to Y' with the price level climbing from P to P.

We already know that fiscal policy would be ineffective because of Ricardian equivalence. Authorities now have three choices—two involving monetary policy and one in which they wait for aggregate supply to recover. In the case of expansionary monetary policy, interventions in the money market would lead to higher consumption, higher investment, and exchange-rate devaluation (figure 15.6). The economy would recover some of the lost growth rate as Y' moves to Y'' but at the cost of soaring inflation (from P to P' to P'').

The next steps depend on the response from agents. Hysteresis and inertia may create a structurally higher unemployment and inflation rate, which is what happened in the United States in the late 1970s.[1]

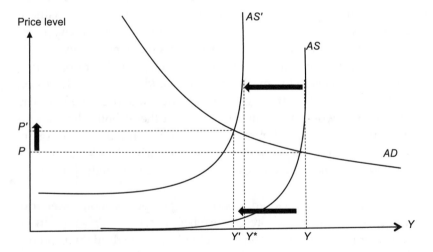

Figure 15.5
Market for goods and services

1. Hysteresis in labor markets is a permanent response to a temporary shock. For instance, a recession causes temporary unemployment. But if skills are tied to learning on the job, this temporary unemployment may cause laid-off workers to lag behind those who keep their jobs. As productivity losses accumulate, a transient situation causes joblessness to rise permanently.

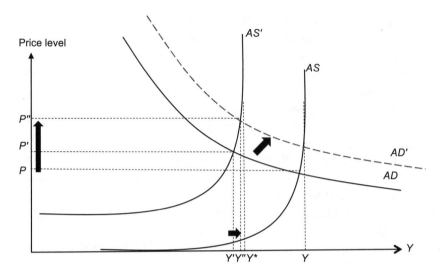

Figure 15.6
Market for goods and services

Another option, taken by the Federal Reserve in the early 1980s, is to try to tame inflation, anchoring it so the following recovery can happen without an escalation in prices. The central bank would perform a contractionary monetary policy through the sale of government bonds, thus reducing money supply. Given that all the transmission mechanisms of monetary policy are operating as expected, this reverberates to the market for goods and services as decreased consumption and investment, softening aggregate demand (figure 15.7). The recession would become worse as Y' moves to Y''', but there should be a dwindling inflationary pressure (at first P moves to P', but it then falls to P''). Again, this mirrors the path that the US economy took in the early 1980s when actions by the Federal Reserve generated a recession but managed to reduce inflation expectations.

The scenarios above apply to a closed economy. In an open-economy scenario, there would be repercussions in the foreign currency market. For instance, if the shock was national or regional (such as energy rationing due to droughts) and not part of a global movement (like an oil crisis), the perceived economic weakness would reduce capital inflows. The currency would devalue (figure 15.8).

As capital inflow dwindles, S_{USD} moves to S'_{USD}. The local currency depreciates from e to e'. Given the nature of pass-through of exchange-rate movements to prices, this could bring even more price instability. If the country is assumed to have an explicit inflation target and if inflation was at its target before the shock, then it is more likely that the central bank will respond with a contractionary

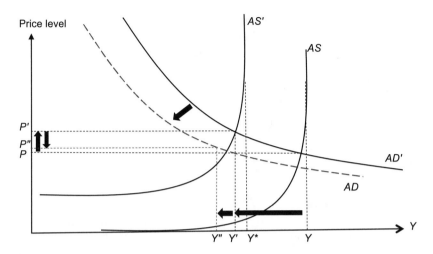

Figure 15.7
Market for goods and services

monetary policy to ensure a reversion of inflation to the target. Again, the likelihood of each policy response is context dependent. If the central bank believes that the shock is temporary and it is right, then the return of supply to its preshock level will result in an equilibrium that is indistinct from the previous one, with inflation at its target rate and full employment.

Another way to view this scenario is by describing the last possible policy response, inaction. If the supply shock is temporary, simply waiting for aggregate supply to recover might bring about full employment without inflationary pressure.

Determining the best policy response depends on the assumptions about the path of the economy, the nature of the shock in aggregate supply, the limits of economic policy, and the reactions by economic agents. A currency overshoot may indicate a more profound problem than a simple adverse shock. If the economy is performing well and the government has credibility, there might be a shock reversion with minimal change in economic policy. Finally, a strained government may find it hard to contain the devaluation and inflation from adverse supply or demand shocks.

Let's take the example of a country in which nominal and primary deficits are high, there is a growth gap and relatively high structural unemployment, the transmission mechanisms of monetary policy work, there is no inflation target and inflation is low, and international investors ascribe a significant risk premium to the country's government bonds. What happens in the scenario of a slowdown in the world economy?

Exchange rate (*x* units of local currency per US dollars)

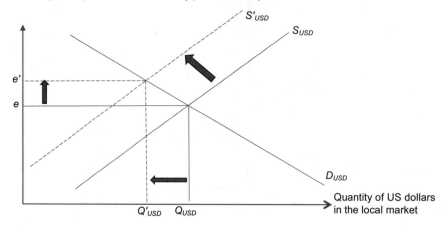

Figure 15.8
Foreign currency market

First, given the context, the country should have a devalued currency (in the case of a flexible-currency regime) or a high interest rate (for a fixed-exchange rate) before the demand shock. Given that it already has a weak economy with high debt and an elevated risk, the equilibrium in the loanable funds and exchange rate markets of the country is already affected by these conditions. For instance, Japan can have a towering public debt with low interest rates and a stable currency in the context of a weak economy, but it can sustain this only because both internal and external agents evaluate the probability of a Japanese default as very low. Otherwise, either capital would flee the country (resulting in a devalued yen), or the monetary authority would have to cut down the money supply (increasing the interest rate and preventing capital flights). Let's see how that works in more detail (figure 15.9).

The situation results in a widening growth gap. As AD moves to AD', growth (already below full employment Y^*) slackens from Y to Y', and prices go down from P to P'. All the restrictions mirror the Greek conundrum in the early and mid-2010s, where the economy was persistently weak and suffered consecutive negative demand shocks. The usual way out of this situation is through anticyclical measures—expansionary monetary and fiscal policies. But because Greece does not have a currency anymore and is part of the euro, it cannot devalue its currency or use expansionary monetary policy. Furthermore, its deficit and debt are high, so it cannot finance increasing public debts without punishing interest rates. The country is stuck.

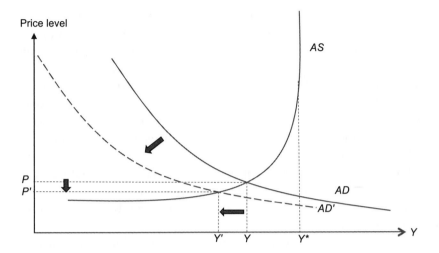

Figure 15.9
Market for goods and services

Conditional forecasts based on scenarios in which the path of the economy is known are easier. Clear growth-gap situations for countries without significant public deficit and debt will lead public authorities to activate expansionary monetary and fiscal policies. Few countries tend to have a smooth public debt trajectory because political incentives increase the likelihood that governments will try to prop up the economy at any sign of economic stress or stagnation. Bureaucrats act like children in front of candy: they cannot show restraint if their bellies are empty or the public coffers are full.

Greece and Paths to Stability

We now have a comprehensive framework to use for modeling the Greek situation. The country cannot use currency or monetary policies because it is part of the eurozone. Fiscal policy relies on market financing for Greece, but there is no space for that. As Greek authorities faced this scenario in the mid-2010s, multilateral institutions advocated austerity to tame the public-debt trajectory. The other option was leaving the eurozone and reviving the Greek drachma (or creating a new legal tender). How could each choice be modeled using the present framework?

Let's start with fiscal austerity. In the short run, austerity would amplify all the effects of adverse demand shocks. There would be deflation and even weaker economic activity. This was the path taken by Greek policymakers shepherded by European and international advisers (from the European Commission, the

European Central Bank, and the International Monetary Fund). Results were as expected. The recession deepened. But there would be a light at the end of the tunnel. If local and international agents expected a more productive Greek economy and a sustainable debt trajectory, aggregate supply and demand would recover over time, resulting in robust growth and stable prices. Trading short-term pain for the hope that in the long run the economy would emerge a stronger one.

But another path could have been chosen. What would be the macroeconomic effects of abandoning the euro? For the moment, we disregard the possibility of a financial crisis and assume a costless transition to a new currency called the new drachma (following the original Greek currency). Economic effects would start in the currency market. Both demand for foreign currency and capital outflows would explode as people tried to arbitrage the relative strength of Europe compared to Greece (see figure 15.8).

Greece probably would experience a currency crisis in which prices would readjust to a devalued currency in lieu of the euro. After this, would the country start a recovery, or would it freefall into an inflationary spiral that would put the country on a worse path than if it had stayed in the euro? Our integrated model helps frame the answer in terms of conditional forecasts. Both scenarios are possible, although not equally likely. The outcome would depend on the reaction of local and international agents (their expectations) and the functioning of transmission mechanisms of economic policies.

Whatever path the economy takes, a financial crisis would make it worse. Leaving the euro would have important implication for the workings of Greece's financial system, especially regarding the balance sheet of its banks. A disorderly withdrawal from the eurozone should result in even bigger economic pain. Nevertheless, assuming financial stability makes it easier to project a possible scenario.

If the government displays some level of competence and economic agents expect sound policies, then the devaluation fosters higher aggregate demand, and the economy starts to recover, albeit with an increase in the rate of inflation (figure 15.10).

The Greek economy starts with a severe growth gap $(Y^* - Y)$. The currency crisis produces a recession combined with rising prices (stagflation as Y moves to Y' and P moves to P'), through a shift in aggregate supply (from AS to AS', step 1). The devaluation in the foreign exchange market gets transmitted to the market for goods and services as larger net exports result in higher AD (that moves to AD', step 2). Growth picks up, but so does inflation. This actually resembles the case of Argentina, described in chapter 5. This is the best-case scenario for Greece. In the long run, the economy would return to normal, aggregate supply would revert to normal, and the business cycle would depend on government policies (good and bad) and the internal and external shocks. Greece would lose the insti-

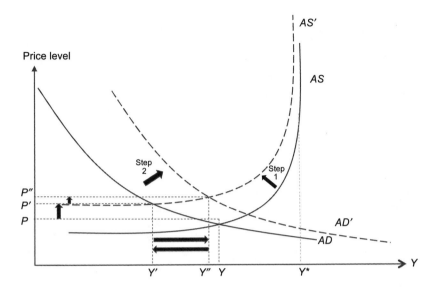

Figure 15.10
Market for goods and services

tutional support of the eurozone and the benefits from integration but would take back sovereignty in terms of monetary and currency policy. Again, there would be short-term pain for the prospect of a brighter future.

Shocks and Long-Run Growth: The Experience of Nigeria

Nigeria is potentially a global power. It is already the most populous country in Africa, and it should have more people than the United States by 2050, becoming the third-most populous country in the world.[2] It has either the largest or second-largest GDP on the continent. Methodological changes in the estimation of GDP by Nigeria and South Africa have resulted in changes in the ranking of the size of African economies.[3]

On average, African countries have lagged behind other emerging regions, like those in Latin America and South Asia. One possible reason for this lies in the quality of local institutions and their governance. Based on this hypothesis, the Mo Ibrahim Foundation (MIF) was established in 2006 with a focus on governance

2. Claire Provost, "Nigeria Expected to Have Larger Population Than US by 2050," *The Guardian*, June 13, 2013, https://www.theguardian.com/global-development/2013/jun/13/nigeria-larger-population-us-2050.
3. Jannie Rossouw, "South Africa Just Leapt Over Nigeria to Become Africa's Largest Economy Again," *Quartz*, August 16, 2016, https://qz.com/758947/south-africa-just-leapt-over-nigeria-to-become-africas-largest-economy-again.

Table 15.1
The top ten overall governance scores for African countries, 2006 to 2015

Rank (out of 54 countries)		Score (1–100)	Change between 2006 and 2015
	Africa	50.0	+1.0
1	Mauritius	79.9	+2.3
2	Botswana	73.7	–0.5
3	Cabo Verde	73.0	+1.9
4	Seychelles	72.6	+4.0
5	Namibia	69.8	+3.6
6	South Africa	69.4	–1.9
7	Tunisia	65.4	+3.4
8	Ghana	63.9	–2.1
9	Rwanda	62.3	+8.4
10	Senegal	60.8	+3.7

Source: Mo Ibrahim Foundation, *2017 Ibrahim Index of African Governance: Index Report*, 2017.

and leadership in Africa.[4] Since then, it has published annual reports with indicators showing the evolution of governance in African countries. Such indicators can easily be related to the framework on long-run growth discussed in chapter 3. A necessary condition for growth is good institutions. Both our version of the Solow model and endogenous growth theory can explain the path of national economies.

According to the MIF, "it is our belief that governance and leadership lie at the heart of any tangible and shared improvement in the quality of life of African citizens."[5] Economic theory justifies that belief. Most countries on the continent have an embedded potential for long-run growth that is still untapped due to poor governance: as governance improves, growth would be expected to follow. Unfortunately, as the MIF 2016 report on African governance shows: "almost two-thirds of citizens live in a country in which safety and rule of law deteriorated in the last ten years."[6] Table 15.1 shows the top ten scores for African countries in terms of overall governance, with the trend over the ten-year period from 2006 to 2015.

Table 15.2 shows data for selected African countries in terms of the Human Development Index, which measures life expectancy at birth, education (expected and mean years of education), and income per capita.

4. For more about the foundation, see "About Us," Mo Ibrahim Foundation, http://mo.ibrahim .foundation/about-us.
5. Ibid.
6. "Mo Ibrahim Foundation: Deteriorating Safety and Rule of Law Have Held Back Progress in African Governance," *Mail & Guardian*, October 3, 2016.

Table 15.2
Economic development data for Norway and selected African countries, 2015

Human Development Index rank	Country	Human Development Index value	Life expectancy at birth (years)	Expected years of schooling	Mean years of schooling	Income per capita (2011 PPP in US dollars)
Very high human development						
1	Norway	0.949	81.7	17.7	12.7	$67,614
High human development						
63	Seychelles	0.782	73.3	14.1	9.4	23,886
64	Mauritius	0.781	74.6	15.2	9.1	17,948
83	Algeria	0.745	75.0	14.4	7.8	13,533
97	Tunisia	0.725	75.0	14.6	7.1	10,249
Medium human development						
108	Botswana	0.698	64.5	12.6	9.2	14,663
111	Egypt	0.691	71.3	13.1	7.1	10,064
119	South Africa	0.666	57.7	13.0	10.3	12,087
Low human development						
185	Burkina Faso	0.402	59.0	7.7	1.4	1,537
186	Chad	0.396	51.9	7.3	2.3	1,991
187	Niger	0.353	61.9	5.4	1.7	889
188	Central African Republic	0.352	51.5	7.1	4.2	587

Note: PPP = purchasing power parity.
Source: United Nations Development Program, *Human Development Report 2016: Human Development for Everyone* (New York: UNDP, 2016).

No African economy is classified as having very high human development, but four out of the fifty-four nations on the continent are in the high development category. Seven of the countries reported to have the best governance on the continent also possess the highest HDI. This correlation highlights how governance, institutions, and economic growth are intertwined. It also shows that the poorest countries suffer from bad governance and poor economic performance. Solving the former would go a long way toward improving the latter.

Nigeria is fraught with mediocre institutions. It ranks thirty-six out of fifty-four countries for overall governance on the continent, one of the worst performers in terms of safety and rule of law (it ranked forty-four with a score of 42.8 out of 100 in 2015). Countries with poor institutions are much more subject to external shocks. Good institutions ensure resilience.

One example of an external shock that affected Nigeria involves the steep decline in the price of oil in 2014 to 2016. The price of a barrel of Brent crude oil was US$112 in June 2014 but declined 45% to US$62 by December. The price did not recover in 2015 and reached a new low of US$27 in January 2017. Nigeria is an oil exporter, one of thirteen countries that form the Organization of the Petroleum Exporting Countries (OPEC). Its oil industry is not as large (relative to GDP) as that the other OPEC nations, but it is a major source of foreign currency and funds most of government spending. In 2016, oil output for all OPEC countries was on average 11% of GDP, but for Nigeria it was 95% of its export earnings and 70% of government revenue.[7] In such a country, a steep drop in the price of its main exported commodity is a major shock.

In a flexible exchange rate regime, a sudden devaluation may engender a contraction in aggregate supply and stagflation. If the regime is a peg, over or undervalued, there is an increase in the possibility of a speculative attack, given that capital flight will result in a deficit in the balance of payment.

Nigeria had an overvalued, crawling peg exchange regime, and the Nigerian naira was allowed to devalue to about 197 nairas per US dollar in March 2015 and stayed at that level until the country chose to transition to a dirty floating system in June 2016.[8] From 2014 to 2016, the decline in the price of oil affected the fixed exchange rate system. Public authorities were afraid to let the currency depreciate because they feared inflation, so they fought hard to maintain the peg. Capital flew out of the country in a mix of speculative attack and hedging against a possible devaluation. To counter this, the central bank used a combination of high interest rates, recrudescing capital controls, and sale of foreign reserves.

Given that the Nigerian exchange rate system had been in place for decades, it was natural that the first action of the central bank was to maintain currency stability. Most central banks are primarily concerned with inflation, but in many emerging countries, the fight for a stable currency is a necessary condition to keep prices stable over time. In fact, the Central Bank of Nigeria stated that the main objectives of its currency policy were to preserve the value of the domestic currency, maintain a favorable external reserves position, and ensure external balance without compromising the need for internal balance and the overall goal of macroeconomic stability.

The fight for the peg was in full display when the government of President Muhammadu Buhari refused to abandon the official exchange rate of about 200 nairas to the US dollar, arguing that to do so would stoke inflation (already higher than 15%) through the higher cost of imports.

---

7. Ministry of Budget and National Planning, "Nigeria's Oil Sector Contribution to GDP Lowest in OPEC—Blueprints," 2014, http://www.nationalplanning.gov.ng/index.php/news-media/news/news-summary/333-nigeria-s-oil-sector-contribution-to-gdp-lowest-in-opec-blueprint.
8. Yukako Ono and Lucinda Elliott, "Nigeria's Currency Tanks against Dollar on Float," *Financial Times*, June 20, 2016, https://www.ft.com/content/b0753e96-36cd-11e6-a780-b48ed7b6126f.

In June 2016, Nigeria finally capitulated and allowed the naira to float. Because its foreign reserves had been depleted to a total of US$26.5 billion; the government decided to maintain some of them instead of engaging in a fruitless attempt to continue with an overvalued peg. Because abandoning a peg on an overvalued currency precipitates an abrupt devaluation, Nigeria followed the script, and the naira plunged 40% soon after its floating.[9]

The slash in oil prices also brought important macroeconomic effects. Nigeria reduced government expenditure by 6% as falling oil prices ate into government revenue. Public employees went unpaid, and states received fewer transfers from the central government. The result was a severe recession in which growth averaged less than 1% from 2013 to 2016. For a poor country, extended periods of middling growth are particularly painful. The present encompassing framework allows us to establish direct links between lower export prices and macroeconomic effects such as higher inflation and lower growth. Effects follow from the foreign currency market to other macroeconomic markets, such as the money market (with the central bank increasing the interest rate to attract foreign capital) and the market for goods and services. Inflation surges because of the devaluation, and recession comes from lower aggregate demand.

Mongolia, the IMF, Profligacy, and Austerity

In Mongolia, as in many emerging countries, growth is a necessary condition for lifting people out of poverty. After the great financial crisis, the country, which was a commodity exporter, was in dire straits. By 2009, its exports had halved after the prices of its exports declined, and it could no longer rely on trade surpluses to service its foreign debt. As in many countries that suffer from a sudden stop in external demand, results are predictable: a currency crisis brings inflation and lower growth but later leads to recovery through a cheaper currency.

The dynamics of a currency crisis followed by recovery were pronounced in Mongolia. In April 2009, the country signed a rescue package of US$229 million with the International Monetary Fund (IMF) that came with conditions to rein in public expenditure and focus on market reforms. The economy started to recover in 2009 and picked up steam in 2010.

The short-run effects of contractionary fiscal policies are well understood. At first, amid a currency crisis, a contractionary fiscal policy would decrease aggregate demand and precipitate a recession with lower inflation (figure 15.11). A currency crisis that shifts aggregate supply to the left (from AS to AS′) is compounded by falling aggregate demand (from AD to AD′).

9. Lumkile Mondi, "Nigeria's Move from a Fixed to a Floating Exchange Rate Policy," *The Conversation*, June 30, 2016, https://theconversation.com/explainer-nigerias-move-from-a-fixed-to-a-floating-exchange-rate-policy-61588.

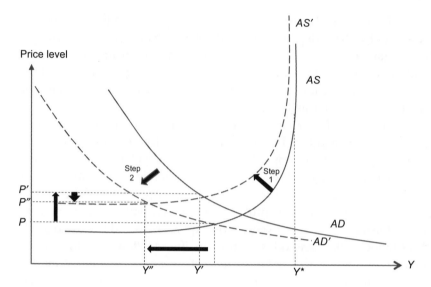

Figure 15.11
Market for goods and services

The desired outcome is for market reforms and fiscal responsibility to generate higher investment, both local and international. There are two possible short-term outcomes of market reforms as preached by multilateral institutions like the IMF. Either the reforms will plunge the economy into a recession that will make them even more costly (increasing the speed of a cyclical downturn), or they can jump-start a recovery, especially in a small economy that is by nature more volatile.

In Mongolia, the second outcome prevailed. Fiscal austerity resulted in a text-book institutional improvement that created growth and prosperity. The deficit was contained, capital arrived, and the economy grew by 8% in 2010 (figure 15.12). The case of Mongolia highlights the relevance of context dependency. Timing is important in terms of economic policy, and even the best policies can be derailed by internal and external shocks. Mongolia's "determined policy implementation," the IMF said, had fostered "a remarkable economic turnaround."[10] Foreign reserves were up, and the budget deficit and inflation were down. Arrears on foreign debts had been paid, and confidence in the currency restored. The honeymoon lasted for three years of double-digit growth. Unfortunately, business cycles are a feature of macroeconomics, and recession follows prosperity. Growth stalled in 2015, and the country experienced another currency crisis.

10. "Bailing Out Mongolia: A Wrong Direction in the Steppe," *The Economist*, October 27, 2016, https:// www.economist.com/news/asia/21709334-government-turns-imf-second-time-seven-years-wrong -direction-steppe.

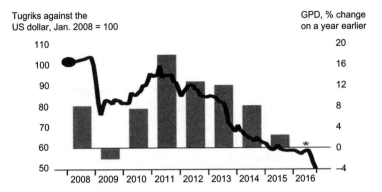

Figure 15.12
Mongolia's exchange rate and GDP growth, 2008 to 2016
Source: "Bailing Out Mongolia: A Wrong Direction in the Steppes," *The Economist*, October 27, 2016.

From 2013 to 2016, the Mongolian tugrik was in a descendent spiral. Mongolia suffered from falling commodities prices, an economic slowdown in China, and waning interest by foreign investors deterred by anti-investment laws and inconsistent policy.[11] One sign of inconsistent policies was fiscal profligacy. Although the IMF praised the government's accountability in reducing the primary deficit in 2010, by 2015 the deficit had ballooned to almost 20% of GDP. Further economic damage was done by the central bank, which chose to increase the interest rate to stall inflation fueled by the deficit and the currency depreciation.

In 2016, the new Mongolian government, elected after the Mongolian People's Party (MPP) won over the Democratic Party (DP), asked the IMF for another bailout. Such a request fits into our comprehensive model and provides some lessons:

• Policymakers should realize that business cycles are real and should prepare for a downturn.
• Many emerging markets have structural current-account deficits and rely on exports or capital inflows to avoid currency crises.
• In emerging countries, the exchange rate is a good signal of the strength of the economy. Currency crises often coincide with recessions, making them worse.
• Balance of payments vulnerabilities diminish the monetary authority power over monetary policy as governments constantly battle for capital inflows with high interest rates.

11. Michael Kohn, "Mongolia Calls for Economic 'Crisis' Plan; Bonds Tumble," *Bloomberg*, August 10, 2016, https://sg.finance.yahoo.com/news/mongolia-finance-minister-calls-economic-100239917 .html.

- Fiscal profligacy, especially in countries with weak institutions, will create budget crises sooner rather than later. Although developed economies can afford debt to GDP ratios of more than 100%, in emerging countries even ratios of 60% make investors squeamish, especially if deficits are high. The poorer a country is, the more its debt trajectories matter.
- Every country that goes to the IMF for a bailout should be prepared to enact market and institutional reforms. As the main collateral for its loans, this important multilateral agency has as its main priority developing good institutions in countries that borrow its funds. Austerity, privatizations, and improved accounting are all elements of the typical IMF recipe.

The recommendations given to Mongolia were no different from the usual made by the IMF—a flexible exchange rate, healthy public finances, banking system improvements, and adjustment costs that protect the poor.[12]

Summing up, the recent history of Mongolia is typical of many emerging markets that are susceptible to external shocks. Economic mismanagement and fragility are portents of doom and part of a vicious circle: weak institutions contribute to bad policies that make the country more vulnerable, and these, in turn, make good policies more costly, reducing incentives for institutional reforms. This is why successful case stories (like South Korea, Japan, and China) are the exception, not the rule, for emerging countries. These countries were able to emerge from poverty through export-oriented industrialization followed by institutional reforms. Such reforms have long-run targets, but recessions may derail many a good idea. Patterns of cyclical currency crises are all too common in emerging countries, and external restrictions make the path toward development even harder for them.

The Washington Consensus, Neoliberalism, and Keynesianism

In the late 1980s, multilateral institutions had their hands full as many countries experienced currency crises. John Williamson first used the term *Washington Consensus* in 1989 to summarize the economic policy prescriptions of the IMF, the World Bank, and other organizations in a set of ten economic policy prescriptions.[13] These policies were supposed to represent the standard reform package promoted by these institutions, and countries in need of a bailout would find easier access to funds if they reformed local markets with these principles in mind.

---

12. Steven Barnett and Julia Bersch, "Mongolia Stages Dramatic Turnaround," *IMF Survey Magazine*, September 13, 2010, http://www.imf.org/en/News/Articles/2015/09/28/04/53/socar091410a.
13. John Williamson, "A Short History of the Washington Consensus," *Law and Business Review of the Americas* 15 (2009): 7.

The consensus is usually regarded as the height of neoliberalism and has been vilified by many intellectuals. According to Charles Gore, "the introduction of the Washington Consensus involved not simply a swing from state-led to market-oriented policies, but also a shift in the ways in which development problems were framed and in the types of explanation through which policies were justified. Key changes were the partial globalization of development policy analysis, and a shift from historicism to a historical performance assessment. ... The demise of the Washington Consensus is inevitable because its methodology and ideology are in contradiction."[14]

Using the present framework to tackle this critique, we can divide the ten consensus policies into short- and long-run growth policies and policy choices that are not universally true or even advisable. First, here are the ten economic policies of the Washington Consensus:

1. Fiscal discipline
2. A reordering of public expenditure priorities (with fewer nonmerit subsidies and more pro-growth and pro-poor expenditure, such as on health, education, and infrastructure)
3. Tax reform (with a tax system that combines a broad tax base with moderate marginal tax rates)
4. Liberalization of interest rates
5. A competitive (freely floating) exchange rate
6. Trade liberalization
7. Liberalization of inward foreign direct investment
8. Privatization
9. Deregulation (with the focus on an easing of barriers to entry and exit and not on abolishing regulations designed for safety or environmental reasons or on governing prices in a noncompetitive industry)
10. Property rights (with a focus on providing the informal sector with the ability to gain property rights at an acceptable cost)

True macroeconomic reforms that are directly associated with short-run growth are fiscal discipline, liberalization of interest rates and foreign direct investment, and floating exchange rates (items 1, 4, 5, and 7 in this list). All the other policies could be argued to have an impact on growth, inflation, and other macroeconomic outputs, but the link is usually indirect, or the policies change only long-term potential output instead of short-run economic growth.

14. Charles Gore, "The Rise and Fall of the Washington Consensus as a Paradigm for Developing Countries," *World Development* 28, no. 5 (2000): 789–804.

Item 1 requires the abandoning of fiscal policy as a countercyclical economic policy. Items 4 and 5 deal directly with the structure of the money and foreign exchange markets. Item 7 is related to capital controls.

What can the present framework tell us about the Washington Consensus? Regarding competitive exchange rates and the liberalization of foreign direct investment, the consensus prescribes a fully flexible exchange rate without capital controls on investment-related flows. Meanwhile, most small countries, with few exceptions (Iceland, for instance), have fixed exchange-rate regimes. There is a clear tradeoff between pegged and floating currencies, with no a priori preference. Williamson, who was the first to describe the consensus, realized that it was a mistake to say that policymakers agreed about prescribing a flexible currency regime: "I fear I indulged in wishful thinking in asserting that there was a consensus in favor of ensuring that the exchange rate would be competitive, which pretty much implies an intermediate regime; in fact Washington was already beginning to edge toward the two-corner doctrine which holds that a country must either fix firmly or else it must float cleanly."[15]

As for fiscal policy, there is no consensus about all the economic impacts of public debt on short- and long-run growth, employment, and inflation. The consequences of extreme decisions related to government spending are easily described, however. Profligacy will lead to inflation if left unchecked, and severe austerity on a growth-gap framework has the potential to lead to an economic depression. Should governments be fiscally responsible regardless of business-cycle effects? Fiscal discipline, as propagated by the consensus, is unclear. In most economic models, the ideal fiscal policy is either neutral or anticyclical. The best anticyclical kind of policy is the one in which governments generate primary surpluses during expansionary periods and spend to revive the economy during recessions. Nevertheless, the political cycle follows its own patterns when incentives for budget deficits loom larger as a country moves closer to a general election. Insomuch as fiscal discipline means avoiding unfettered public deficits, one can easily argue that this is a consensus. Nevertheless, there is no agreement about growth trajectories or ideal levels of public debt.

So far, the Washington Consensus is wrong in promoting fiscal discipline without a qualification of what that would entail, and it fails in advancing a flexible exchange rate as the preferred foreign currency regime. Could it be wrong on every policy prescription? Other measures are easier to defend. Property rights are a clear necessary condition for development, and trade liberalization does increase aggregate output even though it has important income distributive effects. In the early 1990s, privatization did result in improved services in many

15. Williamson, "A Short History of the Washington Consensus," 10.

countries, although it is also fraught with potential corruption if the transfer of public property does not follow rigorous requirements (for instance, Russia and the rise of the oligarchy that benefited from the privatization there).[16]

Summing up, the consensus is a mix of outdated preoccupations (focusing on privatization), solid advice (on trade, government expenditure, and property rights), mistaken recommendations (such as flexible exchange rate regimes), and dubious policy prescriptions (like interest rate liberalization). Regarding interest-rate liberalization, Williamson in 2003 argued that he would like to have written financial deregulation, in a broader sense.[17] It may have been a consensus then, but the great financial crisis showed that unbridled financial systems create systemic risks that can pound the world into a steep recession. The consensus strives for universal rules when economics is context dependent. Some countries need fiscal discipline, whereas others can live with increasing deficits (Japan). The term *neoliberal* was based on the Washington Consensus. Today the consensus is dated, and although some policy prescriptions (like property rights) continue to hold universal appeal, most do not (there are limits to financial deregulations) or are simply wrong (countries should not necessarily adopt flexible exchange rate regimes).

15.2   How Policymakers Act

This textbook is not solely about macroeconomic theory or empirical evidence. Its main theme is the mental models used by policymakers around the world. Governments tend to have similar responses to economic shocks, regardless of ideology. In "liberal" United States, "socialist" Scandinavian countries, or "communist" China, governments try to encourage aggregate demand during a recession and use monetary policy when inflation is high (even though a contractionary fiscal policy would be preferred if the economy faces a growth gap).

Public authorities do not necessarily look for the best economic solutions because their actions are constrained by the political system and the responses of economic agents. Political incentives are not necessarily aligned with the rest of society. For every political action, the groups affected the most have greatest incentives to fight for their own interests, even at the expense of the rest of society. One of the results of this process is that most nations direct public expenditure at older voters instead of the young population, who cannot vote or vote at a much lower rate than their elders. In the United States, Medicare and Medicaid are the

16. Sergei Guriev and Andrei Rachinsky, "The Role of Oligarchs in Russian Capitalism," *Journal of Economic Perspectives* 19, no. 1 (2005): 131–150.
17. John Williamson, "The Washington Consensus and Beyond," *Economic and Political Weekly* (2003): 1475–1481.

cornerstones of a quasi-socialist single-payer healthcare system, and young adults have to buy health insurance or face fines. Most countries face public pension crises in the near future, and authorities find public pension reforms difficult to enact as they risk alienating the gray vote.

Economic theory is far from perfect but still provides the best available road map for solving policy-related dilemmas. In this section, we concentrate on what governments actually do, establishing tradeoffs between action and inaction and between the costs and benefits of each economic policy. Both austerity and prof-ligacy come at a price. Societies make intertemporal choices when they kick neces-sary reforms down the road to benefit one generation over others. More important, choices about foreign currency regimes, inflation targeting, and balanced budgets have their tradeoffs, which are now explicit. The present comprehensive model clarifies why most small countries use fixed exchange rate regimes with some measure of capital controls and why developed and large countries can maintain fully flexible currency regimes.

Most economists agree that countries can run small deficits, adjusted for the business cycle, indefinitely as long as the debt to GDP ratio is low (say, about 50% to 70%), stable, and predictable. They prefer that governments run balanced budgets or small surpluses during expansion periods and then run deficits as the economy contracts.

Unfortunately, predictability is not the forte of governments around the world. Adverse shocks tend to create incentives for disproportionate responses from public authorities, generating all sorts of time-inconsistent attitudes. Benign shocks encourage profligacy.

Monetary policy is no different. It works best when central banks have credibil-ity and act rationally. But building credibility takes time, and their governors face pressure from any adverse shocks. This happens with stagflation or a deep recession, for example. After the great financial crisis, most central banks in devel-oped countries slashed interest rates. They could have waited for the economy to recover without further meddling, but instead they used quantitative easing to try to prop up aggregate demand by printing money and buying all sorts of financial assets.

Many times, governments take actions that work against economic theory and try to manhandle markets. One example is the British pound peg to other Euro-pean currencies in the early 1990s. In that case, the Bank of England lost its gamble and was forced to allow a messy floatation of the pound. In China in 2015, capital flights lowered foreign reserves by US$600 billion, and the government chose to strengthen capital controls to maintain a fixed exchange rate regime and monetary autonomy. Things returned to normal in 2016, but Chinese authorities learned that the trilemma is inexorable, regardless of the size of foreign reserves a country accumulates.

Governments' actions are constrained by multiple simultaneous shocks, time inconsistency, identification, inside and outside lags, and transmission mechanisms. Disentangling all effects to establish the impact of each maneuver by public authorities is almost impossible. Nevertheless, they keep trying and are unlikely to give up. Inaction may be the appropriate response, but we will never know. Any analysis of policymaking involves the context—the connections between all different macroeconomic markets, constraints, and tradeoffs as well as the ideology behind those actions. After labels such as *neoliberalism* or *socialism* are attached to certain actions, the analysis gets even more complicated. This quote bears repeating: "For every complex problem, there is an answer that is clear and simple—and wrong."

15.3   The Limits of Macroeconomics and Open Questions

In this book, the comprehensive model of how national economies work does not follow a single macroeconomic model. Unlike physics and its standard model, economics does not have an all-encompassing theory that explains the intricacies of macro markets and provides a single guideline for public authorities. Context dependency yields different lessons based on the surrounding environment and each country's development path. We do not even know if governments should be active in pursuing their macroeconomic objectives. Countercyclical policies are fraught with issues of identification, calibration, and constraints. The simple selection of a foreign currency regime has many implications for the amount of foreign reserves, the presence of capital controls, and the autonomy of monetary policy, among others. Most small countries prefer fixed exchange rate regimes due to the potential volatility from international shocks, but even emerging countries that adopt flexible arrangements frequently intervene in currency markets. The two-handed economist is born because macroeconomics is not conductive to universal laws and courses of actions.

There are many unresolved questions in macroeconomics, and below are a few that are part of the themes that run throughout this book.

Should Economic Policy Be Active?
Macroeconomic markets are inherently interconnected. Monetary policy is constrained by transmission mechanisms and its effects on public debt and the exchange rate. The impact of fiscal policy depends on how economic agents respond to changes in taxes and spending. Under Ricardian equivalence, fiscal

policy is neutral in the short and long runs. In most countries, public finances are in disarray, but in developed countries, long-term interest rates have hovered at close to zero for almost ten years. Meanwhile, many emerging markets have to contend with high real interest rates that help contain inflationary pressure or avoid rapid depreciation of the local currencies.

In democracies, the political cycle pressures politicians into action. In authoritarian regimes, control is more valued than efficiency, and social welfare is usually a secondary preoccupation. When dictators fear losing their power over institutionally weak nations, the economy suffers. Syria is a contemporary example of the preference for control over social welfare. Members of the Assad regime would rather kill their constituents than relinquish any control over the country. Democracies, theocracies, dictatorships, and plutocracies all behave similarly regarding market interventions: governments rarely let markets adjust unimpeded. There is no counterfactual theory to active macroeconomic policy, and economists simply do not know if business cycles would be more or less volatile without countercyclical policies. Inaction is an impossible hypothesis to test because no government in history has waited for economic shocks to unwind naturally.

Government restraint is usually a consequence of regulations that were put in place by earlier policymakers. The sequence of events begins with a reformist government that wants to build credibility and prevent future governments from straying from new policies. This leads to the adoption of inflation targets and balanced-budget acts and the enshrinement into the constitution of the contemporary understanding of the social contract. But social norms evolve, and policymakers, constrained by earlier decisions, fight to reform or amend the earlier arrangements. Credibility becomes endogenous and never follows the planned route.

The Maastricht Treaty, which became effective in 1993 and set the structure of the European Union, was supposed to restrain profligacy among European governments. But Germany and France, two of the largest European economies and the most difficult ones to punish due to their political influence in the union, were the first to ignore the treaty's limits on public spending.

Economic policies evolve, and no central bank pursues monetary aggregate targets in the way prescribed by original monetarists like Milton Friedman. Many innovations, such as inflation targeting, are introduced. Public institutions learn. China failed in liberalizing, in a tentative way, capital controls while maintaining monetary autonomy and a fixed exchange rate regime. Its US$4 trillion in reserves were not able to overcome the trilemma that limits the alternative schemes of foreign currency markets.

Nevertheless, there is still uncertainty about the results of passive versus active rules for economic policies. Should the United States establish a hard cap on its budget? Would emerging markets benefit from the outsourcing of the administration of new cities to strong foreign institutions (following Paul Romer's idea of charter cities)?[18] Maybe poor economies could look for explicit rules for automatic stabilizers? Should governments concentrate on their major roles as purveyors of national defense and essential public services and relinquish macroeconomic policy altogether (an ultraliberal dream)?

There is one answer to all these questions: we simply do not know. Economists agree that central economic planning that micromanages macroeconomic aggregates simply cannot work. The Soviet Union was doomed to fail, and China could not be the economic powerhouse it is today without abandoning it. Yet there is much to learn regarding the fine-tuning of public policy.

Is Financial Globalization All the Rage?

Developed financial markets are a necessary condition for development. Countries cannot prosper without financial intermediation that guarantees options for borrowers and lenders. Complete and efficient financial markets enhance prosperity. Yet the great financial crisis that started in 2007 destroyed global welfare on an unparalleled scale.

Even before the Washington Consensus, the recommendation for emerging markets has been to globalize to become wealthy. This strategy worked for some countries, especially those open to trade agreements. Nevertheless, there is an optimal level of financial globalization. Complete deregulation carries with it the seeds for devastating currency and financial crises. But in financial markets that are too tightly regulated, sparse markets fail to fund sustained growth, which constrains businesses and savers alike. Most countries today tread carefully when internationalizing their currencies, banks, or markets.

In the United Kingdom, antiglobalization movements prevailed and led to the country's withdrawal from the European Union, and they also inform the policies of countries like Greece as they recoil from the effects of the financial crisis. Ten years after the crisis, two countries where financial systems turned global before collapsing with the crisis, Iceland and Ireland, are little better than before the crisis.

New stringent international regulations emerged, like the recent evolution of the Basel Accord, now in its third version. Central banks are much more eager to fine and punish miscreants—so much so that Minouche Shafik, a deputy governor of the Bank of England, has estimated that the roughly US$275 billion in legal

---

18. Paul Romer, "Technologies, Rules, and Progress: The Case for Charter Cities," Center for Global Development, March 3, 2010, https://www.cgdev.org/publication/technologies-rules-and-progress-case-charter-cities.

costs for global banks in 2008 to 2016 translated into more than US$5 trillion of reduced lending capacity to the real economy.[19]

Until recently, many textbooks did not establish the link between the real and financial sides of the economy. Professors and students just assumed that the transmission mechanisms of monetary policy worked and thus that omniscient central banks could tweak target interest rates to fight inflation or unemployment, in that order. But transmission mechanisms failed after the great financial crisis and have kept sputtering since then. Few economic truisms are known around the globe, but most people know that if governments print enormous quantities of money, inflation ensues. Yet the Federal Reserve, the European Central Bank, and the Bank of Japan printed approximately US$7 trillion from 2009 to 2016, flooding financial markets. This did not result in inflation, growth, or much of anything other than a boost in financial asset prices.

Financial markets in developed markets became dysfunctional after the great financial crisis. Things are not much better in emerging markets, but they already lacked complete and efficient financial markets. Banks and other financial institutions are the grease that should keep the real economy rolling. We are stuck and lack a clear path toward functional financial markets around the world. The status quo of small and medium-sized enterprises (SMEs) is to fight an uphill battle for access to credit. Peer Stein has estimated that the credit gap for SMEs around the world was more than US$2 trillion in 2015.[20] Two-thirds of SMEs are underserved in terms of access to credit, according to the International Finance Corporation, with most of them in developing economies.[21] Printing trillions of dollars did nothing to assuage the credit gap. If anything, access to credit is worse than it was precrisis because banks loathe the idea of filling the balance sheet with unrecoverable loans.

The main regulatory tradeoff remains: too much regulation strangles credit creation, and too little regulation might create the next great financial crisis. There is no sign that a healthy balance will be reached soon. Meanwhile, developed countries need to deal with secular stagnation, and developing countries plod along without all the benefits of globalized financial markets. The new normal is a world with abnormal financial markets. Implications for economic policies are

19. Katy Burne and Aruna Viswanatha, "Bank Legal Costs Cited as Drag on Economic Growth," *Wall Street Journal*, October 20, 2016, https://www.wsj.com/articles/boe-official-bank-legal-costs-since-2008 -reach-275-billion-1476974749.

20. Peer Stein, "Five Steps to Closing the $2 trillion Credit Gap," World Bank, 2015, http://blogs.world bank.org/psd/five-steps-closing-2-trillion-credit-gap.

21. Peer Stein, Oya Pinar Ardic, and Martin Hommes, "Closing the Credit Gap for Formal and Informal Micro, Small, and Medium Enterprises," International Finance Corporation, Washington, DC, 2013, https://www.ifc.org/wps/wcm/connect/4d6e6400416896c09494b79e78015671/Closing+the +Credit+Gap+Report-FinalLatest.pdf?MOD=AJPERES.

manifold and still unexplored. In the mid-2010s, interest rates went negative in many developed countries, even though some said that negative interest rates could not last or were dangerous.[22] The fact that this abnormality became the norm is another sign that financial markets have become dysfunctional.

In the 1980s, John Cox, Jonathan E. Ingersoll Jr., and Stephen A. Ross developed one of the most famous models of the term structure of interest rates. It precluded negative rates by fiat, an assumption that raised no eyebrows because nobody could ever imagine it happening.[23] Economists are playing catch-up by developing models where defective features are persistent, and financial markets do not clear as in the past. There is no consensus or a path to be prescribed to governments. Regular economic theory states that negative rates should boost growth and inflation. Stagnation in developed countries remains. We need a new theory of the relation between the financial and real sides of the economy that unlocks the potential contribution to economic growth from commercial banks and other financial intermediaries. Financial markets are sick, and we do not know how to cure them.

On the Role of a Public Deficit

One of the most common opinions regarding public debt is that it is a tax on our grandchildren. Governments should be responsible and avoid creating obligations for future generations. We are already destroying the planet by not focusing on sustainable business practices and economic policies, but we should not compound this by creating financial liabilities for the unborn. Again, the situation is not as simple as it might seem. Many people equate the economics of governments with household budgeting: people need to meet their obligations, and so should public authorities. Nevertheless, the current public debt is almost irrelevant. It is the trajectory of public deficit and debt that matters, and unlike households, governments can run deficits indefinitely.

Families need to eventually settle their debts because people do not live forever. Would you lend money to be repaid in ten years to somebody who is ninety years old? Governments do not face this constraint because what matters is the ratio of public debt to GDP. As long as the public debt does not get out of control, public authorities will find savers willing to finance it.

A public deficit constrains the actions of governments, and the political cycle allows authorities to postpone the day of reckoning. And therein lies the problem.

---

22. Charles Kane, "Here's Why Negative Interest Rates Are More Dangerous Than You Think," *Fortune*, March 14, 2016, http://fortune.com/2016/03/14/negative-interest-rates-european-central -bank.
23. John C. Cox, Jonathan E. Ingersoll Jr., and Stephen A. Ross, "A Theory of the Term Structure of Interest Rates," *Econometrica: Journal of the Econometric Society* 53, no. 2 (1985): 385–408.

Does a public deficit destroy social welfare? Or is it a boon to nations, in the grand old Keynesian tradition? Countries rarely follow the commonsense path of anti-cyclical fiscal policy, which is saving when the economy is growing and opening the public purse when things get rough. When the economy picks up, politicians tend to increase spending, hoping that the good times will last forever. Whenever the economy tanks, they spend even more, and public spending compounds the natural increase of debt to GDP ratio during recessions.

Governments play an important role in national economies, and fiscal policy is one of their main instruments. Yet we simply do not know all the possible costs and benefits of activating expansionary fiscal policy. But we can state that expansionary fiscal policy is easier to implement in countries with balanced budgets and low debt to GDP ratios. And that loss of credibility in public authorities may accelerate inflation.

There is a gap in our understanding of the connections between fiscal policies and other economic policies. Contractionary fiscal policy may elicit currency appreciation (if confidence in policymakers is high) or devaluation (if recession is the result). Economists have a better understanding of the interplay between monetary and fiscal policy, but it is far from perfect.

Nowhere does context dependency rear its head more than when governments accumulate public debt. Governments are neither evil nor the saviors of poor people against greedy corporations. Their role in national economies has evolved. During the heights of the Keynesian dream of strong governments, they were master puppeteers and arbiters of social welfare. What they are evolving toward remains the unanswered question in macroeconomics.

Demographics, Income Inequality, Sustainability, Secular Stagnation, and Other Contemporary Issues

Demographics and income inequality were not big issues until recently. Countries were relatively young, most people died before reaching old age, and poverty was prevalent. The priority was lifting society's income. The world has changed relatively fast, especially for developed countries. Their populations are aging quickly, and incomes are stagnant for most people other than the very rich. Japan is the epitome of what countries in Europe can expect—a rich society that became less dynamic in as little as thirty years. Even countries that have yet to become prosperous, like China and Russia, are already bracing themselves for changes in demographics and feel the pressure from society because of rising income inequality.

Secular stagnation compounds these issues. Before the great financial crisis, optimism was the norm, China was a rising star, and European countries were advertising themselves as the destination for migration from Latin America. Since the crisis, isolationism has increased as growth has stalled.

The role that public policy plays when addressing income inequality is important. Most economic measures to smooth income inequality come from governments—either through direct transfers, subsidies, or the design of the tax system. There is a tradeoff between equity and efficiency. Governments can err on both sides—by trying to incentivize economic efficiency and generating an extremely unequal society or by fighting for equity while ignoring efficiency.

In the last fifty years, the United States moved from equity to efficiency concerns, which can be seen by looking at the design of the US tax system. The top marginal income tax rate was 91% in the 1960s and only 39.6% in 2017. Income inequality increased because of this tax cut and for many other reasons. Returning to a 91% marginal tax is unfeasible, both politically and because of economic effects, and probably would lower economic growth tremendously.

Demographics also play a role in long-run prosperity. An aging population increases public spending on pensions and reduces the growth of the labor force. Pension reforms have a direct effect on social welfare and income distribution. In 2014, the United Kingdom enacted a pension reform that affected pensioners and employees differently. Before the reform, pensioners had greater incentives to buy annuities or could take out a 25% lump-sum payment from their pensions with the rest being liable to high income taxes. One change allowed pensioners to take out smaller lump-sum payments over time instead. This benefited people with large pension pots more than those with small ones, and it shows how policymakers can affect income inequality through decisions on taxes and subsidies.[24]

What matters is that income inequality and aging populations are significant obstacles to prosperity. Social mobility is key to social justice: if elites entrench themselves, income inequality destroy social welfare by funneling money to a few. Can the United States be called prosperous when almost 10 million Americans are considered to be among the working poor? Will public pensions generate fiscal crises? One trend is for the retirement age to increase. It should be around age sixty-seven in the OECD countries by 2050.[25]

Disregarding income inequality and social mobility has already cost plenty of money for hundreds of millions of people. Although policymakers cannot afford to ignore it anymore, we do not know what is the best approach for this important

24. Patrick Collinson, "UK Pension Reforms: What Do They Actually Mean?," *The Guardian*, October 14, 2014, https://www.theguardian.com/money/2014/oct/14/uk-pension-reforms-what-mean.

25. Organisation for Economic Co-operation and Development, *Pensions at a Glance 2013: OECD and G20 Indicators*, OECD Publishing, 2013, http://www.oecd.org/pensions/public-pensions/OECD PensionsAtAGlance2013.pdf.

issue. We know that some basic income for the poor is extremely relevant in poor countries but that it does not solve everything. Taxing rich individuals may smooth income inequality or destroy social welfare for everybody. And amid such economic worries, part of our economic activity is destroying the planet.

Pollution used to be the price of progress, but if we continue with business as usual, the planet is likely doomed. There are tradeoffs in terms of growth and inequality and growth and sustainability. There are also scenarios in which such tradeoffs disappear. Again, these scenarios are all context dependent. We do not know to what extent the pursuit of economic growth opens the door to income disparity and sustainability issues. We do not know the answer to this question even for a small country, and trying to find a response in a global setting is even more difficult.

There are limits to our knowledge of worldwide economic processes. Will rich countries suffer from secular stagnation? Can poor countries grow and lower the poverty rate without destroying the environment? The world has experienced continued economic growth for the last two hundred years, and although many in poor countries yearn for it, others believe that it disrupts their ways of living. Economists rarely tackle ethical questions like whether people in poor rural villages are better off by maintaining their ways of living or whether growth brings happiness even if it means having to move to large urban centers.

The economics of global business offers material growth—more cell phones, better health care, longer lives, keeping in touch with former colleagues on social media. But it also presents plenty of ethical dilemmas. Economists always assume that poverty is bad and that given a choice people would toil for a modicum of prosperity instead of a quiet way of life—better some growth than nothing. Myanmar, for example, was nearly cut off from the world for the last fifty years and is backward and poor. Many people living there would like to experience economic progress. But plenty of people are content with living a quiet, poor, and predictable way of life. How can ideal economic policies be devised when we do not even know if people actually want economic growth? People should be free to look for a better way of life or be free not to.

When it comes to working, contemporary economics leaves individuals little room for choice. In poor countries, people have two stark alternatives: work or die. Richer countries replace this with a less dramatic but equally uneven choice: work or stop consuming. The seemingly elementary question "Do you want to work?" does not arise. Economic models are ill-equipped to address the query, "What will happen when a society turns away from infinite consumption?" The underlying assumption simply is that more is better. But is it really?

Perfectly balancing all the different aspects of a national economy is impossible, and no path to prosperity is completely smooth. Nevertheless, there have been gains. Living conditions have continued to improve over the last two hundred years, even if not for everybody. The economy has been able to lift more than a billion people out of extreme poverty in the last fifteen years alone. Education and health continue to improve throughout the globe. But we should not become complacent. Governments need to do better. Better institutions and policies would go a long way toward eradicating chronic poverty and improving inequality. They also should do more to protect the environment. True development must not come at the cost of destroying our planet. And it should include everyone.

Index

Page numbers in *italic* indicate figures and tables.